T0178689

Human-Computer Interactions in Transport

Human-Computer Interactions in Transport

Edited by
Christophe Kolski

First published 2011 in Great Britain and the United States by ISTE Ltd and John Wiley & Sons, Inc.

ISTE Ltd
27-37 St George's Road
London SW19 4EU
UK

www.iste.co.uk

John Wiley & Sons, Inc.
111 River Street
Hoboken, NJ 07030
USA

www.wiley.com

Library of Congress Cataloging-in-Publication Data

Human-Computer interactions in transport / edited by Christophe Kolski.
    p. cm.
  Includes bibliographical references and index.
  ISBN 978-1-84821-279-4
  1. Transportation--Automation. 2. Human-machine systems. 3. Transportation--Equipment and supplies--Design and construction. I. Kolski, Christophe.
  TA1230.H86 2011
  629.04--dc23
                                                                        2011020212

British Library Cataloguing-in-Publication Data
A CIP record for this book is available from the British Library
ISBN 978-1-84821-279-4

Printed and bound in Great Britain by CPI Antony Rowe, Chippenham and Eastbourne.

MIX
Paper from
responsible sources
FSC® C013604
www.fsc.org

Table of Contents

Chapter 8. Menu Sonification in an Automotive Media Center:
Design and Evaluation   233
Nicolas MISDARIIS, Julien TARDIEU, Sabine LANGLOIS and Séverine LOISEAU

Introduction

Interactive systems are increasingly present all around us. They are found in companies, public places, training venues, at home and also in the context of leisure activities. They are more or less accessible, useful and usable. Many questions, both practical and theoretical can be asked concerning the analysis, design, realization and evaluation of such systems [SEA 08], [SHN 09], [SEF 09].

Regarding this subject, human-computer interaction (HCI) has been a particularly active area of research in its own right since the 1970s[1]. It is defined as "the discipline dedicated to the design, the implementation and the evaluation of interactive computing systems destined for human use and with the study of major phenomena surrounding them" [HEW 96]. This area is pluridisciplinary by nature, bringing together people particularly from an industrial and academic background, from both the engineering sciences as well as cognitive sciences, related to users with very varied characteristics [ROB 03].

The field of human-computer interactions is vast and constantly evolving; books, guides, theses, conferences and journals have regularly been dedicated to it for a number of years. This book on human-computer interaction reviews a set of principles, knowledge, methods and models, all the while focusing on a single field – that of transport.

The field of transport itself being extremely rich and complex, the central idea of this book is to look at the transport user becoming a user of an interactive system(s)

Introduction written by Christophe KOLSKI, with the help of the authors.

1 The interested reader can consult: (1) the Website of the *Special Interest Group on Human-Computer Interaction* (SIGCHI, www.acm.org/sigchi/) of the ACM (*Association for Computing Machinery*), and (2) the Website of the HCIBIB (HCI Bibliography: Human-Computer Interaction Resources; http://hcibib.org/). For French speakers, see also the Website of the *Association francophone d'interaction homme-machine* (AFIHM): www.afihm.org/.

during the preparation of the trip, or during it, in the context of mobility. He[2] or she then needs information which is qualified as traveler information, in the broad sense, and for this enters into interaction with various systems (information systems, assistance systems, etc.) based on different devices, either personal or not. Moreover, in order to offer the user information which is adapted to his or her needs and preferences at all times, all the while taking into consideration the context, it can be necessary to orient oneself towards approaches based on principles of adaptation and of personalization (Figure 1). Finally, whatever the targeted information system, the focus is to always place the user at the center of its design.

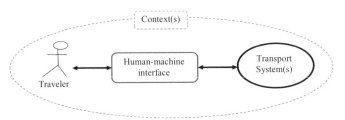

Figure 1. *The traveler as a user of interactive system(s)*

This book on human-computer interactions, the fruit of a common labor, is by no means trying to be exhaustive. Our desire is to above all make available to readers from universities, industry, students or engineers, a summary of available results, of the short-term or long-term ongoing works, in the field of human-computer interaction with transport applications according to approaches centered on their users.

The first chapter was written by Guillaume Uster. It is worth noting that the term multimodal, often used in the literature relating to human-machine interfaces (also called human-computer interfaces or user interfaces in this book) from the point of view of human-machine interaction modes, characterizes in this chapter the use of several means or modes of transport to get from one place to another, which is a source of complexity for the user. He or she must therefore have relevant information made available to him or her according to different forms, interaction modes (thus rejoining the concept of multimodal user interface in HCI) and on different media, either interactive or not, as much during the preparation of the journey as during the journey itself, in a situation of mobility. Guillaume Uster defines multimodal information, in order to then put forward the *Viatic* concept, from the Latin *viaticum* "provisions for the journey", which consists in accompanying the mobility of the traveler each day, from the point of view of innovative information and services. A group of representative research projects,

---

2 Throughout the book, for ease of use, we shall refer to the user simply as "he".

focused on traveler information in a multimodal context are then reviewed by the author, to lead to the concept of reasoned mobility.

The second chapter, written by Pierre Morizet-Mahoudeaux, Annette Valentin and Assia Mouloudi, deals with the integration of the real needs of users in the design of traveler information systems, seen as interactive systems. This approach bases itself on the hypothesis that to be successful in the integration of usage data generated by methods of analysis of the activity, these must be represented in a formalism which is as close as possible to the language of development. The RAMSES approach comes from an experiment on a project of multimodal traveler information system design and has given rise to the design of an aid tool for the specification to be used by designers.

In Chapter 3, Mourad Abed, Abdouroihamane Anli, Christophe Kolski and Emmanuelle Grislin put forward a method called PerMet (*PERsonalization METhodology*) for the analysis, design and modeling of personalized interactive systems. It aims to enable both the implementation of a new personalized interactive system and the personalization of an already existing interactive system. PerMet proposes an iterative, incremental development model and enables a parallel realization, of on the one hand the specific phases linked to the development of services offered by the target system, and on the other hand the specific phases linked to personalization. The chapter also describes a generic personalization system, called PerSyst (*PERsonalization SYSTem*), which can be used conjointly with PerMet for the development of an interactive personalization system. PerSyst is built from an architecture based on agents at the service of the users, which gives it an increased flexibility thanks to the characteristics of adaptability, autonomy, reproducibility and mobility of software agents, among others. A real-world example is presented implementing both the contributions of PerMet and PerSyst for the development of a personalized transport information system.

Multimodal human-computer interfaces enable several media or channels of communication to cooperate on a semantic level (in input and/or in output) in order to increase the communicative abilities of the machine. The objective of the fourth chapter, written by Linda Mohand Oussaïd, Nadjet Kamel, Idir Aït Sadoune, Yamine Ait Ameur and Mohamed Ahmed Nacer, is to present the techniques that currently exist for the modeling and formal verification of multimodal interactive systems; these techniques enable the safe development of the multimodal HCI, conforming to specifications, as well as the verification of the properties of usability of the interface. The authors distinguish, throughout the chapter, between the input and output multimodality and for each of them present the existing works, the formal model proposed, as well as an application of the model to a multimodal HCI used in the field of transport.

The fundamental question raised by Thierry Bellet, Jean-Michel Hoc, Serge Boverie and Guy Boy in Chapter 5 deals with the respective role of the human and technology in the control of the vehicle: must we seek to deliberately be within a substitutive logic (replace the human driver as soon as it is technically possible) or, conversely, must we rather look to focus on the complementarities of the human-machine couple, only assisting the driver when he or she expresses the need and/or when he or she is not able to correctly face the situation ? The co-piloting approach such as it is dealt with here is strictly within this second viewpoint and questions the integrative aspect of an automobile co-pilot in view of guaranteeing a centralized management of the human-machine cooperation.

Bertrand David, René Chalon and Bernard Favre, authors of Chapter 6, present a series of studies dealing with the proper operation of the trucks and buses of the future. This is the vision of ICT (Information Communication Technology) use, and more particularly of their HCI, which is the central point of this presentation, that shows how trucks and buses, placed in appropriate informational contexts such as those put forward by mobile computing, which is *pervasive* and omnipresent, can offer more efficiency and effectiveness in their use and operation, as well as numerous annex services both to the users and the transport operators. According to the authors, it is thanks to the conjunction between embedded computing, wearable computing and fixed computing connected via a computing network that this result can be obtained.

The seventh chapter, written by Annick Maincent, Hélène Tattegrain, Marie-Pierre Bruyas and Arnaud Bonnard, presents the user-centered design approach used to design a truck driving assistance system for reducing accidents with vulnerable users and developed through the VIVRE2 (Industrial Vehicles and Vulnerable Road Users) project. Authors describe the steps applied, from the specification of assistance strategies and human-machine interfaces, based on contextual analysis, to the implementation of technical systems and their assessment using a truck-driving simulator. The specific aspect of this approach was to deal, from a systemic point of view, not only with the actual activity of truck drivers, but also with the vulnerable users' behaviors around delivery trucks. Designed for reducing accidents between vulnerable users (pedestrians, cyclists and motorcyclists) and industrial vehicles in urban areas, the adaptive assistance is based on dynamic strategies according to drivers' and vulnerable user(s)' behaviors for given situations.

The topic of Chapter 8 is the use of the auditory modality in the context of HCI and more precisely the role that sound can play in the interaction process between a user and a system. This question is addressed within the particular framework of menu sonification in an automotive media center, a system that is becoming more and more common in current cars and that essentially allows the driver to manage information of different kinds about the vehicle or the status of various embedded systems (GPS, radio, etc.). In fact, this information is usually given to the driver via visual representations. But, considering that eyes should essentially remain on the road, it can be relevant to consider that ears may constitute a complementary channel for delivering targeted and efficient elements of information. Stakes of this approach are then, first, to secure the driving activity by preventing the driver from looking away too often from the road, and second, to take up ergonomic and qualitative challenges by delivering information through sound. For that purpose, specific studies in the auditory display community are reviewed in the first part of the chapter in order to lead to the definition of an original model for sonification of the aimed application (media center hierarchical menu). Two different implementations of this generic model are then exposed and an experimental procedure for perceptually evaluating these solutions is detailed. Finally, the results obtained are presented, discussed with regards to the preliminary hypothesis and put into perspective for future directions of the work.

The generalization of nomadic tools now enables us to consult a lot of information at any moment and anywhere; the difficulty is then to access relevant information. This is all the more true in the field of transport where, for the duration of the journey, the user must be able to access information regarding his trip, but also services which are adapted to his expectations and needs. However, these are different for each traveler and evolve throughout the trip via a specific experience of the travel time for each individual. This prospective chapter, written by Arnaud Brossard, Mourad Abed, Christophe Kolski and Guillaume Uster, proposes, based on a model-driven method for interactive application design, to take into account, in the applications, the notion of travel time experience of users on public transport. The method is illustrated with several examples in this field, paving the way for numerous research perspectives.

Chapter 10, written by Christophe Jacquet, Yacine Bellik and Yolaine Bourda, is based on the following observation: most of the architecture models for the human-machine interaction do not have an explicit representation for the user. This is a problem in the world of public transport, as we are dealing with mobile users with heterogeneous characteristics: it becomes necessary to take into account both the location and the possible particularities of each user. The authors therefore introduce an architecture model adapted to mobility environments, which explicitly represents information, the presentation devices and the users, the latter occupying a central place. This model was implemented in experiments of providing multimodal information in station- or airport-type environments. These experiments, related in detail in this chapter, demonstrate the benefit of dynamic information presentations, which adapt to users who are present, and offer perspectives on the matter.

Finally, in the last chapter, Gaëlle Calvary, Audrey Serna, Christophe Kolski and Joëlle Coutaz explore the world of transport and access to traveler information in the broad sense, from the point of view of the *plasticity* of user interfaces in ambient intelligence. Plasticity denotes the adaptation ability of interfaces to their context of use with respect to properties based on the user. An analysis of the evolution of the human-computer interaction in ambient intelligence leaves room for potential adaptations. According to two perspectives, user and system, the principles of plasticity are envisaged and illustrated in the world of transport. A space problem for the implementation of the plasticity of user interfaces is proposed at the end of this chapter; this space is intended for designers to help them come up with innovative solutions and to ask the right questions regarding their engineering.

Bibliography

[HEW 96] HEWETT T.T., BAECKER R., CARD S., CAREY T., GASEN I., MANTEI M., PERLMAN G., STRONG G., VERPLANK W., *ACM SIGCHI Curricula for Human-Computer Interaction*, ACM Special Interest Group on Computer-Human Interaction Curriculum Development Group, 1996, available at: http://old.sigchi.org/cdg/cdg2.html.

[ROB 03] ROBERT J.M., "Que faut-il savoir sur les utilisateurs pour réaliser des interfaces de qualité ?", in BOY G. (ed.), *Ingénierie cognitive: IHM et cognition*, p. 249-283, Hermès, Paris, 2003.

[SEA 08] SEARS A., JACKO J.A., *The Human-Computer Interaction Handbook: Fundamentals, Evolving Technologies* (2nd Ed.), CRC Press, New York, United States 2008.

[SEF 09] SEFFAH A., VANDERDONCKT J., DESMARAIS M.C., *Human-Centered Software Engineering: Software Engineering Models, Patterns and Architectures for HCI*, Springer, 2009.

[SHN 09] SHNEIDERMAN B., PLAISANT C., *Designing the User Interface: Strategies for Effective Human-Computer Interaction* (5th Ed.), Addison Wesley, 2009.

Acknowledgements

The Editor would like to warmly thank the authors of the different chapters of this book for having contributed to it and for their comments, which were always relevant and constructive. He also thanks all his contacts at ISTE Ltd and Hermès Science Publishing.

Most of the works described in this book were supported by the National Center for Scientific Research and/or the National Research Agency, the Ministry of Higher Education and Research, the Transport Ministry, the PREDIT, the European Community, the International Campus on Security and Intermodality in Transport, the Nord-Pas-de-Calais region, and the Regional Delegation for Research and Technology. A big thank you to all of these institutions, to the organizers of the "IT in Transport" Forum (IFSTTAR, *GL Journal*), to the establishments to which all the authors belong as well as the industrial partners concerned.

The Editor also thanks his wife Jutta, his daughter Joanna, his family and his family-in-law for many kind little reasons.

Chapter 1

Principles, Issues and Viewpoints of Traveler Information in a Multimodal Context

1.1. Introduction

Traveler information in a multimodal context covers all of the information necessary for the preparation and realization of a journey that uses several means of transport. The term multimodal, often used in literature related to human-computer interaction (HCI) (or more generally human-machine interaction), must be interpreted in the sense of mobility here, that is to say the use of several means or modes of transport. It is rare that a journey is monomodal (only one mode being involved). As an example, the use of an automobile requires the "walking" mode to access or leave the vehicle. In this field, when asked "what is traveler information?" it is customary to answer: "information is what reduces the traveler's uncertainty".

This rough definition allows two main points to be put forward: that it is centered on the traveler, the receiver of information; it highlights the fact that the value of information is measured in the reduction of the resulting uncertainty: any message that does not lead to a reduction in uncertainty must be considered noise.

Surveys [GIL 97] have shown that the traveler awaits "hot" signals from dynamic information, such as information about the arrival of the next metro or bus for example. The main objective of information is therefore to reduce the traveler's uncertainty. The information must be clear, precise and meet the needs of the person and his context of mobility; for example, by giving him the quickest multimodal

Chapter written by Guillaume USTER.

itinerary or the delay for his connecting train. It is worth noting that, from a terminological point of view, traveler information is more closely related to the world of public transportation, whereas in English-speaking literature the term *traveler information* is dedicated to information for road users and essentially concerns road traffic and guidance. The term ATIS (*advanced traveler information systems*) is more generic and is currently eliciting numerous scientific publications, both in engineering sciences and social sciences [LYO 07].

In this chapter, we will present the different aspects of traveler information and show its complexity, depending on the receivers, places and diffusion media. We will then define the multimodal information system enabling a database that classifies all the information relative to the offer of mobility to be constructed, such as train, bus and tram times, the subway train frequency, etc., enabling the traveler to plan his journey and guide him when he carries it out. The viatic research concept, the aim of which is to try to bring added value to the only information linked to mobility by agreement services during the journey and by simplified payment, will be described. We will then present PREDIT (the national program for experimentation and innovation research in terrestrial transport; see www.predit.prd.fr) research projects linked to traveler information. In terms of viewpoints, information becomes increasingly personalized and thus requires highly refined human-machine interfaces.

1.2. A complexity that must be mastered

Like the transport networks that it must enable the use of, traveler information requires a complex domain that is due in particular to the diversity and multiplicity of different *items*:

– the situation of the travelers involved: the regular users or commuters (who make the same journey daily), the occasional users (who do not know the network) and the non-residents (tourists, for example);

– the information producers (the transport system operator and the transport organizing authority[1], which is the public body that finances the transport system, not applicable for countries with privatized transport system, such as Network Rail in the UK);

---

1 Since 1982, a law on the organization of transport within France has provided a guide for regulation. The role of a transport organizing authority is to finance and organize transport under its jurisdiction. For example, in France, four institutional levels coexist: 1) the State is in charge of national transport services; 2) the region for regional rail and road transport; 3) the county for non urban public transport and school transport services; and 4) the commune or group of communes, for urban public transport services in a given territory.

– the travelers' queries (which mode of transport will take me from place A to place B? Which bus timetable should I use? What are the fares for this route? At what time is the next connecting train/bus?, etc.);

– the places where information is made available (at the traveler's home, at the station or on the bus, etc.);

– the media and usable mediums (paper for timetables or network maps, internet for remote access, mobile telephones or mobile objects such as personal assistants, tablets, displays, loudspeaker announcements, face-to-face conversations with transport personnel).

More specifically, the different types of travelers can be characterized according to their intentions with regard to public transportation:

– *Potential travelers*, with no intention of traveling: it is necessary to suggest destinations or motives for travel to them, combined with public transportation services. For example, "to visit that museum, take tramway line B towards the hospital".

– *Travelers in a situation of modal choice*: these travelers have a choice of several modes of transport to reach their destination. It is necessary to increase the chances of public transportation being chosen over other means, and therefore to present the comparable advantages.

– *Travelers "wanting to use public transport"*: these are regular users of the network, but it is nonetheless necessary to help them program and plan their occasional journeys.

– *Travelers in transit*: it is necessary to help them carry out their trips, by guiding them, giving them landmarks and reassuring them throughout their journey. This is achieved, for example, via clear and coherent signage, pictograms and the use of colors that can easily be noticed.

There are many places where information is available and they are not just confined to transport network offices:

– *public places*: in public areas, such as the street, where an arrow will be placed pointing towards the metro stop;

– *private places*: at home, at the work place, in hotels, in a person's own car where information could appear on paper (timetable) or digitally (on a screen);

– *town/transport interface*: at the bus stops with the network map and times, outside trains with the direction of travel and carriage number, at the entrance of stations with the name and destinations they are going to, etc.;

– *within public transportation*: inside the bus with a map of the route or a loudspeaker announcement for the next stop; in station areas with direction signposts and a list of the stations linked by the service; on the platforms with the waiting time displayed before the next subway train, etc.;

– *on ourselves*: this is probably the "place" that will hold the most contextualized and personalized services of traveler information in the future.

In the transport domain, three kinds of information coexist:

– Theoretical information, such as the network map, drawings of public transport lines, or vehicle departure times, has a lifespan of several months to several years.

– Factual information provides details of predicted, planned and programmed events, such as works, construction sites, service cancellations, strikes, etc. Its lifespan is *in theory* known.

– Dynamic information is based solely on using a transport system in real time. It can take the form of waiting time and, in the case of incidents or accidents involving people, a disturbance alert is broadcast, a delay announced, or alternative routes suggested in the event of a prolonged blockage on the line.

Mastering this complexity leads us to adopt a starting point that is focused on the travelers. Based on the questions the client is asking in a given place, at a given time, envisaging which answers to supply, this includes the risk of the client turning away from the public transport network. This philosophy differs from a "technical orientation", in which the possibilities offered by a given technology are first considered in order to apply them to traveler information. The continuous appearance of new information and communication technologies in the domain of data transmission (Bluetooth, WiFi, 3G, 3G+, etc.) such as information-receiving equipment (such as cell phones, personal assistants and nomad computers) has a tendency to cause operators who wish to offer a traveler information services using the latest innovations to throw caution to the wind.

Nonetheless, it is advisable to focus above all on the basics and only a global approach can bring a certain amount of coherence to this ensemble. This so-called functional approach consists of announcing information that must be supplied to the travelers (current or potential), in each place before any technological solution, in order to answer the questions they are asking themselves in each place.

Thus, the functions assigned to a system of traveler information can be distributed according to the four following families:

– the *promotional functions*: meet the commercial objectives of the transport company;

– the *pedagogical functions*: facilitate public transport learning and lead travelers to conform to the user regulations;

– the *operational functions*: facilitate the programming and execution of the trip;

– the *appropriative functions*: facilitate appropriation and mastering of the transport system.

To correctly define the functional approach, it is therefore advisable to answer the following questions:

– what are the *objectives* assigned by the producers of traveler information?

– what are the different types of travelers involved?

– where is the information being made available?

– what are the functions that traveler information will have to fulfill?

We have presented and defined traveler information in the context of a public transport system, as well as the functional approach that its players must adopt, based on [FAI 96]. Nonetheless, during his trip the traveler uses several individual transport systems, such as the car, as well as collective ones, such as the train, bus or tram. The term multimodal information is then used.

1.3. Multimodal information

Specific French laws called *Grenelle de l'environment*[2] defined the main points of sustainable development and were in favor of sustainable mobility. To try and respond to the challenge of sustainable mobility, which involves restoring the balance between the car, on the one hand, and public transport and more generally the soft modes[3], on the other, a concept is starting to emerge in France: multimodal information. The idea is to create a "unique counter", focusing on all of the forms of mobility on offer in a given territory [UST 00]. It is a matter of proposing the global offer including public transport, parking possibilities, how long automobile journeys will take, cycle lanes, taxis, carpooling offers[4], the routes pedestrians take, bicycle or electric scooter hire, etc. All individual and collective forms of urban mobility must be brought together to produce a database allowing us to optimize the mobility resources in a territory. The valuation of such a mutualization of data, called a multimodal information system (MIS), must not only be carried out via services

---

2 http://www.legrenelle-environnement.fr/.
3 Soft modes of transport are those that do not emit CO_2, such as walking, cycling, etc. We also say it is an active mode, to signal that man is the "motor".
4 This consists of a short-term automobile location (a few hours).

destined for the user-client, but also to institutional, professional and economic worlds.

Therefore, the mutualization of data can help the authority organizing the trips and the users of transport to better optimize public spending [PER 02] in the definition of the offer, as well as in the domain of the coordinated use of networks. For example, MIS can make it possible to update inconsistencies in the forms of mobility on offer, with regards to transit, or even redundancies in the same itinerary. A better knowledge of transport demand could also lead to the appearance of new forms of mobility regarding on-demand transport services or car sharing.

This mass of data can help companies that are looking to offer employees a transport solution, in the context of their company mobility plan. The key here is to minimize single-person automobile journeys (without passengers) on the trips between employees' homes and their workplace. For example, regulations enable employees (or employers) to claim a 50% refund on the cost of a season ticket using public transport or bicycle hire. Beyond this incentive, removing parking spaces at the workplace is another, more restricting, aspect. The places that generate flows, such as shopping or leisure centers, are also potential targets for the valuation of the MIS. The availability of this database to players in the information society could also give rise to the development of services with added value, which are more personalized and will eventually have to be paid for.

From an individual point of view, the idea is to create services to help mobility. People living in the city are offered an optimal chain of transport, enabling them to carry out their desired trip:

– by offering global information on all means of transport for a given trip (*preparation for the journey*);

– by accompanying the traveler in his mobility and judiciously advising him, if possible in real time (*realization of the journey*).

This is what we summarize as the two objectives of the MIS [UST 01a]:

– clarification of the modal choice: suggest the global offer of all means of transport in a given trip;

– facilitation of the usage of networks: accompany the traveler who uses transport networks and judiciously inform him.

As the traveler moves through different networks, client sharing is an interesting component to aid the development of a MIS. Therefore, talking to the client and making information available outside the network to address a potential client is a convincing argument for mutualization. The lack of a clear legal answer to the issue of availability and reuse of information concerning mobility has, however, long held back the creation of services. An analysis of the European legislative evolution (2003-98 directives) and its national transposition (ordinance of June 6 and the decree of December 5, 2005) allows the qualification of multimodal information services implemented by the organizing authorities in the context of the LOTI[5] (Art 27-1) of public services, which are of an administrative nature and spread public data. This should be able to remove this obstacle. With regards to Europe, France is definitely behind in the development of MISs, a delay due mostly to its institutional features [UST 01b]. Multimodal information systems are set up in agglomerations, counties and regions, but in a disorganized manner with no real dialog or coherence in many countries worldwide.

In France, from 2001, PREDIT wished to help its development via specific action bringing together individuals from the public and private sectors as well as the scientific and industrial competencies regarding a social issue. It is due to this so-called federative action that Predim was created. Predim (a research and experimentation platform for the development of multimodal information, http://www.predim.org/) aims to improve the complementarity of different modes of transport and travel, both individually and collectively, via the promotion of adequate information mechanisms. From 2000, with the law relative to solidarity and urban renewal, the legislator had called for local authorities from the largest agglomerations to create these kinds of services. Predim contributes to the deployment of multimodal information by completing incentive and mutualization tasks with the help of research, industry and public players.

Following the works of the *Grenelle de l'environment*, AFIMB (the French agency for multimodal information and ticketing), which is dependent on the State, has been created and aims to create homogeneous development of information services over all the French territory. This has been possible thanks to the European standardization efforts, which have served as the basis for implementing added-valued services intended for public use.

In this new organization, the State should be a regulator. As a regulator of the definition of a "universal service of multimodal information", a minimum amount of information is to be exchanged between transport users, involving an open architecture and a common language that needs to be validated in a European approach. It will also be a regulator of the standardization of information exchange, aiding true integration of multimodal information at a national level. It should also help combine the implementation of future ticketing, which will see the disappearance of paper transport tickets to be replaced by new technologies, such as contactless cards or mobile telephones. The realization of a system of multimodal

5 LOTI: orientation law for interior transport.

information will be difficult and sinuous, not only due to the stakes of those involved, but also due to the economic model that needs to be consolidated [PER 04].

1.4. The viatic concept: accompany the traveler

Today, the use of collective means of transport is no longer just restricted to captive users who do not have a personal vehicle. Public transport offers a real modal alternative to its clients. In order to increase modal transfer from the automobile to public transport, however, it is advisable to improve the attractiveness of public transport by simplifying its use. To do this, we have come up with the viatic concept in the context of the Viatic.Mobilité ANR project (National Research Agency) that involves five research laboratories and 10 companies.

Stemming from the Latin *viaticum* meaning "provisions for the journey", Viatic. Mobilité accompanies the mobility of the daily traveler. It aims to offer innovative services and to simplify how they are paid for by making the most of the possibilities made available by information and communication technologies [UST 09].

These services aim to suggest information to accompany the traveler during his travel (multimodal information) and supply complementary information during his journey (news, culture, entertainment, tourism, games): information that is accessible close to the transport systems and on board them. The traveler is not just a user who moves from point A to point B. He is a student, a potential buyer, a tourist, a worker, anxious, someone in a hurry, someone with reduced mobility. Depending on the time, his profile and status, he needs diversified information that he can take with him. The service supply must be present all along his daily or occasional route all along. In the context of the ANR Viatic.Mobility project, an anthropological study monitoring routes has made it possible to highlight the need for information resources to be positioned throughout the traveler's journey.

Based on observations made on the regional express train from Lille to Valenciennes, France, a typology was developed based on ratings, enabling four traveler states to be identified, illustrated by different animals (see Figure 1.1): the beaver works, the marmot is disconnected, the owl is on alert, and the peacock is like an actor. Everyone can identify with this at a given moment in their journey, and informational needs are not always the same depending on the profiles [JUG 07].

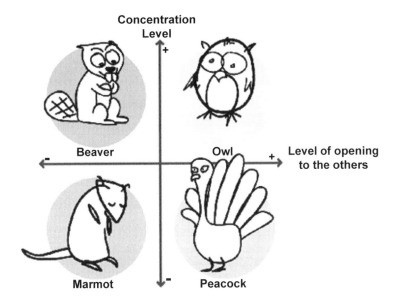

Figure 1.1. *Identification of four traveler states*

The viatic concept materialized through an operational application in the form of an informational fountain, a prototype that can be seen in Figure 1.2. Intuitively, it enables the town to be apprehended using just one finger thanks to its tactile screen. It can be used to search for an address, ask for an itinerary preferentially using public transport and can suggest services that are in close proximity (libraries, cinemas and listings, post offices, swimming pools, opening times, etc.). It also offers information to be used immediately on a big screen that is visible from a distance.

Once the information has been consulted, the traveler can print it off on thermal paper as a "receipt" or send it via SMS. He has then got the information and can carry on with his journey. Viatic provides the traveler with information that will enable him to "take charge of his time" and will contribute to transforming his journey into time spent actively and no longer passively.

The informational fountain was used as a case study in an engineering thesis [BRO 08] led by models applied to the development of personalized human-machine interfaces. Modeling the user according to his psychological profile, at a given moment, means that a more relevant interface can be offered [BRO 09] (see also Chapter 9).

Figure 1.2. *Prototype of the informational fountain from the ANR Viatic.Mobilité project*

In 2009, the continuity of the information service of the viatic concept was also to be found on board a regional express train financed by the Regional Council of the Nord-Pas-de-Calais region in Northern France. An autonomous interactive screen allowed for a general display on a large screen and access to more detailed information on nomad equipment via a WiFi network [UST 09]. This limited trial, partly financed by the i-trans competitivity cluster and supported by a rail industrialist, did not the allow travelers to completely test the benefits offered, but has opened up promising perspectives.

1.5. Other traveler information-based representative research projects in a multimodal context

In this section, several traveler information-based research projects in a multimodal context will be put forward. They give an overview of multimodal information systems that should ultimately be made available to users and which for the most part also envisage new opportunities in terms of human-machine interactions.

1.5.1. *Traveler information and valorization of route time*

The concept of route time valorization was introduced by the French National Institute for Transport and Safety Research (INRETS) in 2003 in the context of the TESS (transport, space and society) project financed by the Research Ministry. The idea was not only to provide information on the journey itself, but also about the urban environment, or even general information involving the interests of the client. One application was able to be carried out in an urban bus run by the Lille metropolis urban community network operator. This vehicle had a geo-localization system giving it its position within the town. The services developed enabled an announcement to be made before the stops as well as regarding cultural and tourist information about the district that it was going through. This information was available on a personal assistant [AMB 08], [GRA 03].

Beyond locating vehicles, which is generally the most frequently studied function, in 2002 research by PREDIT focused on the localization of people moving around in a transport network [UST 03]. The approach was aimed at identifying the effects of this innovation on the development of traveler information services by using a functional approach. It formalized concepts relative to traveler information in order to envisage the potential advantages of localization for these services and by revealing possible avenues for the development of new personalized services, such as:

– "immediate departure" information that informs the traveler, who knows the purpose of his journey but has not organized his trip beforehand, about the best multimodal journey to take in real time;

– information concerning "opportunities in mobility". This is a matter of keeping the traveler informed, during his journey, of the opportunities in the traveled environment that are likely to interest him;

– "assistance" information, which gives the traveler a reassuring way to be helped if a difficult situation arises during the journey; it can also inform the traveler of any incidents detected.

1.5.2. *Traveler information and personalized accompaniment*

The MOUVER.PERSO [GRI 07] research project has enabled the study and implementation of personalized mobility in the context of student daily mobility. Students have a timetable that is initially "static" (but can change each week). Outside this timetable, they use their spare time in different ways: sport and leisure, shopping, culture, etc. The originality of this project is that it accompanied students throughout their occupations in a personalized way:

– in terms of journeys (preferred means of transport, cost);

– in terms of their daily schedules (in relation to the preferences of students and depending on the transport available).

The timetable of students therefore becomes "dynamic". The functionalities associated with the system can thus:

– provide transport information that is relevant to the user;

– plan itineraries;

– manage a personal schedule;

– spread information by ensuring the usability of the human-machine interface;

– manage the presentation of information using different aids.

Its originality lies in offering transport solutions corresponding to the planned events. Indeed, the addition of an event linked to a journey in the schedule sets off the calculation of a corresponding itinerary. Moreover, this itinerary is chosen according to the profile of the user registered in the system. This project is based on the field of multi-agent systems [MAN 02] and research on personalization and learning [ANL 06], [PET 03]. Technical tests have been carried out in order to detect possible defects, introduced in the methodological phase of definition and implementation of the system. The proposed schedule functions by using Webpages as well as a personal digital assistant (PDA).

The laboratory prototype was tested and evaluated by around 20 students with criteria relating to utility and usability, all the while putting emphasis on personalization [SOU 08a], [SOU 08b]. Let us recall here that usability mainly accounts for the quality of human-machine interaction in terms of how easy it is to learn and use. Utility determines whether the interface meets the needs of the user [NIE 93]. In terms of results on utility, 55% of users were very satisfied, 40% were satisfied and 5% were not very satisfied. With regards to usability of the system, the rate of user satisfaction was 41% and 59% were very satisfied. These good results can be explained by the fact that the service is quite simple and was fairly quick and easy to learn. The tests show that the planned personalization functionalities have indeed been carried out, but they also highlight which areas need to be improved. These in particular have to do with the performance of the developed prototype, which demonstrate a need to optimize the research and filter algorithms before being applied on a more large-scale use.

1.5.3. *Traveler information and ergonomics*

Ergonomics is a scientific domain used as an approach to public transport; see for example [LEC 00], [PAT 99]. In the PASS ITS project, an analysis of customer needs was carried out in the public transport network of the agglomeration of Orleans, France. The objective was to identify information that could collectively and individually help users to reach their destination and attenuate any possible disturbances. The sample was refined via hypotheses regarding criteria that could have an impact on the management of the journey, such as network knowledge, IT knowledge and whether the user is of working age or retired, for instance. The profiles of the travelers were thus defined so as to enable the collection of information that could be generalized ([MOU 05], [MOU 07a], [MOU 07b] and refer to Chapter 2 for more on this subject).

As for the population, criteria for the construction of journeys were studied to cover the variability of potential situations regarding modes of travel, places corresponding to the stages of the journey (home, station, transit, public place) and lines (frequency of weak, variable or strong services, types of stations, period (different times, week days, weekend, holidays)). These elements were combined in journey scenarios enabling fictitious disruptions to be managed and to cover the representativity of contexts. For example, the user takes his car as far as a park-and-ride car park, goes to the tram stop, travels by tram, receives a warning message concerning his route, changes to take a bus, travels by bus, gets off the bus and finishes the journey to his destination on foot. Out of the 40 tests carried out, two-thirds of the scenario simulations were done in the lab and a third on site. The information was broadcast by telephone, PDA, laptops, PCs in the lab or on an illustrated board in the case of the proposition of prospective services. Marks enable the usefulness of the service offered to be determined (Does the principle of the service seem interesting to you?) and the usability of the service offered (Does the service seem practical to you in its current state?). It was therefore possible to collect a great deal of information via this very precise analysis of traveler information needs, in a public transport network. It will enable us to refine the kind and form of information to be delivered [MOU 07a].

1.5.4. *Traveler information and intelligent agents*

One of the major difficulties encountered is in elaborating information based on elements contained in different and heterogeneous information systems. This is why it seemed interesting to work on the notion of intelligent agents. These software agents, some of which are adaptive and cooperative, are well adapted tools for browsing and collecting information in a heterogeneous universe. We have used this technology in the context of two PhD theses [ANL 06], [PET 03], following a collaboration between INRETS and the University of Valenciennes, with the aim of intelligent filtering of information. Based on a defined profile and according to a user model, it consists of selecting the information and presenting it in a personalized way, offering greater abundance and relevance than information of a general nature.

In line with this approach, it is advisable to accompany the member of the public during information research and when making a decision about modal choice. We can, for example, cite a PhD thesis about an interactive system of help for multimodal travel [ZID 06]. Furthermore, in order to avoid the traveler having to consult several transport operator Websites to plan his journey, a PhD thesis [KAM 07a] was aimed at conceiving a cooperative mobility information system (CMIS) enabling this route search to be automated, thanks to an integrated information system based on principles that come from multi-agent systems. The CMIS therefore becomes an intermediary between different sources of heterogeneous and distributed information on the one hand and clients on the other. This system must be capable of both finding the right source of information to query it according to various user requirements and grouping information together in such a way as to meet requirements [KAM 05], [KAM 07b]. To provide an itinerary with different components that is optimized according to criteria to be defined, the use of distributed algorithms has been backed up in a patent [KAM 08].

1.5.5. *Traveler information and adjustment to cognitive abilities and the situation of mobility*

For land transport, road information intended for road users has been around for a long time and has seen a lot of public investment to ensure the safety and fluidity of traffic in and around large agglomerations, heavy traffic roads and on motorways. Moreover, personal navigation system equipment for car users that can supply dynamic information concerning disturbances (onboard global positioning system or GPS) has undergone a phenomenal development thanks to a better precision in localization and regularly updated cartography. Even if the latest surveys show a certain dip in its use, the automobile represents around 88% of mobility in France (CCFA, Committee of French Car Manufacturers, 2007). The Mobilurb project [JUG 05] completed the analysis of needs, both of the automobile driver and the multimodal user, via an anthropological approach. The objective was to functionally define a box to aid multimodal mobility. After having qualified the traveler action processes in a disrupted situation, the specifications of a box were thought of, the mission of which would be to provide an appropriate navigational aid and to generate alternative routes when there is a disrupted situation. The originality of this concept lies in its capacity to adapt itself to different user profiles. It is necessary to vary how much the navigational system intervenes so that the tool can adjust itself both to the cognitive competencies of the user and to the mobility situation.

As such, four intervention levels have been differentiated:

– *Passive mode*: MobilUrb would only supply help at the request of travelers. This mode corresponds to the traveler wishing to keep his freedom of circulation, and movement.

– *Pro-active mode*: the terminal, depending on the interventions it gets and the information that it would receive via GPS, would automatically be triggered in a crisis situation to offer alternative solutions. At any moment, it could unplug itself to regain its autonomy.

– *Tutorial mode* would guide the traveler from start to end. MobilUrb would take care of the traveler's journey, remotely video-guided via the intermediary of information that would reach him in real time. This mode would satisfy travelers who are used to following a plan of action to the letter.

– *Personal travel assistant mode* (or distress call) would be piloted by the mobility station by resorting to the help of a physical person who would indicate the way to them and reassure the person. This is the highest degree of intervention that is directed in priority at totally disorientated people.

This project has unfortunately not yet been followed up on for the materialization of the multimodal box, which could have raised interesting issues linked to the design and evaluation of man–machine interfaces.

1.5.6. *Traveler information applied to the bicycle mode*

We could not close this section on transport research projects without mentioning the bicycle mode, which is making a strong comeback in urban centers thanks to the development of cycle hire (Vélo'V in Lyon, Vélib' in Paris). The national research agency (ANR) has thus financed the VIC – Vi(ll)e Cycle project, which aims to rethink the bicycle as it is and to better integrate it into the system of global mobility. The bicycle has evolved little since its creation and, in contrast to the automobile, does not benefit much from new technologies, particularly in terms of safety, assisted movement (electric power) or even steering. Furthermore, information given to the cyclist is practically non-existent. In France in 2009, only a single site in the commune of Tours offered bicycle routes, allowing users to choose between speed and optimal security conditions, such as using cycle paths (http://www.geovelo.fr/).

1.6. Viewpoints

There are already a few small gestures being made on the planet: recycling waste, turning off lights... what is the mobility in these actions? The cost of energy, the protection of the planet, reduction of greenhouse gas emissions and optimization of rare mobility resources are about the extent of topics that the public is aware of. We suggest introducing the concept of reasoned mobility [UST 04]. It is necessary here to take the meaning of the term "reason" from 18th Century philosophers, i.e. a new impetus, an opening towards a more enlightened, more sustainable world. Reasoned mobility in the sense of intelligent mobility! By analogy with an *intelligent transport system*, which is an industry that road and automobile transport in North America and Japan expect a lot of, but with a strong orientation towards public transport, intuition and the responsibility of the public. The stakes of reasoned mobility are to imagine services that help people get around, which accompany the individual in his journey, by guiding him through the mysteries of transport networks and instilling in him the precepts of sustainable development. This involves appreciably bringing him to a change of modal behavior, which is not radical but progressive, and even localized.

In terms of transporting people, broadcasting information is more often general and collective. An initial level of refinement would be to contextualize information, that is to say provide information targeted to a group of people who are in a given situation. Nonetheless, as the possibilities of precise and individual localization and the explosion of new IT services [UST 01c] show, the future is towards "individualization". To limit the amount of information that needs to be sifted though, each person would like to receive information that is useful to them. The personalization of information [UST 00] will be, without a doubt, a major stake in the years to come. The individual is at the center of this device, the communication "knot", through which the thread of information must pass.

Furthermore, a summary of around 40 research projects carried out in the context of the PREDIT [UST 08] has put forward the central position given to the traveler in the mobility system. The projects wish to accompany the traveler in his journey, in the exchange centers, during his shopping or to erase his handicap. Here information plays a fundamental role and has the objective of giving value to all multimodal offers and personalizing services according to his profile. The few demonstrators developed in these projects favor personal nomad tools, personal assistants, cell phones and other nomad computers. In terms of the human-machine interface, however, it seems that information receptors are just simple copies of desktop computers, but in a restricted way.

If the students and young members of the public are familiar with these small screens and can manipulate touch interfaces with dexterity, it is not advisable to neglect older people, the number of whom will considerably increase in France in the years to come. In France, the law on accessibility was voted in on February 11, 2005. Accessibility is an essential condition to enable everybody to carry out acts in daily life and to participate in social life. The law also anticipates the principle of generalized accessibility, whatever a person's handicap (physical, sensory, mental, psychological or cognitive). Access to information for people with reduced visibility, the blind, those with reduced hearing, the deaf, or suffering from a mental disability is therefore a major challenge for the organizing authorities. The idea is still to develop services of digital assistance for mobility that take into account the cognitive profile, handicap and past of each person and offer a human-machine interface that is suitable and friendly. Numerous studies and research still need to be conducted on this, however, with the integration and observation of users in the cycle being carried out within *Living Labs*[6].

1.7. Bibliography

[AMB 08] AMBELLOUIS S., GRANSART C., USTER G., *L'Autobus Communicant – Projet TESS*, rapport INRETS, no. 270, 2008.

[ANL 06] ANLI A., Méthodologie de développement des systèmes d'information personnalisés: Application à un système d'information au service des usagers des transports terrestres de personnes, PhD Thesis, University of Valenciennes and Hainaut-Cambrésis, France, 2006.

[BRO 08] BROSSARD A., L'ingénierie dirigée par les modèles appliquée au développement d'interfaces graphiques personnalisées: une approche à travers les processus métier, PhD thesis, University of Valenciennes and Hainaut-Cambrésis, France, 2008.

[BRO 09] BROSSARD A., ABED M., KOLSKI C., USTER G., "User modeling: the consideration of the experience of time during journeys in public transportation", *ACM Mobility Conference 2009*, ACM Press, Nice, France, 2-4 September 2009.

[FAI 96] FAIVRE J.P., Etude de Faisabilité sur la Mise en Place d'un Système d'Information sur l'Offre de Transport Collectif de Voyageur - Phase 4: Préconisation, Technical report, Paris, France, October 1996.

[GIL 97] GILLES M., Les Attentes des Usagers, FIER Report No. 22, UTP, 1997.

[GRA 03] GRANSART C., RIOULT J., USTER G., "Mobile objects and ground transportation innovative services", *Proceedings of PDPTA '03*, Las Vegas, USA, 2003.

---

6 A *Living Lab* (European quality label) groups together public and private players, as well as players from companies, associations, individuals, with the objective of testing the services, tools and new uses of systems on a "real scale".

[GRI 07] GRISLIN-LE STRUGEON E., ANLI A., PETIT-ROZE C., SOUI M., CONREUR G., DOS SANTOS P., ABED M., KOLSKI C., MOUVER.PERSO, MObilité et mUltimodalité Voyageurs Etudiants, Système d'Information Multimodale Personnalisée, Intermediate report (May 2006) and Final report (July 2007) of Research Contract PREDIT DTT 216-75-01, LAMIH, Valenciennes, France, 2007.

[JUG 05] JUGUET S., BOULLIER D., USTER G., MASSOT M.H., "Pour une assistance informationnelle contextualisée : le projet MobilUrb", *Transport Environnement Circulation*, vol. 185, pp. 49-53, January/March 2005.

[JUG 07] JUGUET S., CHEVRIER S., PETIT C., USTER G., "Radiographie du voyageur : de l'(in)activité aux services à la mobilité", *Actes du Congrès ATEC*, Paris, France, 2007.

[KAM 05] KAMOUN M.A., USTER G., HAMMADI S., "An agent-based cooperative information system for multimodal transport's travelers assistance", *Proceedings IMACS 2005 Scientific Computation, Applied Mathematics and Simulation*, Paris, France, 2005.

[KAM 07a] KAMOUN M.A., Conception d'un système d'information pour l'aide au déplacement multimodal: Une approche multi-agent pour la recherche et la composition des itinéraires en ligne, PhD Thesis, Ecole centrale de Lille and University of Science and Technology of Lille (LAGIS) / INRETS-ESTAS, April 2007.

[KAM 07b] KAMOUN M.A., USTER G., HAMMADI S., "An agent-based cooperative information system for multi-modal route computation", *Proceedings IEEE International Conference on Systems, Man and Cybernetics*, The Big Island, Hawaii, USA, 2005.

[KAM 08] KAMOUN M.A., USTER G., HAMMADI S., Procédé de Recherche et de Composition d'Itinéraires, Patent WO2008017775, 14th February 2008.

[LEC 00] LECOMTE N., PATESSON R., "Le panel des voyageurs: Une étude des activités et des besoins d'information des utilisateurs des transports publics", in: *Actes de la Conférence ERGO-IHM*, D.L. SCAPIN and E. VERGISON (eds), pp. 129-135, Biarritz, France, 2000.

[LYO 07] LYONS G., AVINERI E., FARAG S., HARMAN R., Strategic Review of Travel Information Research, Final Report to the Department for Transport, Contract TDT/149, 2007.

[MAN 02] MANDIAU R., GRISLIN-LE STRUGEON E., PENINOU A., *Organisation et Applications des SMA*, Hermès, Paris, France, 2002.

[MOU 05] MOULOUDI A., LEMARCHAND C., VALENTIN A., MORIZET-MAHOUDEAUX P., "User information guidance in public transportation systems", *Proceedings of the 11th International Conference on Human Computer Interaction*, Lawrence Erlbaum Associates, Las Vegas, USA, July 2005.

[MOU 07a] MOULOUDI A., Intégration des besoins des utilisateurs pour la conception de systèmes d'information interactifs: Application à la conception d'un système d'information-voyageurs multimodal (SIVM), PhD thesis, University of Technology Compiègne, France, 2007.

[MOU 07b] MOULOUDI A., MORIZET-MAHOUDEAUX P., LEMARCHAND C., VALENTIN A., "A proposal of HCI model based on user needs", *Proceedings of IEEE International Human-Machine Interaction Conference Human'07*, Timimoun, Algeria, March 2007.

[NIE 93] NIELSEN J., *Usability Engineering*, Academic Press, London, UK, 1993.

[PAT 99] PATESSON R., LECOMTE N., "User needs analysis: an analysis based on the study of activities of the traveler", *Proceedings of the 8th International Conference on Human-Computer Interaction*, Munich, Germany, 1999.

[PER 02] PERREAU C., Les systèmes d'information multimodale: apports et potentialités dans l'optimisation des déplacements urbains, PhD Thesis, Institute of Political Studies, Paris, France, July 2002.

[PER 04] PERREAU C., USTER G., "Une approche économique de l'information multimodale", *Recherche Transports Sécurité*, vol. 83, pp. 85-98, April-June 2004.

[PET 03] PETIT-ROZÉ C., Organisation multi-agents au service de la personnalisation des informations. Application à un système d'information multimodale pour le transport terrestre des personnes, PhD thesis, University of Valenciennes and Hainaut-Cambrésis, France, 2003.

[SOU 08a] SOUI M., ABED M., "Evaluation of personalized interactive systems in transport applications: criteria and evaluation methods", *27th European Annual Conference on Human Decision-Making and Manual Control, EAM'08*, Delft, The Netherlands, June 2008.

[SOU 08b] SOUI M., KOLSKI C., ABED M., USTER G., "Evaluation of personalized information systems: application in intelligent transport systems", *Proceedings of the 20th International Conference on Software Engineering and Knowledge Engineering, SEKE2008*, pp. 877-880, San Francisco, USA, June 1-3 2008.

[UST 00] USTER G., "Etat des réflexions sur le développement de l'information multimodale en France", *Conférence Internationale UITP "Comment Faire de l'Information Passager votre Meilleur Atout?"*, Hanover, Germany, 2000.

[UST 01a] USTER G., "Développement de l'information multimodale en France: Quels leviers actionner ?", *Annales des Ponts et Chaussées*, vol. 98, pp. 22-26, 2001.

[UST 01b] USTER G., GUIDEZ S., "Pourquoi l'information multimodale ne se développe-t-elle pas en France?", *Actes du congrès ATEC*, Paris, France, 2001.

[UST 01c] USTER G., "Public transport information: towards the information society", *Urban Transport VII*, WIT Press, Massachusetts, USA, pp. 317-326, 2001.

[UST 03] USTER G., VU ANH S., "L'apport de la localisation dans l'information aux voyageurs", *Actes du Congrès ATEC*, Paris, France, 2003.

[UST 04] USTER G., "Pour une mobilité raisonnée", in *Mobilités.net - LGDJ, collection "Questions numériques"*, D. KAPLAN and H. LAFFONT (eds), pp. 324-329, 2004, http://www.lgdj.fr/popup_introduction.php ?Ouvrage=7799.

[UST 08] USTER G., *Services de Mobilité et d'Information*, Innovation et recherche, Paris, Documentation Française, Collection "Le point sur" du PREDIT, 2008.

[UST 09] USTER G., JUGUET S., TALON G., "The Viatic concept: information technology for intelligent travelers", *ITS-T Conference 2009*, Lille, France, October, 20-22, 2009.

[ZID 06] ZIDI K., Système Interactif d'Aide au Déplacement Multimodal (SIADM), PhD thesis, Ecole Centrale de Lille and the University of Science and Technology of Lille (LAGIS), France, December 2006.

Chapter 2

User Needs Analysis Methodology for the Design of Traveler Information Systems

2.1. Introduction

The design of a traveler information system implies a high interdependence of two types of knowledge: knowledge regarding the expectations of the user and the conditions of use; and knowledge regarding the functional and technical aspects of the problem. It is a matter of defining the functional structures of a system that meet the needs of potential users. With this aim, the use of a user-based approach enables the design process to be efficiently organized [ISO 00], [NOR 86]. Furthermore, the management of needs must be adapted to the variability of potential contexts of use, in particular for the consideration of human and technical constraints. The first stage of this approach is therefore the identification of these two bodies of knowledge (human and technical needs). Once identified and validated, it is a matter of defining their adequate formalisms for representation. Finally, it is a matter of building the bridges enabling these data to be linked. In view of this, the descriptive model of the interactive system to be developed must try to take into account the complexity of reality [FAR 98], [WIE 48]. The aim is to summarize the elements of the problem to be solved in order to specify the appropriate solutions. Authors such as Campos and Nunes [CAM 04] or Pasquier *et al.* [PAS 95] speak on this subject of a gap between the problem space and the solution space. The first space consists of the environment of the problem to be solved with its organizational, technical but also semantic and cultural constraints. The second is characterized by a modeling based on representation structures strongly oriented by the design methods.

Chapter written by Pierre Morizet-Mahoudeaux, Annette Valentin and Assia Mouloudi.

These different design components are dealt with by the specialists who bring specific and complementary skills: project manager, technical designer, ergonomist, user representative and quality controller. It is therefore necessary as early as the stage of analysis of the design process to develop an approach that favors the mutualization of knowledge between different players and which therefore ensures the continuity of its transfer to the rest of the stages.

Different design methods enabling us to link the technical aspects and user needs have been put forward. These works in particular concern: the description of technical tools corresponding to the different phases of a project [BOO 99]; the construction of use cases to translate the flow of events [PHI 02]; the descriptions of tasks to link the actions of the user to those of the system [CON 99], [LAU 01]; the modeling of cognitive components [RAS 94]; and the formalization of storyboards by an interface designer [KRU 01]. Other works try to integrate the complementarity of concepts coming from different domains: engineering, psychology, cognitive sciences and computing [HOL 05], [SOU 04].

These approaches nonetheless remain focused on the operational aspects and few works concern the identification and integration of user needs from the phases upstream of the information system design. However, it is more important to understand *what* the system does and *why* it does than to explain *how* it does it [HOL 05]. The methodology of collecting, analyzing, modeling/specifying and evaluating the specifications of interactive information systems, RAMSES, presented in this chapter, is in line with this viewpoint. The implementation of the approach is illustrated by the presentation of the P@ss-ITS project for the design of a multimodal traveler information system (SIVM).

2.2. Traveler information: a pluridisciplinary matter

The development of a traveler information system for the users of a multimodal public transport network raises scientific and technical questions, both for industrialists and researchers. For transport industrialists as well as for urban areas, it represents an asset in terms of quality of service that can greatly improve the attractiveness of public transport [PER 02] and thus increase its use [UST 01]. Furthermore, the elaboration of a multimodal information system is a business that is technically complex. Indeed, it is a matter of aggregating data that are often heterogeneous and come from non-standardized bases [PET 04]. The communication of informative messages on these diverse interfaces requires particular care in terms of relevance, coherence, accessibility and ergonomics [FES 03], [STE 00], [THE 00]. These different aspects take on a particular interest regarding the issues of human–computer interface design and evaluation [VAL 07b]. Finally, the pluridisciplinary nature that can be given to dealing with these questions is in fact a fertile academic ground. Indeed, the growing mobility and availability of new information interfaces generate new uses which represent a large field of cognitive, psychological and sociological study [FRE 96], [JEM 00].

2.3. The example of the P@ss-ITS project

The P@ss-ITS project was funded by the PREDIM program[1]. Its objective was to design a traveler information system enabling us to evaluate the advantages of providing the users of a multimodal public transport network with real-time information, particularly in the event of a disruption (works, accident, expected or unexpected strike). This project was tested in the urban area of Orleans, France. It was developed in association with the research laboratories of UMR CNRS 6599 – Heudiasyc and ODIC of the University of Technology of Compiègne, the National Institute for Research in Terrestrial Transport, and the companies ALSTOM (Transport division) and TRANSDEV.

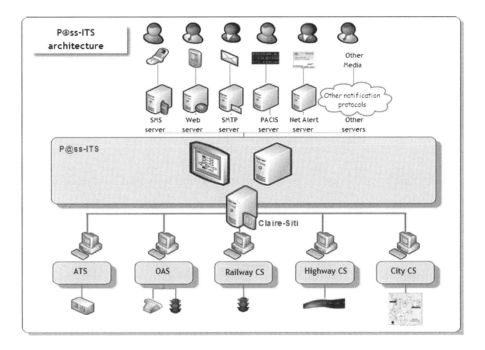

Figure 2.1. *The P@ss-ITS system*

---

1 Research and development platform of multimodal information.

The architecture of the *P@ss-ITS* system presented in Figure 2.1 fulfills three essential functions: (1) the centralization of information coming from different resources describing the functioning and state of the public transport network in real time; (2) the diffusion of relevant and updated information to users; and (3) finally, the elaboration of an answer adapted to personalized requests (itinerary demands, travel schedule, travel modification, search, etc.).

The available information sources are:

– *operating aid systems*, computing applications situated in the operating centers of the different transport modes, the function of which is to assist operators in the management of the network;

– *control stations* that mainly provide real-time information about the state of road traffic in the area;

– *interactive media* that enable information to be distributed to users and ensure the feedback of data to the system. This "dialog" is essential for elaborating a personalized formulation of information in real time.

These data are processed by the system to deliver the relevant real-time message in output. This will enable the user to carry out or pursue his trip, including in the event of a disruption.

The realization of this application has served as a basis for the development of a generic methodology for the design of interactive systems, RAMSES, the principles of which are described in the following section.

2.4. RAMSES methodology for the collection, analysis and modeling of user needs

The design of the *P@ss-ITS* project was based on an ergonomic approach to collecting, analyzing, specifications modeling, and specifications evaluation of an interactive information system. This project has served as a base for the development of a specific study of the links between ergonomic and technological data that are mobilized during the development of an interactive system [MOU 11]. The whole approach has the objective of favoring the transmission of different knowledge that each of the specialists produces during the design process.

2.4.1. *Information flows in RAMSES*

Each design player exerts an activity that generates knowledge. The approach adopted in RAMSES, which stands for "Méthode de Recueil, d'Analyse, de

Modélisation, de Spécification Et d'aide à la Spécification" (Data Collection, Analysis, Modeling, and Specification Method) consists of structuring this knowledge into two flows (see Figure 2.2). The first movement is ascending and represents the *flow of the definition of needs*. It aims to translate the actual activity description into a conceptual representation language along a gradual abstraction process. This flow concerns all the players and begins in the application domain by the identification of the actual user needs. The ergonomist contribution to this step consists of collecting data relative to the use and operation of already existing equivalent systems or contexts. These data are then analyzed to generate the knowledge regarding the needs, expectations and recommendations for improvement and innovation. This knowledge is then transmitted to the designer, who must construct representation models on this basis.

At the end of this phase, the first specifications of the system are drawn up and can be validated in a second flow. The second movement of data is therefore descending and represents *the flow of validation of specifications*. It consists of verifying the appropriateness of the specifications of the system given by the designer against the recommendations of the ergonomist. This iterative phase of definition and validation results in the construction of the functional specifications of a first prototype of the interactive information system (IIS). Once implemented, this prototype will be evaluated by the ergonomist with a panel of users to update the reference source of needs.

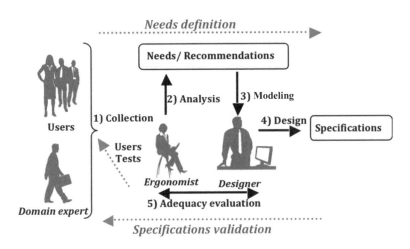

Figure 2.2. *The knowledge flows in RAMSES*

2.4.2. *Generic diagram of information flow*

RAMSES structures knowledge of the design on the basis of a generic diagram representing information flow in an IIS; see Figure 2.3 [MOU 07]. The definition of this diagram implies the specification of the entities involved and their relations, the formalization of use activity of the system by users and the description of the different contexts of use. Indeed, the objective of the design of an information system is to support, assist and/or extend the activity of a user by making relevant information available in its context of use.

The information flows exchanged between the user and the IIS are also illustrated in Figure 2.3. Typically, an information need of a user is transmitted to the IIS via the intermediary of an interface or a medium. The elaboration of a response adapted to this need by the IIS is based on the adequate and available data resources. The system then transmits the information to the user via the adapted interface and medium.

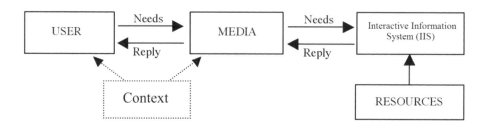

Figure 2.3. *Diagram of information flow in an IIS*

This generic diagram sets the entities to be defined to model the functioning of an IIS. To build this model, the designers must have a methodology that structures both analysis of the problem and construction of the solution. The classic information system design methods propose management of the development cycles that structure the project into phases of analysis, design, realization and validation. It is nonetheless necessary to add an additional approach enabling the generation and transmission of data coming from the analysis of reality (problem, need, specifications) to the design of the system (models, architecture). In other words, it is mandatory to propose a method that enables us to first of all find what the model will need to represent [CAV 00].

2.4.3. *The steps in RAMSES*

RAMSES structures the analysis phase of a project into successive steps. The first step consists of researching and collecting data on information needs. These data are then analyzed and solution recommendations are put forward. At the end of each step, the data and solutions identified are represented in a formalism enabling us to move on to the next step. The progression of the methodology results in a validated model enabling us to begin the phase of IIS development. The following sections describe the four steps of the RAMSES method: data collection, analysis of collected data, modeling/specification and evaluation of specifications.

2.4.3.1. *Data collection*

This first step aims to define user needs and the constraints linked to the information system. Its objective is to understand and characterize the interaction activities of the user with the system in an environment of use. It is carried out by the ergonomist, whose task will be to specify the significant elements from the point of view of the user. Furthermore, a dialog with experts in the application domain is required to define the field of technical and technological possibilities of the system that is to be designed. Different methods can be used to collect these data: survey, interview, discussion groups and observations [SHN 04]. These methods are more or less close to the activity in a situation of use. To favor the consideration of real needs, RAMSES is therefore strongly based on the principles of an ergonomic approach. One of the major properties of this approach is a strict framework for the construction of experiment plans, the definition of the sample of users to be queried and observed, the systematic methods for collecting and the tools for analyzing data [DRO 01], [VAL 06].

The main phases of the data collection steps are:

– *Analysis of the environment of use*: this consists of describing the places in which the user will have access to information delivered by the system (offices, vehicles, outside, etc.), the objectives of the users (tasks prescribed by a procedure or objectives defined directly by the user) and the conditions that can influence the modalities of use (rhythms, flows, temporality, etc.). Second; an inventory of the available and foreseeable media to diffuse the information delivered to the user by the system (computer, cell phone, public terminal, public display, etc.) must be listed. The existing media will then be described according to their ergonomic characteristics (screen sizes, for example) and their technical performance (ability to refresh real time information, for example).

– *Analysis of the operating environment:* this part consists of describing the data resources that are accessible to the system to produce the desired information. Indeed, to elaborate operational recommendations for the design, the ergonomist must know the possible domain of data. He will then be able to recommend their combination to produce information that corresponds to the need that he will have defined with the user. An information system is an application that is based on the operating data and resources (e.g. the available media and its distribution); the IIS can also interact with other systems (e.g. to compare data and put forward emergency solutions in the event of an incident). The functional characteristics of these resources will be described to the ergonomist by experts in the application domain. The ergonomist will endeavor not to limit the proposal to existing systems by projecting it towards the possibilities of new information services for users. A second indicator of the system operating environment concerns the application domain-oriented procedures (in terms of instructions to respect). Indeed, for certain applications the operation of the IIS is restricted by procedures overseeing the security, reliability or organization of the operating environment. With this method, the ergonomist is closest to the constraints of the future system. The previously identified data resources and their functional characteristics will be described to the ergonomist by domain experts so that the considered evolutions will take into account the feasibility constraints.

– *User profile*s: the definition of a representative sample of users targeted by the system is mandatory to correctly specify the relevant criteria for the application. The size of the sample depends on the environment of use. It can nonetheless remain relatively limited as it is a matter of seeking representativeness and not necessarily exhaustiveness of all the combinations of criteria [BRA 04], [NIE 93]. Nielsen, for example, puts forward that it is possible to identify around 80% of software errors that are destined to a specific profile of users with six people of this profile [NIE 00].

The tools recommended for the description of use and the operating environments, as well as for setting the users' profile, are the classical tools for the preparation of activity analysis. The documentary study of the IIS application context (organizational and technical aspects) will be completed with interviews with technical experts. The consultation of organizational and technical documents will also be necessary to define the constraints and rules that govern the application domain of the IIS that is to be designed.

– *Observation of users*: activity analysis is based on the study of users in situations of use. Depending on the constraints of the project (development phase, access to the real environment, availability of new tools, etc.), observations can be made in a real situation or based on scenarios [CAR 00], [ROT 05]. The commentaries of users are solicited in parallel with the observed activity to understand their underlying thought processes.

Data collection can be made by several observers but this may generate discrepancies in the recorded data [HER 01]. Furthermore, the next steps of the method (analysis, implementation and evaluation) require having structured data. According to principles frequently used in ergonomics, the collection of information has therefore been built based on a grid enabling us to make the collection of information systematic (time, place, media, action, commentary, etc.). This medium also contributed to guaranteeing a certain homogeneity of records between the different observers. The medium has been globally organized around activity decomposition into cycles repeated in three phases: preparation of the strategy, implementations of the action plan and capitalization of knowledge after the activity; see Figure 2.4 [MOU 07].

This activity cycle can be repeated several times during an observation. If an event disrupts the progress of an action plan, the user can be called on to make an intermediary assessment, prepare a new plan, pursue its realization, etc. For example, for the observation of a journey on public transport, the support of data collection can be prepared according to the planned steps: planning of an itinerary at the departure station, realization of the travel (travel on a line, connection, commute, etc.), report at the end of the travel; if the travel is disrupted, an intermediary report can be made and a new cycle is launched with a new plan, a new progression, etc.

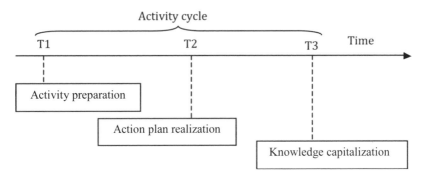

Figure 2.4. *Decomposition of an activity cycle into phases*

2.4.3.2. *Analysis of collected data*

Once the data have been collected, the analysis consists of extracting the specifications of the system linked to the user needs and named *use-oriented specification*. This step calls for using formalisms to represent the activity. The objective of this representation is to bring to the foreground significant elements of the activity of the user into the context of use. The research works undertaken in the domain of human–machine interfaces have given rise to numerous formalisms for the modeling of tasks [DIA 04], [KOL 01]. These models enable us to build logical trees linking user actions to a context represented by conditions and rules.

Task models are frequently used to specify human–machine interfaces. As the functionalities and processing are developed within an information system, the specifications can also be based on one of the numerous formalisms used for the development of computing systems in software engineering.

In RAMSES, the objective of activity analysis is to identify information needs in different contexts of use. It is a matter of accounting for the dynamics of activity in evolving contexts and with a population that has a great variability. Indeed the action depends on circumstances [SUC 87]. An action only has meaning when it is linked to its context of occurrence and restituted in the progress of a general strategy of the user. The analysis of collected data must enable this dynamic to be re-transcribed into a form that is easily shareable, in order to result in the specification of an IIS corresponding to the needs of the target population.

The analysis of needs progresses in two stages. First, the data are re-transcribed in a chronological account of the use activity. Each step of the activity is split into sequences called "action-objective sequences". Each sequence corresponds to an objective of information search situated in its context (description of the environment of use). The media used are also mentioned in order to specify the characteristics that could have influenced the degree of usability of information. The action objective sequences are then submitted to a second processing. Indeed, for the design of the IIS, the analysis of the activity must be centered on the use of information, i.e. the availability, usability and appropriateness of information to the needs and objectives of users. This second processing enables the analysis to be oriented from this point of view.

The first step for data analysis was structured with Quintilien's hexameter (*Who does what, where, when, how and why?*). This tool is frequently cited in the quality approaches, particularly in the Six Sigma method [HAR 00]. The objective is to lean towards a completeness of information enabling the context of an event to be identified. It is a matter of obtaining a precise and factual description of the progress, trying to analyze the components that intervene at each step exhaustively, to still understand the situation [VAL 06]. Each action is situated in space and time (the time and place of the unfolding of the action), and then its content is described by the observer. It is then a matter of specifying with what aim it was undertaken. The motives of the action are partly provided by the commentaries that the users make during the observation of the activity. They can come from past experiences or personal representations. Wiener says on this subject that it is the personal representations of the source and recipient of a message that reveal the meaning of a message [WIE 48]. These motivations will enable us, in the following steps, to update the mechanisms by which the inputs are combined with prior knowledge in order to obtain elaborated strategies [KAY 97]. Thus, these analyses inform as to the motivations and real objectives pursued by users via the actions undertaken.

The modalities of realization of the action are also formalized. The incidents are listed to highlight all the events that could have impeded the progress of the action and the consequences of the action-objective sequence are saved (continuation of the strategy or modification following an incident). This breakdown enables the logic taken by the user to reach his objectives to be reconstituted. Moreover, the first analyses carried out in order to identify the motives of actions enable us to go beyond the explicit elements and to work on the real motivations of an action, which are often conditioned by the possibilities of the moment.

The second level of analysis considers the action-objective sequences more specifically from the point of view of information use. Here it is matter of building a table that highlights the elements of the context that can influence the utility and usability of information. In particular the table describes: the user via his profile; the medium that circulates the information; and the elements of interaction of the user with the information content – information type (according to the typology of the domain), state (accessibility, utility, topicality) and effective use (or not).

The analysis of each action by information descriptors enables us to show the user needs in the context of information use. Each need gives rise to a proposal of information or improvement of the user's information conditions. These proposals are expressed in terms of resources identified during the analysis of the operating domain. This work is carried out by the ergonomist whose expertise in analysis of the activity enables him not only to describe the explicit user actions but to specify his underlying motivations. The realization of this step enables the ergonomist to have a qualified knowledge corpus. This knowledge describes the information use activity and the critical situations corresponding to the needs which are to be satisfied. At the end of these two steps of ergonomics analysis, the ergonomist can make proposals orientated on the usage of the IIS (human–machine interface specifications). The analysis of the operating environment enables us to update these recommendations with regard to the technical possibilities and constraints.

2.4.3.3. *A modeling that favors cooperation*

It is now a matter of having an approach that ensures the transition of the information gathered and analyzed by the ergonomist to the other members of the project. Its objective is to guarantee that the wishes of the ergonomist are respected and that the computing model that will be built based on this analysis is achievable. Furthermore, this model will need to be legible by the ergonomist in the validation phase.

This approach is based on a formal model built based on all the elements previously collected. The objective is to model the knowledge acquired in the experimental phase and to represent it in a structured formalism that makes it operational for the implementation of a logical model. The passage from a representation of needs to a formal model consists of finding a paradigm and associated concepts enabling us to represent the entities that make sense in relation to the problem and to identify the links that join them together. The choice of formalism depends on the ability of concepts to conserve the integrity of the constituted data and on the language that will be used for the implementation of the system.

In this approach, the objective is to look for a formalism and notation that are specific to software development, in order to have a language for the representation of data that is mastered by the computing designer tasked with the realization at the same time as being significant for the ergonomist who analyses needs. This formalism must enable the contextualized user needs to (re)join the formalized data of information resources; all the while preserving the wealth that is inherent in the methodological rigor of data collection and analysis.

To satisfy all the characteristics cited, the object-oriented (OO) approach was chosen. This approach is at the heart of numerous techniques to analyze, design and implement flexible and robust real-world systems, including essential properties such as encapsulation, polymorphism, heritage and reusability [BOO 99], [JAC 92]. It enables the building of the conceptual representations of data issued from the real world and thus allows their implementation [DÉT 94]. The process of object modeling offers a support to the translation of experimental data, according to an ontological description of real world entities and their relations. It enables the structural, dynamic and functional aspects of an activity to be translated [CHA 03]. This model will be completed by the inheritance analyzed by the designer in order to build the descriptive model of development.

UML (*Unified Modeling Language*) was adopted as an object modeling standard by the *Object Management Group* (OMG) in 1997. UML enables multiple views of a system to be represented, with the help of a variety of graphical diagrams such as the use case diagram, class diagram, sequence diagram or communication diagram. In so far as the proposed approach is based on the study of use cases, UML is a particularly well adapted language. Furthermore, works have shown that the use case model acts as a powerful communication tool between developers and users [AGA 03]. A class-state diagram gives the dynamic or static structure of a system, whereas a state diagram gives the dynamic or behavioral nature in terms of state transitions. As for the sequence and communication diagrams, they are two types of interaction diagrams. The sequence diagram explicitly shows the sequencing of messages, and the communication diagram highlights the relations between objects. Both are useful to develop a dynamic model of a system in terms of interaction between objects. An interaction diagram is therefore used to show the interaction patterns between objects for a particular use case. The objects then communicate with each other by sending messages.

Though work still needs to be carried out to merge the progress of human–machine interface research in mainstream UML-based software design methods [PAL 03], OO developers perceive UML as an approach that is intuitive and effective to implement, particularly for use case diagrams and state diagrams [AGA 03]. The developers that have more experience in OO analysis and design techniques also perceive class diagrams and interaction diagrams as easy to use [AGA 03]. In the case of IIS, certain works have already put forward ways for improvement. For example, da Silva and Paton propose an extension of UML that enables us to directly integrate the interface specifications by incorporating a new notation in UML [DAS 03]. UML*i* enables us to express the relations between the use case, tasks, views and particularly the relations that exist between tasks and the data on which they act. More recently, Razali and his colleagues have shown in their survey the benefit of using a method of formalization in UML that is based on a cognitive framework which enables each player to share a notation and a common formalism [RAZ 08]. The object modeling in RAMSES implies a dialog between ergonomist and computing designer. It must be ensured by a designer who masters the OO methods. It progresses according to two axes: a static modeling and a dynamic modeling.

Static modeling or domain modeling describes the use and operating environments of the IIS. The definition of the information flow diagram enables the construction of a class diagram representing the elements of the problem. Each element of the environment (place, media, operator, etc.) previously identified is represented in the form of a class. Activity analysis enables us to exhibit the components, which describe these elements. These components appear as the attributes and methods of these classes. Thus, the ergonomic analysis of the previous step has enabled us to define users' profiles. These profiles represent the instances of a user class. Each user is an instantiated object based on this class. Similarly, the media and resources have been described by the ergonomist in environments of use and operation. These elements contribute to the definition of IIS classes (classes, attributes and methods).

The classes were then linked by associations describing their interactions in the process of production and diffusion of information between the system and the users. The specification of the system at this step is to describe the functions expected after the analysis of user needs. Based on these observations of an existing system or scenarios of contexts, the ergonomist will be able to give the orientation of the IIS functionalities to produce information that meets the user's needs and the conditions to fulfill and guarantee the usability of this information in the environment of use.

The second modeling axis concerns the dynamic aspects of users' activity. This model explains the interactions of the user with the entities created in the static model. These interactions are represented by the description of the activity of users observed. Each action-objective sequence represents the request for an object. It is therefore a call for a class method that could possibly lead to its change of state. The construction of this model must enable the expectations of the user to be situated in relation to an object or a situation of information use. The classes that have been described in the model of the domain will then be able to be enriched with characteristics corresponding to the needs observed.

The static model of the domain has been built on the basis of a class diagram describing the defined entities and their relations. The basic diagram will be built on the four entities described in the generic diagram in Figure 2.3.

The dynamic model of the activity was built on the base of a use case diagram. This diagram must exhaustively describe the types of interaction of the user with the IIS. The construction of this requires the abstraction of objectives that are recurrently found with all users and contrary to the specific and particular objectives. This abstraction work is carried out based on the representation of information use activity [MOU 07].

System modeling is carried out by the designer. Indeed, the modeling and drafting of specifications of the system are strongly linked to development technologies and to technical constraints. However, the method aims to integrate the ergonomic proposals into the system as well as possible. Data representation of activity analysis is carried out with this aim. Thus, the data concerning the needs are qualified by the elements referring back to the classes of the static model. The modeling can be noted in a formalism that is adequate for implementation.

2.4.3.4. *Evaluation of specifications*

Given the previous representation, it becomes possible to model the satisfaction of a user need by an IIS in the form of a function linking the activity of use to the data resources of the IIS. An information need is identified when a user is searching for a solution to a given problem in his context of use. Once identified, each need gives rise to the construction of a solution. In other terms, the satisfaction of a user need (S_B) is a projection of a situation defined by an event E and a context of use C in a space of solutions expressed in terms of data resources P_R:

$$S_B: (E,C) \rightarrow P_R$$

A context of use is made up of the objects, user, media and place. The couple (event and context) constitutes a situation of use that generates an information need. Each situation of use is linked to one or several possible solutions put forward by the ergonomist to meet this need. This proposal is expressed in terms of data resources that are needed to build it. The function of satisfaction need (S_B) thus defined, is surjective and not injective. Indeed, a solution proposal can be associated with several distinct situations of use. The (S_B) function is therefore not injective. Furthermore, a function is surjective when any element of the target ensemble can be associated with an element of the domain. The function (S_B) is therefore surjective, as for any proposition P_R there is an associated situation of use. Thanks to the formatting of this function and to the previous modeling, it becomes possible to implement a specification aiding tool to be used by the designer. Indeed, modeling enables us to build a view of the problem in terms of classes and objects linked by methods. The implementation of these classes according to the function of satisfaction of the need then leaves us to consider the generation of a tool enabling us to search for and manage knowledge that qualifies the user needs and solutions that are associated with them. These recommendations are expressed in terms of entities of the domain model.

2.5. RAMSES in the context of the P@ss-ITS project

As was said in the introduction, the traveler information system design project, *P@ss-ITS*, offered a favorable ground for the implementation of the RAMSES approach. Indeed, the highly iterative aspect of the application, the diversity of the players involved and the variability of situations of use were of particular interest for the collection and analysis of data.

The operational timeframe of the project was nonetheless constrained to an implementation of RAMSES in two distinct phases. The first phase was integrated in the project; it covered the steps of ergonomic collection and analysis, then it contributed to the use-oriented specifications of *P@ss-ITS*. A second phase unfolded in parallel to the realization of the project; based on real data, it consisted of studying the phases of modeling, specification and evaluation of specifications via the MASSIV application.

The initial phase of the project enabled us to identify the information that can help users, both collectively and individually, to reach their destination and attenuate the impact of possible disruptions. As for any design of a "general public" product, this analysis phase implies taking into account the variability of the population, contexts and objectives of use in order to put forward tools that are adapted to the greatest number of potential situations. The preparation of collections therefore required the definition of the samples to be studied: population, contexts, travels [VAL 10a]. The collections were then carried out according to principles of an ergonomic approach, by observation of the activity in an actual situation. Tools of chronological re-transcription were then defined to keep the context of the observed actions. Next, each step was analyzed to identify the information needs of the travelers.

2.5.1. *The preparation of collections*

The strategy of collecting information was elaborated by defining profiles representative of the targeted population and the potential contexts of use.

2.5.1.1. *Population sample*

The variability of the population was defined on the notion of a traveler. Socio-demographic data provided markers for the profiles of network users. Criteria that had an impact on motives, times and constraints of trips were taken into account. For example, people that work have frequent home/work journeys with specific times; people travelling for a leisure activity circulate more easily in the middle of the day; and the elderly can have mobility difficulties.

Aspects that can modify the information that is sought have also been integrated. For example, knowledge of the network conditions information needs in terms of maps and meshing of the network; possible disabilities can require particular modalities (e.g. for the visually impaired) or specific needs (e.g. points accessible to wheelchairs). Students represent an important part of subscribers; people outside the urban area have longer journeys with more connections.

The criteria that characterize the population (student, senior, active, with knowledge of the network, etc.) have been used to build a sample of 36 people. These profiles were combined to enrich the number of cases studied, for example: active and season ticket holder, senior and stranger to the urban area, student in a wheelchair and who does not know the urban area, etc. The sample was then constructed to respect a representativeness of at least six people per criterion: six external, six seniors, six active, etc. According to Nielsen [NIE 93] or Brangier and Barcenilla [BRA 03], this number allows the collection of nearly 80% of needs for the corresponding profiles.

2.5.1.2. *Sample of contexts*

The experiment domain of the project was an urban area of average size: the town of Orleans and the 22 surrounding communities, with a transport network comprising a tramway line and around 30 bus lines. This agglomeration size enables us to have an important variability of contexts.

The lines' timetable varies according to the function of the transport mode and the sectors served. The tram line and certain bus lines have a high frequency and a regular rhythm, but other lines have variable frequencies according to days or time of day. The network proposes numerous connections. A few stations are very important (12 lines at the center of the agglomeration in the Orleans station, eight lines at the Léon Blum bus stop, etc.) and most of the connections have two or three lines.

The criteria characterizing the network (transportation modes, sectors, frequency of lines, types of connection) have enabled a sample of contexts to be defined that must take the observations into account [VAL 06]. For example: the tram line with a high frequency; reliably frequent bus routes; bus routes with a low frequency; average stations with two connections in north and south sectors; great connections with many exchanges in the center of town and towards the outside; small stations; etc.

2.5.2. *The methodology of data collection*

The collection of data concerning the use of transport and information needs of users has been carried out by observing real situations and according to two types of protocol: the monitoring of users making a journey that they had planned and the actualization of scenarios that enable certain tests to be planned and expanded upon.

2.5.2.1. *Actual or constructed journeys*

For passengers, the contexts are linked to the notion of journeys. The choice of observation protocol was therefore made by monitoring users during their travels on real life trips to observe how they manage information in a context in which things are working normally. Having said this, the study was oriented towards disrupted situations, whether planned (demonstrations, road/engineering works) or unforeseen (traffic jams, accidents, breakdowns). It was necessary to be sure of being able to observe disruptions during the data collection phases. The decision was therefore made to construct scenarios with one or several fictitious disruptions (blocked connection, interrupted line or inaccessible station). This method is often used at different phases of the design [DRO 01], [MAL 94], [VAL 93]. In the P@ss-ITS project, the journeys constructed therefore made it possible to introduce numerous potential events and to manage the distribution of journeys in the network to take the variability of contexts into account.

Each public transport user was requested for around two hours, which allowed them to carry out a return journey. For example, starting from the university at noon, "you will go to the village hall of Saint Pryvé to take a document"; this journey meant walking to the tram station, taking the northbound tram, and changing at the Quai de l'Horloge station, taking a bus line towards Candolle. At this stage the observer signaled a "disruption" requiring the person to get off before Candolle to change bus line, etc.

2.5.2.2. *Observations in a real situation*

The ergonomic approach is based on the activity analysis in a real situation and places observation at the center of methods [DAN 04], [NAR 95]. In this project, data collection was carried out by direct observations, following users during their travels in the public transport network (Figure 2.5).

Figure 2.5. *Examples of observed situations: prepare a journey, check times, and take the tram [VAL 10a]*

The observations were collected by several observers. Specific collecting media enable the recording of actions carried out, the information sought after, used or expected, incidents encountered, etc., to be made systematic. Explanations were asked for in parallel (simultaneous verbalizations) to understand the choices of the user. At the end of the journey, an interview enabled us to assess the events encountered.

2.5.3. *The analysis of collections*

The collected elements were analyzed in two steps: first of all in the form of a chronological re-transcription; then from the more specific point of view of information processing.

2.5.3.1. *Chronological re-transcription*

Chronological re-transcription was structured to keep the progression and the context of journeys by using Quintilien's hexameter (top part of Figure 2.6). In this project, the hexameter was used as tables to follow the progress of the stages of a traveler [VAL 06].

Time	Where	What	Why	What for	How	Incident	Result
...							
1.10pm	Station	Looking for a map	To find the quickest way	To go quickly = to avoid connections	Compares few travels	The map is damaged	Has to find another map
...							

Ref	Chr	Line	Media	Level	Objective/actions	Proposals
A3	89	Station	7	1	To find the quickest way	To show travel times
A3	90	Station	7	1	To avoid connections	To propose this criterion
A3	91	Station	7	1	Compares few travels	A table of comparisons
...						

Figure 2.6. *Analysis of collections*

The user (*Who*) was followed throughout the journey. He was therefore not recalled in the table. The other participants were mentioned with the detail of the operations involved. The tables contained the following elements:

– when: the chronology, the times, recorded in particular at the changes of steps; time of entrance/exit of a mode of transport, time of arrival/departure of a connecting node of transportation;

– where: the places (station, bus, tram, etc.); examples: bus line 6, Lorette station;

– what: observable and relatively generic actions, which can be shared between numerous travelers; examples: look for a map, look at a synoptic;

– why: specifications regarding the goal to be reached – examples: to look for the destination, to calculate the length of the travel, etc. – or references to previously acquired knowledge – examples: there is always a network map on the platform; the tram comes regularly;

– how: the modalities of carrying out actions, the operations carried out – examples: the user locates the town and then the town hall, he multiplies the number of stations by the length of a segment, he asks the driver.

Each end of step was shown by two columns. The *Incident* column highlighted disrupting elements, for example the display device is out of order or there is no information about the waiting time. The *Result* column gave the elements obtained, for example the journey is defined, the user obtains his ticket, he waits for the Zénith stop.

2.5.3.2. *Information use analysis*

The objective of the study was to identify the information needs of travelers. The chronological tables being purely descriptive, another table was then built to more specifically analyze the use of information (lower part of Figure 2.6). For this analysis, all the components of the realization of journeys were taken into account: actions, objectives, calling on knowledge, modalities and incidents. Indeed, each element was able to correspond to the expression of needs for the future system. Furthermore, the profile, chronology, places and media used were standardized to facilitate comparative processing.

Analysis later confirmed that this mode of collecting data in various situations (real or simulated) provides very rich results. For example, around 160 needs were defined in the observation phase of the existing network. It is also advisable to highlight the importance of the diversity of profiles. Indeed, analysis by criteria (age, knowledge of the network, disability, etc.) and attempts at reducing the sample showed that it is better to increase the variability of profiles than to increase the number of people with similar profiles. In particular, integrating people with reduced mobility (visually impaired, in a wheelchair, etc.) greatly enriched the identification of needs. Similarly, expertise does not necessarily guarantee the maximum provision of information. For example, people having a poor knowledge of the network have more needs than those who know the network well. However, the proposals put together are potentially useful for all. For example, placing lifts on a station map can help a person in a wheelchair, a person who has a walking stick or a child in a pram; voice announcements in the tram are useful for the visually impaired but also if crowds are blocking the visual displays, etc. [VAL 10b].

The *items* corresponding to similar formulations have therefore been grouped together, for example the user compares the number of stations; he is hesitating between two connections; "we should have taken number 30, it arrives closer to our destination". In these examples, the events all correspond to journey comparisons, but on different criteria. Each event was translated by proposals. Bringing together events of the same type also enabled us to group together proposals, for example to provide a comparative table enabling the choice of a journey according to the length, number of stations and connections, duration of walking, etc.

In this approach, the incidents correspond to the difficulties encountered by certain users and missing or erroneous information during the journeys monitored in

Orleans. The successful strategies highlight positive points to be reinforced, transferred or facilitated. Each event is likely to correspond to a potential need shared by numerous travelers in numerous contexts. For example, the lack of a map of the area was able to be pointed out at Candolle station with a student using the tram line who did not know the sector very well. The corresponding need: "being able to consult a map of the area" is potentially applicable for any traveler who does not know this sector well.

2.5.4. *The definition and evaluation of new services*

Needs concerning the different services of aid to travelers have been identified in the project, for example:

– *at home* (Website): a network map with the display of disruptions and actual timetables, an itinerary computation taking into account disruptions, comparative table of the travel modes, warnings concerning a line or an itinerary, area map with the announcement of works, etc.;

– *during travel* (mobile site): the sending of text messages regarding disruptions, the actual timetables taking into account early/delays, an updated computation of the itinerary that integrates real times and disruptions, etc.;

– *in vehicles*: a dynamic synoptic of progress on the line, the times of the line connecting at the next stop, the possible warnings and emergency solutions, etc.;

– *at stops*: the display of real times and possible disruptions, a station map for connections, a map of the area with the position of other stops and list of possible works, etc.

In a later phase of the project, the identified needs were structured in the form of services diffused via the means of computerized media [VAL 10a]: Website, mobile site, telephone (Figure 2.7).

Given the diversity of situations and profiles, the order of actions is potentially very variable. The design was therefore centered on objects [SHN 04]: current objects (network map, area map, etc.) or missing objects (real time disruptions, real times the trains come, etc.). The objective is to facilitate access to information and to limit the number of entry points by grouping together the objects concerned, for example: map (consult, zoom, print, etc.); this structuring mode is particularly well adapted to the design of new products.

Prototypes were developed, for example the computation directly accessible on the network map and integrating the disruptions in real time. Fictitious images were also created to simulate public displays on potential media (but not available in the whole network): display devices at stops, dynamic synoptic in vehicles, etc. The evaluation of services was defined once again on the basis of case simulations in order to adjust the proposed services.

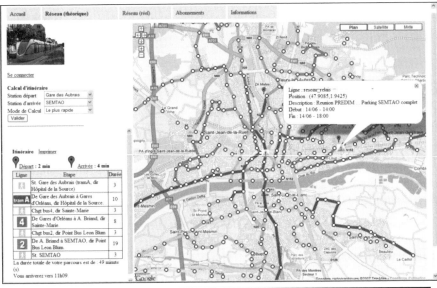

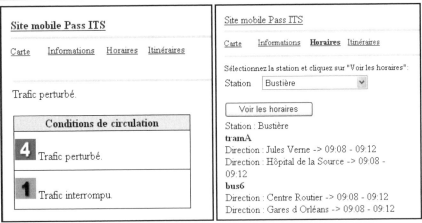

Figure 2.7. *Examples of the prototype screens [VAL 07a]: at the top, network map and computation of an itinerary integrating the real times of vehicles; at the bottom, mobile services (smaller screen) – list of disruptions and times in real time*

2.5.5. *Modeling and specification based on P@ss-ITS data*

The data obtained in the previous phase built a reference source of the real needs of users and the services that they are associated with. To fuel discussion about the approach to integration of needs in the design of the information system, the *P@ss-ITS* domain data were used to produce the modeling of a traveler information system. The modeling was structured according to two axes: a static model of the domain and a dynamic model of the activity. The whole model was then transcribed in UML to obtain a representation that can be interpreted for the implementation.

The static model was structured around the generic diagram of information flow (Figure 2.3), which constitutes a *package* model according to the UML norm. This structure was then developed within a class diagram with the help of inheritance and association mechanisms (Figure 2.8). Note that the static class diagrams come from the codification of the observation collections analysis step (user profiles, places, media, etc.).

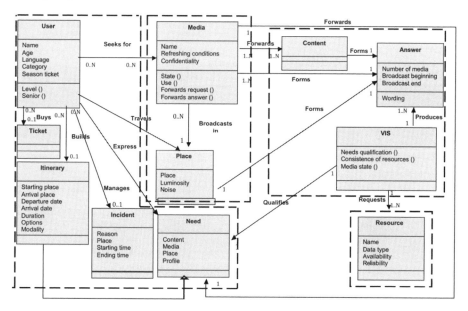

Figure 2.8. *Summary model of the domain classes*

The dynamic of the system from the point of view of the user was modeled starting with a use case diagram. In UML, a diagram of use case represents all the configurations that characterize the behavior of a system. In RAMSES, use cases are built based on the needs of users from decomposition of the activity into action-objective sequences. The first step required defining the blocks of sequence corresponding to situations which are characteristic of the use of information (objectives in the contexts). These use cases were then developed in sequence diagrams or activity diagrams in order to describe their mode of operation [MOU 07].

2.5.6. *MASSIV*

The modeling phase provided a class diagram representing the application domain and a diagram of the use case broken down into sequence diagrams describing the activity of use. The implementation phase consisted of translating the classes and their relations with the help of an OO programming language: Java. The MASSIV application (specification of the traveler information system aid module) was then built on the basis of *P@ss-ITS* collections, following the MVC (model-view-controller) *design pattern* [FRE 05]; see Figure 2.9.

Figure 2.9. *Execution of MASSIV for a visually impaired user*

This application enables the designer to choose the criteria of the situation of use (event, context) and in return obtain a state of needs corresponding to the situation. For a given user profile (e.g. someone who is visually impaired), and the expression of a need (e.g. the knowledge of waiting time at a station), MASSIV enables us to display the situations of real use observed and, for each, the associated solution(s) proposed and the resources that enable it to be implemented. It is also possible to refine the search by specifying the type of medium, a reference to a particular use case, or the state and accessibility of the available information.

This automated translation of data represents a step in the transmission of the real needs of users towards the technical design. Indeed, formalization in terms of objects and access by criteria enable us to hope for a better understanding of the user issues by the system designers. Furthermore, this implementation of use data could be an interesting tool for the evaluation of prototypes. Indeed, the realization of the experimental protocol on an existing device, then on a prototype (or two prototypes separated with an iteration) allows us to create two databases of action-objective sequences. The MASSIV tool will then enable us to compare the use of two systems in relation to the same reference source of situations of use.

2.6. Conclusion

This chapter allowed the empirical and theoretical genesis of a methodology that structures analysis for the design of an IIS to be presented. The methodology comes from experimental work carried out in the context of the *P@ss-ITS* project involving development of a multimodal traveler information system. Feedback from this experiment enabled RAMSES to be built; a formal methodology for the collection, analysis, modeling/specification and evaluation of specifications of an interactive information system. This methodology combines the benefits of paradigms that come from the ergonomics and software engineering, with the aim of helping the design of systems useful and usable to varied populations in a great variability of situations of use.

This study enabled us to validate the RAMSES method for the phase concerning the transformation of users' real needs in functional specifications. It will be advisable to validate its application in the context of a design project enabling its complete deployment. Thus, the benefit of a tool for management of needs of the final users (MASSIV) could be tested before even making prototypes. It would thus be a matter of evaluating its benefit in terms of covering needs, facilitating inter-player communication and/or the degree of transmission of use-oriented specifications for the technical design.

A way to improve RAMSES would be to add iteration circles. As user-centered approaches recommend [ISO 00], it is a matter of analyzing the real use of new services by the panel of travelers – after the realization of a prototype – then in a real situation. The evaluation would be carried out with MASSIV, which would then enable us to verify the response to the needs for each iteration.

2.7. Bibliography

[AGA 03] AGARWAL R., SINHA P., "Object-oriented modelling with UML: A study of developer's perceptions", *Communications of the ACM*, vol. 46, no. 9, pp. 248-256, September 2003.

[BRA 03] BRANGIER E., BARCENILLA J., *Concevoir un Produit Facile à Utiliser*, Editions d'Organisation, Paris, France, 2003.

[BRA 04] BRANGIER E., LANCRY A., LOUCHE C., *Les Dimensions Humaines du Travail: Théorie et Pratiques de la Psychologie du Travail*, Presses Universitaires de Nancy, Nancy, France, 2004.

[BOO 99] BOOCH G., RUMBAUGH J., JACOBSON I., *The Unified Software Development Process*, Addison-Wesley, Boston, USA, 1999.

[CAM 04] CAMPOS P., NUNES N., "CanonSketch: A user-centered tool for canonical abstract prototyping", R. BASTIDE, P. PALANQUE, J. ROTH (eds), *Engineering Human Computer Interaction and Interactive Systems, Joint Working Conference EHCI-DSVIS*, LCNS 3425, Springer Verlag, Hamburg, Germany, pp. 146-163, July 2004.

[CAR 00] CARROLL J.M., *Making Use: Scenario-Based Design of Human-Computer Interactions*, MIT Press, Cambridge, MA, USA, 2006.

[CAV 00] CAVARERO J., LECAT R., *La Conception Orientée objet, Évidence ou Fatalité, Informatique Technosup*, Ellipses, Paris, France, 2000.

[CHA 03] CHAUVIN C., "Modélisation "objet" d'une activité de conduite de navire", SPERANDIO J.C., WOLFF M. (eds), *Formalismes de Modélisation pour l'Analyse du Travail et l'Ergonomie*, pp. 111-136, PUF, Paris, France, 2003.

[CON 99] CONSTANTINE L., LOCKWOOD L., *Software for Use: A Practical Guide to Models and Methods of Usage-Centered Design*, Addison-Wesley, Massachusetts, USA, 1999.

[DAN 04] DANIELLOU F., BÉGUIN P., "Méthodologie de l'action ergonomique: approches du travail réel", FALZON P. (ed.), *Ergonomie*, pp. 335-358, PUF, Paris, France, 2004.

[DAS 03] DA SILVA P.P., PATON N., "User interface modelling in UMLi", *Software IEEE*, vol. 20(4), p. 62-69, July-August, 2003.

[DÉT 94] DÉTIENNE F., "Assessing the cognitive consequences of the object-oriented approach: A survey of empirical research on object-oriented design by individual and teams", *Interacting with Computers*, vol. 9, pp. 47-72, 1994.

[DIA 04] DIAPER D., STANTON N., *The Handbook of Task Analysis for Human-computer Interaction*, Lawrence Erlbaum Associates, New York, USA, 2004.

[DRO 01] DROUIN A., VALENTIN A., VANDERDONCKT J., "Les apports de l'ergonomie à l'analyse et à la conception de systèmes d'information", KOLSKI C. (ed.), *Analyse et Conception de l'IHM, Interaction Homme-Machine pour les Systèmes d'Information*, vol. 1, pp. 51-83, Hermès, Paris, France, 2001.

[FAR 98] FARENC C., BARTHET M.F., "L'évolution de l'intégration de l'ergonomie dans le développement des applications informatiques", *Actes du Colloque Recherche et ergonomie*, pp. 67-71, Hermès, Paris, France, February 1998.

[FES 03] FESENMAIER D.R., RICCI F., SCHAUMLECHNER E., WOBER K.W., ZANELLA C., "DIETORECS: Travel advisory for multiple decision styles", *Conference on Information and Communication Technology in Tourism*, pp. 232-241, Helsinki, Finland, 2003.

[FRE 05] FREEMAN E., SIERRA K., BATES B., BALAND M.C., *Design Patterns*, Editions O'Reilly Media, Sebastopol, CA, USA, 2005.

[FRE 96] FRENAY P., "De l'importance des facteurs psychosociaux dans le choix modal", *Recherche Transports Sécurité*, no. 55, pp. 47-65, 1996.

[HAR 00] HARRY M., SCHOEDER R., *Six Sigma*, Campus Fachbuch. 2005.

[HER 01] HERTZUM M., JACOBSEN N., "The evaluator effect: A chilling fact about usability evaluation methods", *International Journal of Human-Computer Interaction,* vol. 13, no. 4, pp. 421-443, 2001.

[HOL 05] HOLLNAGEL E., WOODS D.D, *Joint Cognitive Systems: Foundations of Cognitive Systems Engineering*, CRC Press, February 2005.

[ISO 00] ISO-18529, Ergonomics – Ergonomics of Human-system Interaction – Human-centered Lifecycle Process Descriptions, International Organization for Standardization, Geneva, Switzerland, 2000.

[JAC 92] JACOBSON I., *Object-Oriented Software Engineering: a Use Case Driven Approach*, Addison-Wesley, Reading, Massachusetts, USA, 1992.

[JEM 00] JEMELIN C., KAUFMANN V., JOYE D., Entre Rupture et Activités: Vivre les Lieux du Transport, Rapport final du projet A4 (PNR41) : OFCIM, Berne, Switzerland, 2000.

[KAY 97] KAYSER D., *La Représentation des Connaissances*, Hermès, Paris, France, 1997.

[KOL 01] KOLSKI C., *Analyse et Conception de l'IHM: Interactions Homme-machine pour les SI*, vol. 1, Hermès, Paris, France, 2001.

[KRU 01] KRUCHTEN P., AHLQVIST S., BYLUND S., "User interface design in the rational unified process", *Object Modeling and User Interface Design*, Addison-Wesley, Massachusetts, USA, 2001.

[LAU 01] LAUSEN S., "Task and support – task descriptions as functional requirements, *Proceedings of AWRE*. pp. 83-91. 2001.

[MAL 94] MALINE J., *Simuler le Travail*, ANACT, Montrouge, France, 1994.

[MOU 07] MOULOUDI A., MORIZET-MAHOUDEAUX P., "Design process of interactive information systems", *Intelligent Decision Technologies, an International Journal*, vol. 1, no. 3, pp. 127-138, 2007.

[MOU 11] MOULOUDI A., MORIZET-MAHOUDEAUX P., VALENTIN A., "RAMSES: A method for the design process of interactive information systems", *International Journal of Human-Computer Interaction*, vol. 27, no. 2, pp. 107-130, 2011.

[NAR 95] NARDI B., "Studying context: a comparison of activity theory, situated action models, and distributed cognition". In: *Context and Consciousness: Activity theory and Human Computer Interaction*, pp. 69-102, MIT Press, Cambridge, MA, USA, 1995.

[NIE 93] NIELSEN J., *Usability Engineering*, Academic Press, London, UK, 1993.

[NIE 00] NIELSEN J., *Why You Only Need to Test with 5 Users*, www.useit.com/alertbox/20000319.html, 2000 (accessed 9.5.11).

[NOR 86] NORMAN D., DRAPER S.W., *User Centred System Design*, Lawrence Erlbaum, Mahwah, NJ, USA, 1986

[PAL 03] PALANQUE P., BASTIDE R., "UML for Interactive Systems: What Is Missing", *Proc. of the IFIP INTERACT Workshop: Closing the Gap: Software Engineering and Human-Computer Interaction*, Zürich, Switzerland, September, 2003.

[PAS 95] PASQUIER C., ROUCOULET P., LANASPÈZE M., *L'Approche Objet*, Hermès, Paris, France, 1995.

[PER 02] PERREAU C., Les systèmes d'information multimodale : apports et potentialités dans l'optimisation des déplacements urbains, PhD Thesis, Institut d'études politiques, Paris, France, July 2002.

[PET 04] PETIT-ROZÉ C., ANLI A., GRISLIN-LE STRUGEON E., ABED M., USTER G., KOLSKI C., "Système d'information transport personnalisée à base d'agents logiciels", *Génie logiciel*, no. 70, pp. 38-47, 2004.

[PHI 02] PHILIPS C., KEMP E., "Support of user interface design in the rational unified process", *Proceedings of the Third Australian User Interface Conference*, pp. 21-27, 2002.

[RAS 94] RASMUSSEN J., PEJTERSEN A., GOODSTEIN L.P., *Cognitive Systems Engineering*, John Wiley & Sons, New York, NY, USA, 1994.

[RAZ 08] RAZALI R., SNOOK C, POPPLETON M., GARRATT P., "Usability assessment of a UML-based formal modeling method using a cognitive dimensions Framework", *Human Technology*, vol. 4, no. 1, pp. 26-46, May 2008.

[ROT 05] ROTH E., PATTERSON E.S., "Using observational study as a tool for discovery: uncovering cognitive and collaborative demands and adaptative strategies", *How Professionals Make Decisions*, Lawrence Erlbaum, Mahwah, NJ, USA, pp. 379-393, 2005.

[SHN 04] SHNEIDERMAN B, PLAISANT C. *Designing the User Interface*, Addison-Wesley, Boston, USA, 2004.

[SOU 04] SOUSA K., FURTADO E., "Upi – a unified process for designing multiple uses", ICSE (Ed.), *ICSE 2004, Workshop Bridging the Gaps between Software Engineering and Human-Computer Interaction*, Scotland, 2004.

[STE 00] STEPHANIDIS C., "From user interfaces for all to an information society for all: Recent achievements and future challenges", CNR-IROE, *6th ERCIM Workshop "User Interfaces For All"*, Florencia, Italy, October 2000.

[SUC 87] SUCHMAN L., *Plans and Situated Action: the Problem of Human-machine Communication*, Cambridge University Press, New York, USA, 1987.

[THE 00] THEVENIN D., CALVARY G., COUTAZ J., "La multimodalité en plasticité", *Colloque sur la Multimodalité*, IMAG, Grenoble, France, May 2000.

[UST 01] USTER G., "Développement de l'information multimodale en France: quels leviers actionner?", *Annales des Ponts et Chaussées*, no. 98, pp. 22-26, 2001.

[VAL 93] VALENTIN A., VALLERY G., LUCONGSANG R., *L'Évaluation Ergonomique des Logiciels: une Démarche Itérative de Conception*, ANACT, Montrouge, France, 1993.

[VAL 06] VALENTIN A., LEMARCHAND C., MOULOUDI A., MORIZET-MAHOUDEAUX P., "Identifying relevant objects in users' activities with Quintilian's hexameter", *16th Congress of the International Ergonomics Association*, The Netherlands, July 2006.

[VAL 07a] VALENTIN A., LEMARCHAND C. *Tests de P@ss-ITS: Synthèse des Principaux Éléments*, 2007 (available at: www.predim.org/spip.php?article2757, accessed 9.5.11).

[VAL 07b] VALENTIN A., LANCRY A., LEMARCHAND C., MOULOUDI A., MORIZET-MAHOUDEAUX P., "L'action située dans la conception de produit: L'exemple d'un serveur d'informations d'aide aux voyageurs", *42th Congrès de la SELF: Ergonomie des Produits et des Services*, Saint-Malo, France, 2007.

[VAL 10a] VALENTIN A., L'ergonomie dans une conception orientée objet des produits logiciels ; D'une démarche centrée utilisateur vers une démarche fondée sur les situations, PhD Thesis, University of Picardy Jules Verne, Amiens, France, December 2010.

[VAL 10b] VALENTIN A., LANCRY A., LEMARCHAND C., "La construction des échantillons dans la conception ergonomique de produits logiciels pour le grand public: Quel quantitatif pour les études qualitatives?" *Le Travail Humain*, vol. 73, pp. 261-290, 2010.

[WIE 48] WIENER N., *Cybernetics*, MIT Press, Cambridge, USA, 1948.

Chapter 3

A Generic Method for Personalizing Interactive Systems: Application to Traveler Information

3.1. Introduction

Following the wide development of distributed and networked information sources, more specifically on the Internet, the advantage of benefiting from reference points, such as "portal" sites that offer facilitated, even personalized access to all available resources became apparent. The personalization of information systems (ISs) aims to provide an adaptive and intelligent human-machine interaction with the goal of improving the efficiency of the interaction as well as the usability (in the sense of [NIE 93]) of systems [MOU 09]. It must offer the possibility of accessing ever greater quantities of information on increasingly varied media and support increasingly different interaction modes.

In order to meet the usability criteria and enable the user to easily find the information he wants, personalization appears to be an appropriate solution [MOU 09], [PET 03a]. In addition to the personalization of delivered information, other aspects of the interaction can be subject to personalization in this context, such as the consideration of different interaction modes (vocal, textual, etc.), the consideration of different interaction platforms (PC, personalized digital assistant or PDA, cell phone, etc.) and user assistance. Our objective is to provide a support to the design of personalization systems that covers these different aspects. The

Chapter written by Mourad Abed, Abdouroihamane Anli, Christophe Kolski and Emmanuelle Grislin.

consideration of interaction modes and platforms used means, for us, that the personalization system must integrate them into its reasoning in relation to the preferences of the user. The personalization system must be able to know or deduce, for example, that for a given piece of information the user would prefer to listen to it from his cell phone, rather than read it on his PDA.

This notion of personalization is inscribed in the continuity of current research, which has been very active in man-machine interactions since the beginning of the 1980s, and targets new, increasingly adaptive and intelligent interactions [HOO 00], [KOL 98], [MOU 09], [KOL 92] (see also the *User Modeling and User-Adapted Interaction* journal). Initially, through its approach centered around adaptation to the user, personalization in human-computer interaction (HCI) can also be seen as very complementary to current research on plasticity, which currently most often puts emphasis on adaptation to the platform and the interaction environment [CAL 03], [CAL 07], [KOL 04,] (see also Chapter 11 in this book).

This chapter is based on different documents, including [ANL 05a], [ANL 05b], [ANL 05c], [ANL 06b], [ANL 07], [GRI 07,], and especially [ANL 06a] (a PhD thesis co-financed by Archimed in Lille and the Nord-Pas-de-Calais region of France). It begins with a non-exhaustive review of personalization systems at the origin of the proposal, which is the focus of this chapter. Then, an approach called *PERsonalization METhodology* (PerMet) for the development of personalized ISs, as well as a personalization system called *PERsonalization SYSTem* (PerSyst), which differs from the others in its distributed and evolving aspect, will be presented. Giving the main points, we then describe an application developed for the validation of our approach in the domain of transport; it is meant for itinerary planning based on the personal calendar of the user. A discussion and a conclusion will end this chapter.

3.2. Personalization in HCI: examples of existing approaches, at the origin of the approach proposed

Several systems are contributing to progress in the domain of personalization in human-machine interactions. These systems are, for the most part, destined to aid navigation on the Web (for example, Web browsers). They ensure the observation of user behavior, and the research, filtering and presentation of this information.

Arising from the works of Lieberman [LIE 01], Letizia saves the URLs chosen by the user, reads the pages and draws up a profile of the user as he visits pages; based on this, it searches for other pages that are likely to interest the user and presents its results in an independent window.

IFWeb [ASN 97] carries out the search and filtering of documents by taking into account the specific needs of the user; when a document is selected by a user, the system searches the web for similar documents and shows them to the user, ranking them in order of relevance.

IFM (*Intelligent File Manipulator*) [VIR 02] is a system that aids the graphic handling of file systems; it intervenes automatically and suggests advice when a user makes inconsistent approaches or commits handling errors. IFM bases itself on stereotypes and includes a mechanism for recognizing the goals of the user.

InfoSleuth [NOD 00] relates the queries of the user to the corresponding service providers. The work of InfoSleuth agents is based on the use of ontologies, which enable them to specify the queries or to break them down, and then to fuse collected information together based on heterogeneous and distributed sources.

WebMate [KEE 00] is an agent for aiding information search on the web. It learns the profile of the user, prepares personalized news for him and helps him improve his information search. The profile of a user is an ensemble of keywords found in the pages that he has selected. These pages are positive examples of the machine learning algorithm; this algorithm uses the frequency of appearances of words in the pages. There is a mechanism of keyword "expansion": the addition of words with a similar connotation to a given keyword in order to specify its meaning.

Stemming from previous works at the Laboratoire d'Automatique, de Mécanique et d'Informatique industrielles et Humaines (LAMIH), MAPIS (MultiAgent Personalized Information System) [PET 03a], [PET 04], [PET 06] is a Web application based on software agents that help users of public people transport with their itinerary choice. The profile of the user corresponds to the associated weighting given in relation to the different modes (bus, train, metro, walking, etc.), the length of the journey, the number of changes and the cost of the journey. MAPIS uses a reinforcement learning mechanism for management of the user profile.

Other systems are based on the profile of the user to provide personalized information in specific domains, such as *Gulliver's Genie* [OHA 03] for tourism and Smart Radio [HAY 04] for music. The former uses localization, direction and user preferences to search for cultural or tourist places that could be of interest to him, and sends this personalized information on a PDA. The system is based on the *Beliefs, Desires and Intentions* or BDI model [RAO 91] to infer the mental state of the user. The latter enables users to listen to their favorite music or to a musical program recommended by the system. In order to know their musical tastes, Smart Radio asks its users to rate an ensemble of musical pieces, or musical programs, from one to five (five being the highest mark), in order to establish user profiles.

The user therefore has the possibility of creating a personal *playlist* and can later listen to his favorite tracks. Thanks to this profile, the system can find one or more users with common tastes in terms of music and thus recommend to each person another person's or other people's playlist(s).

Another category of systems aims to facilitate the design of personalized ISs. They generally appear in the form of an application ensuring the representation of the user profile and the inference mechanisms for choosing which solution to suggest. Independent of the browser used, BroadWay [TRO 99] is a system that bases itself on user navigation to recommend links to a particular user, using a case-based reasoning motor for this.

The *Belief, Goal and Plan Maintenance System* or BGP-MS [KOB 95], [PHO 99] is a user modeling system that enables the goals, beliefs and knowledge of the user to be taken into account. It functions according to different types of inferences, from hypotheses based on an initial questionnaire, observed actions and the knowledge of an ensemble of predefined subgroups. This system can be used in a server with multiple users and applications.

The Eperson project [DIC 03] aims to provide a common open platform enabling software agents to be able to assist the user, all the while preserving the confidentiality of information about him. The system appears as a server providing Web services for the management of user profiles. The user data is organized as an ontology [CHA 99].

NetP 7 (www.tornago.com) is a system that enables prediction of the hobbies and interests of users for electronic commerce. The prediction is made based on inferences of data provided explicitly by the user and the data implicitly collected by user queries and commands (purchase of products). This system can be used for web applications, telephone call centers, e-mail, publicity catalogs, etc.

PassPort.Net [OPP 04] is a user profile server. The user joins the service, giving personal data. These data are used by external applications (integrating their own methods of personalization) to provide the user with personalized services corresponding to his profile.

In the WebSphere suite (www.ibm.com), a software application allows the detection of user trends and preferences. This application manages the content and the structure of the commercial site by adapting them in relation to the client. It has been used for the personalization of information on sites selling hardware and software, for example.

Table 3.1 presents a summary of the different personalization systems that have served as a basis for the discussion that led to our proposal.

		Systems	Multi-application	Distribution	Upgradeability	Information search	Information collection	Type of filtering	Type of personalization
Free or academic systems	Agent based	Letizia	-	-	-	√	implicit	[C]: Terme frequency-Inverse Document Frequency (TF-IDF)	Recommendation of a web page
		IFWeb	-	-	-	√	implicit	semantic networks [P]	Filtering and sorting of information
		ConCall	-	-	-	√	implicit/ explicit	[P][RC]: stereotypes and TF-IDF	Filtering, sorting and recall of information
		InfoSleuth	-	√	√	√	implicit/ explicit	[P]: ontology	Reformulation of the request
		Gulliver's Genie	-	√	-	√	implicit/ explicit	[P][C]: Belief, Desire and Intention (BDI)	Recommendation of touristic places, guiding
		WebMate	-	-	-	√	implicit/ explicit	[P]: TF-IDF	Information filtering
		MAPIS	-	-	-	√	implicit/ explicit	[P]: reinforcement learning	Information filtering
		Eperson	-	√	√	√	implicit/ explicit	[P][FC]: ontology	Information filtering
	Others	RESCUER	-	-	-	-	implicit	[C]: human plausible reasoning	Help and advice
		IFM	-	-	-	-	implicit	[C]: stereotype, human plausible reasoning	Help and advice
		Smart radio	-	-	-	√	implicit/ explicit	[FC]: Pearson	Music recommendation
		BGP-MS	√	-	-	-	implicit/ explicit	[P] [RC]: modal logic	Adaptation of the interface
		BroadWay	√	-	-	-	implicit/ explicit	[FC]: case based reasoning	Link recommendation
Commercial systems		NetP 7	√	?	?	?	implicit/ explicit	Different data mining techniques	Recommendation of products, personalization of content
		PassPort.Net	√	-	-	-	Left to third party applications	Left to third party applications	Left to third party applications
		WebSphere	√	?	?	?	implicit/ explicit	Different data mining techniques	Recommendation of products, personalization of content

Table 3.1. *Comparative study of personalization systems at the origin of the proposal [ANL 06a] ([FC]: collaborative filtering; [P]: profile-based filtering; [C]: contextual filtering; and [RC]: community recommendation)*

Two approaches can be distinguished for the construction of personalization systems.

The first approach consists in providing an interactive system that itself (*ad hoc*) incorporates personalization, such as IFM, RESCUER and SmartRadio. These systems generally appear as software agents (see Letizia, IFWeb, Concall, InfoSleuth, Gulliver's Genie, WebMate and MAPIS), which ensure search, filtering and information presentation functions. These systems have the advantage of being directly in contact with the user, which facilitates the collection of data regarding user behavior for a more subtle personalization. Their main disadvantage is in the fact that reuse of the systems is very limited.

The second approach consists of providing a system that is dedicated to personalization and interacts with a third party for personalization (see e-Person, BGP-MS, Broadway, NetP 7, Passport.Net and WebSphere). The main functions of these systems include managing the user profile and the selection of relevant data that the third party applications are tasked with presenting to the user. These systems are much more flexible than the previous ones. They are generally used to personalize several applications likely to be used by the same users. Of course, a communication protocol is necessary to enable communication between the personalization system and the third party applications. Besides the advantages that final users will benefit from (the same profile for different applications, use of user experiences from one application to another by the system, etc.); the development costs of personalized applications are dramatically reduced.

The existing systems are generally meant for a particular kind of personalization and incorporate well-defined methods of personalization. It is very rare to find a system that ensures personalization of the container as well as the content, for example. This would require the integration of different (often cumbersome) methods of collection and management of the user profile in a single system. The ideal would be to have a personalization that is generic enough (which can support the different types of personalization) and favors an incremental integration of the different methods of personalization. As the existing systems do not do this or only to a small extent, we propose an approach for the design of a personalized information system (PIS) to satisfy this need[1].

---

1 The approach put forward, called PerMet, is based on an ensemble of foundations coming from state-of-the-art, available in [ANL 06a], several development models (enriched or not from the point of view of human-machine interactions [KOL 01]) and methods of analysis and design coming from the literature, representative of several classes of methods. Of these classes let us in particular note: MERISE (method for the computing study and realization of business systems) [NAN 01], which is representative of the systemic methods of analysis and design of information systems; *Two Track Unified Process* [ROQ 07], which is representative of object-oriented analysis and design methods, such as UP [JAC 99]; WAE (*Web Application Extension*) [CON 00], which is representative of web applications analysis and design methods; and AODPU (*Agent-Oriented Design Process with UML*) [CHE 00], which is representative of methods for the analysis and design of software systems based on software agents.

3.3. PerMet: method for the development of personalized information systems

The approach proposed by PerMet is in line with approaches that separate the IS from the PS, as [KOB 95] and [TRO 99] did initially. This choice of separation between IS and PS is driven by the personalization objective of the former, which possibly already exists. In transport, this is important if we wish to use information coming from different operators of modes of travel.

This separation is also necessary in order to meet the multi-application criteria that enables the unique *Single Sign On* (SSO, authentication or identification allowing a user to access several IT applications or secured websites) [PFI 04]. It must also favor personalization of the multi-modal, multi-channel and multi-platform HMI (according to the initial objective of these works [ANL 05a], [ANL 05b], [ANL 05b]).

The IS is considered an ensemble of services. A personalized service corresponds to a functional unit enabling a personalized HMI. A PIS can therefore be seen as an IS providing at least one personalized service.

To meet the objective of distributiveness and upgradeability, like [DIC 03] and in the continuity of works initially carried out [MAN 02], [PET 01], [PET 03a], [PET 06] at the LAMIH, we advocate the use of a PS based on software agents. The distributiveness is ensured thanks to the characteristics of autonomy, communicability and mobility of software agents, which can be seen as being at the service of users [GRI 01], [KOL 98]. Upgradeability is favored thanks to the characteristics of adaptability and reproducibility.

The PerMet method adheres to a development model following three parts (Figure 3.1). The IS part concerns the development of an IS service. The PS part concerns the adaptation and the configuration of a PS composed of software agents to meet the objectives of service personalization. These two parts, IS and PS, follow a classical development model that can take place in parallel and join together to form the middle part. As we can see in the figure, it starts from a requirements analysis (see Chapter 2 on this subject).

The PerMet development model is iterative and incremental. Each iteration gives rise to an increment aiming to improve the usability of the service. However, it is not necessary to specify all the services to be personalized in an IS. The other services can be specified and developed according to needs. There are different platforms made up of agents (Jade or *Java Agent DEvelopment Framework* [BEL 07] currently being the most well known). Thus, the effective realization of different phases can vary slightly according to the platform used.

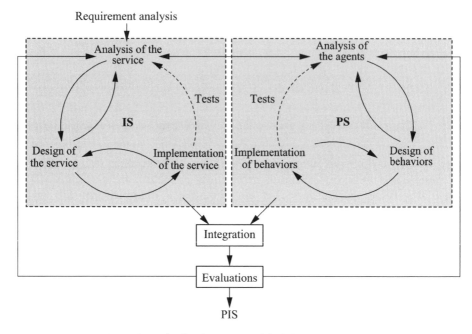

Figure 3.1. *The development model of the PerMet method*

3.3.1. *Analysis of the service*

This phase implies that a preliminary study has been carried out and that the personalized service to be implemented has been identified. It follows the analysis model of the 2TUP method [ROQ 07] to meet the evolution constraints of the service. The analysis phase therefore comprises four stages:

– The *capture of functional needs* describes the service to be developed. It consists of an exhaustive description of the functional and operational needs for the modeling of behaviors expected of the service. Certain use cases can be specified by scenarios, in particular through sequence and/or activity unified modeling language (UML) diagrams.

– *Functional analysis* describes the structure of the service based on functional needs. It consists of structuring and representing objects of the business domain of the service through a series of class diagrams. The behavior of the service is then described using dynamic diagrams (sequence, activity and transition-state diagrams). It is also in this stage that data models (modeled by class diagrams) exchanged between the service and the PS are defined.

– The *capture of technical needs* makes an inventory of all the constraints that do not deal with the description of the business domain or the service. It consists of the specification of tools (software), structure of the hardware to use and constraints for integration with what already exists. The material configuration is modeled through diagrams of deployment and the software specification is modeled via component diagrams.

– *Generic design* defines the elements that are necessary for construction of the technical architecture independently of the functional aspects and functional analysis. The architecture must be constructed so as to favor its reuse. This generic design can lead to the development of one or several prototypes in order to verify and validate the principles defined. The models used in the generic design essentially concern diagrams of class and components.

3.3.2. *Design of the service*

The design aims to specify the analysis model in such a way that it can be implemented with the elements of the architecture. It is a matter of expressing static and dynamic models that will be directly translated in the form of codes, which can be executed in the analysis phase of the service. The class diagram of the analysis phase of the service (functional analysis and generic design) is developed to enable a direct passage from the design model to implementation. The types of attributes of classes and types and parameters of inputs/outputs of the methods need to be specified. Dynamic diagrams are used to specify the states of classes (state-transition diagrams), the algorithm of methods (activity diagrams) and interactions between the different classes (by sequence diagram, for example). The component diagrams that come from the analysis phase will be completed and specified after the design of all the classes useful to the development of the service.

3.3.3. *Implementation of the service*

This is the stage of effective realization of the service. The service is developed in accordance with the conceptual models defined during the design phase. During implementation, the developer will make sure that the design model exactly reflects the IT code produced. Service tests can be carried out by data simulation (in accordance with data models defined in the analysis phase) to be provided to the service (these data will come from the PS when the integration phase is over). These tests can lead to a revision of the analysis model of the service, which will require another realization of different phases of the IS and PS parts.

3.3.4. *Analysis of agents*

This can start at the end of functional analysis of the service analysis phase. The models of agents, behaviors, communication links and deployments of agents are identified here for personalization needs. They are structured into four subphases:

– The *analysis of agent models* identifies the types of agents necessary for the realization of functional needs. The agent models can be identified following the rules below:

- rule 1: an agent model by the functionality expected from the service. For example, the functionality "itinerary search" will be translated by an agent model of "itinerary search",

- rule 2: an agent model by type of interaction platform. For example, an agent model for a PDA, another model for a PC, etc.,

- rule 3: an agent model by external resource with which the system must interact. For example, an agent model for itinerary search on transport operator servers, another for the search of restaurants on web services, etc. In this stage of analysis of agent models, the diagrams for use and deployment cases of the analysis phase are taken up again from the angle of personalization. Only the aspects that are judged as being part of personalization are considered;

– The *identification of communication links* describes relations between the different agents and their beliefs regarding the abilities of various individuals. Here, relationships of the interactions of each agent are modeled. The modeling of communication links can be done via UML extensions put forward by [ODE 99] which are used in *Agent-Oriented Design Process with UML*.

– *Behavior analysis*, for each agent to adequately attain its objective. This analysis determines the granularity necessary for breaking down behaviors. This will therefore depend on the intuition and know-how of the developer. The main rule to apply consists of breaking down a behavior for as long as the task associated with this behavior can be associated with another behavior.

– *Deployment information* describes the different physical locations where the agents go to be executed. This description can concern information of static location (the agent is located at a same place and never changes place) as well as information of dynamic location (the agent can dynamically change place according to the tasks it wishes to accomplish). The deployment information is modeled via deployment diagrams.

3.3.5. *Design of agent behaviors*

This phase enables the models that have come out of the agent analysis phase to be refined to become models that can be directly translated into code. Class diagrams directly modeling the behaviors of agents are specified to enable direct implementation of agent behaviors. The services provided by the behaviors are modeled using activity diagrams. State proactive actions can be represented by state-transition diagrams.

3.3.6. *Implementation of agent behaviors*

This consists of the effective realization of agent behaviors. For each behavior, unitary tests are carried out. The creation of agents, their deployment and the integration of their behavior is possible thanks to tools for agent administration. After having deployed the agents, tests by simulation of PS must be carried out, to check whether the multi-agent system (MAS), which constitutes the PS, meets the objectives defined in the agent analysis phase. These tests can lead to a revision of the analysis model of agents, which will require another realization of the different phases of the PS part.

3.3.7. *Integration*

This is the phase of integration of IS with PS to form the PIS. It consists of making the IS and PS communicate for adaptation of the service developed in the IS part. This phase can also be seen as a classic problem of electronic data interchange [MAN 01]. Several methods are put forward in the literature for communication between heterogeneous applications [ABO 03]. The approach that is most currently used consists of communication by Web service [MON 04].

3.3.8. *Evaluations*

At the end of the integration phase, it will be a matter of testing and evaluating the personalized service obtained. These evaluations can be qualitative (the quality of the personalization realized), quantitative (global performance of the PIS and scalability) or ergonomic (constituting a research domain in its own right, for which numerous methods are possible [HUA 08], [SEA 08]; see also [SOU 10] for works in the domain of PIS evaluation). These evaluations can lead to iteration of the IS part and/or PS part again.

3.4. PerSyst: personalization system supporting the PerMet method

PerMet separates the IS from the PS to take into account the personalization process of different input-output modalities (sound, image, Braille, etc.), different communication channels (Internet, SMS, e-mail, etc.) and different interaction platforms (PC, smartphone, television, etc.). The PerMet method emphasizes the need for an *evolving and distributed* PS that can take into account different types of personalization.

To do this, PerMet recommends the use of a PS based on software agents. In what follows, the general architecture and the design of the PerSyst PS will be described, as well as general models that are useful for the development of a PIS. This is described in full in [ANL 06a].

3.4.1. *General architecture and design of PerSyst*

The two main characteristics that the PS must have are: the possibility of communication with external applications (not necessarily based on software agents); and upgradeability. It is therefore natural that the architecture of PerSyst comprises an agent enabling this communication (communication agent) and an agent enabling the upgradeability of the MAS which makes up the PS (administration agent) that is to be managed. Other agents could then appear in the PS depending on the needs of a project (these agents are established during progression of the PS part of the PerMet method). To make the link between the different agents of the PS, another agent (a coordination agent) has been defined.

Indeed, as the agents are completely autonomous and can be located at various points in the network, it is necessary to have a reference source that will allow the developer to locate the agents and possibly interact with them (evolve their skills, change their location, etc.). This coordination agent also intervenes for the transmission of different messages that agents can exchange between themselves to meet a global objective of the PS. The general architecture of the PerSyst therefore consists of different agents. Figure 3.2 presents the general architecture of PerSyst and its interactions with the existing ISs.

The three agents of communication, coordination and administration (contained in the ellipsis with the grey background in Figure 3.2) form the core of PerSyst. The other agents, which we call applicative agents (A for *Assistant*, P for *Profile*, and S for *Search*), are examples of agents (they are the most used agent models for the construction of PISs), which could be defined to meet specific objectives according to a particular project.

The behaviors and coordination mechanisms of these agents are therefore established in the phases of agent model analysis and PerMet method of behavior design. The only constraint that these agents must respect is to have a communication link with the coordination agent, in order to be located for upgradeability needs. It is not necessary that it be a direct contact link. There need only be a "contact path" linking an agent with the coordination agent. For example, if agent A1 has a communication relationship with the coordination agent, all that is necessary is for agent A2 to have a communication relationship with A1 in order for PerSet to be able to locate it in the system.

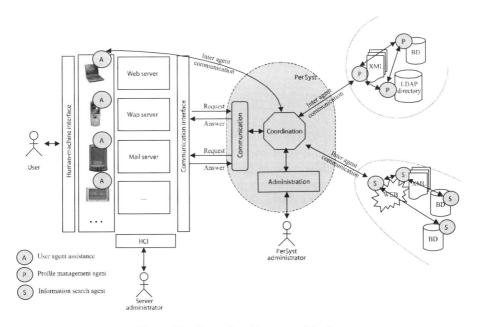

Figure 3.2. *General architecture of PerSyst*

3.4.2. *The coordination agent*

The coordination agent enables the communication link to be made between the different agents that constitute PerSyst. The coordination agent ensures three roles:

– The coordination of the tasks of applicative agents. The coordination agent coordinates the messages exchanged between the various applicative agents. PerSyst recommends only managing the coordination of messages exchanged between agents of different business areas at this level. The coordination between agents in the same business area is delegated to another applicative agent. This avoids overloading the coordination agent and allows for better structuring of the system (for maintenance requirements). The analysis of agent models enables the different business areas of the agents to be distinguished. An agent model is an abstraction of a type of agent carrying out the same activities. Agents that come from the same model can be organized according to a hierarchical structure that does not reflect the physical organization of agents that come out of these models in any way. However, this hierarchical organization informs as to the activity areas to which the agents resulting from these models belong.

– Coordination with external applications. Messages exchanged between external applications and applicative agents transit via the coordination agent. Of course, transformation of the messages is carried out (by the communication agent, described hereafter) in order for the messages sent by external applications to be understood by software agents and vice versa. It is the coordination agent that distributes messages to the applicative agents concerned and sends the responses back to the external applications.

– Coordination with the user. Messages exchanged between the user and applicative agents transit via the coordination stage. The queries of the user are interpreted by the administration agent (described further on in section 3.4.4) and then transmitted to the coordination agent that deals with sending the request to the concerned agent. The transmission of user messages is ensured thanks to the skill the coordination agent has. This skill provides services enabling administration queries to be transmitted to a particular agent.

3.4.3. *The communication agent*

The communication agent enables the translation of queries sent by external applications into messages comprehensible to the coordination agent and vice versa. It is broken down into two parts:

– The first part deals with communication with external applications. It uses the *Simple Object Access Protocol* (SOAP) [NEW 02] for interaction with external applications which can be written in any programming language. It provides four communication primitives (*Ask*, *Request*, *Perform* and *Send*) presented in the form of Web services [MON 04]. The first two primitives enable synchronous communication and the two others enable asynchronous communication.

– The second part deals with interaction with the coordination agent. It recuperates messages from communication with the external applications part to translate them into queries comprehensible to the coordination agent. This part is provided in the form of an API Java, which can be imported into a Java application independently of PerSyst.

3.4.4. *Administration agent*

The administration agent enables the management and administration of PerSyst. Its main role is to enable a user (in the case of PerSyst, a developer) to interact with software agents for the adaptation and configuration of PerSyst. In view of all these constraints imposed by the existing tools of different agent platforms, PerSyst provides its own administration tool. This tool appears in the form of an agent that has the necessary skills enabling the administration and management of agents (it is explained in [ANL 06a]). It is associated with a graphic interface (see Figure 3.3).

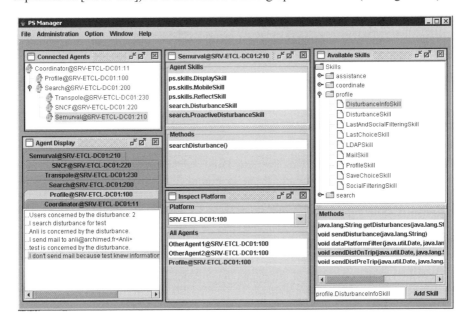

Figure 3.3. *The administration agent of PerSyst*

The administrator has a view of active agents, their organization and location (*Connected Agents* window), on skills (*Agent Skills*) and the content of their exchanges (*Agent Display*). It can create and remove agents, as well as acting on each of them to add or delete one of the available skills (*Available Skills*). It can also connect to an existing agent (*Inspect Platform*) or remove it from PerSyst.

3.5. Application to the public transport of people: itinerary search

This section describes an application of the PerMet method using the PerSyst PS. This application deals with a personalized itinerary search service in the area of the terrestrial transport of people. The objective is to facilitate access to multi-mode information for a user wishing to make a trip.

Indeed, the user is often confronted with an ensemble of disparate information (times and fares issued by the different operators, cards or tickets, etc., on paper, interactive terminals or by Internet) which sometimes turn out to be difficult to integrate into a specific and unique plan for a trip, adapted to their needs and preferences. In this context, personalization turns out to be a promising approach to take up this challenge. In the context of information to users, which integrates several modes of transport and their connections, our objective is to help the user in his approach to an information search and to provide him with a personalized result, i.e. all the necessary information and only the necessary information. The user provides the starting place, the arrival place and the arrival time. The system suggests an itinerary to him according to his preferences. The user has the possibility of validating the proposal or choosing another itinerary.

3.5.1. *Scenario*

The scenario acting as a base for illustration of the concepts is the following. It deals with the transport network given in Figure 3.4, simplified on purpose, but initially based on real data. In fact, it would have been possible to add other modes of transport, both current and future (see Chapter 1 on this subject): these modes can be individual (bicycle, rollerblades, electric or non electric wheelchair, Segway, etc.), public (tramway – one is being inaugurated in Valenciennes in parallel with our simulations), cyber-vehicles [MEL 10], [SER 08], auto-sharing, etc. Other modes, such as the taxi or carpooling, can be considered, both individual and public, according to their management system.

Thus, this simplified network (see Figure 3.4), describes the connection points enabling a user to carry out a trip from the LAMIH laboratory at the University of Valenciennes and Hainaut-Cambrésis, to the Archimed company in Lille (Valenciennes and Lille are two towns separated by 60 km). Three transport operators intervene in the realization of the journey:

– Semurval (bus operator), at the time of our first simulations, ensured the movement of the user in the town of Valenciennes and its surroundings. The transport modes considered in this scenario are mainly the bus, the car and walking.

– Transpole (bus and metro) is set up in the region of Lille. The transport modes considered in this scenario are mainly the bus and the metro.

– The SNCF (train) links the two towns of Valenciennes and Lille by the TER (regional express train) of the Nord-Pas-de-Calais region. We have also included the possibility that a user takes a car to go from the LAMIH to Archimed, without going via the public transport network.

We consider that the user has nine possible itineraries to go from LAMIH to Archimed. In the context of this search, the IS used is a Web portal developed based on the MASC[2] platform of the Archimed company.

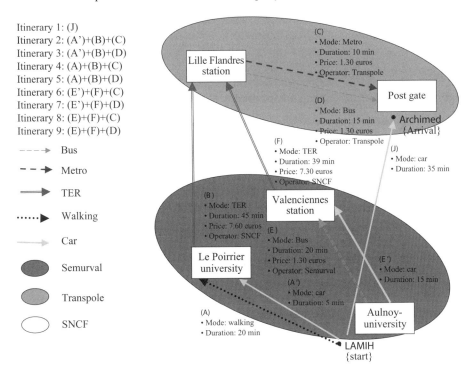

Figure 3.4. *Choice of itineraries from the trip, example*

3.5.2. *Analysis of the personalized transport service*

The main stages useful for global understanding of the personalized transport service analysis will be presented in succession. The interested reader will find a complete description in [ANL 06a].

3.5.2.1. *Capture of functional needs*

The functional needs have been modeled using use case diagrams. Figure 3.5 presents the functional needs for an itinerary search service.

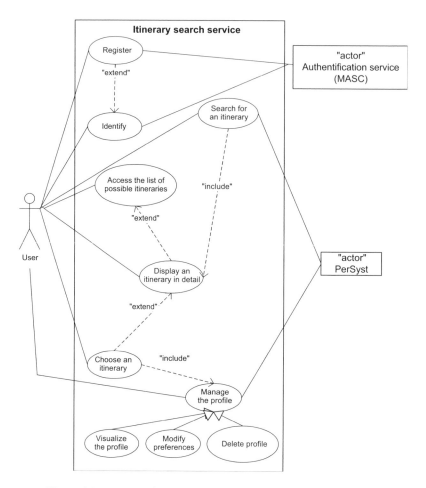

Figure 3.5. *Use case diagram of personalized itinerary search service*

The use case (each being associated with a textual description file) can be structured into three categories:

– the first category concerns identification of the user: use case *register* and *identify oneself*. These functionalities are already provided by the MASC platform and are directly used by the itinerary search service;

– the second category groups together the functionalities for the personalized itinerary search: use case search for an itinerary, access the list of possible itineraries, display the specifics of an itinerary and choose an itinerary;

– the third category concerns the use case for manipulation of the user profile: *manage the profile, visualize the profile, modify preferences and delete the profile.*

3.5.2.2. *Functional analysis of the personalized service*

Starting from the use case diagram stemming from the capture of functional needs, a static modeling of the business objects of the itinerary search service is carried out (see Figure 3.6).

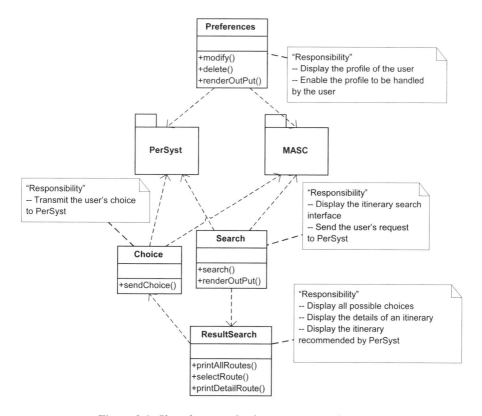

Figure 3.6. *Class diagrams for the itinerary search services*

The classes necessary to ensure the different responsibilities are defined. The modules that are not part of the service (but are useful to it) are represented in the form of *packages*. To refine the static model, a series of dynamic models was established. For example, Figure 3.7 presents a scenario for the itinerary search by giving details of the interactions between different objects of the service. After connecting to the MASC, the user begins his request using the personalized itinerary search service, *Search*, which asks the name of the user connected to MASC and sends the completed request of the user name to PerSyst. PerSyst sends all the possible itineraries answering the request to *Search* and recommends an itinerary that is likely to interest the user. *Search* creates *ResultSearch*, which provides the personalized results to the user.

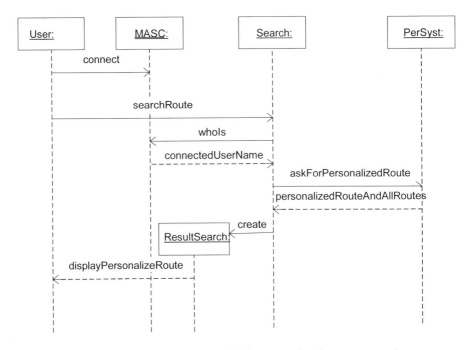

Figure 3.7. *Sequence diagram for the personalized itinerary search*

The data models that the service should exchange with the PS are defined (see Figure 3.8).

A request specifies the username of the user (DN) and the data (*Departure, Arrival, ArrivalTime,* etc.) for the itinerary search. A response (*Response*) takes the request (with the DN) and adds all the possible itineraries (*Result*).

This response is associated with a choice (*Choice*), which enables the itinerary likely to interest the user to be referenced. An itinerary (*Result*) is made up of several ways (*Way*) and includes its own characteristics (*Criteria*).

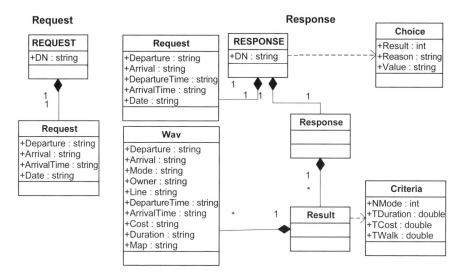

Figure 3.8. *Data models exchanged between the itinerary search service and PerSyst*

3.5.2.3. *Capture of the technical needs*

The application has a server where *Windows 2003 Server* is installed. All the software components are installed on this server. The user accesses the itinerary search service from his own work station (which can be a personal computer, a PDA, etc.) using the Internet network (see Figure 3.9).

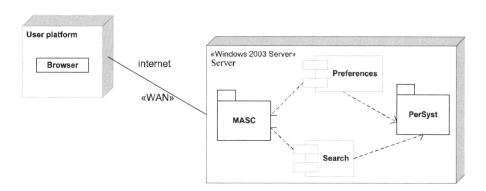

Figure 3.9. *Capture of technical needs for the itinerary search service*

3.5.2.4. *Generic design of the personalized service*

The service is broken down into three subsystems (manipulation of user preferences, itinerary searches and access to PerSyst; see Figure 3.10). Each subsystem corresponds to a grouping of modeling elements providing the same behavior unit. For example, the "access to PerSyst" subsystem contains the *PersonalizeSystem* class.

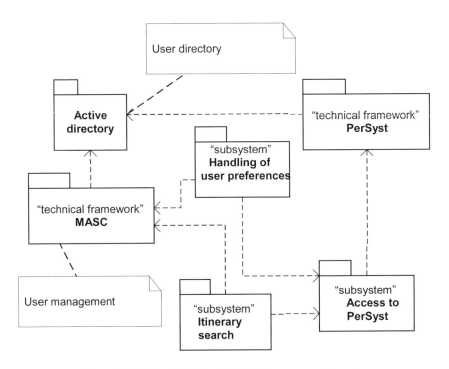

Figure 3.10. *Generic design for the itinerary search service*

3.5.3. *Design of the personalized service*

The service being a Web application, we have used the UML extensions put forward by [CON 00] for conceptual modeling of the service.

Figure 3.11 presents the diagrams of conceptual classes for personalized itinerary search (without the classes for handling of the user profile, nor those for authentication of the user).

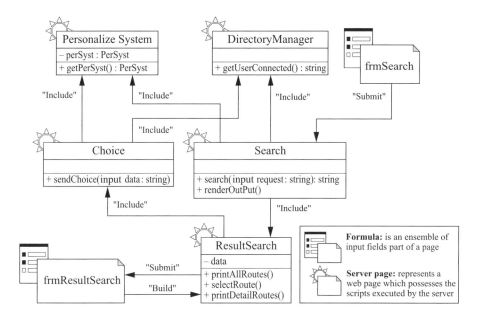

Figure 3.11. *Diagram of design classes for the itinerary search service*

3.5.4. *Implementation of the personalized service*

The applications (*Search*, *ResultSearch*, *Choice*, etc.) have been implemented through *ASP.NET* pages. Implementation of the *PersonalizeSystem* module provides a function (*getPerSyst*) that has the objective of sending back an object enabling PerSyst primitives to be invoked.

This object determines the data that the service and PerSyst should exchange while respecting the data models defined in the phase of service analysis. These data are transcoded in the XML format (Figure 3.12 gives an example of XML data for an itinerary search request)[2].

The presentations are carried out via an XSLT transformation using Archimed's JSE[3] transformation motor. Figure 3.13 presents the itinerary search page also enabling the visualization and modification of user preferences.

---

2 XML (*eXtensible Markup Language*, www.w3.org) is a standard for the exchange of data between applications. It also facilitates the development of an adaptive interface [HAB 04] that is multi-targeted [PUE 02] and multi-modal (with VoiceXML [ROU 04] or UsiXML [STA 05]) and even multi-context [LIM 05].

```
– <REQUEST>
    <DN>LDAP://SRV-ETCL-
       DC01:389/cn=john,OU=Sitp,DC=DOMTRANSPORT,DC=local</DN>
  – <Request>
       <Departure>LAMIH</Departure>
       <Arrival>Archimed</Arrival>
       <DepartureTime>07:00</DepartureTime>
       <Date>12/07/2006</Date>
    </Request>
  </REQUEST>
```

Figure 3.12. *Example of XML data for an itinerary search request*

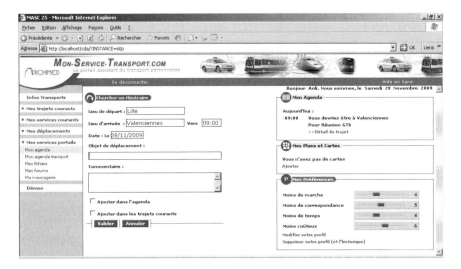

Figure 3.13. *Itinerary search page including the visualization
and modification of the user profile*

At the end of implementation of the service, preliminary tests of usability and verification of the functionalities of the PS were conducted. Even if these tests used simulated data (in the *PersonnalizeSystem* module), they were useful as they enabled us to add attributes (*Reason*, *Value*) in the *Choice* class of the data model of responses sent by PerSyst. These attributes were necessary to provide the user with an explanation of the recommendations made by the PS.

3.5.5. *Analysis of constitutive agents of the personalized system*

3.5.5.1. *Analysis of agent models*

The use case diagram in Figure 3.14 shows PerSyst as a user of itinerary search service. In this application, we assume that there is a federative authority that groups together the databases of the Transpole, Semurval and SNCF operators. We have simulated this authority by creating an XML database enabling the itinerary search for a trip from Valenciennes to Lille. The user information is stored in the *Lightweight Directory Access Protocol* (LDAP) directory, which is the same one that MASC uses for user management.

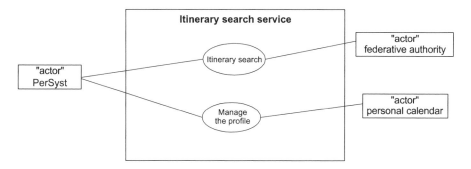

Figure 3.14. *Use case diagram of the itinerary search service seen from the perspective of personalization*

By analyzing this use case diagram and following the rules of the PerMet method for agent model analysis (see section 3.4.4), we obtain an agent model for the itinerary search and an agent model for management of the user profile. Indeed, rule 1 (an agent model of expected functionality of the service) and rule 3 (an agent model by external resource), led us to an agent model for the itinerary search and for the management of user information. Rule 2, which stipulates that one agent model is needed per interaction platform, will not be applied here because in this application the objective is to leave management of the interaction between the user and service to the MASC platform. The user accesses the service via a Web browser. The different roles that these agents must play are described in Figure 3.15.

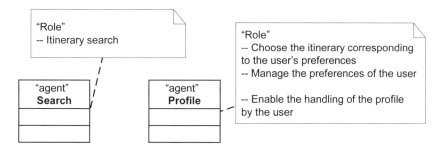

Figure 3.15. *Agent models for the itinerary search service*

3.5.5.2. *Identification of contacts*

Figure 3.16 represents the interactions of the agents for the itinerary search. Let us note the intervention of the two PerSyst agents: the communication agent that enables the transmission of messages which come from the itinerary search service integrated into MASC; and the coordination agent that ensures coordination of messages between the *Search* agent and the *Profile* agent. The analysis of this diagram enabled us to define the communication links described in Figure 3.17.

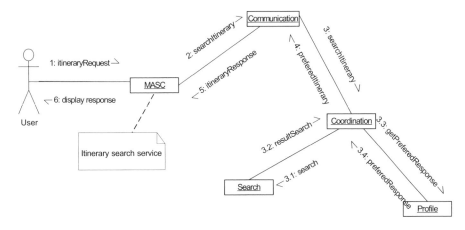

Figure 3.16. *Interaction between agents for the itinerary search service*

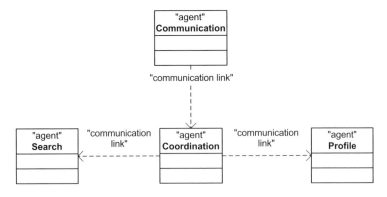

Figure 3.17. *Communication links between agents for the itinerary search service*

3.5.5.3. *Analysis of behaviors*

We have analyzed the behaviors that each agent model must have in order to carry out its roles. The analysis of agent models enabled us identify the behaviors of the *Search* and *Profile* agents.

For example, Figure 3.18 presents the behaviors required by the *Profile* agent for the itinerary search service.

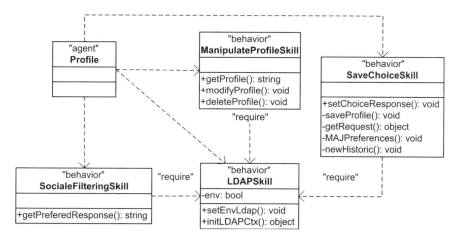

Figure 3.18. *Profile management agent skills*

3.5.5.4. *Deployment information*

In the context of our prototype, all PerSyst agents are located in the same machine (see Figure 3.19). It is the same machine as the one where the itinerary search service is deployed.

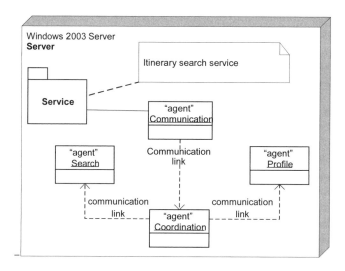

Figure 3.19. *Agent deployment*

3.5.6. *Design of agent behaviors*

In this phase, for each agent model we have refined and specified the agent behaviors. For example, for the profile management agent we have applied our user model put forward in [ANL 06a].

This model is made up of three parts:

– static data represent the authentication information (*login*, password) and the user's personal data (surname, name, place of work, etc.). These data come from the LDAP directory where MASC saves the user's information when he registers;

– the weighted data models the preferences of the user in relation to transport criteria (least connections, the quickest, least amount of walking, the cheapest). Each criterion is associated with a mark between 0 and 10, which represents the degree of preference of the user in relation to this criterion;

– the history keeps track of the user interactions with PISs. This can act as a knowledge base for the updating of static and weighted data. Analysis of the information can, for example, inform the system that the user lives in Valenciennes and works in Lille (as the user leaves for Lille in the morning and comes back to Valenciennes in the evening, except on bank holidays). By analyzing the itineraries chosen by the user, the system can deduce the preferences of the user in relation to the modes of transport.

This user model is stored with the profile management agents in the form of an XML document (an example is available in [ANL 06a]). Figure 3.20 presents the activities carried out during the execution of the internal action *MAJPreferences* for the skill *SaveChoiceSkill*. The objective here is to deduce the preferences of the user according to criteria associated with the itineraries (least connections, the quickest, the least amount of walking, the cheapest).

Figure 3.21 presents the activities carried out during the execution of the *getPreferedResponse* service of the *SocialFilteringSkill* skill. To select the itinerary that is likely to interest the user, a majority vote (select the itinerary that was the most chosen by users) is carried out on the itineraries if the current user has no profile. If the user possesses a profile, and has already made his request, the itinerary that he chose will be recommended. If the user has a profile but has never made a request, a collaborative filtering[3] (it is the collaborative filtering method based on the preferences and the behaviors of user which is applied) is carried out to choose which itinerary to propose. This model therefore combines a cognitive method (recommendation in relation to the profile) and social methods (majority vote and collaborative filtering).

---

3 A synthesis of collaborative filtering techniques is available in [SU 09].

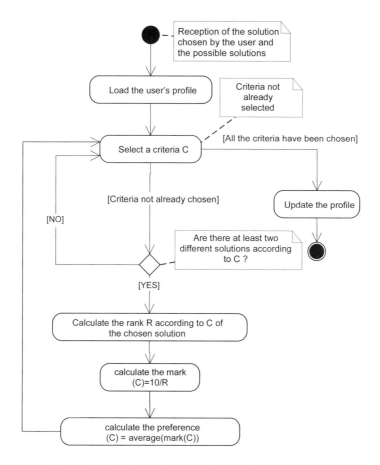

Figure 3.20. *Activities for the updating of user preferences*

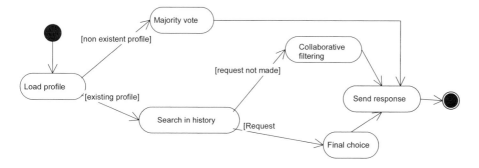

Figure 3.21. *Activities for the choice of itinerary*

3.5.7. *Implementation of the agent behaviors*

The agent skills were implemented and tested as they were being developed. The creation of agents, the association of their skills and deployments were carried out via the graphic administration interface of PerSyst. After the deployment of agents, verification tests for the smooth running of MAS, which makes up PerSyst, were carried out by a simulation of data that should come from external applications.

3.5.8. *Integration*

The communication between the applications of the itinerary search service and PerSyst goes via the *PersonalizeSystem* module. The *getPerSyst* function was implemented for it to provide a reference of an object enabling the primitives of PerSyst to be invoked via SOAP messages [NEW 03]. The data coming from PerSyst are displayed on the Web pages of itinerary search service (see Figure 3.22). The *Request* primitive was used for the itinerary search to enable the user to visualize his profile. The *Send* primitive was used to send the user's choice to PerSyst and for modification of the user profile.

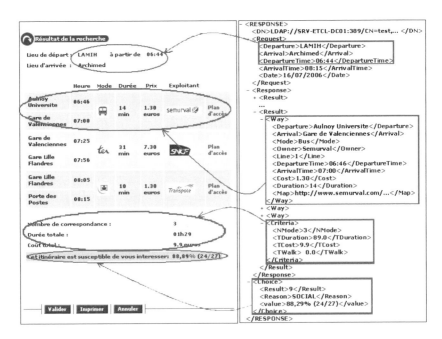

Figure 3.22. *Use of data coming from PerSyst by itinerary search service*

3.5.9. *Evaluations*

Here, it is a matter of a global evaluation combining the IS part and PS parts. More specifically, different evaluations were carried out. Three of them are described in the following; they are within the context of the PREDIM Mouver.Perso project (Mobility and mUltimodality travelers studying in the Nord-Pas-de-Calais region – personalized multimodal information system) [GRI 07], bringing together LAMIH, INRETS and Archimed.

3.5.9.1. *Functional and technical evaluations*

The functional evaluations were fairly quick as they had already been carried out in the implementation phase of the service. We checked in particular that the functionalities of the service at the end of the integration phase still conformed to those defined in the stage of capturing functional needs. Technical evaluations of the service were carried out. The conformity of the HTML code produced in relation to several browsers was also checked.

3.5.9.2. *Performance evaluation*

We carried out tests to evaluate the performance of the personalized itinerary search service. These tests involved the gathering of service response times for an itinerary search request. We measured the average response time in relation to the number of users contained in the user base. Figure 3.23 presents the response times according to the filtering method used with the profile management agents. A cognitive method (filtering based on the profile of the user: last made choice) and two social methods (the first is that of the majority vote; the second is a method of collaborative filtering based on the preferences and behaviors of users on the basis of a Bayesian network, put forward in [ANL 06a]) were tested. We expressly chose these three methods as they are included in the activity model of the profile management agent for the choice of itinerary.

The results obtained show that when it is a matter of a majority vote, the response times increase according to the number of responses registered in the system, but that these times remain acceptable (less than a second for 500 users). For filtering based on a Bayesian network, the response time is exponential from 100 users. Above 100 users, the response time exceeds 3 seconds. We believe we can improve performances by improving the algorithm implemented. For filtering based on the user profile, the number of users registered in the system does not influence the performance of the system. Other performance evaluations have been envisaged, for example evaluation of the performance of the service in relation to the number of users simultaneously connected to the service or study of the impact of the physical distribution of PerSyst agents on the global performance of the IS.

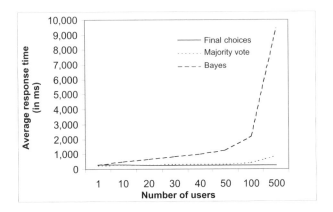

Figure 3.23. *Response time of the system according to the number of users registered with the service*

3.5.9.3. *Ergonomics evaluation*

The objective of this evaluation was to gather, in the field, the opinions of the people mainly targeted by the application. We therefore carried out a study in a student population at the University of Valenciennes in France [GRI 07] (see Figure 3.24).

Figure 3.24. *Subjects using the PIS on PDA and PC*

An original evaluation approach [SOU 07], [SOU 08a], [SOU 08b] was put forward, broken down into three phases[4]:

– A preparation phase: the evaluator must choose tasks that are representative of the system and prepare a general questionnaire on the experimentation subjects and one form per criterion evaluated. The task chosen here is the itinerary search after

---

4 This research on the evaluation of a PIS was extended in the context of a thesis [SOU 10].

the addition of a rendezvous. This task has the uniqueness of requiring the consultation of at least three application interfaces.

– A test phase of the model: the evaluator presents the chosen tasks to the subjects as well as the evaluation criteria and their definition, and asks them to select the most important criteria according to their needs and preferences. Then the subjects evaluate the system according to the defined criteria, during the execution of tasks, with a mark representing their level of satisfaction. Forms allowing the possible problems to be noted are also available. Twenty-three people participated in this evaluation (two evaluators-experts, 20 students-subjects and one technician). The length of an evaluation period was around three hours per subject.

– An analysis phase: the evaluator calculates the level of satisfaction of each user relatively to each criterion, and their average levels of satisfaction.

The system is evaluated according to seven criteria, of which three are linked to content and four are to the container:

– *Personalization of the content* (see Figure 3.25): 47% of users are very satisfied, 41% are satisfied, 6% not very satisfied and 6% of users are not at all satisfied. Figure 3.25 shows that the subjects are favorable to the quality of personalization linked to preferences and to the experiment (average > 0.6). Concerning the experiment, subjects spoke of the lack of help during first use. The consideration of interests (professional or personal) is less satisfying.

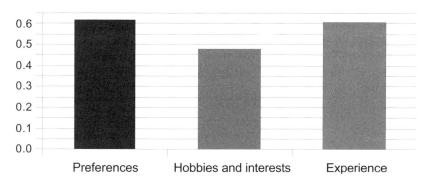

Figure 3.25. *Average satisfaction levels according to criteria linked to content*

– *Personalization of the container* (see Figure 3.26): the satisfaction rate is 33% for very satisfied subjects, 17% for satisfied subjects and 50% for not very satisfied subjects. After having tested the application using two different interactive media (PC and PDA), the subjects gave a favorable opinion for adaptation of the system to the interactive platform. As for the adaptation to behavior (adaptation to the goals and plans of the user), most respondents gave a neutral response. Students had an unfavorable opinion concerning the adaptation of the application to the physical capacity of the user and to the environment (luminosity, noise and geographic localization). With accessibility, a problem cited several times, respondents commented on the smallness of characters, which resulted in poor legibility. A recurring problem with behavior was the lack of "feedback" during validation actions.

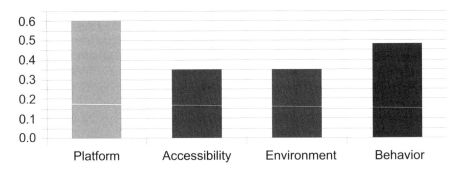

Figure 3.26. *Average satisfaction levels according to criteria linked to the container*

Other general results linked to utility and usability (in the sense of [NIE 93]) were obtained:

– Utility determines whether the interface meets the needs of the user: 55% were satisfied (satisfaction level [0.75; 1.0]), 40% satisfied ([0.5; 0.75]) and 5% not very satisfied ([0.25; 0.5]). Users make few mistakes.

– Usability accounts for the quality of the human-machine interaction in terms of how easy it is to learn and use. The satisfaction rate of the users in terms of usability is 41% satisfied and 59% very satisfied. These good results can be explained by the fact that the service is relatively simple, and learning it is quick and easy.

Such results are promising and call for other experiments and developments.

3.6. Discussion about the possibility of generalization relative to personalization

Elements of personalization applied to traveler information have been described in this chapter. However, it seems to us that it is possible to go much further in terms of personalization if we generalize the idea of having a detailed schedule of the activities of the user, made available to intelligent software agents at their service.

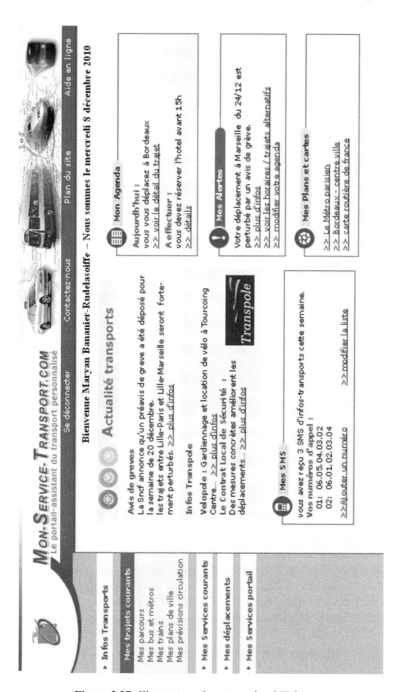

Figure 3.27. *Illustration of a personalized Web page*

Figure 3.27 can provide us with an insight into this matter. It takes the elements of a demonstrator developed in the context of the PREDIT AGENPERSO project (human-machine interfaces based on PERSOnnal software AGENts of information to the collective transport users) [PET 03b], bringing together LAMIH, INRETS and Archimed. The personalized Web page, visible in this figure, is exclusively meant for an identified user. The system knows via the intermediary of his schedule that he must go to Bordeaux. The agents put themselves at the service of the user by recuperating information that is relevant to him: the need to reserve the hotel before 3pm, collection of plans likely to be useful in the context of this trip, etc. The agents also anticipate future trips. For example, several days later the user must go to Marseille, but the intelligent agents detect that there is advanced notice of a strike that could disrupt the trip; the user perhaps needs to consider a re-planning the journey and is warned via the intermediary of the personalized system.

By generalization, other elements of personalized information can be expressed with mobility information, via knowledge of the preferences of the user in terms of leisure, for example.

Intelligent agents can indeed go in search of information likely to complement the user's trip by informing themselves as to the possibilities of shows and events at the destination place, as well as about the *best* restaurants (best in the sense of the adaptation to the user's criteria), the most *interesting* museums (for example, "the museum of pans, dishes and other kitchen utensils" if the user enjoys cooking), all the while preparing the *best* way (according to the user's criteria) to access it. Agents can obtain information about television programs if the user is too tired to leave the hotel in the evening (the study taking into account the hundreds of channels that might be available). Numerous other generalization ideas can of course be envisaged, which opens up new research avenues.

3.7. Conclusion

This chapter has described a contribution to the personalization of ISs, in view of improving the HMI and moving towards adaptive, intelligent HMIs, within a huge international research movement. We have put forward a method called PerMet (*PERsonalization METhodology*) for the development of PISs. This method enables both the implementation of a new PIS as well as the personalization of an already existing IS. PerMet proposes an iterative and incremental development model and allows the specific phases linked to the development of services and the specific phases linked to personalization to be carried out in parallel. We have also put forward PerSyst (PERsonalization SYSTem), which is a PS that supports the PerMet method, consisting of agents at the service of users. PerMet and PerSyst were validated in different applications based on real or simulated data for the personalization of terrestrial transport information for people. One of these applications was presented in this chapter.

The research perspectives are numerous. It would be possible to improve both the PerMet method as well as the PerSyst system. As explained in the discussion (section 3.6), other perspectives of these works would consist in using PerMet for the personalization of information connected to transport (hotels, restaurants, museums, etc). It would also be interesting to work on new machine learning methods for the personalization of transport information. In the end this should contribute to new, friendlier and more personalized interactive services.

3.8. Bibliography

[ABO 03] ABOU-HARB G., RIVARD F., *L'EAI au Service de l'Entreprise Évolutive*, Maxima, Paris, France, 2003.

[ANL 05a] ANLI A., GRISLIN-LE STRUGEON E., ABED M., "A Generic Personalization Tool based on a Multi-agent Architecture", in: STEPHANIDIS C. (ed.), *Proceedings HCI International (Las Vegas, Nevada, July 22-27, 2005), Volume 7 - Universal Access in HCI: Exploring New Interaction Environments,* Lawrence Erlbaum Associates, Mahwah, USA, pp. 1-8, July 2005.

[ANL 05b] ANLI A., GRISLIN-LE STRUGEON E., ABED M., "Une plate-forme de personnalisation basée sur une architecture multi-agents", *Revue des Nouvelles Technologies de l'Information (RNTI-E)*, vol. 5, pp. 95-100, 2005.

[ANL 05c] ANLI A., KOLSKI C., ABED M., "Principes et architecture pour la personnalisation d'information en interaction homme-machine, application à l'information transport", *Proceedings of IHM 2005*, International Conference Proceedings Series, pp. 123-130, ACM Press, Toulouse, France, September 2005.

[ANL 06a] ANLI A., Méthodologie de développement des systèmes d'information personnalisés - Application à un système d'information au service des usagers des transports terrestres de personnes, PhD thesis, University of Valenciennes and Hainaut-Cambrésis, Valenciennes, France, October 2006.

[ANL 06b] ANLI A., ABED M., "PerSyst: Un système de personnalisation de l'information transport multimodale", *Sciences et Technologies pour l'Automatique*, vol. 3, pp. 1-6, 2006.

[ANL 07] ANLI A., ABED M., "PerMet, méthode pour le développement de systèmes interactifs personnalisés: application au transport collectif de personnes", in: I. SALEH I., REGOTTAZ D. (eds), *Interfaces Numériques*, Hermès, Paris, France, pp. 71-89, 2007.

[ASN 97] ASNICAR F.A., TASSO C., "IfWeb: a prototype of user model-based intelligent Agent for document filtering and navigation in the World Wide Web", *Proceedings of the Workshop "Adaptive Systems and User Modeling on the World Wide Web"*, pp. 3-12, Chia Laguna, Italy, June 1997.

[BEL 07] BELLIFEMINE F.B., CAIRE G., GREENWOOD D., *Developing Multi-Agent Systems with JADE*, Wiley Series in Agent Technology, 2007.

[CAL 03] CALVARY G., COUTAZ J., THEVENIN D., LIMBOURG Q., BOUILLON L., VANDERDONCKT J., "A unifying reference framework for multi-target user interfaces", *Interacting with Computers*, vol. 15, no. 3, pp. 289-308, 2003.

[CAL 07] CALVARY G., *Plasticité des Interfaces Homme-machine*, Mémoire d'Habilitation à Diriger des Recherches, University of Grenoble, France, November 2007.

[CHA 99] CHANDRASEKARAN B., JOSEPHSON J.R., BENJAMINS V.R., "What are ontologies, and why do we need them?", *IEEE Intelligent Systems*, vol. 14, no. 1, pp. 20-26, 1999.

[CHE 00] CHELLA A., CONSSENTINO M., LO FASO U., "Designing agent-based systems with UML", in: *International symposium on Robotics and Automation, ISRA'2000*, Monterrey, Mexico, November 2000.

[CON 00] CONALLEN J., *Concevoir des Applications Web avec UML*, Eyrolles, Paris, France, 2000.

[DIC 03] DICKINSON I., REYNOLDS D., BANKS D., CAYZER S., VORA P., "User Profiling with privacy: A framework for Adaptive Information Agents", in: KLUSH M. *et al.* (eds), *Intelligent Information Agents,* LNAI 2586, pp. 123-151, Springer-Verlag, Berlin, Germany, 2003.

[GRI 01] GRISLIN-LE STRUGEON E., ADAM E., KOLSKI C., "Agents intelligents en interaction homme-machine dans les systèmes d'information", in: KOLSKI C. (ed.), *Environnements Évolués et Évaluation de l'IHM. Interaction Homme-machine pour les SI*, vol. 2, pp. 209-248, Hermès, France, Paris, 2001.

[GRI 07] GRISLIN-LE STRUGEON E., ANLI A., PETIT-ROZE C., SOUI M., CONREUR G., DOS SANTOS P., ABED M., KOLSKI C., MOUVER.PERSO, MObilité et mUltimodalité Voyageurs Etudiants, Système d'Information Multimodale Personnalisée, Intermediate report (May 2006) and Final report (July 2007) of Research Contract PREDIT DTT 216-75-01, LAMIH, Valenciennes, France, 2007.

[HAB 04] HABIEB-MAMMAR H., TARPIN-BERNARD F., PREVOT P., "Adaptive presentation of multimedia interface case study: Brain story course", *Lecture Notes in Computer Science*, vol. 2702/2003, pp. 15-24, 2004.

[HAY 04] HAYES C., CUNNINGHAM P., "Context boosting collaborative recommendations", *Knowledge-Based Systems*, no. 17, pp. 131-138, 2004.

[HOO 00] HÖÖK K., "Steps to take before intelligent user interfaces become real", *Interacting with Computers*, vol. 12, pp. 409-426, 2000.

[HUA 08] HUART J., KOLSKI C., BASTIEN C., "L'évaluation de documents multimédias, état de l'art", in: MERVIEL S. (ed.), *Objectiver l'Humain? Volume 1, Qualification, Quantification*, pp. 211-250, Hermès, Paris, France, 2008.

[JAC 99] JACOBSON I., BOOCH G., RUMBOUGH J., *The Unified Software Development Process*, Addison Wesley Longman, UK, 1999.

[KEE 00] KEEBLE R.J., MACREDIE R.D., "Assistant agents for the world wide web intelligent interface design challenges", *Interacting with Computers*, vol. 12, no. 4, pp. 357-381, 2000.

[KOB 95] KOBSA A., POHL W., "The user modeling shell system BGP-MS", *User Modeling and User-Adapted Interaction*, vol. 4, pp. 59-106, 1995.

[KOL 92] KOLSKI C., TENDJAOUI M., MILLOT P., "A process method for the design of "intelligent" man-machine interfaces: case study: "the decisional module of imagery"", *International Journal of Human Factors in Manufacturing*, vol. 2, pp. 155-175, 1992.

[KOL 98] KOLSKI C., GRISLIN-LE STRUGEON E., "A review of intelligent human-machine interfaces in the light of the ARCH model", *International Journal of Human-Computer Interaction*, vol. 10, pp. 193-231, 1998.

[KOL 01] KOLSKI C. (ed), *Analyse et Conception de l'IHM*, Hermès, Paris, France, 2001.

[KOL 04] KOLSKI C., PETIT-ROZE C., ANLI A., ABED M., GRISLIN-LE STRUGEON E., EZZEDINE H., TRABELSI A., "La plasticité vue sous l'angle de la personnalisation ou selon les besoins vis-à-vis de l'information transport", *Journées thématiques de l'AS Plasticité du RTP 16 IHM*, Namur, Belgium, August 2004.

[LIE 01] LIEBERMAN H., FRY C., WEITZMAN L., "Exploring the web with reconnaissance agents". *ACM Conference on Human-Computer Interface*, ACM Press, pp. 69-75, August 2001.

[LIM 05] LIMBOURG Q, VANDERDONCKT J., MICHOTTE B., BOUILLON L., LOPEZ-JAQUERO V., "USIXML: A language supporting multi-path development of user interfaces", in: BASTIDE R., PALANQUE P., ROTH J. (eds), *Engineering Human Computer Interaction and Interactive Systems, Joint Working Conferences EHCI-DSVIS 2004*, pp. 200-220, Hamburg, Germany, July 11-13 2005.

[MAN 01] MANOUVRIER B., *EAI: Intégration des Applications d'Entreprise*, Hermès, Paris, France, 2001.

[MAN 02] MANDIAU R., GRISLIN-LE STRUGEON E., PENINOU A. (eds), *Organisation et Applications des SMA*, Hermès, Paris, France, 2002.

[MEL 10] MELKI A., HAMMADI S., SALLEZ Y., BERGER T., TAHON C., "Advanced approach for the public transportation regulation system based on cybercars", *RAIRO-Operations Research*, vol. 44, no. 1, pp. 85-105, 2010.

[MON 04] MONFORT V., GOUDEAU S., *Web services et Interopérabilité des SI: WS-I, WSAD/J2EE, Visual Studio.Net et BizTalk*, Dunod, Paris, France, 2004.

[MOU 09] MOURLAS C., GERMANAKOS P., *Intelligent User Interfaces: Adaptation and Personalization Systems and Technologies*, IGI Global, Hershey, USA, 2009.

[NAN 01] NANCI D., ESPINASSE B., *Ingénierie des Systèmes d'Information: MERISE, 2ème Génération*, Vuibert, Paris, France, 2001.

[NEW 02] NEWCOMER E., *Understanding Web Services: XML, WSDL, SOAP, and UDDI*, Addison-Wesley Professional, Boston, USA, 2002.

[NIE 93] NIELSEN J., *Usability Engineering*, Academic Press, Boston, USA, 1993.

[NOD 00] NODINE M., FOWLER J., KSIEZYK T., PERRY B., TAYLOR M., UNRUH A., "Active information gathering in Info Sleuth", *International Journal of Cooperative Information Systems*, vol. 9, no. 1/2, pp.3-28, 2000.

[ODE 99] ODELL J., VAN DYKE PARUNAK H., BOCK C., Representing agent interaction protocols in UML, OMG Document/ad99-12-01, Intellicorp Inc, December 1999.

[OHA 03] O'HARE G.M.P., O'GRADY M.J., "Gulliver's Genie: a multi-agent system for ubiquitous and intelligent content delivery", *Computer Communications*, vol. 26, pp. 1177-1187, 2003.

[OPP 04] OPPLIGER R., Microsoft.NET passport and identity management, Information Security Technical Report, vol. 9, no. 1, pp. 26-34, January-March 2004.

[PET 01] PETIT-ROZÉ C., GRISLIN-LE STRUGEON E., "Interaction with agent systems for intermodality dans transport systems", in: M.J. SMITH, G. SALVENDY, D. HARRIS, R. KOUBEK (eds), *Usability evaluation and Interface design: Cognitive Engineering, Intelligent Agents and Virtual Reality*, vol. 1, Lawrence Erlbaum Associate Publishers, London, pp. 494-498, 2001.

[PET 03a] PETIT-ROZE C., Organisation multi-agents au service de la personnalisation de l'information, application à un système d'information multimodale pour le transport terrestre de personnes, PhD thesis, University of Valenciennes and Hainaut-Cambrésis, Valenciennes, France, January 2003.

[PET 03b] PETIT-ROZE C., ANLI A., GRISLIN-LE STRUGEON E., ABED M., KOLSKI C., AGENPERSO: Interface Homme-machine à Base d'AGENts Logiciels PERSOnnels d'Information aux Usagers des TC, Final report of project PREDIT, LAMIH, Valenciennes, France, January 2003.

[PET 04] PETIT-ROZE C., ANLI A., GRISLIN-LE STRUGEON E., ABED M., USTER G., KOLSKI C., "Système d'information transport personnalisée à base d'agents logiciels", *Génie Logiciel*, 70, pp. 29-38, 2004.

[PET 06] PETIT-ROZÉ C., GRISLIN-LE STRUGEON E., "MAPIS, a multi-agent system for information personalization", *Information and Software Technology*, vol. 48, pp. 107-120, 2006.

[PHO 99] PHOL W., "Logic-based representation and reasoning for user modeling shell systems", *User Modeling and User-Adapted Interaction*, vol. 9, no. 3, pp. 217-282, 1999.

[PFI 04] PFITZMANN B., Privacy in enterprise identity federation – policies for Liberty 2 single sign on, Information Security Technical Report, vol. 9, no. 1, pp. 45-58, January-March 2004.

[PUE 02] PUERTA A., EISENTEIN J., *XIML*: A Universal Language for User Interfaces, White paper, 2002.

[RAO 91] RAO A.S., GEORGEFF M.P. "Modeling rational agents within a BDI architecture", *Proceedings of the Second International Conference on Principles of Knowledge Representation and Reasoning (KR'91)*, pp. 473-484, 1991.

[ROQ 07] ROQUES P., VALLEE F., *UML2 en Action*, 4th edition, Eyrolles, Paris, France, 2007.

[ROU 04] ROUILLARD J., *VoiceXML, Le Langage d'Accès à Internet par Téléphone*, Vuibert, Paris, France, 2004.

[SEA 08] SEARS A., JACKO J.A., *The Human-Computer Interaction Handbook: Fundamentals, Evolving Technologies*, 2nd edition, CRC Press, Washington, USA, 2008.

[SER 08] SERRATE O., BERGER T., TABARY D., KOLSKI C., "Towards context-aware interactions between humans and a self-organized cybercar system", *27th European Annual Conference on Human Decision-Making and Manual Control, EAM'08*, Delft, The Netherlands, June 2008.

[SOU 07] SOUI M., ABED M., KOLSKI C., GHÉDIRA K., "Criteria devoted to evaluate personalized interactive systems", in: M. ABID, A. HADJ KACEM, M. JMAIEL, M. LAHIANI (eds), *Nouvelles tendances technologiques en génie électrique & informatique, GEI'2007*, Edition CPU, Sfax, Tunisia, pp. 119-125, 2007.

[SOU 08a] SOUI M., ABED M., "Evaluation of personalized interactive systems in transport applications: criteria and evaluation methods", *27th European Annual Conference on Human Decision-Making and Manual Control, EAM'08*, Delft, The Netherlands, June 2008.

[SOU 08b] SOUI M., KOLSKI C., ABED M., USTER G., "Evaluation of personalized information systems: application in intelligent transport system", *Proceedings of the 20th International Conference on Software Engineering and Knowledge Engineering, SEKE2008*, pp. 877-880, San Francisco, USA, July 2008.

[SOU 10] SOUI M., Contribution à l'évaluation des systèmes d'information personnalisés, Application au transport collectif de personnes, PhD thesis, University of Valenciennes and Hainaut-Cambrésis, Valenciennes, France, February 2010.

[STA 05] STANCIULESCU A., LIMBOURG Q., VANDERDONCKT J., MICHOTTE B., MONTERO F., "A transformational approach for multimodal web user interfaces based on UsiXML", in: LAZZARI G., PIANESI F., CROWLEY J.L., MASE K. and OVIATT S.L. (eds), *Proceedings of the 7th International Conference on Multimodal Interfaces*, ICMI 2005, pp. 259-266, Trento, Italy, October 4-6, 2005.

[SU 09] SU X., KHOSHGOFTAAR T.M., "A survey of collaborative filtering techniques", *Advances in Artificial Intelligence*, vol. 19, Article ID 421425, 2009.

[TRO 99] TROUSSE B., JACZYNSKI M., KANAWATI R., "Using user behavior similarity for recommandation computation: The broadway approach", in: *Proceedings of the 8th International Conference on Human Computer Interaction (HCI'99)*, BULLINGER H.J. and ZIEGLER J. (eds), pp. 85-101, Munich, Germany, 1999.

[VIR 02] VIRVOU M., KABASSI K., "IFM: An intelligent graphical user interface offering advice", *2nd Hellenic Conf. on AI, SETN-2002*, Thessaloniki, Greece, pp. 155-164, April 2002.

Chapter 4

A Formal Framework for Design and Validation of Multimodal Interactive Systems in Transport Domain

4.1. Introduction

The birth of new interaction devices (touch screens, feedback gloves, etc.), the use of machines in different situations with different users, the use of different modes (visual, auditory, etc.) has led to a complexity in the use of machines. The integration of these different media has given rise to a new type of human-computer interface called the multimodal human-computer interface (multimodal HCI).

The use of multimodal HCI enables the user to intuitively communicate with the machine; however, the use of several interaction modalities in a sequenced or even simultaneous manner (speech, gesture, etc.) makes the representation of information exchanged more arduous and involves a more complex development and validation process.

The introduction of computerized interactive systems in transport systems, generally critical, requires them to be highly reliable and imposes safe design approaches guaranteeing the specifications are respected. These approaches, normally dedicated to the development of the functional core of systems, are now turning towards the development of interfaces – an integral part of the system that also plays a determining role in this type of system; such is the importance of communications.

Chapter written by Linda Mohand Oussaïd, Nadjet Kamel, Idir Aït Sadoune, Yamine Aït Ameur and Mohamed Ahmed Nacer.

This gave birth to works that are concerned with the formal modeling and verification of multimodal interactive systems.

In this chapter, we will try and address the formal design of multimodal HCI. In section 4.2 we will present the main concepts linked with multimodality. In section 4.3 we will succinctly expose the principles of design and formal verification approaches. Sections 4.4 and 4.5 are dedicated to input and output multimodality, respectively, and we will present the main modeling and multimodality works, as well as the formal models of input and output that have been proposed. For each formal model we define the syntax and the semantics, then illustrate the model via a multimodal HCI referring to the world of transport.

4.2. Concepts of multimodality

Before addressing the different representations of modeling and multimodal HCI validation techniques, it is advisable to define the terminology relative to multimodality that is necessary for understanding the approaches proposed. In the literature [NIG 96], there are definitions that differ according to the point of view (user, technology) or the level of abstraction. We will try and clarify these concepts by presenting the definitions considered below:

Mode: state or manner in which an action is carried out, and that determines its interpretation when it is made by the user (vocal, direct handling) or system (visual, auditory and tactile).

Media: physical device in a computing system enabling the transmission of information (human/machine) that has the role of a sensor (microphone, camera, keyboard or mouse) or effecter (screen or loudspeaker).

Modality: refers to the structure of information (command) during the interaction, when it is introduced by the user: speaking, gesture, click; or when it is perceived by the user: text, audible warning or vibration.

Statement: command that calls (at input) or information that restitutes an elementary function of the functional core (at output).

Interactive task: complex or elementary informational exchange between user and machine in input (in view of realizing a goal) or in output (in view of presenting information).

Input multimodality: type of interaction that consists of fusing information provided by the user via several modalities. For example, the interaction in which the user expresses the phrase "*put that there*" by clicking on an object an then on a site of the interface, constitutes a multimodal input interaction by using the information respectively introduced via *speech* modalities via microphone media, and *direct handling* via the mouse media.

Output multimodality: type of interaction that consists of fissioning (decomposing) the information generated by the functional core and giving the information to the user by taking advantage of the different output modalities according to the interaction context. For example, in the interaction in which the user asks for the list of trains from town A to town B, the system responds by vocal synthesis "your request can be met by the four following trains" and displays a detailed list of trains at the same time. It is an output multimodal interaction responding to the user's request by the information "your request can be met by the four following trains" and lists the trains, by the means of speech modalities via loudspeaker medium, and text via the screen medium.

Multimodal system: system that enables several media and modalities to be combined in a dynamic way in input and/or output and to a semantic level.

Multimodal systems were implemented in various application domains. Input modality has elicited more interest, and is therefore more widespread than output modality. Thus, there are exclusively input multimodal systems, of which some have been developed for real needs. Examples of these are the system [MER 00] that helps surgeons place a screw in the pedunculate of a vertebra by using two input modalities: a pointer and a three-dimensional optical locater, and the VICO (*Virtual Intelligent CO-Driver*) system [BER 01] used to help automobile driving. The latter uses two input modalities: the touch screen and speech. Other systems have been developed with the aim of studying multimodal interaction, such as [JUS 04, NED 03] and others are developed in an experimental context in research laboratories, such as the MATIS system [NIG 94]. In parallel, exclusively output multimodal systems have been developed. Among these we will mention: COMET [FEI 91] used in the automatic generation of diagnoses for the repair and maintenance of military portable radios by combining visual modalities (textual and graphic); AlFresco [STO 93] used for access to information on 14th Century Italian frescoes by the coordination of visual modalities (text and images); PostGraphe [FAS 96] used for the generation of statistical reports by the coordination of visual modalities (texts and graphs); and MAGIC [DAL 96] for the generation of post-operative cardiovascular *debriefings*, using visual and auditory modalities. Finally, there are input and output multimodal systems, such as SmartKom [REI 03] enabling the management of diverse applications: address book, access to information services, hotel reservations, control of household devices, etc. It is a symmetrical multimodal system using the same modalities (speech, gesture and facial expressions) both in input and output.

Multimodality can be envisaged in different ways. Thus, several works have been dedicated to the characterization of multimodal HCI with the aim of evaluating and comparing them. Among these works we will discuss the CASE design space [CAE 91] (system oriented) that expresses: the temporality, the succession of statements and their contribution to the interactive task, and the CARE properties

[COU 95] (user oriented), which enable the usability of the interface to be verified via properties of flexibility[1] and robustness[2].

4.2.1. *Types of multimodality: CASE space*

The CASE space [CAE 91] proposes classing the multimodality according to two axes:

– *the usage of media (parallel or sequential)*, which specifies whether the media are used sequentially (one after the other) or in parallel (at the same time);

– *the links between information (combined or independent)*, which specify whether there is a semantic link between the information exchanged during the interactive task (introduced in input or presented in output) by the different modalities.

The crossing of two values of each of these axes below gives birth to the following four types of multimodal interaction:

– *concurrent (parallel and independent)*: the use of media is parallel and the information expressed by the different modalities is semantically independent. For example the redimensioning of a graphic object by the user sliding the mouse at the same times as opening a new window by vocal command by microphone;

– *alternated (sequential and combined)*: the use of media is sequential and the information expressed by the different modalities are semantically dependent. For example, the result of the train times request, given to the user by the phrase "*the train times are the following*" by vocal synthesis on a loudspeaker followed by the timetable displayed on the screen;

– *synergistic (parallel and combined)*: the use of media is parallel and the information expressed by the different modalities is semantically dependent. For example, the vocal command "destroy this" on a microphone given when clicking on the object of the interface;

– *exclusive (sequential and independent)*: the use of media is sequential and the information expressed by the different modalities are semantically independent. For example, giving the temperature on the screen followed by the announcement of the humidity level on the loudspeaker.

The CASE space was refined, in [BEL 92, BEL 95], with the aim of distinguishing the parallelism relative to the production of statements. It proposes to cross three axes: production of statements (sequential/parallel), use of media (exclusive/parallel) and the number of media by statement (one/several). This results in seven types

---

1 System ability to offer several possibilities to perform a task.
2 System ability to prevent errors and increase the user success probabilities.

of multimodality (the configuration sequential production of statements and simultaneous use of the media being impossible): exclusive, alternated, synergistic, parallel, exclusive, simultaneous parallel, alternated parallel and synergistic parallel.

4.2.2. *The CARE properties*

HIC3 can be characterized by four properties [COU 95] that describe the relations existing between the different modalities for the accomplishment of a task. These properties enable us to appreciate the *flexibility* and *robustness* of a multimodal HCI:

– *Complementarity*: several modalities intervene in the interactive task and each modality used is necessary for the interactive task. Example: the command *"put that there"*, which combines speaking the phrase and clicking the mouse to select the object and the site. *Speech* and *direct handling* are therefore complementary.

– *Assignation (specialization)*: the same modality (or subset of modalities) is chosen for a given interactive action. Example: the change from one window to the next is always done by the click of the mouse.

– *Redundancy*: several modalities intervene in the interactive task and the modalities express the same semantics. Example: the presentation of the information that *"there is no train that meets your request"* is done by vocal synthesis and by displayed text. Thus, these two modalities are redundant for this task.

– *Equivalence*: the interactive task can be carried out by using different modalities enabling the same result to be obtained with a cognitive cost that may be different. Example: the presentation of information: *"there is no train that meets your request"* is done by vocal synthesis or by text displayed; these two modalities are equivalent for this task.

Thus, equivalence and redundancy that offer the user interaction variations favor the flexibility and robustness of the interface. On the contrary, the assignation that means the user has to use a particular modality for an interactive task contributes to the rigidity of the interface and goes against the principles of flexibility and robustness. Similarly, several modalities intervene in complementarity that are assigned to different aspects and are complementary to the execution of an interactive task; consequently, it is like assignation, source of a certain rigidity of the interface.

4.3. Formal design

Formal design consists of developing a system (software or material) by strictly respecting a set of specifications. It is based on formal models and mechanisms of validation either *prior* (proof of theorems, *model checking*) or *after the fact* (test).

4.3.1. *Formal models*

A formal model uses a syntax associated with a rigorous and non-ambiguous semantics enabling us to carry out mathematical and logical reasoning. With rules of deduction or inference[3], it is possible to verify the particular properties of a system specified with the help of these models. Finally, the formal models use an abstract description of the system. This is why certain modeling approaches propose refinement mechanisms to derive the concrete system.

Formal models can be classed according to the theories that they originate from [MON 96] (sets, algebra types, automatons and high order typed logic) as are discussed in the following sections.

4.3.1.1. *Set models*

Set models are based on the theory of sets. They suit the specification of so-called sequential systems. The most well known representatives of this family of models are: the Z notation [SPI 88], the VDM language [JON 92] and the B method [ABR 96]. The Z notation not enabling complete refining of the specifications is restricted to the functional specifications. This is why it is not accompanied by obligations of particular proofs. Conversely, the VDM and B methods propose refinement mechanisms involving proof obligations. B method being more elaborate, complete and tooled, is undergoing a considerable expansion in the industrial sector. Indeed, it is based on a process of progressive refinement leading to a practical description that can be automated. The process of proof has to do with the coherence of the mathematical model and on preservation of the properties of the initial model by the successive refinements. Method B has a tool called *Atelier B* that includes a generator of proof obligations and an assistant for proof.

4.3.1.2. *Algebra models*

Algebra models, used for sequential and concurrent systems, use high-order and algebra logic. Indeed, a system is modeled by using the concept of data abstract type that correspond to a type of data class, the description of which is independent of any implementation. The refinement is carried out by corresponding a practical type to each abstract type by means of a function of practical expression. The refinement mechanism used requires us to carry out certain proof, which ensures the coherence between abstract and concrete types. The process of proof is often supported by tools that use rewriting techniques [BAA 99], solving of equations [LEH 05] or recurrence. The algebra models are very little tooled (*ACT ONE* [DEM 92], *LPG* [BER 00]); this is why they are not used in practice, with the exception of *LOTOS* [EIJ 89], which is considered a hybrid model combing the algebra mode of ACT ONE for

---

3 Rules producing new facts from assumptions and axioms.

the description of abstract data types to the algebraic model CCS [MIL 80] for specification of the behavior of processes and their interactions. This combination of models adapts LOTOS language to the description of concurrent systems.

4.3.1.3. *Models based on extended states automatons*

The models based on extended states automatons [HOP 07] are concerned with changes in the state of the system; they are therefore adapted to the specification of the dynamic and reactive systems. The system is modeled by processes communicating via messages or shared variables, where each process is an extended finished state machine evolving by transitions The models based on extended states automatons associate an algebra model for the static description of the system in their specification. They inherit the refinement and proof mechanisms. The dynamic part of the specification offers the possibility of the specification using a temporal logic in order to verify the properties at a high level of abstraction via the model checking verification technique (see section 4.3.2.2) or by techniques of proof (see section 4.3.2.1). The models that are based on automatons with extended states, which are the most well known, are *SDL* [ELL 97] and *Estelle* [EST 97].

4.3.1.4. *Models based on the logic of a higher order*

The logic of a higher order is a logic that has a high level of expressivity as it enables us to consider a predicate as an object that can vary or even be used as an argument of a function or a predicate [MON 96]. This logic is combined with a type system. It proposes a different mechanism by extraction of the program that enables it to simultaneously develop a functional program and to prove it. The high degree of expressivity offered by the logic of higher order enables it to specify a variety of systems but increases the complexity of the proof process. Among such models we can cite *Coq* [HUE 07], *HOL* [GOR 93] and *Isabelle* [PAU 93].

4.3.2. *Formal verification*

Formal verification consists of verifying that the desired properties are respected by a given system (model). This verification is done by confronting a formal expression of the properties of a system with a mathematical model, based on a formal language, which represents the system. The mechanism of verification must examine whether the desired properties are met by the behaviors of the system. There are two main approaches to formal verification: *theorem proof* and *model checking*.

4.3.2.1. *Theorem proof*

Introduced by Hoare [HOA 69], this approach is based on mathematical proof. It involves describing the system and its properties in an axiomatisable model of semantics (expressed by axioms) and demonstrating that the properties can be obtained based on the system by using inference rules. It is used in tools such as B-Tool or Coq [HUE 07], etc. This approach has the advantage of being able to process systems with an infinite number of states. It is not based on an explicit and exhaustive construction of a behavior model of state/transition type, which is very costly in memory, as it is able to directly infer conclusions based on a description of events or operations enabling the system to evolve. Nonetheless, the main limitation of the formal proof of the theorem is its complexity, which restrains its use to systems of a limited size.

4.3.2.2. *Model checking*

Model checking is an algorithmic approach that is based on the enumeration of all the possible states of a system, in order to ensure that none of these states contradicts the behaviors desired for the system. Due to the fact that *model checking* proceeds by exhaustive enumeration of the system states to be verified, the representation of all possible behaviors of a system with a large number of states rapidly uses up the memory storage capacities. This phenomenon is known as combinatory explosion. It is the subject of several research projects that have given rise to abstraction techniques enabling us to address the verification of large size systems [CLA 94].

4.4. Use of formal methods for input multimodality

4.4.1. *Existing models*

In [PAL 03, SCH 03, NAV 05], the authors use the formalism of *interactive cooperative objects* (ICOs) [BAS 94] to represent the fusion of two modalities: gesture and speech. The ICOs are dedicated to the specification of modeling and the implementation of interactive systems. They use the concepts of object-oriented approaches (dynamic instantiation, classification, encapsulation and heritage) for the description of the static part of the system, and Petri networks for the dynamic part (behavior). To take into account the specificities of the multimodal interaction, the formalism of ICOs has been extended, with a set of mechanisms such as communication by production and consumption of events. This mechanism enables a set of transitions in relation to an event to be synchronized, and to emit an event when a stage transition is being crossed. Interactions of a virtual reality application have been presented in [PAL 03]. The interactions are modeled at several levels of abstraction of which the first level concerns the physical interactions that involve modalities.

[JOU 06, BOU 06] have used the Lustre data stream of synchronous language data flow synchronous language in their works [HAL 91] to carry out software tests to verify whether the system developed meets the desired properties. These works use the Lutess synchronous reactive software verification tool [BOU 99] to verify a multimodal interactive system developed with the ICARE platform [BOU 05]. Lutess automatically builds a generator of test data for the program being tested. In these works, the CARE properties were specified in Lustre; then verified with the help of the Lutess tool. These works do not use formal methods during the design of the system but they call on it at the end of the multimodal system development in order to carry out software tests.

Method B [ABR 96], in its event-driven version, was used in the [AIT 06b, AIT 06a] works for formalizing the specifications of an operational interactive system all the while ensuring certain ergonomic properties. The system was modeled by a set of guarded events (the event is then set off as soon as its guard is fulfilled). The properties were expressed in the form of invariants (properties always needing to be checked) in the higher order logic. The authors have proposed a development methodology based on refinement [AIT 06b] and a validation of tasks expressed with the CTT process algebra [AIT 06a]. A representation of the CARE properties in B was also addressed in [AIT 06a].

4.4.2. *A general formal model for input multimodality*

In this section, we present a formal model of the design of the input multimodal interaction put forward in [KAM 06]. It is meant to be used in the design phase in the development life cycle of a multimodal interactive system. It is a model that formalizes the refined CASE space informally defined in [BEL 92, BEL 95]. A formal model inspired by the algebra of the CCS process [MIL 80] and Lotos is defined for each multimodal HCI class of this space. The syntax of the model is given by grammar rules and semantics of the words of this grammar are given by labeled transition systems.

4.4.2.1. *Syntax*

The syntax of the model is given by grammar containing two rules. The first rule S is used to generate the model according to the user tasks from a high level of abstraction to an elementary level, which are the statements. The latter are tasks that set off an elementary function of the functional core of the application. The second rule E generates the statements by composing basic interactive actions (which cannot be broken down): a of set A representing the interactive actions of the system. Am_i is the set of actions produced by modality m_i. The basic interactive actions, the statements as well as the tasks are composed with the help of a set of operators: $;$, $\gg$, $[]$, $||$ and $|||$ that respectively refer to prefixing, sequence, choice, the parallel operator and interleaving. The symbol δ is used to designate the stopping or end of a process. The semantics of these operators is presented later.

4.4.2.2. *Types of HCI*

Exclusive type: in this type of interface, the statements are produced in a sequential manner. This implies that the parallelism operator must not be used to compose the statements. Only the operators from the ($[]$) choice and the ($\gg$) sequence are present in rule S. A statement is composed of actions stemming from a single modality. If the basic actions that participate in the formation of a statement come from modality m_i, it is noted E_{Am_i}. In rule E, which describes it, only the actions of set Am_i are accepted. The syntax of the model corresponding to this type of interface is given by the following BNF grammar rules:

$$S ::= S[]S \mid S \gg S \mid E_{Am_i}$$

$$E_{Am_i} ::= a_i; \quad E_{Am_i} \mid \delta \text{ with } a_i \in Am_i$$

An example of this type of HCI is illustrated via the case study presented in section 4.4.4.

Alternated type: as for the exclusive type, the statements in an alternative type interface are composed sequentially. However, a statement can be produced by several modalities. Thus, the statements in the first S rule are indexed by set AM, which is a set of actions produced by a subset of system modalities. The syntax of the model corresponding to this type of interface is given by the following BNF grammar rules:

$$S ::= S[]S \mid S \gg S \mid E_{AM}$$

$$E_{AM} ::= a; \quad E_{AM} \mid a|||E_{AM} \mid \delta \text{ with } a \in AM$$

Synergistic type: in synergistic type HCI, the statements are composed sequentially. Thus, in the S rule we will only keep the sequence and choice operators. The statements can be produced by several modalities, as well as the actions that participate in their realization, which are considered in set AM. The basic interactive actions can be produced in parallel or interleaved, which explains the use of parallel operators ($||$) and parallel interleaved ($|||$) in the rule that generates statements. The syntax of the model corresponding to this type of interface is given by the following BNF grammar rules:

$$S ::= S[]S \mid S \gg S \mid E_{AM}$$

$$E_{AM} ::= a; \quad E_{AM} \mid a|||E_{AM} \mid a||E_{AM} \mid \delta \text{ with } a \in AM$$

Exclusive parallel type: contrary to the three previous types of HCI, in this type of interface the statements can be produced in a parallel or sequential manner. This explains the use of the interleaved parallel operator in the S rule. Each statement is composed of actions that come from a single modality and this is why each statement in the grammar is indexed by the set Am_i, made up of the interactive actions produced by modality m_i. In this type of HCI, the use of two actions at the same time is not tolerated. This justifies the absence of the parallel operator in the S rule of the grammar. Thus, the syntax of the model corresponding to this type of interface is given by the following BNF grammar rules:

$$S ::= S[]S \mid S \gg S \mid S|||S \mid E_{Am_i}$$

$$E_{Am_i} ::= a_i; \quad E_{Am_i} \mid \delta \text{ with } a_i \in Am_i$$

Simultaneous parallel type: this type of HCI has the same constraints on the statements as the previous type does but several modalities can be used at the same time. Thus, the parallel operator is used in the S rule of the grammar. The syntax of the model corresponding to this type of interface is given by the following BNF grammar rules:

$$S ::= S[]S \mid S \gg S \mid S||S \mid S|||S \mid E_{Am_i}$$

$$E_{Am_i} ::= a_i; \quad E_{Am_i} \mid \text{ with } a_i \in Am_i$$

Alternated parallel type: in this type of HCI, a statement can be produced by several modalities interleaved in parallel. This explains the presence of the interleaved parallel operator in the second rule that generates the statements. The statements are indexed by all the interactive actions AM that produce them and are produced by a subset of modalities. The syntax of the model corresponding to this type of interface is given by the following BNF grammar rules:

$$S ::= S[]S \mid S \gg S \mid S|||S \mid E_{AM}$$

$$E_{AM} ::= a; \quad E_{AM} \mid a|||E_{AM} \mid \delta \text{ with } a \in AM$$

Synergistic parallel type: in this type of HCI, the statements are composed in a parallel or sequential manner. This involves the presence of all the operators in the S rule. Each of the statements can be produced by several modalities, hence the indexation of the statements by set AM. Several actions can be set off at the same time thanks to the presence of the parallel operator in the two rules (S and E_{AM}). The syntax of the model corresponding to this type of interface is given by the following BNF grammar rules:

$$S ::= S[]S \mid S \gg S \mid S||S \mid S|||S \mid E_{AM}$$

$$E_{AM} ::= a; \quad E_{AM} \mid a|||E_{AM} \mid a||E_{AM} \mid \delta \text{ with } a \in AM$$

4.4.2.3. *Semantics*

The dynamic or operational semantics describes the dynamic behavior of the system. The operational semantic associates a model in the form of a system of labeled transitions with a grammatical term. The description of models is done by defining the set of states made up of the terms of the grammar and a relation of transition $\rightarrow$ between these terms. The actions are the a elements of set A. Let P, P', Q and Q' be terms of the grammar and a, a_1 and a_2 actions of set A.

$P \xrightarrow{a} Q$ reads: P has a transition by a leading to Q, and signifies that in the behavior of P we observe action a and that the later behavior corresponds to that of Q. The transition system of a term of the grammar is obtained by a structural induction according to the style of [PLO 81] by the means of rules of the form:

$$\frac{\text{Premises}}{\text{Conclusion}}.$$

We present the semantic rules of the following operators:

– The stop δ is a term that expresses the state of arrest. It corresponds to the STOP process of the CCS algebra [MIL 80]. It is a state from which no action is possible.

– The prefixing operator; is an operator borrowed from CCS. A state corresponding to the term $a; P$ can carry out a transition by executing the action a and passing to the state corresponding to the term P.

– The choice operator $[]$ is an operator of CCS and Lotos. There are two transition rules for this operator: one rule to define the composition on the left; and another to define the composition on the right. If a transition is possible from a state corresponding to the term P (resp. Q) to go to the other corresponding to the term P' (resp. Q'), then in the composed system corresponding to the term $P[]Q$, the same transition remains possible and moves the system to the state corresponding to the term P' (resp. Q').

$$\frac{P \xrightarrow{a} P'}{P[]Q \xrightarrow{a} P'} \quad \frac{Q \xrightarrow{a} Q'}{P[]Q \xrightarrow{a} Q'}$$

– The sequence operator $\gg$ is an operator borrowed from Lotos. The rules of this operator express the behavior of the sequencing of two terms P followed by Q. The two rules express the fact that $P \gg Q$ behaves like P until it reaches the end of its execution then it will behave like Q:

$$\frac{P \xrightarrow{a} P' \text{ and } P' \neq \delta}{P \gg Q \xrightarrow{a} P' \gg Q} \quad \frac{P \xrightarrow{a} P' \text{ and } P' = \delta}{P \gg Q \xrightarrow{a} Q}$$

– The interleaved operator $|||$ is an operator borrowed from Lotos. The rules of this operator express the parallel interleaving behavior by two terms. If, from the state P, the system transits by a to P', then the state composed of $P|||Q$ transits by a to the state composed of $P'|||Q$. Similarly, if from state Q the system transits by a to the state Q', then the state composed of $P|||Q$ transits by a to state $P|||Q'$:

$$\frac{P \xrightarrow{a} P'}{P|||Q \xrightarrow{a} P'|||Q} \qquad \frac{Q \xrightarrow{a} Q'}{P|||Q \xrightarrow{a} P|||Q'}$$

– Parallel operator $||$ is an operator borrowed from Lotos. Conversely to the previous operator, which only enables a single action to be executed at a time, parallel operator $||$ authorizes the execution of an action of the first system or even an action of the system or these two actions at the same time. We have imposed a condition on the modalities of actions put in parallel. We will consider that a modality cannot produce two actions at the same time.

$$\frac{P \xrightarrow{a} P'}{P||Q \xrightarrow{a} P'||Q} \qquad \frac{Q \xrightarrow{a} Q'}{P||Q \xrightarrow{a} P||Q'}$$

$$\frac{P \xrightarrow{a1} P' \text{ and } Q \xrightarrow{a2} Q' \text{ and } \text{modality}(a_1) \neq \text{modality}(a_2)}{P||Q \xrightarrow{a1,a2} P'||Q'}$$

4.4.3. *Verified properties*

Once the HCI is modeled and the system of transitions describing its dynamic behavior is generated, the verification of these properties can be carried out according to two techniques. The CARE properties are part of the properties of usability of the multimodal HCI, thus two formal models were defined for CARE. The first is operational and it describes the property with a system of transitions [KAM 07]. This model is based on the same syntaxical and semantic elements as those used for the model of multimodal interactions presented in the previous section. The technique of verification used in this case is based on the comparison of transition systems of the multimodal HCI and the property that needs to be verified.

The second model is logical and describes the properties by the declarative expression in a logic interpreted in a transition system. In this model, the verification is carried out with the help of the *model checking* technique. Two techniques were tested: the SMV (*symbolic model verifier*) technique [MCM 92], where the properties are expressed in the CTL temporal logic [KAM 04, KAM 05]; and the Promela/Spin technique [HOL 91], where the properties are expressed in the LTL temporal logic [PNU 77]. In this section, we present the expression of CARE properties in LTL logic with the SPIN tool. For this we will go ahead with the abstraction of actions of interaction by replacing each of the actions by the modality that generates it. Thus, the variable *mod* is introduced. It contains the value of the modality that enabled the interactive action that labeled the transition to be carried out.

4.4.3.1. *Complementarity*

Two modalities – m_1 and m_2 – are called complementary for task T to be carried out if the next formula is verified by the system:

$$G((state = stateI) \Longrightarrow ((mod = m_1 \lor mod = m_2) \cup (state = stateF))) \quad [4.1]$$

$\land$

$$G(not((state = stateI) \Longrightarrow ((mod = m_1) \cup (state = stateF)))) \quad [4.2]$$

$\land$

$$G(not((state = stateI) \Longrightarrow ((mod = m_2) \cup (state = stateF)))) \quad [4.3]$$

This formula means that in the system of transitions of the multimodal HCI (all the traces of execution):

(1) if a state is identified as being the initial state of the task $T(state = stateI)$, then all the states that follow it are reached either by modality m_1 or m_2 $(mod = m_1 \lor mod = m_2)$ until ($\cup$) the end of the realization of this task $T(state = stateF)$;

(2) there is no execution where if a state is identified as being the initial state then all the states that follow it are reached with m_1 modality until ($\cup$) the final state of the task T;

(3) there is no execution so if a state is identified as being the initial state then all the states that follow it are reached with the m_2 modality until ($\cup$), the final state of the task T.

4.4.3.2. *Assignation*

A modality m_i is assigned to task T if the following formula is verified by the multimodal HCI system:

$$G((state = stateI) \Longrightarrow ((mod = m_i) \cup (state = stateF)))$$

This formula means that in the transition system of the HCI (all the execution traces), if $stateI$ is identified as being the initial state of task $T(state = stateI)$, then all the states that follow it are reached by modality m_i until the end of the realization of task $T(state = stateF)$.

4.4.3.3. *Equivalence*

Two modalities – m_1 and m_2 – are said to be equivalent for the realization of task T if the following formula is verified by the system:

$$G((state = stateI) \Longrightarrow (((mod = m_1) \cup (state = stateF))$$
$$\lor ((mod = m_2) \cup (state = stateF))))$$

This formula means that in the transition of the HCI (all the execution traces), if $stateI$ is identified as being the initial state of task T, then all the states that follow it are reached by m_1 modality until reaching the $stateF$, which identifies the end of task T, or they are reached by m_2 modality until they reaching $stateF$ identifying the end of task T.

4.4.3.4. *Redundancy*

To express the property of redundancy in the LTL temporal logic, we must enumerate all possible combinations between the modalities in each state. We have not been able to represent this properly in a generic expression of LTL logic. It requires a richer logic, enabling us to express the parallel operator.

4.4.4. *Case study*

To illustrate the approach previously described, we have chosen MATIS (*Multimodal Airline Travel Information System*), the multimodal application described in [MAC 98, NIG 94]. It enables a user to extract information regarding the times of flights using voice, direct handling with the keyboard and the mouse, or a combination of these modalities, by basing itself on the individual or synergistic use of numerous input modalities. For each request, a window is created following an order from the user. It contains fields filled in with values corresponding to the parameters of the request, such as the names of the flight departure and arrival towns. The user can fill in these fields by saying town names that are recognized by the system or by clicking on the fields before selecting a town from among the suggested list.

4.4.4.1. *Modeling of the input interaction*

For reasons of simplification, we will model an multimodal HCI that will enable the user to formulate a single request. We will consider two modalities: speech and direct handling with the mouse. A_{speech} and A_{handle} are the set of actions of the system generated, respectively, by the speech and direct handling modalities using the mouse:

$$A_{\text{speech}} = \{\text{'show me flights', 'from', 'this', 'City', 'To', 'Boston', 'Oslo'}\}$$

$$A_{\text{handle}} = \{\text{ClicBoston, ClicOslo, ClicFrom, ClicTo, ClicNrequest}\}$$

With the following basic actions made using the mouse:

– *ClicBoston, ClicOslo*: click the mouse on the town of Boston and the town of Oslo, respectively, from a list of towns;

– *ClicFrom, ClicTo*: click the mouse on the text field, respectively *From* and *To* of the form for request input;

– *ClicNrequest*: click the mouse on the button attributed to the creation of a new request. The click on this button engenders the creation of a new window in a form for request input.

An expression of an multimodal HCI of an exclusive type can be broken down according to tasks as follows:

$$(CreateReq) \gg (FillinFrom) \gg (FillinTo)$$

Here, *CreateReq* is the task that enables us to create a new window to formulate a request. *FillinFrom* is the task that enables the From field to be filled in, corresponding to the town of departure in the form of the request. *FillinTo* is the task that enables us to fill in the *To* field corresponding to the destination town. Each of these tasks can be carried out in two different ways, which corresponds to the definition of two different statements for the realization of each of the tasks. Each of these statements is defined according to basic interactive actions as follows:

$$\text{Create1Req} = \text{'show me flights'}; \delta$$
$$\text{Create2Req} = \text{clicNrequest}; \delta$$
$$\text{Fillin1From} = \text{ClicFrom}; \text{ClicBoston}; \delta$$
$$\text{Fillin2From} = \text{'From'}; \text{'Boston'}; \delta$$
$$\text{FillinTo} = \text{ClicTo}; \text{ClicOslo}; \delta$$
$$\text{Fillin2To} = \text{'To'}; \text{'Oslo'}; \delta$$

Finally, the expression of the multimodal HCI according to the basic actions is obtained by replacing each of the statements by its expression according to the basic actions:

$$(('show me flights'; \delta)[](\text{ClicNrequest}; \delta)) \gg$$
$$(('From'; 'Boston'; \delta)[](\text{ClicFrom}; \text{ClicBoston}; \delta)) \gg$$
$$(('To'; 'Oslo'; \delta)[](\text{ClicTo}; \text{ClicOslo}; \delta))$$

The corresponding transitions system is given in Figure 4.1.

Figure 4.2 shows a part of the Promela code that implements this transitions system.

The *random* variable was introduced to carry out non-determinism. The instruction $if..fi$, randomly chooses the two instructions guarded by the same guard *random* = 1. The transitions are carried out in an uninterrupted manner with the instruction *atomic*{}.

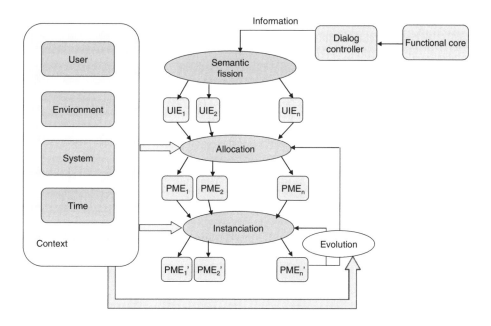

Figure 4.1. *Transitions system of the exclusive multimodal HCI*

4.4.4.2. *Verification of the properties of usability*

The properties of complementarity and equivalence of the two modalities *speech* and *direct handling*, for the realization of the task *fillinFrom*, have been verified in transitions, with the help of the SPIN checker. Each property is expressed by a LTL temporal logic formula. The two formulae are obtained by replacing in the generic formula, the values *stateI* and *stateF* of the variable state by the values 2 and 5 corresponding to the initial and the final state of the task, as well as the modalities values m_1 and m_2 of the variable mod by the values corresponding to the modalities *speech* and *direct handling*. The result of this verification concludes that the property of complementarity is not satisfied by the exclusive type multimodal HCI, whereas the equivalence property is fulfilled.

4.5. Use of formal methods for output multimodality

4.5.1. *Existing models*

As with the multimodality in input, works have focused on modeling the design process for multimodality in output, nonetheless the design models put forward remain informal. We cite among these works the design space, the *Standard Reference Model* (SRM) symbol and the *What, Which, How, Then* (WWHT) model.

```
mtype = {parole, manipulation, nil}; % modalities of the system
byte state, random;
mtype action; % variable designating the modality used
proctype exclusive()
{  random=1;
% initialization of the system at state 1. The modality is initialized
% either by speech or by direct handling

    if
       ::random==1 -> atomic{action=speech; state=1};
       ::random==1 -> atomic{action=handling; state=1};
    fi;
    goto E1;

% first transition to state 2. The modality either goes to speech
% or direct handling in a random way
E1 : ···
```

Figure 4.2. *Promela code corresponding to the exclusive type multimodal HCI*

4.5.1.1. *Bernsen's design space*

In [BER 94], Bernsen specifies the outputs of the multimodal system by a generative approach that consists of combining the elementary or pure modalities in order to get more complex representations. The modalities are classed according to four criteria:

– static or dynamic: expresses the intervention of the time factor in the evolution of the modality, a text displayed is a static modality whereas speech is a dynamic modality;

– linguistic or non-linguistic: highlights the existence of linguistic components in the modality, a text displayed is a linguistic modality whereas a sound beep is a non-linguistic modality;

– analog or non-analog: gives the correspondence of the modality with objects of the real world, a photograph is an analog modality unlike a histogram that is a non-analog modality;

– arbitrary or non-arbitrary: expresses whether it is necessary or not for the user to learn a new semantic system to be able to interpret the modality. For example, the photograph modality is non-arbitrary since the user does not need to learn a particular semantic system to identify what a photograph represents (interpretation of the modality), whereas the modality symbol is arbitrary as it requires the user to know the semantics of all the symbols (correspondence table) in order to interpret the different symbols.

4.5.1.2. *The SRM model*

The SRM model [BOR 97] represents the process of the construction of the output interaction based on the goal. It involves five layers:

– *Control layer*, which consists of selecting the next goal to be reached (output interactive task) or the presentation command to be executed;

– *Content layer*, which first refines the goal into more specialized sub-goals, then selects the couple (modality, media) as well as the content of the presentation for each elementary goal;

– *Design layer*, which fixes the morphological attributes (e.g. size of the font used) and spatial and temporal (chronology and arrangement on the interface) of couples (modality, media);

– *Realization layer*, which deals with effectively generating the presentation;

– *Presentation display layer*, the role of which is to distribute the different components of the presentation to the appropriate media and to coordinate the different components in order to result in the presentation.

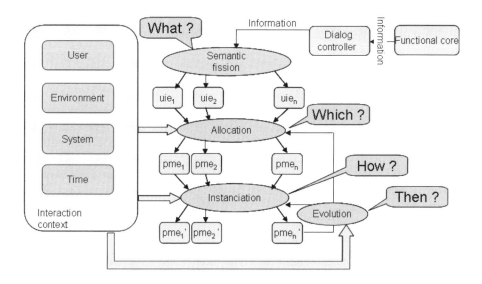

Figure 4.3. *The WWHT (What, Which, How, Then) model*

4.5.1.3. *The WWHT model*

The design model WWHT [ROU 06] comes down to asking the following questions during the design process of an output interface:

– *What*: what information should be presented?

– *Which*: which multimodal information should be chosen?

– *How*: how can this presentation be instantiated?

– *Then*: how to evolve this presentation?

The answers to these questions lead to follow of the output multimodal presentation design process presented in Figure 4.3. It involves several stages:

– semantic fission: semantic decomposition of the information produced by the functional core in elementary information UIE to present to the user;

– allocation of the presentation: selection, for each elementary information unit, of the multimodal presentation PME adapted to the current state of the context of interaction, and grouping together the PME into a same multi-modal presentation;

– instantiation: determination, according to the interaction context, the lexico-syntaxical content and the morphological attributes of presentation modalities (PME');

– evolution: evolution of the multimodal presentation according to the change in context. This evolution can bring back the design of the presentation, depending on the degree of change of the context, either to the allocation phase or to the instantiation phase.

4.5.2. *Formal model*

The formal model that we propose enables us to formally specify a output multimodal HCI. It takes the first two stages of the process of generation of a multimodal presentation based on the WWHT model (semantic fission, allocation) in a formal framework and enriches it by the introduction of additional operators. This model formalizes the different successive representations of the information in output throughout the refining process generated by the functional core until resulting in the multimodal presentation.

4.5.2.1. *The model of semantic fission*

It expresses semantic fission or decomposition of the information generated by the functional core in elementary units of information to present to the user. The description of the model of semantic fission includes the description of the syntax and the static and dynamic semantics. We will also present a parameterized model that describes the syntax of each of the four types of CASE space.

4.5.2.2. *Syntax*

Let I be the set of continuous[4] information to be fissioned, and UIE the set of units of elementary information. The syntax of the fission model is expressed in BNF grammar as follows:

$$I ::= UIE \mid (op_{temp}, op_{sem})(I, I) \mid It(n, I) \text{ with } n \in \mathbb{N}, \text{ where:}$$

$- op_{temp}$ is a temporal binary operator belonging to $TEMP$:

$$TEMP = \{An, Sq, Ct, Cd, Pl, Ch, In\};$$

$- op_{sem}$ is a binary semantic operator belonging to SEM:

$$SEM = \{Cc, Cp, Cr, Pr, Tr\};$$

$- It$ is a binary temporal operator expressing the iteration.

The temporal and semantic binary operators are defined on traces of events expressing the production of information $i_i \in I$.

$$op_{temp} : I \times I \longrightarrow I$$
$$op_{sem} : I \times I \longrightarrow I$$
$$It : \mathbb{N} \times I \longrightarrow I$$

Let i_i, i_j be two information belonging to I. Then:

$- i_i \, An \, i_j$: i_i anachronic i_j expresses that i_j occurs after a period of time following the end of i_i;

$- i_i \, Sq \, i_j$: i_j sequential to i_i expresses that i_j occurs right at the end of i_i;

$- i_i \, Ct \, i_j$: i_j concomitant to i_i expresses that i_j occurs after the beginning of i_i and that it finishes after i_i;

$- i_i \, Cd \, i_j$: i_i coincident with i_j expresses that i_j occurs after the beginning of i_i and ends before the end of i_i;

$- i_i \, Pl \, i_j$: i_i parallel to i_j expresses that i_i and i_j start and finish at the same time;

$- i_i \, Ch \, i_j$: choice between i_i and i_j expresses the deterministic choice between i_i and i_j;

$- i_i \, In \, i_j$: independent order between i_i and i_j expresses that the temporal relation between i_i and i_j is unknown.

---

4 Information whose restitution to the user takes a significant time.

The approach defined being generic, we do not know the effect of the elements of set I, so a function of interpretation will specify its meaning. The knowledge of this function will allow us to establish the properties relative to this interpretation. Let the function of interpretation of information be int, which enables us to associate the semantic interpretation to an element of information that characterizes multimodality. It is defined as follows:

$$int : I \longrightarrow D$$

where D is the interpretation domain associated to the information. D is defined according to the system studied, the user or the HCI designer. This domain is not specified in this chapter – it concerns the functional core. Nonetheless, it is essential to define the interpretation function to establish the characteristics of complementarity, independence, redundancy, etc.:

– $i_i \; Cc \; i_j$: i_i concurrent to i_j expresses that the interpretations of i_i and i_j are independent;

– $i_i \; Cp \; i_j$: i_i complementary to i_j expresses that the interpretations of i_i and i_j are complementary without being redundant;

– $i_i \; Cr \; i_j$: i_i complementary and redundant to i_j expresses that the interpretations i_i and i_j are complementary and that a part of their interpretations is redundant;

– $i_i \; Pr \; i_j$: i_i partially redundant to i_j expresses that the interpretation of i_i is entirely included in the interpretation of i_j or that the interpretation of i_j is entirely included in the interpretation of i_i;

– $i_i \; Tr \; i_j$: i_i totally redundant to i_j expresses that the interpretations of i_i and i_j are equivalent.

The relations of complementarity, independence and redundancy on domain D need to be specified for each system studied.

Let i be an information belonging to I, and n a natural number greater or equal to 1, $It(n, i)$ expresses the iteration n times of the information i.

4.5.2.3. *Static semantics*

The static semantics of the fission model define the duration of restitution of information i expressed for each elementary information by its temporal boundaries by means of temporal relation T.

Let us consider $Time = \{t_j\}$ the set of the discrete instants and the functions deb and end defined on I as follows:

$deb : I \rightarrow Time \; \forall i_i \in I deb(i_i)$ is the start of i_i event occurrence;

$end : I \rightarrow Time \; \forall i_i \in I end(i_i)$ is the end of i_i event occurrence.

Let T be the temporal relation which associates the start and end instant with each information:

$$T : I \longrightarrow Time \times Time$$

$\forall i_i \in I \; \exists (deb(i_i), end(i_i)) \in Time \times Time$ such as $deb(i_i) < end(i_i)$ and $T(i_i) = (deb(i_i), end(i_i))$.

4.5.2.4. Dynamic semantics

The dynamic semantics of the fission model describe the temporal ordering of i_i. It defines the temporal operators by means of the temporal relation T:

$\forall op_{temp} \in \{An, Sq, Ct, Cd, Pl, Ch, In\}$

$\forall i_i, i_j \in I,$ with $T(i_i) = (deb(i_i), end(i_i)), T(i_j) = (deb(i_j), end(i_j))$

$\exists i_k \in I,$ with $i_k = i_i \; op_{temp} \; i_j$ and:

$T(i_k) = (deb(i_i), end(i_j))$ iff $op_{temp} = An$ and $end(i_i) < deb(i_j)$

$T(i_k) = (deb(i_i), end(i_j))$ iff $op_{temp} = Sq$ and $end(i_i) = deb(i_j)$

$T(i_k) = (deb(i_i), end(i_j))$ iff $op_{temp} = Ct$ and $deb(i_i) < deb(i_j) < end(i_i) < end(i_j)$

$T(i_k) = (deb(i_i), end(i_i))$ iff $op_{temp} = Cd$ and $deb(i_i) < deb(i_j) < end(i_j) < end(i_i)$

$T(i_k) = (deb(i_i), end(i_i))$ iff $op_{temp} = Pl$ and $deb(i_i) = deb(i_j) \wedge end(i_i) = end(i_j)$

$i_k = i_i \vee i_k = i_j$ iff $op_{temp} = Ch$

$T(i_k) = (deb(i_k), end(i_k))$ iff $op_{temp} = In$

The binary temporal operator It is defined as follows:

$$\forall i_i \in I, \; n \in \mathbb{N}^* \quad It(n, i_i) = \underbrace{(\ldots ((i_i \; Sq \; i_i) \; Sq \; i_i) \ldots \; Sq \; i_i)}_{n \; times}$$

4.5.2.5. Modeling of the CASE space

The formal model of the CASE space is based on the formal model that was previously described, by defining the syntaxes relative to the four types of multimodality of the space. We start by defining the temporal and semantic operators authorized for each of the two values of the two axes of the space (use of media and link between information). Then we give the grammar of the syntax of the four axes resulting from crossing of the two axes (concurrent, alternated, synergistic and exclusive):

– *use of media*: this axis relates to the temporal ordering and thus conditions the use of temporal operators:

- sequential: reduces the grammar to the temporal operators excluding the use of parallelism: anachronic, sequential, choice and iteration,

- parallel: limits the grammar to the temporal operators using the different types of parallelism: concomitant, coincidental and parallel;

– *link between the information*: this axis relates to the semantic relation between the information and thus conditions the semantic operators:

- combined: reduces the semantic operators for the operators: complementary, complementary and redundant, partially redundant and totally redundant,

- independent: limits the semantic operators for the concurrent operator.

Thus, the four types of multimodalities can be defined as follows:

– *Concurrent type*: by using the temporal operators that are concomitant, coincidental and parallel combined with the concurrent semantic operator:

$$I ::= UIE \mid (op_{temp}, op_{sem})(I, I) \text{ with } op_{temp} \in \{Ct, Cd, Pl\} \text{ and } op_{sem} \in \{Cc\}$$

– *Alternated type*: with the anachronic, sequential, choice and iteration temporal operators combined with the semantic operators that are complementary and redundant, partially redundant and totally redundant:

$$I ::= UIE \mid (op_{temp}, op_{sem})(I, I) \mid It(n, I) \text{ with } n \in \mathbb{N}$$

$$\text{with } op_{temp} \in \{An, Sq, Ch\} \text{ and } op_{sem} \in \{Cp, Cr, Pr, Tr\}$$

– *Synergistic type*: by using the concomitant, coincidental and parallel temporal operators combined with the semantic operators – complementary, complementary and redundant, partially redundant and totally redundant:

$$I ::= UIE \mid (op_{temp}, op_{sem})(I, I) \text{ with } op_{temp} \in \{Ct, Cd, Pl\}$$

$$\text{and } op_{sem} \in \{Cp, Cr, Pr, Tr\}$$

– *Exclusive type*: with the anachronic, sequential, choice and iteration temporal operators combined with the concurrent operator:

$$I ::= UIE \mid (op_{temp}, op_{sem})(I, I) \mid It(n, I) \text{ with } n \in \mathbb{N}$$

$$\text{with } op_{temp} \in \{An, Sq, Ch\} \text{ and } op_{sem} \in \{Cc\}$$

4.5.2.6. *Allocation model*

The proposed allocation model is based on the second stage of the refinement process relating to the WWHT model. It includes the operators proposed in the allocation phase, complementary and redundant, and adds two operators – choice and iteration. Thus, the formal allocation model formalizes the allocation for each information unit the corresponding couple (modality, media) combined with the operators – complementary, redundant, choice and iteration – in view of applying the usability choices made for the output HCI.

4.5.2.7. Syntax

The syntax of the language describing the allocation model is described by two types of grammar: the first defines the multimodal presentation pm corresponding to information i; the second defines the elementary multimodal presentation pme corresponding to elementary unit of information UIE.

Let PM be the set of multimodal presentations and PME the set of multimodal elementary presentations. The multimodal presentation pm corresponding to i is the combination of different elementary multimodal presentations pme corresponding to the elementary information UIE units that constitute i. Consequently, there is a morphism of relation between (I, op_{temp}) and (PM, op'_{temp}), and (I, op_{sem}) and (PM, op'_{sem}).

The syntax for PM is described as follows:

$$PM ::= PME \mid (op'_{temp}, op'_{sem})(PM, PM) \mid It'(n, PM) \text{ with } n \in \mathbb{N} \text{ or:}$$

– op'_{temp} is a temporal binary operator belonging to $TEMP'$.

$$TEMP' = \{An', Sq', Ct', Cd', Pl', Ch', In'\}.$$

– op'_{sem} is a binary semantic operator belonging to SEM'.

$$SEM' = \{Cc', Cp', Cr', Pr', Tr'\}.$$

– It' is a binary temporal operator expressing the iteration.

The temporal and semantic binary operators are defined based on traces of events expressing the production of multimodal presentations $pm_i \in PM$:

$$op_{temp'} : PM \times PM \longrightarrow PM$$
$$op_{sem'} : PM \times PM \longrightarrow PM$$
$$It' : \mathbb{N} \times PM \longrightarrow PM$$

Let pm_i and pm_j be two multimodals belonging to PM. Then:

– pm_i An' pm_j: pm_i anachronic to pm_j expresses that pm_j occurs after an interval of time at the end of pm_i;

– pm_i Sq' pm_j: pm_j sequential to pm_i expresses that pm_j occurs just at the end of pm_i;

– pm_i Ct' pm_j: pm_j concomitant to pm_i expresses that pm_j occurs after the beginning of pm_i and that it ends after pm_i;

– pm_i Cd' pm_j: pm_i coincident with pm_j expresses that pm_j occurs after the beginning of pm_i and ends before the end of pm_i;

– pm_i Pl' pm_j: pm_i parallel to pm_j expresses that pm_i and pm_j start and end at the same time;

– pm_i Ch' pm_j: choice between pm_i and pm_j expresses the determinist choice between pm_i and pm_j;

– pm_i In' pm_j: independent order between pm_i and pm_j expresses that the temporal relation between pm_i and pm_j is unknown.

As with the definition of the interpretation function int, we define the interpretation function int' for PM as follows:

$$int' : PM \longrightarrow D'$$

where D' is the interpretation domain associated with the multimodal presentations. D' is also defined according to the context of the HCI or of its designer and is not developed in this chapter:

– pm_i Cc' pm_j: expresses that the interpretations of pm_i and pm_j are independent;

– pm_i Cp' pm_j: expresses that the interpretations of pm_i and pm_j are complementary without being redundant;

– pm_i Cr' pm_j: expresses that the interpretations of pm_i and pm_j are complementary and that a part of their interpretations is redundant;

– pm_i Pr' pm_j: expresses that the interpretation of pm_i is entirely included in the interpretation of pm_j or that the interpretation of pm_j is entirely included in the interpretation of pm_i;

– pm_i Tr' pm_j: expresses that interpretations of pm_i and pm_j are equivalent.

Let pm be multimodal presentation belonging to PM, and n a natural number greater or equal to 1, where $It'(n, pm)$ expresses the iteration n times the presentation pm.

Let MOD be the set of output modalities and MED the set of output medias. Let the relation $rest$ determine whether a modality can be resituated by a medium:

$$rest : MOD \times MED \longrightarrow \{true, \, false\}$$

$\forall mod_i \in MOD, \forall med_j \in MED, mod_i\ rest\ med_j$ expresses that mod_i can be restituted by med_j.

Let us consider the set of couples (modality and medium), such as the modality is restituted by the media:

$$ITEM = \{(mod_i, med_j)\ \text{such as}\ mod_i \in MOD \wedge med_j$$
$$\in MED \wedge mod_i\ rest\ med_j\}$$

Let the function $affect$ which associate a couple (modality and media) with an elementary unit of UIE information in $ITEM$.

$$affect : UIE \longrightarrow ITEM$$

The syntax of PME is expressed by the following BNF grammar:

$$PME ::= affect(UIE) \mid iter(n, PME) \mid affect(UIE)\ compl\ PME \mid$$
$$affect(UIE)\ redun\ PME \mid affect(UIE)\ choice\ PME\ \text{with}\ n \in \mathbb{N}$$

where $Iter$ expresses the iteration n times an elementary multimodal presentation pme:

$$Iter : \mathbb{N} \times PME \longrightarrow PME$$

Let the representational interpretation function of the multimodal presentations $repres$ defined as follows:

$$repres : PME \longrightarrow DR$$

where DR is the representational interpretation domain associated with the multimodal presentations. Thus the operators $compl, redun, choice$ express:

– $compl$: the representational complementarity between two elementary multimodal presentations for the restitution of an elementary unit of information UIE;

– $redun$: the representational redundancy between two elementary multimodal presentations for the restitution of an elementary unit of UIE information;

– $choice$: the representational choice between two elementary multimodal presentations for the restitution of an elementary unit of UIE information:

$$compl : PME \times PME \longrightarrow PME$$
$$redun : PME \times PME \longrightarrow PME$$
$$choice : PME \times PME \longrightarrow PME$$

4.5.2.8. *Static semantics*

The static semantics of the allocation model express the duration of multimodal presentation pm and elementary multimodal presentation pme.

It is defined by their time boundaries respectively, via temporal relations T' and T'', and a set of properties defined on the syntaxical elements of the model enabling us to describe the usability properties of the HCI, let us consider the functions deb' and end' defined on PM as follows:

$deb' : PM \to Time \; \forall pm_i \in PM \, deb'(pm_i)$ is defined at the beginning of the pm_i;

$end' : PM \to Time \; \forall pm_i \in PM \, end'(pm_i)$ is the moment of the end of pm_i.

Let T' be the temporal relation, which associates to each elementary multimodal presentation associates its start and end moment:

$$T' : PM \longrightarrow Time \times Time$$

$$\forall pm_i \in PM \; \exists (deb'(pm_i), end'(pm_i)) \in Time \times Time \text{ such as:}$$

$$deb'(pm_i) < end'(pm_i) \text{ and } T'(pm_i) = (deb'(pm_i), end'(pm_i))$$

Let us consider the functions deb'' and end'' defined on PME as follows:

$deb'' : PME \to Time \; \forall pme_i \in PME \; deb''(pme_i)$ is the moment of the beginning of pme_i;

$end'' : PME \to Time \; \forall pme_i \in PME \; end''(pme_i)$ is the moment of the end of pme_i.

Let T'' be the temporal relation which associates the moment of the start and end to each elementary multimodal presentation:

$$T'' : PME \longrightarrow Time \times Time$$

$$\forall pme_i \in PME \; \exists (deb''(pme_i), end''(pme_i)) \in Time \times Time$$

such as $deb''(pme_i) < end''(pme_i)$ and $T''(pme_i) = (deb''(pme_i), end''(pme_i))$

There are usability constraints of the interface in output that can be linked to: the environment (e.g. the noise which detracts from the use of the vocal mode); the system (the use of a PDA is an argument in favor of graphic modality rather then textual one); and the user (a hearing impaired user will favor visual mode to auditory mode). In the aim of describing these constraints we will introduce the following static properties:

– the mode used for the media: $mode(med_i) \in \{visual, auditory, tactile\}$. For example, $mode(loud\text{-}speaker) = vocal, mode(screen) = visual$;

– the shareability of media: $shar(med_i) \in \{true, false\}$, which expresses the possibility of whether or not to share the media between more than one modality of the same or different kinds. For example, $shar(screen) = true$, $shar(loud\text{-}speaker) = false$. The introduction of this property enables us to avoid the collisions[5] on a media. The property of absence of collisions was expressed in the formal model proposed in [MOH 09];

– the priorities between modalities: $priority(mod_i) \in \mathbb{N}$. For example, $priority(speech) > priority(text)$;

– the priorities between modes: $priority(mode_k) \in \mathbb{N}$. For example, $priority(visual) > priority(auditory)$ (hearing impaired user case).

4.5.2.9. *Dynamic semantics*

The dynamic semantics of the allocation model describe the temporal ordering of pm_i and pme_i. It defines the operators An', Sq', Ct', Cd', Pl', Ch', In', It', $iter$ and $choice$ with the help of the relation T':

$$\forall pm_i \in PM, \ \forall pm_j \in PM, \ \text{with} \ T'(pm_i) = (deb'(pm_i), end'(pm_i)),$$

$T'(pm_j) = (deb'(pm_j), end'(pm_j)) \ \exists pm_k \in PM, \ \text{with} \ pm_k = pm_i \ op'_{temp} \ pm_j$
and:

$$T'(pm_k) = (deb'(pm_i), end'(pm_j))$$
$$\text{iff} \ op'_{temp} = An' \ \text{and} \ end'(pm_i) < deb'(pm_j)$$

$$T'(pm_k) = (deb'(pm_i), end'(pm_j))$$
$$\text{iff} \ op'_{temp} = Sq' \ \text{and} \ end'(pm_i) = deb'(pm_j)$$

$$T'(pm_k) = (deb'(pm_i), end'(pm_j))$$
$$\text{iff} \ op'_{temp} = Ct' \ \text{and} \ deb'(pm_i) < deb'(pm_j) < end'(pm_i) < end'(pm_j)$$

$$T'(pm_k) = (deb'(pm_i), end'(pm_i))$$
$$\text{iff} \ op'_{temp} = Cd' \ \text{and} \ deb'(pm_i) < deb'(pm_j) < end'(pm_j) < end'(pm_i)$$

$$T'(pm_k) = (deb'(pm_i), end'(pm_j))$$
$$\text{iff} \ op'_{temp} = Pl' \ \text{and} \ deb'(pm_i) = deb'(pm_j) \wedge end'(pm_j) = end'(pm_i)$$

---

5 Representing two modalities in the same temporal window, on a non shareable media such as presenting, at the same time, a tone with a sentence produced by speech synthesis.

$$pm_k = pm_i \lor pm_k = pm_j \text{ iff } op'_{temp} = Ch'$$

$$T'(pm_k) = (deb'(pm_k), end'(pm_k)) \text{ iff } op'_{temp} = In'$$

$$It'(n, pm_i) = \underbrace{(\dots ((pm_i \ Sq' \ pm_i) \ Sq' \ pm_i) \dots Sq'pm_i)}_{n \text{ times}}$$

The temporal binary operator $iter$ is defined by using the sequential operator Seq:

$$\forall pme_i \in PME, \quad n \in \mathbb{N}^*$$

$$iter(n, pme_i) = \underbrace{(\dots ((pme_i \ Seq \ pme_i) \ Seq \ pme_i) \dots Seq \ pme_i)}_{n \text{ times}}$$

The sequential operator Seq is defined via the temporal relation T'' as follows:

$$\forall pme_i, \ pme_j \in PME \times PME \text{ with } T''(pme_i) = (deb''(pme_i), end''(pme_i)),$$

$$T''(pme_j) = (deb''(pme_j), end''(pme_j)) \text{ and } end''(pme_i) = deb''(pme_j)$$

$$\exists pme_k \in PME \text{ such as } pme_k = pme_i \ Seq \ pme_j$$

$$\text{and } T''(pme_k) = (deb''(pme_i), end''(pme_j))$$

The *choice* operator is defined as follows:

$$\forall pme_i, \ pme_j \in PME \times PME \ \exists pme_k \in PME \text{ such as}$$

$$pme_k = pme_i \ choice \ pme_j \implies pme_k = pme_i \lor pme_k = pme_j$$

4.5.3. *Case study*

To illustrate the formal model described above, we use an interaction scenario in output inspired by the SmartKom system [REI 03]. It is a system for the management of different applications relative to communication services (telephone, fax, email, etc.) of access to diffuse computing devices, localization services and navigation and road information. SmartKom is a symmetrical multimodal system whose output multimodality is supported by the conversational agent Smartakus, which has an inventory of gestures, postures and facial expressions.

The scenario of output multimodal interaction modeled consists of a dialog between Smartakus and the user, who is asking for a map of the town of Heidelberg. The conversational agent Smartakus responds to the user request by vocal synthesis: *"Here you can see the map of the city"* while displaying the map of the town of Heidelberg.

4.5.3.1. *Modeling of the output interaction*

In what follows, we model the interface that enables a system to respond to a request according to the scenario described above. We consider I the set of information in output output information constituted of the singleton $i =$ "*here you can see the map of the city*" combined with the image of the map of the town of Heidelberg, UIE the set of elementary information units constituted of elements $uie_1 =$ "*here you can see the map of the city*" and $uie_2 =$ image of the map of Heidelberg. We also consider the sets:

$$MOD = \{speech, \ facial \ expression, \ image\}$$

$$MED = \{screen, \ loud\text{-}speaker\}$$

$$ITEM = \{(speech, \ loud\text{-}speaker), (facial \ expression, \ screen),$$
$$(image, \ screen)\}$$

4.5.3.2. *Semantic fission*

$I = \{i\}$ with $i =$ "*here you can see the map of the city*" combined with the image of the map of Heidelberg:

$$UIE = \{uie_1, uie_2\}$$

with: $uie_1 =$ "*here you can see the map of the city*", $uie_2 =$ image of the map of Heidelberg.

The fissioned information i is expressed by the parallel temporal combination:

$$i = (Pl', Cp')(uie_1, uie_2)$$

Thus, we deduce that the interface was designed according to the type of synergistical multimodality.

4.5.3.3. *Allocation*

The elementary multimodal presentations pme_1 and pme_2 respectively corresponding to the elementary information units uie_1 and uie_2 are:

$$pme_1 = (speech, loud\text{-}speaker)(uie_1) \ compl \ (facial \ expression, screen)(uie_1)$$

The information uie_1 is expressed by the speech modality on the *loud-speaker* completed by the facial expression on the screen (restitution of the dialog of the conversational agent):

$$pme_2 = (picture, screen)(uie_2)$$

The information uie_2 is expressed by the picture modality on the screen (restitution of the map).

The multimodal presentation pm corresponding to i is the temporal parallel and semantic complementary combination of the elementary multimodal presentations pme_1 and pme_2:

$$pm = (Pl', Cp')((speech, loud\text{-}speaker)(uie_1)\ compl\ (facial\ expression, screen)$$
$$(uie_1)), (picture, screen)(uie_2)).$$

4.6. Conclusion

This chapter has dealt with the design of HCI, and in particular multimodal HCI. They are increasingly present in transport systems, particularly critical systems, and few works have concerned themselves with their formal validation.

We focused on the formal modeling of these HCIs. The benefit of approaches put forward is twofold. On one hand, these approaches enable us to, *a priori*, master the complexity of the development process of the interface. This complexity is accentuated by the presence of synchronization primitives and of semantic reference between information, which come from the particularities introduced by the multimodal nature of these HCIs. On the other hand, once the formal model has been established, these approaches enable us to establish or verify certain properties of usability of the interface *beforehand*. We have made sure to present formal modeling of these properties in the same model, which served to describe the multimodal HCI studied.

Furthermore, the approach proposed enables us to define the multimodal HCI models in a progressive and iterative manner by introducing the different characteristics throughout the modeling phase. Finally, we made a special case study to define a generic model, taking into account different design spaces and enabling the processes of both input and output multimodality. This enables us to target different validation techniques that support the verification of the desired properties.

Several extensions of these works can be envisaged. We gave two. With regards to the definition of HCIs, it seems important to us to define other instantiations of the model proposed on other design spaces or approaches of multimodal HCI descriptions, both in input and output. With regards to formal verification, it is a matter of defining generic properties guaranteeing the quality of HCIs modeled and transformations, preserving the semantics of the system modeled, which extend a modelization following the model put forward in a target formal technique which supports the verification of properties.

This work has partially been addressed in the case of input multimodality but must be dealt with in the case of output multimodality.

4.7. Bibliography

[ABR 96] ABRIAL J.-R., *The B-Book*, Cambridge University Press, 1996.

[AIT 06a] AIT-AMEUR Y., AIT-SADOUNE I. and BARON M., "Etude et comparaison de scénarios de développements formels d'interfaces multi-modales fondés sur la preuve et le raffinement", *MOSIM'06: 6ème Conférence Francophone de Modélisation et Simulation. Modélisation, Optimisation et Simulation des Systèmes : Défis et Opportunités*, Rabat, 2006.

[AIT 06b] AIT-AMEUR Y., AIT-SADOUNE I., BARON M. and MOTA J., "Validation et vérification formelles de systèmes interactifs multi-modaux fondées sur la preuve", *18° Conférence Francophone sur l'Interaction Homme-Machine (IHM)*, Montréal, pp. 123–130, 2006.

[BAA 99] BAADER F. and NIPKOW T., *Term Rewriting and All That*, Cambridge University Press, 1999.

[BAS 94] BASTIDE R. and PALANQUE P., "Petri net based design of user-driven interfaces using the interactive cooperative objects formalism", *Interactive Systems: Design, Specification, and Verification, DSV-IS'94*, Springer-Verlag, pp. 383–400, 1994.

[BEL 92] BELLIK Y. and TEIL D., "Les types de multimodalités", *IHM'92: 4èmes Journées sur l'Ingénierie des Interfaces Homme-Machine*, France, Telecom Paris, pp. 22–28, 1992.

[BEL 95] BELLIK Y., Interfaces multimodales : concepts, modèles et architecture, PhD thesis, LIMSI, University of Orsay, 1995.

[BER 94] BERNSEN O., "Foundations of multimodal representations. A taxonomy of representational modalities", *Interacting with Computers*, vol. 6, no. 4, pp. 347–371, 1994.

[BER 00] BERT D., ECHAHED R. and REYNAUD J.-C., Reference manual of the LPG specification language and environment, 2000.

[BER 01] BERNSEN N. and DYBKJAER L., "Exploring natural interaction in the car", *International Workshop on Information Presentation and Natural Multimodal Dialogue*, Verona, Italy, pp. 75–79, 2001.

[BOR 97] BORDEGONI M., FACONTI G., MAYBURY M., RIST T., RUGGIERI S., TRAHANIAS P. and WILSON M., "A standard reference model for intelligent multimedia presentation systems", *Computer Standards and Interfaces*, vol. 6, no. 4, pp. 477–496, 1997.

[BOU 99] BOUSQUET L.D., OUABDESSELAM F., RICHIER J.-L. and ZUANON N., "Lutess: a specification-driven testing environment for synchronous software", *International Conference of Software Engineering*, ACM Press, pp. 267–276, 1999.

[BOU 05] BOUCHET J., NIGAY L. and GANILLE T., "The ICARE component-based approach for multimodal input interaction: application to real-time military aircraft cockpits", *The 11th International Conference on Human-Computer Interaction*, Las Vegas, Nevada, USA, 22-27 July, Lawrence Erlbaum Associates, 2005.

[BOU 06] BOUCHET J., MADANI L., NIGAY L., ORIAT C. and PARISSIS I., "Formal testing of multimodal interactive systems", *DSV-IS2006, The XIII International Workshop on Design, Specification and Verification of Interactive Systems*, Lecture Notes in Computer Science, Springer-Verlag, 2006.

[CAE 91]   CAELEN J. and COUTAZ J., "Interaction homme-machine multimodale : problèmes généraux", *IHM'91*, Dourdan, France, 1991.

[CLA 94]   CLARKE E.M., GRUMBERG O. and LONG D.E., "Model checking and abstraction", *ACM Trans. Program. Lang. Syst.*, vol. 16, no. 5, pp. 1512–1542, 1994.

[COU 95]   COUTAZ J., NIGAY L., SALBER D., BLANDFORD A., MAY J. and YOUNG R., "Four easy pieces for assessing the usability of multimodal interaction: the CARE properties", NORDBY K., HELMERSEN P., GILMORE D. and ARNESEN S. (Eds.), *Proceedings of INTERACT '95 - IFIP TC13 Fifth International Conference on Human-Computer Interaction*, Lillehammer, Norway, pp. 115–120, Chapman & Hall, London, June, 1995.

[DAL 96]   DALAL M., FEINER S., MCKEOWN K., PAN S., ZHOU M., HÖLLERER T., SHAW J., FENG Y. and FROMER J., "Negotiation for automated generation of temporal multimedia presentations", *ACM Multimedia'96*, Boston, USA, pp. 55–64, November 1996.

[DEM 92]   DE MEER J., ROTH R. and VUONG S., "Introduction to algebraic specifications based on the language ACT ONE", *Computer Networks and ISDN Systems*, vol. 23, no. 5, pp. 363–392, Elsevier Science Publishers B.V., 1992.

[EIJ 89]   VAN EIJK P.H.J., VISSERS C.A. and DIAZ M., *Formal Description Technique Lotos: Results of the Esprit Sedos Project*, Elsevier Science Inc., New York, NY, USA, 1989.

[ELL 97]   ELLSBERGER J., HOGREFE D. and SARMA. A., *SDL: Formal Object-Oriented Language for Communicating System*, Prentice Hall PTR, 1997.

[EST 97]   ESTELLE, ISO 9074, A formal description technique based on an extended state transition model, 1997.

[FAS 96]   FASCIANO M. and LAPALME G., "PostGraphe: a system for the generation of statistical graphics and text", *Workshop on Natural Language Generation*, Sussex, UK, pp. 51–60, 1996.

[FEI 91]   FEINER S.K. and MCKEOWN K.R., "Automating the generation of coordinated multimedia explanations", *Computer*, vol. 24, no. 10, pp. 33–41, IEEE Computer Society Press, 1991.

[GOR 93]   GORDON M.J.C. and MELHAM T.F., *Introduction to HOL, A Theorem Proving Environment for Higher Order Logic*, Cambridge University Press, 1993.

[HAL 91]   HALBWACHS N., CASPI P., RAYMOND P. and PILAUD D., "The synchronous dataflow programming language LUSTRE", *Proceedings of the IEEE*, vol. 79, no. 9, September 1991.

[HOA 69]   HOARE C.A.R., "An axiomatic basis for computer programming", *Communications of the ACM*, vol. 12, no. 10, pp. 576–580, 1969.

[HOL 91]   HOLZMANN G.J., *Design and Validation of Computer Protocols*, Prentice Hall Int., 1991.

[HOP 07] HOPCROFT J.E., MOTWANI R. and THEORY J.D.U.A., *Automata Theory, Languages, and Computation*, Addison Wesley, 2007.

[HUE 07] HUET G., KAHN G. and PAULIN-MOHRING C., The Coq proof assistant: a tutorial, Report, Logical project, 2007.

[JON 92] JONES C.B., *VDM: une méthode rigoureuse pour le développement de logiciels*, Masson, 1992.

[JOU 06] JOURDE F., NIGAY L. and PARISSIS I., "Test formel de systèmes interactifs multimodaux : couplage ICARE - Lutess", *ICSSEA'06: 19ème Journées Internationales "Génie Logiciel & Ingénierie de Systèmes et leurs Applications" Globalisation des Services et des Systèmes*, Paris, France, 2006.

[JUS 04] JUSTER J. and ELVIS D.R., "Situated speech and gesture understanding for a robotic chandelier", *Sixth International Conference on Multimodal Interfaces*, ACM Press, pp. 90–96, 2004.

[KAM 04] KAMEL N., "Utilisation de SMV pour la vérification de propriétés d'IHM multimodales", *16° Conférence Francophone sur l'Interaction Homme-Machine (IHM'04)*, Namur, Belgique, pp. 219–222, 2004.

[KAM 05] KAMEL N. and AIT-AMEUR Y., "Mise en oeuvre d'IHM multimodales dans un système de CAO. Une approche fondée sur les méthodes formelles", *Revue Internationale d'Ingénierie Numérique*, vol. 1, no. 2, pp. 235–256, Lavoisier et Hermes Science, 2005.

[KAM 06] KAMEL N., Un cadre formel générique pour la spécification et la vérification des interfaces multimodales. Cas de la multimodalité en entrée, PhD thesis, University of Poitiers, France, 2006.

[KAM 07] KAMEL N. and AIT-AMEUR Y., "Formal model for usability properties in multimodal HCI", *2nd International Workshop on Multimodal and Pervasive Services(MAPS07), at IEEE International Conference On Pervasive Services (ICPS07)*, Istanbul, Turkey, July 2007.

[LEH 05] LEHNING H., *Les équations algébriques*, Pôle, Collectif Tangente, 2005.

[MAC 98] MACCOLL I. and CARRINGTON D., "Testing MATIS: a case study on specification based testing of interactive systems", *Formal Aspects of HCI (FAHCI98)*, Sheffield-Hallam University, pp. 57–69, 1998.

[MCM 92] MCMILLIAN K., The SMV system, Report, Carnegie Mellon University, 1992.

[MER 00] MERLOZ P., LAVALLEE S., TONNETTI J. and PITTET L., "Image-guided spinal surgery: technology, operative technique and clinical practice", *Operative Techniques in Orthopaedics*, vol. 10, no. 1, pp. 56–63, January 2000.

[MIL 80] MILNER R., *A Calculus of Comunicating Systems*, vol. 92 of *LNCS*, Springer-Verlag, New York, NY, USA, 1980.

[MOH 09] MOHAND-OUSSAÏD L., AÏT-AMEUR Y. and AHMED-NACER M., "A generic formal model for fission of modalities in output multi-modal interactive systems", *VECoS '2009 - 3rd International Workshop on Verification and Evaluation of Computer and Communication Systems*, Rabat, Morroco, July 2009.

[MON 96] MONIN J.-F., *Comprendre les méthodes formelles*, Masson, 1996.

[NAV 05] NAVARRE D., PALANQUE P., BASTIDE R., SCHYN A., WINCKLER M., NEDEL L. and FREITAS C., "A formal description of multimodal interaction techniques for immersive virtual reality applications", *INTERACT 2005*, Rome, Italy, Lecture Notes in Computer Science, Springer-Verlag, pp. 25–28, September 2005.

[NED 03] NEDEL L.P., FREITAS C., JACOB L. and PIMENTA M., "Testing the use of egocentric interactive techniques in immersive virtual environments", *INTERACT 2003 – Ninth IFIP TC13 International Conference on Human-Computer*, IOS Press, pp. 471–478, 2003.

[NIG 94] NIGAY L., Conception et modélisation logicielle des Systèmes interactifs : application aux interfaces multimodales, PhD thesis, Joseph Fourier University, Grenoble, 1994.

[NIG 96] NIGAY L. and COUTAZ J., "Espaces conceptuels pour l'interaction multimédia et multimodale", *Technique et Science Informatiques, Spécial Multimédia et Collecticiel*, vol. 15, no. 9, pp. 1195–1225, 1996.

[PAL 03] PALANQUE P. and SCHYN A., "A model-based for engineering multimodal interactive systems", *9th IFIP TC13 International Conference on Human Computer Interaction (Interact'2003)*, 2003.

[PAU 93] PAULSON L.C., The Isabelle reference manual, Report, University of Cambridge, Computer Laboratory, 1993.

[PLO 81] PLOTKIN G., A structural approach to operational semantics, Report, Department of Computer Science, University of Aarhus DAIMI FN 19, 1981.

[PNU 77] PNUELI A., "The temporal logic of programs", *FOCS*, 1977.

[REI 03] REITHINGER N., ALEXANDERSSON J., BECKER T., BLOCHER A., ENGEL R., LÖCKELT M., MÜLLER J., PFLEGER N., POLLER P., STREIT M. and TSCHERNOMAS V., "SmartKom: adaptive and flexible multimodal access to multiple applications", *ICMI'03*, Vancouver, British Columbia, Canada, pp. 101–108, November 2003.

[ROU 06] ROUSSEAU C., Présentation multimodale et contextuelle de l'information, PhD thesis, University of Paris sud XI-Orsay, 2006.

[SCH 03] SCHYN A., NAVARRE D., PALANQUE P. and NEDEL L.P., "Description formelle d'une technique d'interaction multimodale dans une application de réalité virtuelle immersive", *Proceedings of the 15th French Speaking conference on Human-Computer Interaction (IHM'03)*, Caen, France, pp. 25–28, November 2003.

[SPI 88] SPIVEY J., *The Z Notation: A Reference Manual*, Prentice Hall Int., 1988.

[STO 93] STOCK O., "ALFRESCO: enjoying the combination of natural language processing and hypermedia for information exploration", *Intelligent Multimedia Interfaces*, pp. 197–224, American Association for Artificial Intelligence, Menlo Park, CA, USA, 1993.

Chapter 5

From Human-Machine Interaction to Cooperation: Towards the Integrated Copilot

5.1. Introduction

This chapter aims to introduce and discuss the concept of *copiloting* applied to the specific context of automobile driver assistance. For the past few years, we have seen a massive inflow of embedded information devices (at the forefront of which are the navigational aid systems), as well as the emergence of technologies for the partial automation of driving (such as automatic speed regulators). All these evolutions make the development of integrated copiloting devices necessary. Such devices must be able to harmoniously cooperate with the driver and adapt their assistance according to the driving context. As such, similar to what happened in aeronautics during the 1980s, the problems of human-machine cooperation are now a particular focus of attention in the automobile sector.

The fundamental question concerns the respective roles of humans and technology in control of the vehicle. Must we seek to deliberately adhere to the substitutive logic (replace the human driver with automaton as soon as it is technically possible) or, *conversely*, should we seek to count on the complementarities of the human-machine couple, only assisting drivers when they express the need for it and/or when they are not correctly able to manage the situation? The "copiloting" approach, as it is dealt with in this chapter, is strictly from the latter point of view: the objective is for technology to act as *support* for

Chapter written by Thierry BELLET, Jean-Michel HOC, Serge BOVERIE and Guy BOY.

human activity, and not on the contrary replacement for it (i.e. where the activity of the driver would be defined "by default", leaving the human with residual tasks outside the automaton's reach).

After a concise introduction of the context and the stakes of ergonomic research in terms of human-machine cooperation (section 5.2), we present a few examples of cooperative assistance devices on which the different authors in this chapter are working (section 5.3).

The first of these devices (section 5.3.1) aims to prevent collision risks. The specific challenge of this research project is to design an *adaptive* technology that is able to jointly take into account external driving conditions (how critical a situation is, as it can be measured by time to collision with an obstacle, for example) and the driving behaviors implemented by the human driver, in order to determine in real time whether the latter is properly managing the risk or needs assistance.

The second device (section 5.3.2) is concerned with the prevention of risks of exiting lanes and aims to guarantee a *secure driving trajectory* from the point of view of lateral control. This research enabled different philosophies of human-machine cooperation to be investigated from a *perceptive* mode centered on the diffusion of information to the implementation of a *mode of delegation of the function* aiming to entrust lateral control to the automaton via a *mutual control mode*. These different modes of cooperation are presented and then discussed with regards to recent experimental results.

The last device (section 5.3.3) adheres to the logic of driver *monitoring* and deals more specifically with accident risks induced by the driver falling asleep at the wheel. The objective is to design a warning system able to diagnose a critical decrease in vigilance and to compensate, as the case may be, for this type of human failure. It is also a matter of enabling adaptation of interaction modalities and/or human-machine interfaces, according to the driver's vigilance level.

Finally, beyond these three specific aid functions − by nature limited in their respective objectives − we ask ourselves about the integrative aspect of what a true automobile "copilot" should be, while at the same time trying to guarantee centralized and harmonious management of human cooperation, whatever the subjacent aid functions on which it is based. This point is more specifically the focus of a discussion in section 5.4, and will enable us to propose a first hint of generic architecture for such a copiloting device adapted to the specificities of automobile driving.

5.2. Copiloting and human-machine cooperation: context and stakes for the automobile

With the massive development of embedded information systems and recent progress in terms of automation of driving, the whole activity of the human driver is radically changing. Under the combined effect of these two technological revolutions, it is now a matter of extricating a general framework for human-machine cooperation in automobiles, in view of designing the vehicle of the future. This approach is necessary for improving security, acceptability and the user friendliness of driving assistance. On the one hand, the diversity technology on offer and the multitude of aid systems that are already available means that their integration within more complex devices needs to be considered in order to be able to guarantee a good interaction with the human driver. This is necessary, as much to avoid certain problematic effects (negative interference with the activity of the driver, for example, or a distraction with regards to the road), as to improve the legibility of aids (harmonization of the aid, whatever the device in charge of providing it at time *t*). It equally involves trying to get a greater benefit from existing technology on offer (for example, by the mutualization of certain technical components between different assistance devices).

On the other hand, drivers do not all necessarily need to be assisted in the same way or in the same situations. When the driver is perfectly in control of the situation, he does not care about assistance. However, sometimes he can have real difficulties or is unaware of a potential danger, which fully justifies the intervention of a driving aid. It is therefore advisable for technology to be able to appreciate the difficulties that the human is facing *at that moment,* in order to provide assistance that is adapted in its nature and form, to the actions of the driver at the time and to the driving conditions at that moment. All these evolutions are heading towards integrated "intelligent copiloting" devices that are able to harmoniously cooperate with the driver and likely to adjust their assistance according to the context of use. Though this approach is necessary and has been the subject of research in the context of embedded information systems (for example, the European projects CEMVOCAS[1] and AIDE[2]), it nonetheless becomes much more acute as soon as the assistance devices are able to directly intervene in the commands.

Indeed, just like the technological revolution that radically changed aeronautics at the end of the 1970s [BIL 91], [BOY 03], [STA 92], automation is now appearing in the automobile sector, with the automaton able to take control of the vehicle

---

1 CEMVocAS (European project 1997-2001) *CEntralised Management of Vocal interfaces aiming at a better Automotive Safety* [BEL 02, BEL 03].

2 AIDE (European project 2004-2008): *Adaptive Integrated Driver-vehicle interfacE* [TAT 05, BEL 07b].

under certain conditions [YOU 07b]. Eventually, the entire activity of the human driver is likely to radically change: from a piloting task that is totally the responsibility of the human driver (in perception, decision making and sensorimotor control). Automobile driving is slowly changing into a task of automaton supervision, potentially calling for completely different skills. The question of human-machine cooperation is now different[3], depending on whether the automatic devices are engaged at the driver's initiative (as is the case for speed regulators, for example) or those that are spontaneously set off when the situation requires it (for example, collision avoidance devices). It is nevertheless true that the question of copiloting – considered from the point of view of distribution of tasks and responsibilities between the human and automaton – is now central to automobile driving. From an activity that had been the exclusive prerogative of the human, we are now heading towards co-managed driving under the joint authority of a complex entity: the human-machine system.

These notions of system and human-machine cooperation were initially productive in aeronautics [BOY 91], [HUT 95], [WIE 93], before establishing themselves in the automobile context [BEL 03], [HOC 09]. Moving the notion of machine "system" towards the "human-machine" structure as a whole is the result of two realizations.

First, recognizing that in many situations automation without taking the human operator into consideration is not a possibility. In automobile driving, full automation is a utopia that ignores the extraordinary complexity of the driving environment (this environment is much more simple in aeronautics). Apart from situations where the abilities of the driver are very degraded and for which simplification is required (an emergency stop, for example) or situations in the hypothesis of future road sections that would be entirely dedicated to automated driving, the notion of copiloting is unavoidable.

Second, the viewpoint of the human-machine system makes us consider that a task common to the human and the machine exists for which a distribution of

---

3 As long as the automatic devices are in line with the activity of the human driver (as is the case with breaking aids), the problems of human-machine cooperation are (all proportions conserved) relatively simple to resolve: the driver decides on an action (to brake, for example) and the automaton consequently acts on the vehicle in order to optimize the action (and decision) of the human. In this context, human-machine coupling is quite natural (even if it is not trivial on an ergonomic level): the human driver decides on an action and the automaton assists him in its implementation. However, as soon as we come close to more decisional levels (whether or not to engage an action on the brake), the integration of the assistance technology in human activity becomes infinitely more complex. The conflict between the driver and automatic devices becomes a more recurring issue, with the problems of acceptability and responsibility in the event of an accident at the forefront of this.

functions is necessary. In other words, the "task" of the machine or human operator, considered in isolation, can have no meaning without integrating them into the global task. It is the *joint cognitive systems* as a whole that becomes the central player [HOL 83], [HOL 05]. Thus, for example, an *antilock braking system* (ABS) involves both the driver (stepping on the brake pedal, linked with an analysis of the situation) and the machine (implementation of breaks so that the wheels do not lock). What meaning would the action of the driver have without that of the machine completing it? What would the action of the machine be without the prior action of the driver (analysis of the situation and action on the pedal)? As soon as the notion of the human-machine system is concerned and that the intelligence of the machine increases, in the sense of its adaptive abilities and a certain autonomy, the issue of human-machine cooperation becomes of increasing interest [HOC 01]. It goes beyond the single notion of a human-machine system by considering the human operator and the machine as two agents or partners of the same team tasked with driving. For the rest, it has been proven that humans have a tendency to attribute cooperative abilities to machines as soon as they perceive their "intelligence" [NAS 96].

This issue of cooperation proposes considering that as well as their private activities, the cooperative agents carry out cooperative activities. The latter are at the disposal of interference management (negative, as much as positive), created by interdependencies between the goals of the agents in order to facilitate tasks (individual or collective). This means that we agree to not plan the activity of the human-machine system too rigidly to leave the necessary room for maneuver for unforeseen conditions. For example, the distribution of functions can change according to circumstances. The user trained in the use of an adaptive cruise control (ACC)[4] speed regulator knows under what conditions he can delegate longitudinal control or regain control.

Human–machine cooperation goes further than single shared control (co-action on the environment). It also integrates the action of an agent on the activity of another agent. The most well-known form in aeronautics is *mutual control*, when both agents check what the other is doing, thus facilitating the prevention, detection and correction of errors [WIE 93]. In this case, it is a matter of positive interference between agents. In driving assistance, mutual control can go beyond a simple sound, visual or haptic warning, as far as the haptic suggestion of action on the wheel or pedals [NAV 07], [SUZ 03]. It can also occur that the drivers are objectively failing (distracted, surprised, victim of a dizzy turn), or that the driving situation becomes too difficult to manage on their own, given their abilities at the time (imminent

---

4 ACC: a device for the automatic regulation of longitudinal control, ensuring that a target cruise speed is kept (in the event of driving alone) and slowing if necessary in order to keep a secure inter-vehicle distance with the vehicle in front).

collision risk), thus justifying an action from the automaton. In all these cases, the device "criticizes" the behavior of drivers and consequently assists them to improve safety.

Here we are starting to address one of the key questions of automobile copiloting: on the one hand the machine must "support" human activity by facilitating the common objective of the human-machine system as a whole being reached. Good cooperation in this case implies the sharing of a *common frame of reference* [HOC 01], [PAC 02], [TER 90] between agents (adopted in [HOC 01]), i.e. a certain agreement in the analysis of the situation and on what each of the agents is or must carry out. This sharing is greatly facilitated if each of the agents has a basic model of the way the other functions (which can imply training from the driver's point of view and the integration of a driver model into the machine from a technological point of view).

Nonetheless, a "good" copilot must also know how "relay" to the failing human driver when he commits an obvious error or when himself unable to correctly control the situation. Ultimately, copiloting aims to get the best out of the respective abilities of the human and the machine. The human has abilities of analysis that are often unequalled by the automaton, and are not soon going to be equaled, but he can also make a mistake or reach his own limitations, thus justifying the relayed assistance. It is therefore not about rejecting the substitutive philosophy that is inherent to the automation of driving; in fact quite the opposite. It looks to distinguish the situations for which this option fully justifies itself, from those where other solutions would be better. Such is the real stake of "intelligent copiloting": to choose, in the range of possible human-machine interactions (from the diffusion of information to taking control of the car) the action that will best meet the needs of *this* driver and the specific requirements of *this* situation [BEL 03]. From the point of view of the ergonomist, the (total or partial) automation of driving does not constitute an end in itself. It is only a means, one mode of assistance among others, which has its advantages but also its limitations and problematic effects that it is advisable to control.

Evidently, incorporating automobile copiloting into the logic of human-machine cooperation is not without consequence from a technological point of view, and this implies the active participation of social science researchers alongside engineers. It is advisable to provide the machine with the ability to analyze the situation as well as the activity of the driver (diagnose how critical a situation is, for example, and judge how adequate the human behavior is [BEL 06]). It is also advisable to give it a "knowledge of how to cooperate" [MIL 98], [MIL 03] in view of guaranteeing good coordination of the copilot's activity, to anticipate the negative interference risks between the human activity and the automaton and, as the case may be, to resolve these conflicts if they occur. This is essential if we envisage going beyond the strict framework of a *vertical cooperation* (the driver is the only master on board and the automaton only intervenes under his control). In order to subscribe to the logic of *horizontal cooperation* [MIL 95], aiming to give the machine real decision-making powers that are potentially very useful, particularly in a critical situation.

These questions, which reveal the ergonomics as much as the cognitive engineering [BOY 03], are at the heart of current discussion in terms of driving assistance. They were partially addressed by the authors of this chapter via different research thematics that we present in the following section. The first thematic deals with the prevention of collision risks and seeks to differentiate situations in the context of adequately managing the risk, to those where assistance would be required. The second concerns making the trajectory secure in its lateral dimension, and in particular enabling us to explore the different modalities of human-machine cooperation in depth. The last one addresses the question of the diagnosis of certain human failures, such as inattention or falling asleep, in real time.

5.3. Three realizations of cooperative devices for the purposes of automobile copiloting

5.3.1. *Preventing collision risks*

The avoidance of collisions is a major stake for road safety. If we only consider the risks of collisions between vehicles, the figures for the national observatory of road safety[5] indicate that in France this type of collision represented more than 63% of corporal accidents in 2007 (that is 51,548 cases out of a total of 81,272 accidents) and more than 51% of fatal accidents on the road (2,385 people killed out of 4,620). If we integrate collisions with pedestrians, these numbers go to nearly 80% for corporal accidents (64,526) and 63% for fatal accidents (2,911), respectively.

In terms of human-machine cooperation, collision avoidance is a particularly delicate question. It is a matter of appreciating the critical nature of the road situation, which is in itself a complex task from a technological point of view (extract targets relevant to the road scene and estimate the probability of occurrence and imminence of trajectory conflicts). Nonetheless, this is far from being sufficient. If we exclude the extreme conditions for which the time to collision is so brief that no human intervention is likely to avoid the accident, all the configurations require the activity of the driver to be taken into account in view of appreciating the effective risk of collision with precision.

---

5   ONSIR: http://www2.securiteroutiere.gouv.fr/infos-ref/observatoire/accidentologie/le-bilan-de-l.html.

As an example, a fall in collision time from 3.0 to 1.5 s during the arrival of a slow vehicle does not mean the same thing depending on whether the driver: (i) keeps the speed and trajectory stable; (ii) engages the brakes; or (iii) has activated the left indicator. If, in the first case, the absence of reaction can potentially be interpreted as a deficiency in the detection or estimation of the speed of the obstacle (which could justify an alert), things are radically different in the two other configurations. The action on the brake proves an awareness of the presence of an obstacle, but nonetheless does not prejudge the efficiency of the engaged regulation procedure (a breaking aid can be envisaged in this case). As to activation of the indicator, it very probably reveals an intention to overtake, which it would be unadvisable to counter by the diffusion of a collision avoidance alert, at the risk of unnecessarily disturbing an overtaking maneuver, which in essence requires the complete attention of the driver.

Evidently objective parameters, even as relevant as the time to collision or the inter-vehicle distance, for example, are often insufficient to make the right decisions in terms of human-machine interactions. It is precisely with the objective of bringing these elements of decision into *real time* that the IFSTTAR laboratory of ergonomics and cognitive science began (ARCOS[6] program supported by the PREDIT[7]) the design and development of a device for the automatic analysis of the driving situation. The ultimate ambition of this was to enable an adaptive management of interactions between the driver and a collision avoidance device.

Summarily (see Figure 5.1) the objective is to enable a joint analysis of the driver's activity (i.e. the actions that he engages on the commands and their effects on the dynamics of the vehicle) according to the data enabling us to characterize the driving situation (via information coming from perception technologies, as well as mapping data), and this in order to:

– *Detect* situations that could potentially cause accidents (rapid approach towards a slower vehicle, the arrival of a fixed obstacle on the road, the presence of vulnerable users on the road, whether it be pedestrians or cyclists, etc.).

– *Analyze*, in real time, the behaviors of the driver with regards to objective characteristics of the road situation (for example, how critical it is).

– *Assess* the adequacy of the behaviors implemented by the driver and diagnose driving errors (for example, non detection of an obstacle).

---

6 ARCOS (2001-2004): *Action de Recherche pour une COnduite Sécurisée* (Research Action for Safe Driving).

7 PREDIT: *Programme de REcherche et D'Innovation dans les Transports* terrestres (Research and Innovation Program in Terrestrial Transport).

– *Identify* the type of assistance (help for monitoring, anti-collision, overtaking, etc.) and interaction mode (from the diffusion of warnings to taking partial or total control of the vehicle) that is most adequate in the situation.

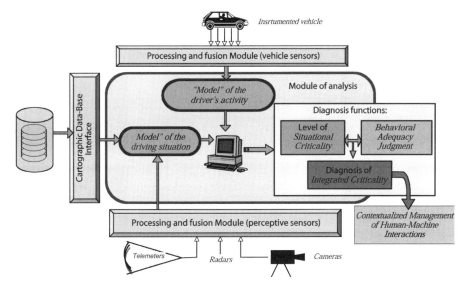

Figure 5.1. *General architecture of a device for the adaptive management of collision risks*

On a methodological level [BEL 06], data were gathered on an open road from a group of 10 experienced drivers (five men and five women, with an average age of 39). First of all, the drivers were asked to carry out one of the two predefined experimental routes (one of 60 km and the other of 180 km) at the wheel of an instrumented vehicle. Their activity, as well as the road environment, was then recorded on video. At the end of the driving phase, the situations when a collision risk occurred, even if very small (112 cases collected for a total of 1,200 km covered), were then the subject of individual *debriefing* interviews based on the technique of self-confrontation: the drivers watch the film of their own activity *in situ*, then the experimenter asks them to clarify their actions, decisions, reasoning, etc. The benefit of using the self-confrontation method lies in the possibility of accessing information that is not directly observable, such as the way in which the drivers *mentally represent a situation to themselves* [BEL 07a], [BEL 09], assesses the *criticality* [BAN 08] or make a particular decision in view of managing risks. Figure 5.2 gives an example of data collected during this experiment.

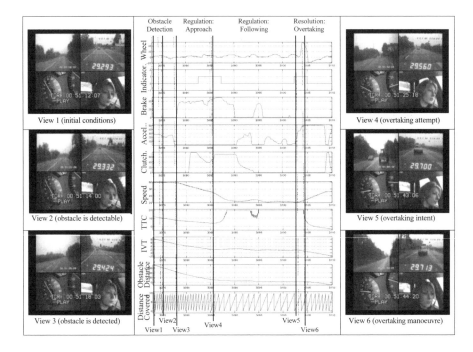

Figure 5.2. *Example of data collected and analysis of the activity, in a situation of arrival at an obstacle (slow vehicle). The lines in the center respectively correspond to: the angle of the steering wheel (in degrees), the state of the indicators, and the percentage the pedals are pushed in: brake; accelerator; clutch; the speed of the vehicle (in km/h); the time to collision in seconds; the time headway in seconds; the distance to the obstacle (in meters); and the distance covered (each "peak" corresponds to 10 m covered)*

The situation reproduced here represents 38 s of driving upon the arrival of a slow vehicle (tractor equipped with a revolving light) in the rain. *View 1* corresponds to the initial driving situation before the obstacle is detectable (exit from a bend at 80 km/h): the tractor is situated at around 200 m but it is still masked by lateral vegetation. In *View 2*, the obstacle is situated at 180 m. It is detectable for the first time. It progresses at an estimated speed of 25 km/h. The *time to collision* (TTC) is around 12 s, and the *time headway* (IVT) greater than 8 s. The current speed of our female driver is still 80 km/h, and no particular regulation procedure has been engaged at this instant. In *View 3*, the obstacle is around 110 m ahead. The time to collision is around 8 s and the IVT around 5 s. The driver has just engaged a regulation procedure: she took her foot of the accelerator pedal and now presses on the break (40%). The speed of the vehicle is still 80 km/h however. In *View 4*, the obstacle is around 30 m ahead and the left indicator is active, as the driver hopes to be able overtake immediately after the passage of a vehicle coming the other way.

The speed is "under control" (at 50 km/h), but still twice as fast as that of the obstacle (TTC of 4 s and IVT of 2 s). The vehicle going the other way now having passed, the driver detects the presence of other vehicles and the overtaking procedure is momentarily abandoned (indicator is reset). The driver then acts on the break in view of reducing her speed and engaging in a stabilized phase of monitoring (speed of 20-25 km/h, distance of monitoring the tractor of around 10 m, and TTC greater than 20 s).

A new overtaking attempt begins 5 s after *View 4* (i.e. she presses on the accelerator pedal, provoking a TTC fall to 10 s and a slight increase in speed), but it is abandoned (press on the brake pedal) due to the presence of opposing vehicles. At the approach of the last vehicle coming the other way, corresponding to *View 5*, the driver takes the decision to overtake and anticipates her overtaking action (activation of the left indicator and pressing of the accelerator). All her attention is now on the opposing lane (marked lateral offset of the chest and head), in order to ensure the absence of all other vehicles. In *View 6* overtaking finally occurs (offset of the vehicle of around 50% at this moment in time): the left indicator is still active, the steering wheel angle is 48°, and the pressing of the accelerator pedal is 50%, rapidly causing an increase in the speed of the vehicle.

As in the case presented in Figure 5.2, all the situations of arrival at an obstacle collected on the open road were subject to a detailed analysis in order to identify the behavioral and situational markers. This enabled us to propose a model for the analysis of the driving activity in real time in the form of a "transition-states" graph (the *states* corresponding to *activity phases*, via the implementation of particular regulation procedures, and the *transitions* corresponding to conditions required to pass from one activity phase to the next).

Synthetically, in addition to the initial phase of *driving without an obstacle* (corresponding to *View 1*), this activity model distinguishes four main phases:

– The *risk awareness* phase: corresponding to the detection of an obstacle on the road and a "break" in the driving situation, thus requiring an appropriate reaction on the behalf of the driver (*Views 2* and *3*).

– The *regulation* phase: occurring during the approach to the obstacle in view of avoiding the collision (i.e. progressive deceleration between *Views 3* and *4*). In the frame of a critical event, the regulation is based on emergency maneuvers (such as emergency braking).

– The *stabilized* phase (i.e. situation is under control and the risk of collision is managed): it can be car-following phase, as is the case in Figure 5.2, or slowing to a "stationary" position if the obstacle is fixed.

– The *resolution* phase (begin overtaking, in the case of Figure 5.2) ends in the disappearance of the obstacle (it has been overtaken, or has turned off the road, for example) and the return to the initial driving conditions ("driving without an obstacle").

These different activity phases are not systematically required (overtaking can occur as early as the phase of obstacle detection) and do not always proceed in a sequential logic. It is more a matter of a "regulation cycle" (modeled here in the form of an automaton of defined states) composed of an ensemble of potential states enabling us to move from one activity phase to another, according to certain transition conditions.

These transition rules can be based on behavioral indicators (the fact that the driver presses the brake, for example), as much as on variations of situational parameters (for instance the distance to the obstacle). Beyond the identification of the *activity phases* in real time, the objective of the model was to judge how adequate the implemented behaviors were with regards to the criticality of the situation (estimated from the TTC), thus leading to an "integrated" criticality diagnosis (see Figure 5.1). The stake was then to estimate whether or not these different activity phases were mastered by the driver, and to specify the nature of the assistance required in real time (aid for detection of the obstacle, decision making, carrying out an action, etc.).

The results obtained at the end of the project [BEL 06] have enabled us to show the benefit of this approach from an ergonomic point of view, and to prove its scientific and technical feasibility (80% good diagnosis in the situation of approaching a fixed or slow vehicle), as soon as the critical events were correctly detected by the perception technologies.

Though the developed prototype is still far from being operational, this research project (above all focused on the diagnosis stakes) shows us how to resort to models for the analysis of human activity in real time to enable adaptive management of human-machine interactions (Does the driver need assistance? What does the aid provide? In what form?). It nonetheless has not enabled us to explore the effective implementation and comparative evaluation of different modalities of human-machine cooperation in a driving situation. This was possible, however, in the monitoring research case.

5.3.2. *Lateral control and securing a trajectory*

The questions of human-machine cooperation have been the subject of a particularly in-depth investigation, via a series of experiments dealing with securing the trajectory in its lateral dimension (ARCOS and PARTAGE[8] projects run by ANR-PREDIT). Depending on the year, country and consequences, the accidents involving involuntary lane exits represent 40 to 70% of cases.

Four principal cooperation modes were examined, on a simulator and test track: a *perceptive* mode, a *mutual control* mode, a *function delegation* mode and, more recently, a *continuous shared control* mode. The central idea, in certain of these experiments, was to start from devices that would be able to take automatic control of the vehicle, but restricting their use, to take partial control of the vehicle. It was a matter of applying the philosophy of the projects mentioned that considered the driver to be the main entity in charge of driving.

The *perceptive mode* uses the perceptive abilities of one of the agents to enrich the perception of the other. From the machine to the driver, it is something that we can envisage with "head-up display" visualization devices (i.e. information presented on the windshield), even though they still pose a few problems. In any case, it is possible to identify where the gaze must be drawn in a turn in order to improve the trajectory and show the positive effect of such visual assistance ([MAR 08], see Figure 5.3). This experiment explored the relative efficiency of highlighting different points situated on the road, including the tangent point (circled in Figure 5.3). Similarly, after having shown that the signposts indicating dangerous turns have no effect on underestimating the bend on the tightest turns, it is advisable to turn towards the production of visual information that enters more directly into the sensorimotor loops [MIL 07]. Driving assistance has too often been limited to the production of symbolic information, requiring specific processing of the meaning, rather than research of the most efficient perceptive (sub-symbolic) information. Though these two types of information are complementary, the processing of perceptive information is quicker. Being a matter of obtaining better adaptation of the driver to the bend in a turn, a (symbolic) warning sign can enable us to better regulate the approach speed. However, for the steering wheel angle to be relevant, it is preferable to base research on the perceptive characteristics of the turn (markings, for example).

8 PARTAGE: Safe trajectory shared control between driver and car-driving assistance (http://www.projet-partage.fr/)

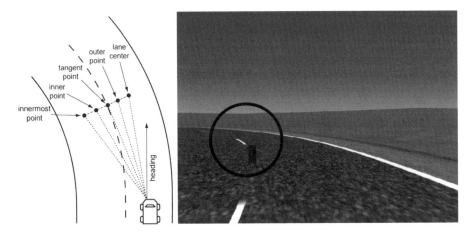

Figure 5.3. *Guiding of the gaze by showing the tangent point or different acentric points in a turn (according to [MAR 08])*

The *mutual control* mode uses one of the agents to verify the adequate nature of the activity of the other. It is translated by the production of critical information by an agent on the behavior of the other agent. In the context of lateral control, two mutual control types have been examined: the warning mode, producing an auditory or haptic critique; and the action suggestion mode, acting more specifically on the action effector (oriented oscillation of the steering wheel). These modes have been examined in critical situations close to the lane exit [HOC 06], [NAV 07]. On a simulator and on the track, the warning mode (nonspecific sound and/or oscillation of the wheel) proved to be effective. The action suggestion mode proved to be much more effective than the warning mode on the simulator. This mode acts directly on the production of the response (at the level of the applied energy), whereas the other intervened more indirectly in the diagnosis. Nonetheless, the effect of the two modes is modulated by the level of risk that the driver attributes to the situation [DER 11]. When the gap at the center of the lane is not very significant, the effect of assistance is not as great. Thus, the assistance does not produce an irrepressible response, which leaves the driver free to take action, particularly when an obstacle must be bypassed and the assistance must not be followed.

The *function delegation* mode, as its name suggests, consists of sustainably delegating a function to another agent. Numerous works have been dedicated to the delegation of longitudinal control in the context of cruise control devices (e.g. ACC), of which some have shown difficulties with regaining control at the limits of the validity of the device [YOU 07a]. The ACC not being a collision avoidance device, it is up to the driver to brake when the obstacle is fixed or if it has a significant speed differential compared with his own vehicle.

The delegation of lateral control to an automatic device was examined on the track [HOC 06]. In particular, there was significant difficulty in regaining lateral control in situations where obstacles were bypassed that required the device to be countered (without it requiring effort). This difficulty, like that concerning the ACC, could partly be due to a complacency effect, often described in aeronautical literature, linked to the negligence of supervision of the delegated function. Young and Stanton [YOU 02] have put forward some experimental evidence regarding a more radical hypothesis, however. According to this hypothesis, the delegation of a function would globally reduce the mobilized attention resources, including ensuring other functions that remain the responsibility of the driver. Such a hypothesis deserves further investigation, due to its severity.

Finally, in the specific frame of the PARTAGE project, a new mode is currently under development: the *continuous shared control* mode. On the basis of a cybernetic model of driver trajectory control, its aim is to provide the driver with part of the steering torque, in order to increase comfort and safety [SAL 11]. This mode is therefore between mutual control and function delegation because it acts on the vehicle but without taking the full control of the function.

5.3.3. *Prevent driver failures*

The final research theme that we present in this section deals with the question of diagnosis of driver failures in real time, considered here from the specific point of view of the detection of hypovigilance[9] states and the prediction of risks of falling asleep at the wheel. The state of tiredness or drowsiness of the driver is responsible for 10–20% of accidents according to [HOR 99], but this percentage could be a lot higher on the motorway [GAR 98], which is a particularly monotonous driving environment, taken for long journeys that favor the appearance of states of tiredness. These questions have been examined in the context of different European projects (AWAKE[10], SENSATION[11], or AIDE[12]). These projects aim to design driver *supervision* devices to assess their level of vigilance in real time, be it to guarantee driving safety or to adapt the interfaces (sound, visual or haptic) according to the estimated level of vigilance (by varying their intensity, for example). At one of the

---

9 Hypovigilance: decrease in vigilance, corresponding to more or less advanced states of falling asleep.

10 AWAKE (European project 2001-2004): System for Effective Assessment of driver vigilance and Warning According to traffic risK Estimation. See: http://www.awake-eu.org/.

11 SENSATION (European project 2002-2006): Advanced Sensor Development for Attention, Stress, Vigilance and Sleep/Wakefulness Monitoring. See: http://www.sensation-eu.org/.

12 AIDE (European project 2004-2008): Adaptive Integrated Driver-vehicle interfacE (2004-2008). See: http://www.aide-eu.org/.

extremes of the chain, we can give the example of the driver who feels faint and the imperative need, in these conditions, for the automaton to take total control of the vehicle. This is in order to immediately alert the other drivers (or pedestrians) of the danger but also, and especially where possible, to enable the stopping and secured parking of the vehicle (SAVE[13] project). Beyond this dramatic, but relatively rare, case, it is above all a matter of diagnosing states of driver hypovigilance and to alert them so he becomes aware of the change in their abilities and/or so that he can correct a driving error before it causes an accident.

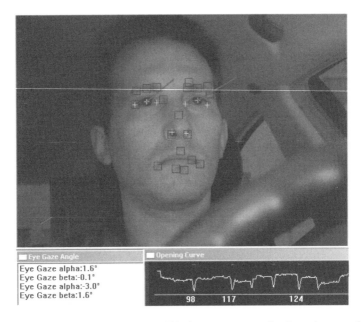

Figure 5.4. *Analysis of eye movements and blinking to estimate the driver's state of vigilance*

This diagnosis in real time can rest on behavioral measures (such as eye movements and/or visual strategies, see Figure 5.4, posture in the driver's seating area, more or less atypical actions on the commands, etc.). It can also rest on physiological data (such as the cardiac frequency or the measure of cerebral activity with electroencephalograms) or the analysis of driving performance (exposition of the vehicle on the lane, unusual deviation from the trajectory, dramatic and recurrent variations in distance monitoring).

---

13 SAVE (European project 1995-1998): System for effective Assessment of the driver state and Vehicle control in Emergency situations.

Nonetheless, resorting to physical measures such as electroencephalograms is not foreseeable in the context of a commercial application, for obvious practical reasons, as well as for reasons of acceptability from drivers. The development of "non intrusive" technologies, particularly based on the analysis of ocular activities, is therefore favored. Initial technological realizations are already operational in this field, such as SAFETRAC[14], *Driver State Sensor* (DSS)[15] or *PERcent of the time eyelids are CLOSed* (PERCLOS)[16] devices, even if their performances in real driving conditions are still far from being optimal. For a concise report regarding these devices, see [GON 04]. Regarding this, the *Driver Monitoring System* (DMS) device, based on the video analysis of eyelid movements (the time it takes them to close, for example) coupled with an analysis of driving performance in terms of lateral control of the vehicle [BOV 08], has promising results.

Experiments carried out on the open road [BOV 05] have enabled us to show a good correlation between:

– physiological measures characteristic of states of drowsiness that are estimated based on electroencephalograms (Figure 5.5) and electro oculograms;

– the diagnosis of hypovigilance in real time proposed by the DMS device (see Figure 5.5);

– a diagnosis of a decrease in vigilance estimated based on the average duration of eyelid blinking (*means blink duration* in Figure 5.5); and

– a diagnosis of decrease in vigilance based on the calculation of the PERCLOS system [GRA 01].

This supervision device of the state of the driver is not limited to the single hypovigilance diagnosis; it can also provide relevant elements of a solution with regards to problems of inattention and/or distraction at the wheel. It is precisely in view of this that the DMS system has been used in the context of the European AIDE project, dedicated to the adaptive management of driving assistance [TAT 05]. In this particular context, the objective was to use the *state of vigilance* of the driver and couple it with a diagnosis of "availability"[17] of the driver [BEL 07b], to adapt it to human-machine interfaces (from the specification of intervention modalities to management of the intensity of warnings).

---

14 http://www.assistware.com/.

15 http://www.seeingmachines.com/product/dss/.

16 http://www.attentiontechnology.com/pro-per.html [GRA 01].

17 The concept of *availability*, such as it defined in the context of this project, corresponds to the ability of the driver to perceive and deal with information delivered by an assistance device, given the requirements (effective or potential) of the current driving situation [BEL 07b].

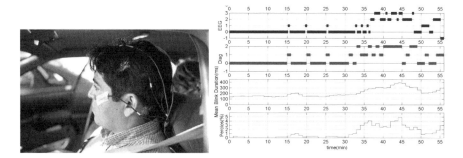

Figure 5.5. *Example of the diagnosis of hypovigilance of the driver monitoring system device and comparison with EEG measures (taken from [BOV 05])*

Evidently, this type of supervision technology is very complementary to the assistance devices described in sections 5.3.1 and 5.3.2.

First of all, the levels of vigilance and distraction of the driver directly influence driving behaviors (in terms of reaction time when faced with an obstacle, for example, and lateral trajectory management). The receptivity of the human to information and warnings also has such effects [GRE 06]. These are therefore two essential issues for the design of cooperative devices for collision avoidance and/or keeping the vehicle in a secure trajectory.

The real time analysis of driving performance in terms of lateral and longitudinal control could give rise to inter-device mutualizations (sensors, analysis algorithms, or diagnosis functions). The three examples of cooperative devices therefore illustrate that we can not only improve device's respective performances (or to "make them more robust"), but also reduce the costs of implantation on the vehicle.

There is therefore every reason, ultimately, to try and combine these different analyses and/or assistance functions. It is the potential mutualization of embedded "intelligence" as a means of acquisition (measure instruments, for example) required by these different devices, as well as on the "integrative" purpose of a future automobile copilot, that we will now discuss.

5.4. Discussion: towards an "intelligent" and "integrated" copilot

The different research projects we have presented only constitute part of the necessary functions that an automobile copilot should have. We could add numerous other functions, going far beyond stakes of strict security, such as favoring economic driving [BAR 06] or increasing the comfort of the driver. As it stands, most assistance devices are designed, developed and then implanted in the vehicle independently of each other (particularly if these pieces of equipment are integrated by car manufacturers themselves). This "cumulative" logic of assistance, designed in juxtaposition to autonomous systems, is quickly reaching its limits. At the end of the day, indeed, there is only one driver whose attention must primarily be on the road, and for whom the integration of assistance is a more than imperious requirement. Conversely, there is not only a major risk of perceptive and cognitive overload, but it can also be a source of human error (ambiguity regarding the origin or effective sense of certain information, potential confusion from the point of view of commands to be activated, etc.). This problem, though it has already been identified in the field of embedded information systems, also deserves to be investigated in depth regarding devices for the automation of driving.

What would happen if two different devices recommended or engaged contradictory driving actions at the same time? (This could include breaking to respect a speed limit versus accelerating to safely join another stream of traffic, keeping the vehicle in the lane to guarantee a safe trajectory versus leaving the lane in order to avoid an obstacle, etc.) Ideally, it would be advisable to design these assistants in synergy with each other from the start: a cruise control device would have a lot to gain from being part of a collision avoidance function, for example when a monitoring situation suddenly becomes critical. This would be all the more relevant as these two assistance functions, artificially disassociated from a technological point of view, are *in continuum* from the point of view of human activity.

This is not necessarily easy to implement from an industrial point of view, and the "integrated" and "organic" development of all the assistance functions in a single device is no doubt not realistic, in the short term anyway. However, there is nothing to say that it is not possible to move forward in a more pragmatic fashion, based on the logic of *distributed intelligence* (to which we will return in the conclusion). This is headed by the first-rate assistance devices of copiloting meta-function, designed as an *integrative* layer in charge of guaranteeing efficient coordination of driving aids in favor of harmonious cooperation with the human driver.

This integrative dimension of an automobile copilot must furthermore be completed by an *adaptive* dimension. As we specified in the introduction, not all drivers need to be assisted in the same way or at the same time. The machine must therefore "listen" to the human operator, all the while taking into account the requirements of the driving situation. Ultimately, it is therefore a matter of heading towards ergonomics "in real time" via the adaptive nature of assistants, to provide a contextualized aid conscious of the effective needs and the potential difficulties that the driver might have at a moment in time *t*. An important stake at this level resides in the ability of the copilot to adopt a critical eye regarding human decisions and actions. Evidently, it will be a matter of accompanying human activity as well as possible, when it is relevant (i.e. compatible with the objectives of comfort, performance and security to which the driver and/or human-machine system is aspiring to). A copilot is certainly not meant to maintain the drivers in error and back up their decision if they make an obvious mistake. On the contrary, it will be a matter of making them aware of the danger, to try and persuade them not to engage in a situation in which they will be unable to appreciate the critical nature, or to assist them in mastering risks via an adequate corrective action.

Finally, the development of an automobile copilot invites us to go beyond the strict frame of the "human-machine interaction" to inscribe the human-machine relation in the context of a true "cooperation". It is indeed the human-machine system as a whole that is in charge of driving, driver and assistants joining their efforts and skills in order to reach a common objective. This requires the abilities of observation, interpretation and cooperation on the behalf of the copilot. A successful cooperation can pass directly in the sensorimotor activities. Great progress has been made in modeling these processes, but very delicate questions arise when we wish to act with the best efficiency and at the best time. Furthermore, since the driver is most able to provide a rich analysis of the situation, any interventions of the automatic devices must be able to be modulated by this analysis. All the cooperation modes pose the same problem of sharing a common frame of reference between the driver and the automaton. Differences that are too large between the risk levels evaluated by the two agents can put the efficiency of assistance devices in jeopardy. In particular, the incoherence between information that is perceived or received by the driver and the interventions by the device considerably affects confidence [LEE 04]. Consequently, a key issue that will need to be dealt with more directly is that of communication between the driver and the automatic devices, whether this communication is based on information of a symbolic nature (vocal messages or visual pictograms) or on a sub-symbolic mode (vibration of the steering wheel or hardening of the pedals, for example). It is thanks to this communication that the common frame of reference will regularly be able to be updated, all the while looking to reduce cognitive costs for the human driver.

The three fundamental principles that should rule over an automobile copilot are "integrative", "adaptive" and "cooperative". On the basis of this analysis, it is possible to propose a general architecture of the copiloting device adapted to driving of the vehicle (see Figure 5.6).

The copilot *inputs* correspond to the data coming from:

– the road environment (i.e. from the embedded perceptive sensors or directly transmitted by the infrastructure, other vehicles or by a control post tasked with regulating traffic);

– the drivers (by their actions on commands, their postures or visual strategies, etc.) and the vehicle (its speed, lateral and longitudinal accelerations, position in the lane, or possible malfunctions of the vehicle itself or some of its components, such as the state of the tires in the event of a puncture).

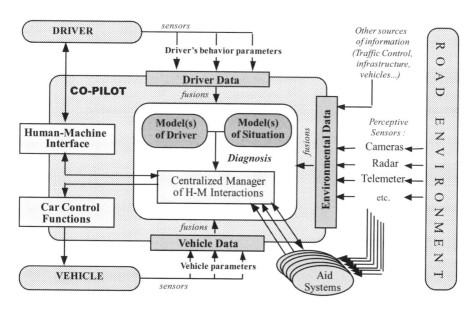

Figure 5.6. *Generic architecture of an automobile copilot (inspired by [BEL 03])*

The copilot *outputs* can be based on the diffusion of information and/or warnings (via *human-machine interfaces*) or require the direct intervention of automaton on the vehicle controls (via the *control-command* functions).

As for the heart of the device, it is made up of one (or several) *model(s) of the situation*, in charge to represent the human driver in the machine. These models must be elaborated or updated in real time, based on information coming from the environment and the vehicle. They constitute the main foundation for the elaboration of a *common frame of reference* between the driver and the automaton.

A copilot must also have *centralized management of human-machine interactions*. This module – based on the *common frame of reference* and/or *diagnosis functions* that come from the analysis of human and situational reflections – would then have the main function of ensuring the coordination and adaptation of assistance with regards to the state, the difficulties encountered and the specific needs of the human driver at the time. Home of the *knowledge of how to cooperate,* its role would be to supervise the first-rank assistance devices, by controlling their modalities of interaction with the human driver (from the diffusion of information to automatic piloting of the vehicle, via a mode of *mutual control*). We can also envisage that it orientates the reasoning of these same devices (by assisting their processing algorithms and/or decision functions, for example) or even that it takes the initiative of activating them as soon as the driving situation requires (according to the criticality level of the driving conditions, imminence of a problem, or emergency nature of an intervention, for example).

Evidently, this generic architecture only constitutes a first line of investigation calling on multiple complementary research efforts to result in an operational prototype. It nonetheless enables us to insist on the essential functions that should make up a future automobile copilot.

5.5. Conclusion

The aim of this chapter was to present a general framework for automobile copiloting. An initial level of analysis, developed section 5.2, enabled us to address the issue of human-machine cooperation, in the particular context of automobile driving. In order to make this theoretical discussion more grounded, three examples of cooperative devices were then presented and discussed. Respectively based on the prevention of collision risks, securing of the lateral trajectory and driver's state of vigilance, each of these devices provides a specific illumination regarding the stakes of human-machine cooperation and on the difficulties it is advisable to resolve, in order to meet the effective needs of human drivers.

Evidently, this is only a very small part of the future assistance functions that are likely to be implanted in a vehicle and numerous other systems are currently being developed in research laboratories and by automobile constructors. Indeed, after the first revolution of embedded information systems during past 20 years, a new generation of assistance devices is starting to emerge on the market. Based on a partial automation of driving, these aids are likely to take control of the vehicle, radically changing the driving task and activity of the driver. Whether desired or not, copiloting is now an effective reality in terms of driving aids.

In light of the abundance and complexity of the technology on offer, both current and potential, implantation "as things happen" has led to the decision that considering each device individually is no longer acceptable, at the risk of posing serious risks for road safety in the long term. It has therefore become imperative to define a frame for the integration of these different assistance devices. This was the objective of our discussion, with the ambition of proposing generic architecture for a future automobile copilot (see Figure 5.6).

At first glance, the task can seem disproportional. Nonetheless much scientific knowledge and many technological components likely to have such a use already exist, whether in terms of embedded sensors and perception technologies, algorithms for processing or fusion of data, human-machine cooperation, control-command functions or interfaces with the driver.

In addition, it is not necessarily a matter of designing an "omniscient" copilot, which has a "universal" intelligence. Much more pragmatic and no doubt more realistic from an industrial approach, would be to proceed according to the logic of *distributed intelligence*, i.e. maintaining a "local" intelligence that is specific to the level of each of the assistance functions (such functions include mapping knowledge and itinerary management skills for the navigational aid devices; estimation of the criticality of the situation and regulation of the speed via collision avoidance devices and ACC; lateral control abilities via functions to maintain a secure trajectory; or diagnosis of falling asleep and/or inattention via a driver supervision device, etc.). It is necessary to restrain the skills of the copilot to the fundamentals of its integrative function: the *knowledge of how to cooperate*[18] [MIL 98] and the *adaptive nature* of assistance [BEL 03] required in order to guarantee the proper functioning of a human-machine as a whole.

Thus defined, the automobile copilot is no longer just a pipe dream. It is a conceptual framework for *human-machine coupling* [AMA 92], assorted with ergonomic specifications enabling us to define an *integrated and coordinated* design strategy of future aid devices. This is achieved by favoring the optimization of assistance functions by the mutualization of technical means and the coupling of human and machine competencies in view of improving the reliability of the human-machine system tasked with piloting the vehicles of tomorrow.

5.6. Acknowledgements

This work has been carried out with the support of the GDR CNRS 3169 Psycho Ergo and the ANR-PREDIT projects PARTAGE, PREVENSOR and ARCOS. Some of the results presented in this chapter are from projects that have also received funding from the European Commission's Framework Programs (FP6 and FP7), more particularly under the grant agreements of CEMVOCAS, AWAKE, SENSATION, SAVE and AIDE projects.

---

18 The knowledge of how to cooperate between two agents refers – as a minimum – to: (i) the ability of these agents to manage interferences between their respective goals; and (ii) to the ability of each agent to facilitate the other agent reaching its goals.

5.6. Bibliography

[AMA 92] AMALBERTI R., DEBLON, F., "Cognitive modelling of fighter aircraft process control: a step towards an intelligent on-board assistance system", *International Journal of Man-Machine Studies*, vol. 36, pp. 639-671, 1992.

[BAN 08] BANET A., BELLET T., "Risk awareness and criticality assessment of driving situations: a comparative study between motorcyclists and car drivers", *IET Intelligent Transport Systems*, vol. 2, no. 4, pp. 241-248, 2008.

[BAR 06] BARBÉ J., BOY G., "On-board system design to optimise energy management", *Proceedings of the European Annual Conference on Human Decision-Making and Manual Control (EAM'06)*, Valenciennes, France, September 27-29, 2006, http://www.univ-valenciennes.fr/congres/EAM06/program_topics.htm.

[BEL 02] BELLET T, BRUYAS M.P., TATTEGRAIN-VESTE H., FORZY J.F., SIMOES A., CARVALHAIS J., LOCKWOOD P., BOUDY J., BALIGAND B., DAMIANI S., OPITZ M., "Real time analysis of the driving situation in order to manage on board information", *Proceedings E-SAFETY International Conference* (CD-ROM), Lyon, France, 16-18 September 2002.

[BEL 03] BELLET T., TATTEGRAIN-VESTE H., CHAPON A., BRUYAS M.P., PACHIAUDI G., DELEURENCE P., GUILHON V., "Ingénierie cognitive dans le contexte de l'assistance à la conduite automobile", in: G. BOY (ed.), *Ingénierie Cognitive: IHM et Cognition*, pp. 379-410, Hermès, Paris, France, 2003.

[BEL 06] BELLET T., "Driving activity analysis and modelling for adaptive collision avoidance systems design", *Proceedings of the 16th World Congress on Ergonomics (IEA 2006)*, Maastricht, The Netherlands, July 10-14, 2006.

[BEL 07a] BELLET T., BAILLY-ASUNI B., MAYENOBE P., GEORGEON O., "Cognitive modelling and computational simulation of drivers mental activities", In: P.C. CACCIABUE (ed.), *Modelling Driver Behaviour in Automotive Environment: Critical Issues in Driver Interactions with Intelligent Transport Systems*, pp. 315-343, Springer Verlag, London, 2007.

[BEL 07b] BELLET T., MANZANO J., "To be available or not, that is the question: A pragmatic approach to avoid drivers overload and manage in-vehicle information", *Proceedings of the 20th International Technical Conference on the Enhanced Safety of Vehicles ESV2007)*, Lyon, France, 18-21 June 2007.

[BEL 09] BELLET T., BAILLY-ASUNI B., MAYENOBE P., BANET A., "A theoretical and methodological framework for studying and modelling drivers' mental representations", *Safety Science*, vol. 47, no. 9, pp. 1205-1221, 2009.

[BIL 91] BILLINGS, C.E., Human-centered Aircraft Automation: a Concept and Guidelines (Technical Memorandum). Moffett Field, CA: NASA, Ames Research Center, 1991.

[BOV 02] BOVERIE S., "A new class of intelligent sensors for the inner space monitoring of the vehicle of the future", *Control Engineering Practice*, vol. 10, no. 11, pp. 1169-1178, 2002.

[BOV 05] BOVERIE S., GIRALT A., "Driver monitoring systems, a key technology for solving ADAS challenges", *Technical Symposium on Intelligent Vehicles, Salon Internacional del Automovil de Barcelona* (CD-ROM), Barcelona, Spain, May 11, 2005.

[BOV 08] BOVERIE S., GIRALT A., LE QUELLEC J.M., "Diagnostic fusion in vehicle driver vigilance assessment", *Proceedings of the 17th World Congress of the International Federation of Automatic Control (IFAC'08)*, Seoul, South Korea, July 6-11, 2008.

[BOY 91] BOY G., *Intelligent Assistant Systems*, Academic Press, London, 1991.

[BOY 03] BOY G., "Introduction à l'ingénierie cognitive", in G. BOY (ed.), *Ingénierie Cognitive: IHM et Cognition*, Hermès, Paris, France, pp. 23-51, 2003.

[DER 11] DEROO M., MARS F., HOC, J.M., "Can drivers modulate the effect of a motor priming assistance device during lane departure?", in: DE WAARD D., GÉRARD N., ONNASCH L., WICZOREK R. and MANZEY D. (eds.), *Human Centred Automation*, Shaker Publishing, Maastricht, The Netherlands, in press.

[GAR 98] GARDER P., "Continuous shoulder rumble-strips – A safety evaluation", In: *CSRS Seminar*, Linkoeping, Sweden, August 1998.

[GRA 01] GRACE R., "Drowsy driver monitor and warning system", *Proceedings of the International Driving Symposium on Human Factors in Driver Assessment, Training and Vehicle Design*, Aspen, USA, August 14-17, 2001.

[GON 04] GONZALEZ-MENDOZA M., Surveillance temps-réel des systèmes Homme-Machine, Application à l'assistance à la conduite automobile, PhD thesis, INSA of Toulouse, France, 2004.

[GRE 06] GREEN P., "Driver status and implications for crash safety", *Proceedings of the Convergence 2006 Conference (SAE paper 2006-21-0028)*, Detroit, USA, 2006.

[HOC 01] HOC J.M., "Towards a cognitive approach to human-machine cooperation in dynamic situations", *International Journal of Human-Computer Studies*, vol. 54, pp. 509-540, 2001.

[HOC 06] HOC J.M., MARS F., MILLEVILLE I., JOLLY E., NETTO M., BLOSSEVILLE J.M., "Evaluation of human-machine cooperation modes in car driving for safe lateral control in curves: delegation and mutual control modes", *Le Travail Humain*, vol. 69, pp. 155-185, 2006.

[HOC 09] HOC J.M., YOUNG M.S., BLOSSEVILLE J.M., "Cooperation between drivers and automation: implications for safety", *Theoretical Issues in Ergonomics Science*, vol. 10, pp. 135-160, 2009.

[HOL 83] HOLLNAGEL E., WOODS D.D., "Cognitive systems engineering: new wine in new bottles", *International Journal of Man-Machine Studies*, vol. 18, pp. 583-600, 1983.

[HOL 05] HOLLNAGEL E., WOODS D.D., *Joint Cognitive Systems: Foundations of Cognitive Systems Engineering*, Taylor & Francis, London, 2005.

[HOR 99] HORNE J., REYNER L., "Vehicle accidents related to sleep – a review", *Occupational and Environmental Medicine*, vol. 56, pp. 289-294, 1999.

[HUT 95] HUTCHINS E., "How a cockpit remembers its speed", *Cognitive Science*, vol. 19, pp. 265-288, 1995.

[LEE 04] LEE J.D., SEE K.A., "Trust in automation: designing for appropriate reliance", *Human Factors*, vol. 46, pp. 50-80, 2004.

[MAR 08] MARS F., "Driving around bends with manipulated eye-steering coordination", *Journal of Vision*, vol. 8, no. 11, pp. 1-11, 2008.

[MIL 95] MILLOT P., MANDIAU R., "Man-machine cooperative organizations: formal and pragmatic implementation methods", in: HOC J.M., CACCIABUE P.C., HOLLNAGEL E. (eds), *Expertise and Technology: Cognition & Human-Computer Cooperation*, Lawrence Erlbaum Associates, Hillsdalep, USA, pp.213-228, 1995.

[MIL 98] MILLOT P., PACAUX-LEMOIGNE M.P., "An attempt for generic concepts toward Human Machine Cooperation", *IEEE SMC*, San Diego, USA, October 1998.

[MIL 03] MILLOT P., " Supervision et coopération homme-machine: approche système", in : BOY G. (ed.) *Ingénierie Cognitive: IHM et Cognition*, Hermès, Paris, France, pp. 191-224, 2003.

[MIL 07] MILLEVILLE-PENNEL I., HOC J.M., JOLLY E., "The use of hazard road signs to improve the perception of severe bends", *Accident Analysis & Prevention*, vol. 39, pp. 721-730, 2007.

[NAS 96] NASS C., FOGG B.J., MOON Y., "Can computers be teammates?", *International Journal of Human-Computer Studies*, vol. 45, pp. 669-678, 1996.

[NAV 07] NAVARRO J., MARS F., HOC J.M., "Lateral control assistance for car drivers: a comparison of motor priming and warning systems", *Human Factors*, vol. 49, pp. 950-960, 2007.

[PAC 02] PACAUX M.P., DEBERNARD S., "Common work space for human-machine cooperation in air traffic control", *Control Engineering Practice*, vol. 10, pp. 571-576, 2002.

[SAL 11] SALEH L., CHEVREL P., MARS F., LAFAY J.F. CLAVEAU F. "Human-like cybernetic driver model for lane keeping", *Proceedings of the 18th World Congress of the International Federation of Automatic Control (IFAC 2011)*, 2011.

[STA 92] SARTER N., WOODS D.D. "Pilot interaction with cockpit automation. I: operational experiences with the Flight Management System", *International Journal of Aviation Psychology*, vol. 2, pp. 303-321, 1992.

[SUZ 03] SUZUKI K., JANSSON H., "An analysis of driver's steering behaviour during auditory or haptic warnings for the designing of lane departure warning system", *Japan Society of Automotive Engineers Review*, vol. 24, pp. 65-70, 2003.

[TAT 05] TATTEGRAIN-VESTE H., BELLET T., BOVERIE S., KUTILA M., VIITANEN J., BEKIARIS E., PANOU M., ENGSTRÖM, J., AGNVALL A., "Development of a driver situation assessment module in the aide project", *Proceedings 16th World Congress of the International Federation of Automatic Control (ifac'05)*, Prague, Czech Republic, July 6-11, 2005.

[TER 90] DE TERSSAC G., CHABAUD C., "Référentiel opératif commun et fiabilité", in: LEPLAT J. and DE TERSSAC G. (eds), *Les Facteurs Humains de la Fiabilité*, Octarès, Toulouse, France, pp. 110-139, 1990.

[WIE 93] WIENER E., KANKI B., HELMREICH R., *Cockpit Resource Management*, Academic Press, New York, USA, 1993.

[YOU 02] YOUNG M.S., STANTON N.A., "Malleable attentional resources theory: a new explanation for the effects of mental underload on performance", *Human Factors*, vol. 44, pp. 365-375, 2002.

[YOU 07a] YOUNG M.S., STANTON N.A., "Back to the future: Brake reaction times for manual and automated vehicles", *Ergonomics*, vol. 50, pp. 46-58, 2007.

[YOU 07b] YOUNG M. S., STANTON N.A., HARRIS D., "Driving automation: Learning from aviation about design philosophies", *International Journal of Vehicle Design*, vol. 45, pp. 323-338, 2007.

Chapter 6

ICT and New Human-machine Interactions for Trucks and Buses of the Future: *e-Truck and e-Bus* Perspectives

6.1. Introduction

Efficiency in operating trucks and buses has always been a major concern for OEMs (Original Equipment Manufacturer)/vehicle manufacturers, and especially for owners and operators. Indeed, the acquisition and operating costs are such that the truck and bus are on the road as much as possible. From this point of view, they are very similar to airplanes, with which they share certain characteristics such as operability, but they also have their specificities. For the truck it is being able to change itinerary at will, the route not (yet) being constrained by a prior declaration (authorization). For the bus, operating efficiency is also targeted, but user satisfaction is a priority, particularly in terms of punctuality and comfort. These collective means of ground transport are not as highly monitored and controlled as the plane and do not yet have as much on-board ICT. Research on computerization, in the broad sense, in transport has been the subject of a lot of work, both in universities as well as in private or semi-public organizations. The research came to fruition and many aspects and solutions have been industrialized and implemented. We will establish a typology of concerns that relate to the truck and bus, which are at the centre of our studies. The industrialization of the different concerns highlighted is not the same. However, it is certain that the logistical aspect has been the most studied, notably in terms of its economic impact, which explains numerous

Chapter written by Bertrand DAVID, René CHALON and Bernard FAVRE.

successful and applied solutions. Nonetheless, other aspects are still being researched and it is this in particular that interests us, as members of public and private research structures. From this point of view, instead of establishing a bibliographical list, we refer readers to an excellent Website that presents a series of conferences entitled FORUM Systems and software for the New ICT in transport [FOR]. This is organized by INRETS (which became IFSTTAR after merging with LCPC in January 2011) in conjunction with the CNAM, which for five years has twice yearly summarized different research issues and their progress. We will recap on certain European projects which are related to these issues at the end of the chapter.

Around 15 years ago, we conducted an initial project introducing ICT in the car [DAV 91], [LAB 92], [LAB 94]. At the time, our study looked at helping the driver through the implementation of a screen presenting an array of information possibilities and aids for driving. Since then, various industrialized solutions have been proposed and put on the market. We have recently taken up this subject again with the students of the Ecole Centrale, in an initially informal cooperation with Renault Trucks. We have studied this issue in the context of computerization of a truck or, more generally, a fleet of trucks. Indeed, the current technological environment allows new and more complete solutions to be envisaged compared to those that we put forward in the past.

This first study coincided with the creation of a competitiveness cluster LUTB (*Lyon Urban Truck and Bus*) in Lyon, which we have joined in our collaboration with Renault Trucks and Volvo IT, as well as with the other members of the LUTB (section 6.11). Within this framework, again with the students of the Ecole Centrale de Lyon, we conducted two preliminary studies, the issues of which came out of the LUTB *Think Tank*s. These studies have contributed to the proposal of joint projects approved by LUTB and currently carried out by collaborative *consortia* made up of people from universities and industrial companies under the aegis of LUTB, which receives institutional funding. We present the two issues where the ICT plays, or will play, an essential role in the delivery of goods in towns or the dynamic driving lane management. These studies being ongoing and protected by intellectual property rights, we only present this preliminary work conducted with students at the Ecole Centrale to lay the groundwork for these different issues. In the last part, we present the latest state-of-the-art developments by briefly presenting a number of recent or ongoing European projects, as well as a few Renault Trucks projects that are not covered by trade secrets, to show the active and attractive nature of work being conducted in this area.

6.2. Trucks in the context of ICT

First of all, we conducted a global discussion to reveal the informational context in which we could place a truck (or a fleet of trucks) to significantly increase yield thanks to contributions from the ICT. It was a matter of envisaging all the possible cases for the introduction of computer tools to all of the stages and work situations of a truck, to extrapolate a coherent proposal of desirable tools. The result of this preliminary study was the following list:

– *truck itself*: its technical state (incidents, accidents, overhaul, maintenance);

– *truck on the road*: dynamic behavior, communication with the infrastructure, etc.;

– *truck and its crew*: driving time, driver management, hotels;

– *truck and its load*: optimization of journeys, cargo management and all logistics.

In the context of road transport of the future, as the ongoing work shows, a truck benefits or will be able to benefit from different connections allowing it to communicate with:

– the *transport infrastructure*, providing it with varied information about the road that can be either static (curving, turning, uneven road surfaces, widening or narrowing) or dynamic (due to ice, traffic jams, diversions or accidents);

– the *satellite*, allowing drivers to remotely monitor their driving (speed, fuel consumption and stops), know their itinerary and geographic location, communicate with their logistical base, collect information concerning the state of the vehicle for maintenance or in the case of breakdown;

– *vehicles that are in proximity* going in the same direction (in front or behind) with a view to synchronizing driving (speed adaptation, communication of changes in trajectory and braking) which can ultimately lead to the implementation of a "virtual train of vehicles" in which only the first driver will be active, the others maintaining a passive watchfulness. Here other drivers can intervene to take control of the vehicle only in the event of a problem [CHA].

All these aspects are directly related to the possibilities offered by the ICT and this applies to all the vectors of computerization: storing, processing, distribution (network) and information exchange, more specifically between users and the system. Based on these initial observations, we first established a summary diagram showing how the different aspects can be materialized. This diagram came out of our informal discussions with Renault-Trucks in Lyon. It is shown in Figure 6.1.

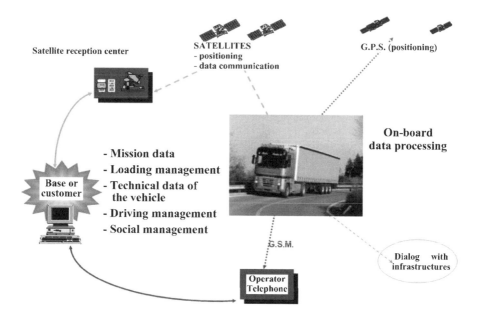

Figure 6.1. *General context of the e-Truck project*

6.3. Informational context of the truck

A more in-depth study enabled us to bring out a UML (Unified Modeling Language) specification comprising different use cases, based on the different relations between users and the truck in different parts of the study, characterized both by accessible communications and the reasons for exchange between players [ECL 06]. In this way, specific sequence diagrams were elaborated, showing exchanges between the main users and objects identified. A fairly detailed class diagram resulted in a development proposal. A collaboration diagram enabled us to formalize the exchanges between the different objects and users. We outline the information exchanges identified, less formally than in UML but more easily understood, in Figure 6.2. The main users are positioned around the driver and his truck. These include the transport company, the customer, the mechanic, the weather forecast service, the road maintenance services and the local transport infrastructure service.

The exchanges can be characterized in the following way:

– commercial exchanges between the customer, the transport company and the driver;

– the company management exchanges between the transport company, the driver and his truck;

– the exchanges of truck management information between the maintenance services and the truck, with the participation of the driver;

– driving exchanges between the driver, his truck and the services that enable him to organize and manage his trips while respecting safety, efficiency and profitability guidelines.

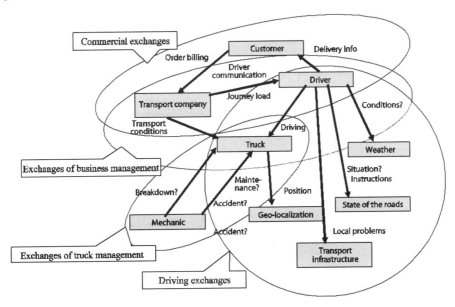

Figure 6.2. *Informational context of an e-Truck*

6.4. Bus in the context of ICT

The same reasoning applied to buses has to led to fairly similar results. In the case of buses, it is necessary to make the distinction of hire for specific journeys (schools and sports teams, for example) where the issues are very similar to trucks, with one important difference. Indeed, it is not about transporting products and inert material, but humans, with specific transport constraints, in particular concerning journey times, refreshment stops, etc. The second category concerns buses used for city, intercity or even long-distance transport, where it is a matter of planned itineraries and times with passengers being able to choose their places of departure and arrival. This leads to new constraints being taken into account, in particular with respect to time, at every stage of the journey.

As compared to the informational context established for trucks, in the case of transport of travelers new aspects need to be taken into consideration, notably involving communication between the driver and passengers, information as to the progress of the journey (delay, connections, etc.) and informational access given to passengers (the Internet, for example). It is a matter of making the journey pleasant and possibly productive for them, if they so wish: continuing professional activities, such as the writing e-mails, schoolwork (homework, revision) or entertainment (films, games and television).

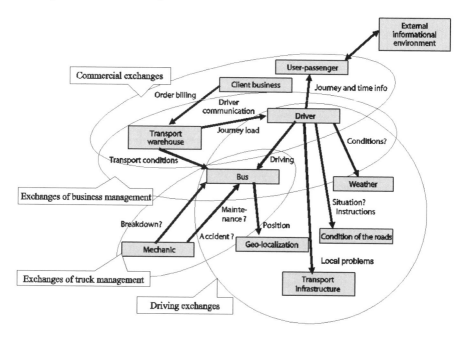

Figure 6.3. *Informational context of an e-Bus*

The corresponding diagram (see Figure 6.3) is therefore similar to Figure 6.2, but with specificities.

Thanks to these analyses, we have been able to make the link between these issues and the *HelpMeToDo* (HMTD) project [DAV 06] on which we have been working for several years in the LIESP laboratory at Ecole Centrale of Lyon and the aim of which is implementation of a "real augmented environment" at the service of activities requiring exchange and assistance. In the next section, we outline the main principles of IMERA (mobile interaction in the real augmented environment) and HMTD.

6.5. Principles of IMERA and HMTD

The IMERA project [DAV 07b] aims to take into account a real augmented environment and to introduce the users, mobile, who can carry out activities using their hand-held computers, the means of mobile interaction. We base ourselves on the principles of mobile and ubiquitous computer use [WEI 91], on the principles of *Mobile Learning* [MEY 06] (which we will define further on) and augmented reality [WEL 93]. In this context, our main concepts are:

– MI (mobile interaction): consists of proposing user interfaces for hand-held computers (PDA, Smartphones, Tablet PC) and other devices adapted to mobile situations;

– RAE (real augmented environment): we target the deployment of an augmented environment in the sense of mixed reality and ubiquitous computing;

– MOCOCO (mobility, cooperation, contextualization): this dimension deals with tasks carried out collaboratively by several mobile users, who have access to specific and contextualized data;

– proactivity is all the more important in these conditions: it consists of the ability of the human-machine interface (HMI) to adapt itself to the actions of the user and to the context in which he is interacting (in a logic of ambient intelligence) by showing the ability to think ahead.

The *HelpMeToDo* (HMTD) project [DAV 07a] has the aim of using these new mobile communication means for the general public and professionals in activities requiring help. The need for information, training, assistance and help with maintenance and breakdown in individual, collective, industrial or general public contexts are therefore taken into account. The HMTD project aims to study this issue in both a generic way and also a way which is transferable into those contexts where the constraints and requirements are both specific, but which can be "derived" from generic situations.

6.6. RAE (real augmented environment) for *e-Trucks* and *e-Buses*

In the context of *e-Trucks* and *e-Buses*, RAE takes the form described in Figure 6.1 for the *e-Truck*. Indeed, the different users are all emitters, receptors and/or transformers of information. They are then dispatched to other users who also use them. The truck GPS, the driver's mobile phone and mobile Internet phone connections are elements of RAE. We can also add more local elements to this, in the truck or between the truck and the infrastructure, in the form of active or passive

RFID[1] labels [FIN 03], *ad hoc* networks, WiFi, IR (infrared) or ZigBee. All these elements contribute to the set up of the RAE. We will comment more specifically on the main concepts deployed hereafter.

Wearable computing assumes all its importance in this context. It consists of a recent trend in computing where different devices are "embedded" in the mobile user and are interconnected via a computer accessory, the heart of the system with other, often distant, elements. Wearable computing raises new stakes [PLO 04], [TAP 09].

Augmented reality (AR) is mainly defined as the addition of digital or virtual elements to objects of the real world. The aim is to create new tools, similar to everyday tools, but augmented with specific abilities brought about by computing. Visual augmentation is most often perceived by the user through a visualization headset allowing the overlay of digital images onto the direct vision of the real world with the help of a semi-transparent mirror. However AR is not limited to vision and can involve all the senses: hearing, touch and, why not, smell and taste on the condition of having *ad hoc* devices.

Context is a very important notion; we define it in the same way as [DEY 00] which puts three aspects forward (environment-platform-user preferences) which translate our concerns very accurately. The consideration of the context is unavoidable as, once it is captured and interpreted, it enables us to appropriately assist the user, that is to say by taking into account his situation (place and preoccupations: environment, platform: the computer accessory he is using, as well as his personal preferences). It is via this consideration in particular that the user interface can be adaptable and proactive.

In situ storage is a vital characteristic, for in the mobile applications sensitive to context it is important to easily access information describing and characterizing this context. Environmental objects (bar-codes, RFID tags, ZigBee or other markers) can provide this static information to the mobile devices which detect them, or enable them to access a richer content by acting as user ID to the distant server, accessible via the wireless network containing a PDMS (product data management system).

Nonetheless, in certain mobile applications, it is not possible to systematically count on network access availability and in this case it is necessary to have contextualized information on site to ensure efficiency. The *in situ* storage of dynamic information therefore constitutes an important requirement for certain

---

1 Radio-identification, most often designated by the acronym RFID (*Radio Frequency IDentification*), is a method for memorizing and recuperating remote data by using markers called "radio-labels".

applications. RFID technology can be a solution to this problem as its storage capabilities are increasing more and more.

The *traceability* of operations is a strong requirement in sensitive situations necessitating a possibility for verification *after the fact*. It is a matter of saving the operations carried out in order to be able to retrace them. The operations in question are carried out by memorizing, for each operation, the part involved and the tool used. For this, tagging by RFID of all the parts as well as the tools (screwdriver, clamp, hammer and other more sophisticated tools) enable information to be collected "naturally" in the operations carried out. Afterwards, it is possible to retrace all the operations carried out on each part, as well as the use of different tools. For this the information collected is either centralized in a database or stored locally on the RFID labels [SRI 05].

The prescription of operations is complementary to traceability, as it enables the actions to be carried out under control, in other words we are aiming here for the guided execution of the necessary professional process. Indeed, it is a matter of ensuring the safety and robustness of operations. This control can be, on the one hand, of identity, and therefore the qualification of the user, who must identify himself by his RFID badge and, on the other hand, of the process itself, during which the sequence of actions and parts and tools used are controlled. In practice, this means becoming familiar with the sequence of operations carried out and of the ensemble of tools and parts handled during this time, by controlling the coherence of what the user does in respect to what is being asked and notifying him of his inappropriate choices, where applicable. These different aspects and concepts progressively appear in the work described hereafter.

6.7. HMI (Human-Machine Interface) needs for the e-Truck and e-Bus

6.7.1. *HMI of driving activity*

In driving activities, HMI is mainly based on an integrative screen on which all the useful information is shown. By integration, we qualify the approach in which a single screen is used (so as not to transform the cab of the truck into a plane's cockpit) to display, each in turn and selectively, at the demand of the system or the user, information and the human-machine interfaces linked to the different activities. If everything is accessible when stationary, including driving activities, presentation of the state of the vehicle, road instructions as well as navigational guiding, the functioning of the car radio, telephone, etc., when driving, a natural selection must be set up according to the context in order not to disturb the main driving task, both in the e-Truck and the e-Bus. This context takes into consideration the present situation characterized by the main activity (driving), the state of the car, the state of the road and other immediate elements, as well as the profile of the driver. The switch towards another activity comes into effect at a deliberate demand from the system: sudden breakdown, incoming telephone call, road safety message, etc.

Work which we carried out in the 1990s [DAV 91], [LAB 92], [LAB 93] is still current at least from a conceptual point of view. Technologies need to be adjusted, but the principle, which considers that it is a matter of implementing an adaptive human-machine interface, is based on three important models, which are the functioning model, which describes the system possibilities in the form of user tasks, the situational model, which describes the immediate state of the global system (state of the vehicle, incoming events such as external calls) and the user model, his profile expressing his abilities, his specificities. The choice of human-machine interaction for the selected task, as well as the elements of interaction and constituent presentation, depend on these different models and the way in which we integrate the corresponding computer in the e-Truck or the e-Bus.

6.7.2. *Wearable HMI in mobility situations*

When the driver is not at the wheel of the bus or the truck, but is occupied with loading or unloading goods, or managing a breakdown, incident or accident, he needs a different interaction than the one which is fixed in his cab, used for driving. It must be mobile to enable him to act in the trailer, or outside, depending on the need. Tasks which are at least partially different in relation to those mentioned for driving are necessary. In fact, a partial overlap between certain tasks similar to driving and those used in mobility is normal. Nonetheless, new, more contextualized tasks must be proposed. These are linked to the cargo, either to the functioning or malfunctioning of the truck. In both cases, contextualization is essential.

Indeed, the merchandise to be delivered must be dealt with contextually. It is the same for a breakdown situation or malfunctioning of the truck [BES], [DAV 06]. To help the driver diagnose the defect or failure, it is necessary to collect adequate information and to analyze it and correctly aggregate it. The computer accessory which has the appropriate peripherals [MAS 06], the RFID label reader in particular can help in both cases, as much during the contextual management of merchandise as during the contextualization of breakdown situations. This contextualization can go as far as the presentation in augmented reality of instructions, actions and interventions to be carried out on the equipment (Figure 6.4).

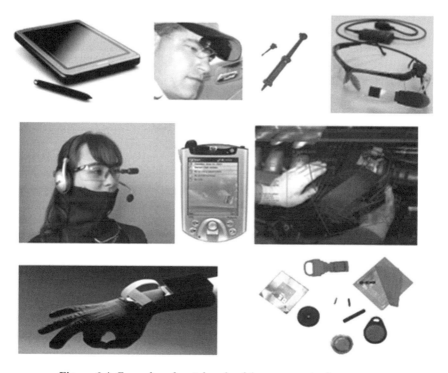

Figure 6.4. *Examples of peripherals of the computerized accessory*

The communication must be correlated with the technologies of appliances, machines or equipment on which the user wishes to intervene. Three forms of relation between the computerized accessory and equipment need to be distinguished (Figure 6.5):

– when the equipment offers no means of connection with the computerized accessory, it is up to the user to ensure the link between the information provided by the computerized accessory and the situations that are observed or to be produced on the equipment (Figure 6.5a);

– when the equipment is able to receive commands via, for example, an infrared interface, it is possible to establish a unilateral contact from the computerized accessory to this equipment, to command it. The other way, which should provide the computerized accessory with information observed on the equipment, remains the responsibility of the user (Figure 6.5b);

– when the equipment is able to establish a two way communication with the computerized accessory, it is possible to substitute the interface proposed by the accessory for the original interface of the equipment. In this case the new interface, completely deported, can be specific to the requirements of the user (Figure 6.5c).

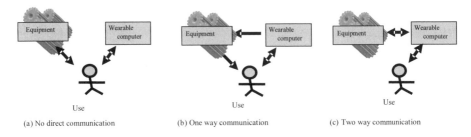

(a) No direct communication   (b) One way communication   (c) Two way communication

Figure 6.5. *Types of communication between the computerized accessory and the equipment*

6.8. *Mobile Learning* **from e-Truck and e-Bus perspectives**

Among the activities which can take place in the *e-Truck* and *e-Bus* context, *Mobile Learning* holds a unique place, as it can involve both transport professionals and users. *Mobile Learning (M-Learning)* is a form of learning which uses mobile devices; it is the result of the development of mobile technologies, including wireless networks and the evolution of learning methods. One of the most significant definitions of *M-Learning* is "any kind of learning which occurs when the learner is not static, in a specified location, or learning which occurs when the learner takes advantage of the learning possibilities offered by mobile technologies" [OMA 03]. Without going into more detail faced with the different *M-Learning* taxonomies [MEY 06], we can only separate *M-Learning* into two categories according to whether or not the context is taken into account. The first category considers the learning activity as totally independent of the localization of the learner and the context in which he involves, only taking into account the possibility of using mobile devices with a view to learning (in the cafeteria, during lesson breaks, etc.). On the other hand, our second category indicates a learning activity in relation to the location (physical, geographical, logical) of the learner and the context in which he evolves. We focus on this second category of *M-learning* where the context plays an important part (the driver learns to use and repair his truck, he manages distribution while respecting constraints imposed by a customer). Contextualized *M-learning* targets the consideration of the situation and *Just in time Learning, Learning by Doing* and the *Learning & Doing* approach. Among the previously introduced *M-Learning* situations, we made a distinction between situated and non-situated *M-Learning*. The former is directly linked to the context in which the learner finds himself, the latter is independent from this. In transport, we find these two versions of *M-Learning*, as we will see.

6.8.1. *Non-situated Mobile learning*

Non-situated *M-Learning* concerns both transport professionals and users. For professionals, it is a matter of learning activities that are fundamentally independent of their immediate activity. Language learning, for example, during the driving period or during rest periods, is an activity independent of the context (of the place, the state of the vehicle). These learning activities are therefore part of the parallel activities of professionals on business trips, in addition to entertainment activities (DVD, television, video games, etc.). For transport users, it is this context independent learning activity which can become very important. Students who do their homework in public transport are double winners, both in time (the transport time is masked by a more important activity) and in behavior (useful activity). In this case, the devices used are often mobile, such as Tablet PC or eBooks, either autonomous or connected information access devices such as Internet via WIMAX or G3 networks.

6.8.2. *Situated M-Learning: from maintenance to e-maintenance*

For transport professionals the situated *M-Learning* aspect is important, as it is directly linked to their concerns: mastering their work tool and if necessary repairing or maintaining it. In this context, it is possible to deploy mobile, contextual and collaborative learning, which can be very useful in case of a breakdown or incident. The driver can consult a computerized instruction booklet indicating the steps to follow. If he considers that he does not have the necessary skills, he can either consult and learn the actions and skills necessary to carry out small repairs, or enter into contact with the repair shop to receive explanations and instructions and therefore learn at the same time as doing. Augmented reality can also facilitate this learning.

Figure 6.6 presents the general organization of the repair set-up – contextualized learning and the corresponding support documents. The learning system production approach is based on the following elements: the documentation of the driver, a task tree corresponding to the generic activities [DEL 04] [DAV 07c] which are generally found to "master" the targeted equipment. The specialization process of the generic tree is currently carried out in an assisted manner; in fact the automation of this process is still the focus of research. The collection of information is not limited to the textual description of work which needs to be carried out (and therefore learned), but also to collecting diagrams, photos, figures and models of elements (parts that make up the equipment, its front panel, its control panel …). The aim is to build a computing model which is as complete as possible to be able to base oneself on it to support the diagnosis, repair process and build appropriate learning objects.

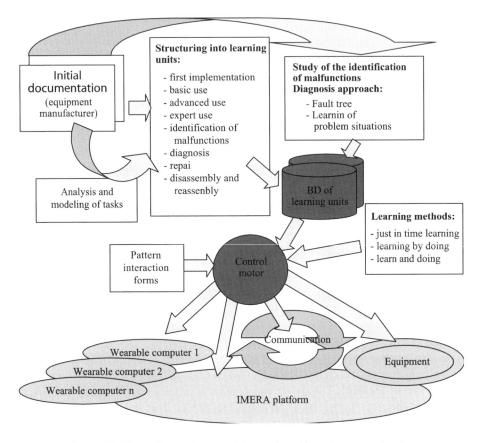

Figure 6.6. *General organization of the work and learning support system*

As far as diagnosis and repair is concerned, it is necessary to go beyond the reproduction of tasks; it is necessary to find the significant variables, directly or indirectly observable, which play a role during the diagnosis. We are currently working on two complementary approaches: the first is based on the fault tree analysis, which gives the impact of different identified variables on the state of the system, the second aims to collect problem situations and progressively construct a system capable of reasoning on breakdowns as [MOU 06] recommends. After having collected the information and constructed the corresponding model, it is possible to proceed to an effective implementation. This leads to building the learning (and action) system that is contextually satisfying and functioning in the practical environment. The latter is based on the choice of the means of contextualization (in particular RFID labels and readers) and on the configuration of the interaction devices of the computerized accessory. The instantiation of generic tasks can then take place. The interaction patterns [BOR 01], the aim of which is to propose stereotyped interactions which facilitate both the deployment by the developer and the mastering of the interaction by the user help this instantiation.

The set up of the augmented reality approach requires the precise geometric locating of physical elements, in order to adjust the visualization to the appropriate scale of virtual elements. Indeed, if we wish to be able to indicate which screw to unscrew first, it is necessary to be able to place the arrow at the appropriate place, which implies knowing the position (distance) of the subject and the direction in which they are looking (and therefore which way their head is turned) in relation to the targeted elements.

The aim of the control engine is to animate learning and link it with work interventions. It plays the role of conductor which uses the databases of learning units described in IMS-LD [NOD], an internationally recognized format of description and characterization of learning units. We use XML to make portable and easily transformable what is written, to be able to take into account the display and interaction means linked to the different configurations of the wearable computer.

6.9. ICT in city delivery

A second study conducted, situated in the domain of the HMTD and IMERA issue, is entitled *Computerized Management of deliveries in a large town* or e-delivery.

The objective of this project is to study the deployment of a distributed and mobile ICT environment enabling all the goods transportation participants (traffic management, suppliers, customers, transporters-deliverers, traffic controllers, etc.) to benefit from and/or act with a view to a better use of infrastructures and delivery areas to make traffic in large towns safer and more freely flowing.

Among the objectives of the project there are the following aspects in particular: it is necessary to be able to dynamically prohibit truck access to certain places in the town (near schools when the pupils are going in or coming out) and make the delivery areas more efficient through a prior booking, which can evolve dynamically, as necessary. For this, it is a matter of equipping the transportation participants with a means of communication which allows them to receive and/or emit useful information.

The augmented environment must be able to ensure these information exchanges by capillarity (as in the blood network). The issues of this project can be reformulated in the following way:

– offer an urban freight transportation support, by providing delivery assistance, in the form of an information system used by different mobile or static, active or passive participants;

– identify the participants involved (responsible for the organization of the delivery areas and traffic in town, logisticians preparing the routes for delivery, drivers, etc.);

– transpose the principle of the computerized management of rooms to the reservation of delivery areas;

– carry out a delivery area reservation, then dynamically modify in the event of a delay, or take place immediately if the delivery area has not been reserved for the upcoming period;

– also study different approaches leading to a greater or lesser on-site provision of reservation information: an information panel in front of the delivery area or the display of this information only on the mobile device (PDA, mobile telephone) of the participant involved;

– have a maximum of features to increase the efficient and appropriate use of delivery areas while respecting the traffic constraints (parking for as short a time as possible by authorized users only). In particular, the idea is to avoid private individual car parking;

– identify the medium and the interaction (PDA, Smartphone, etc.) to access relevant, therefore contextualized, information by choosing the presentation form appropriate for each user.

We can characterize the targeted objectives in the following manner:

– identify all the participants: transport users, management of town traffic, delivery customer, transport logistician, transporter, deliverer, traffic operator and associate them with authorized operations from two main categories: (1) to be informed, for the passive participants and (2) to take action, for the active participants; it is also a matter of identifying the types of information to be handled;

– use the fixed interaction devices sooner for the managers (logisticians) and new mobile devices (telephone, PDA, Tablet PC) for the transporters-deliverers and traffic operator (policeman being able to give a fine in the event of illegal parking);

– make information available in the form appropriate to the task;

– enable the collaboration between different participants (signal traffic problems such as accidents, dynamically re-allocate the journey in the event of a problem, ask for an infracting vehicle to be fined, etc.).

The most important operations are the following:

– define the dynamic prohibition of truck circulation;

– know the current situation of traffic prohibitions for trucks;

– know the provisional occupation of the delivery areas involved;

– know the immediate occupation of delivery areas concerned and take action (take the space if free, change a reservation, etc.).

The proposed solution is based on the principles previously described (HMTD and IMERA) with three main concepts that we designate by the term MOCOCO (mobility, collaboration, contextualization): the concept of mobility suggests using miniature portable (or worn as an accessory) appliances offering appropriate services which are applicable in the context of global communication. That of collaboration (local or remote) brings the possibility of involving multiple participants with diverse competencies, who are not necessarily co-localized, to manage the particular situation. The concept of contextualization suggests making contextualized information available at the site of the action and more generally to all the users. Nomadism is taken into account by the use of lightweight appliances which can access the system and which are connectable – disconnectable – reconnectable and which support the user in his activities: these are *wearable computers* or *handheld computers*.

The mobility of users is situated on the scale of the town or the agglomeration, where it is a matter of ensuring the accessibility of the users or through them the common information system and the delivery areas. The consideration of the location is of utmost importance, not only geographically but also logically (in proximity to a given delivery area for example). For this the notion of attentive environment (which is alert to the situation), which we qualified beforehand as augmented, is essential. Indeed, thanks to the sensors which observe the environment and update the perceived state, the system knows the situation of the moment and can take it into account.

Taking into account the context deals for example with the identification of objects and users (who), the physical location of objects and users (where), and the interaction history (when). The augmentation communication mobile objects are mainly drawn from three categories:

– autonomous mobile objects which contain the essential minimum required to function (user interface, network interface, location possibility). For example it could be a PDA or a SmartPhone;

– environment embedded objects which are not mobile, but can be moved. For example they might consist of information terminals which can be placed at the most opportune place in relation to the activity which requires support;

– passive objects which are not directly connected by a network, but can be so via the intermediary of another object which is. For example RFID stickers which provide information via the RFID when placed in proximity to it. These objects have the objective of ensuring communication between the user and physical objects, and between mobile or fixed (augmented) physical objects.

Following the description of the issues and the objectives, the work carried out with the students of the Ecole Centrale of Lyon consisted of reformulating this issue in the form of a requirement, and then the elaboration of specifications in line with the software engineering approach, relying on UML modeling: use cases, sequence diagrams, class diagrams, transition-state diagrams for each significant class, collaboration diagram, architecture diagram and deployment diagram.

The approach for the design of interactive applications was also carried out by building the different models recommended by [CAL 03] with in particular the task model, for each of the identified participants shown in CTT (*Concurrent Task Trees*) [PAT 00], design model, dialog model and the abstract and practical interfaces which take into account the reusable interaction *patterns* [CHA 07]. The study of the choice of configuration for the wearable computer for each mobile user was also done with an explicit and precise evaluation based on the approach described in [MAS 06]. Particular attention was given to the following mobile users: transporter-deliverers and traffic wardens (policemen given the task of booking in the event of improper use of delivery areas by non authorized motorists) taking into consideration the range of applications of their wearable computer. The envisaged contextualization medium was the RFID label, but the use of other sensors does not call the development of the modeling into question.

The study enabled the consideration of both the forecasting of deliveries and the adjustment in real time of the deliverer's routes, depending on the disruptions that occurred. To have a clear perception of the different aspects of the daily lives of deliverers, three situations increasingly representative of reality were successively taken into account:

– the static, theoretical vision, with no disruption. This consists of taking into account real data regarding deliveries to be made and to make deliveries in an ideal context, with no disruptions;

– the predictable dynamic. This consists of taking into account predictable disruptions such as road works and planned closures;

– the non-predictable dynamic. This consists of taking into account disruptions, as well as accidents, during the delivery journey and to dynamically adjust the route in view of the situation. The deliverer himself can do this, but if the situation becomes too complex, he speaks to his logistician, who deals with it.

The collection of information to be archived in order to ensure traceability, was one of the priorities among the targeted objectives. Figures 6.7, 6.8 and 6.9 give examples of suggested solutions.

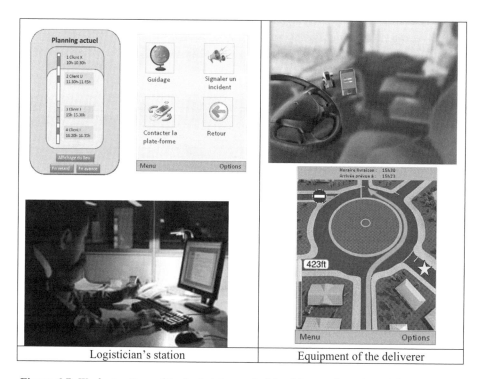

| Logistician's station | Equipment of the deliverer |

Figure 6.7. *Work situations of the logistician and of the deliverer from the e-delivery project*

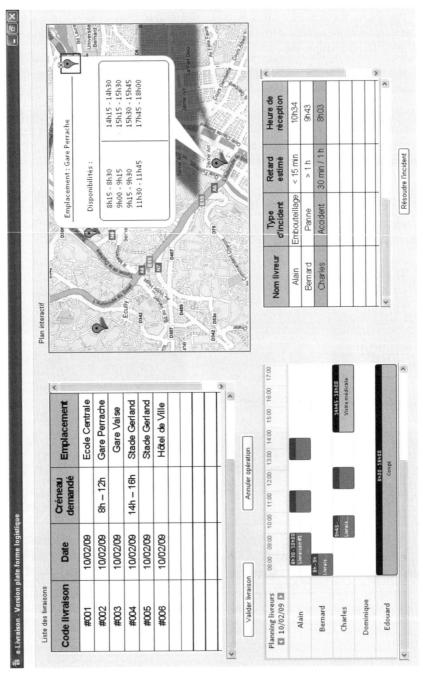

Figure 6.8. *Suggested interface of the e-delivery logistician*

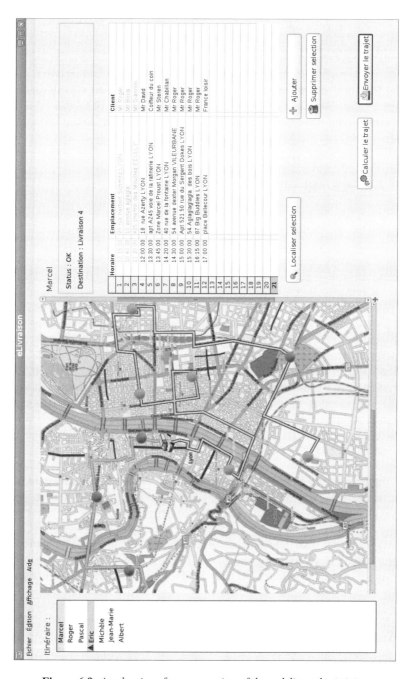

Figure 6.9. *Another interface suggestion of the e-delivery logistician*

This preliminary work enabled the issue of computerized management of delivery areas, such as it is perceived by ICT specialists, to be harnessed. This contribution was the starting point for the *Delivery area of the future* project, carried out in the context of the competitiveness cluster LUTB (*Lyon Urban Truck and Bus*) bringing together several participants of the cluster concerned by this issue. First approved by the cluster and then submitted to the PREDIT 4 GO 4 call for tender, it was accepted and financed by the ministry of Ecology, Energy, Sustainable development and the Sea.

6.10. ICT in the dynamic management of road networks

A third study which we present concerns the dynamic management of road traffic, which is regularly increasing, both in towns and outside agglomerations.

A first approach leads to development such as increasing the number of lanes; the second aims to segment traffic according to categories (individual cars, heavy vehicles, public transport, priority vehicles) by proposing specific development and traffic rules, with in particular the creation of specialized lanes (bus, tram, trolley). This second choice can lead to satisfying solutions on the condition that there is enough space.

When space is lacking and the frequency of this type of specialized traffic is not sufficient, there is a sense of waste and poor management. A third solution then saw the light of day, that of the dynamic allocation of lanes to different types of transport. A significant work of data gathering, analysis and classification was done by J. Nouvier of CERTU (Centre for studies on networks, transports, urbanism and public construction) [NOU 07].

He shows very varied solutions, from the more physical (the *ad hoc* movement of low walls with trucks) to the more informational (signposts with variable displays) enabling a greater or lesser rapidity of dynamicity.

Today it is true that telematic or embedded and/or mobile ICT can provide solutions leading to a very large dynamicity (clear a lane for a bus or an ambulance in real time) on the condition of sufficiently informing the different users and ensuring both the respect of regulations in terms of transport (or suggestions to modify it) and in particular the safety of all the users. Hereafter we give a brief description of the ICT vision, in a system perspective, such as we see it in our IMERA–HMTD logic. Figures 6.10, 6.11 and 6.12 present a number of situations which seem interesting and more or less complex to implement.

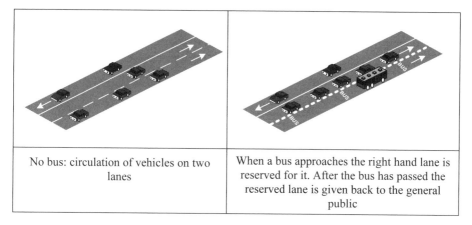

No bus: circulation of vehicles on two lanes	When a bus approaches the right hand lane is reserved for it. After the bus has passed the reserved lane is given back to the general public

Figure 6.10. *Case 1 – transformation of the right hand lane into a bus lane*

From the simplest (cases 1 and 2, Figures 6.10 and 6.11) to the very complex (last case, Figure 6.12), each requires an appropriate infrastructure.

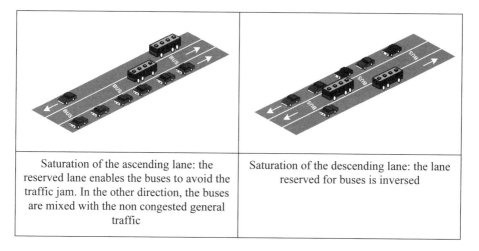

Saturation of the ascending lane: the reserved lane enables the buses to avoid the traffic jam. In the other direction, the buses are mixed with the non congested general traffic	Saturation of the descending lane: the lane reserved for buses is inversed

Figure 6.11. *Case 2 – change in a direction of a bus lane*

The alternative use of the two previous solutions according to the number of buses arriving in the single lane section, gives the complex case presented in Figure 6.12.

Bus descending on its own: the single lane section is open in the descending direction	
Bus ascending on its own: the single lane section is open in the ascending direction	
Crossing of two buses in the single lane section: an additional reserved lane opens taken from the general traffic lanes for the ascending bus, enabling the descending bus to simultaneously use the single lane section	

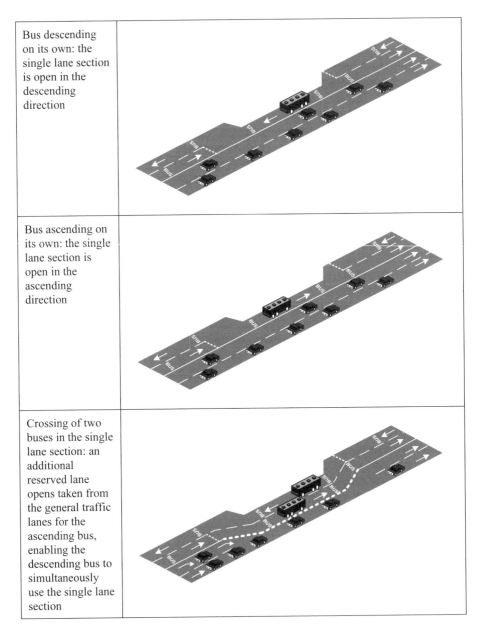

Figure 6.12. *Complex case – roads with lanes with a two directional bus lane which has a single lane section (narrowing of the road)*

The implementation of a dynamic management system for the lanes must be based on a set of sensors, displays and activators placed in strategic places: on the lane (sensors as well as displays and activators), with the active users involved, and therefore requestors (bus drivers, ambulances, firemen, possibly trucks), passive users "subjected to" the imposed modifications (displays only) and external – traffic regulators, as indicated in Figure 6.13.

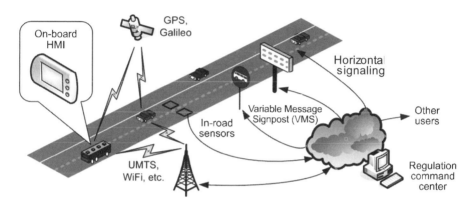

Figure 6.13. *Diagram of the system architecture*[2]

6.10.1. *System perspective*

All the elements, the appropriate functions of which are to be identified, as well as the technologies which can bring them about, must be integrated within the global system, collecting, aggregating, processing and diffusing the appropriate information to all users. It is this system which will be able to be simulated first, with the appropriate simplifications which need to be chosen. It is the one that gives the base for the implementation of the digital simulator. The diagram of Figure 6.14 presents the main elements of the system which are to be deployed.

This system perspective (Figure 6.14) brings into play the main elements which are:

– the sensors in the lane concerned by the collection of information regarding the state of the traffic and priority requests;

– the vehicles of users who request priority and who receive information regarding the state of the lanes (allocation of lanes, authorized or not dynamic priority requests) for *on-board* display;

---

2 Wireless network: UMTS, WiFi, etc. VMS: variable message sign.

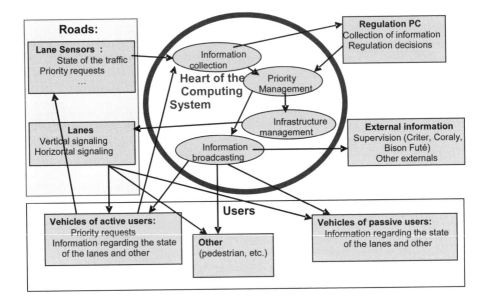

Figure 6.14. *System perspective of the support of dynamic road network management*[3]

– the vehicles of passive users who cannot take action, but who receive information regarding the state of the lanes (whether or not they are dynamically allocated to different categories of users: prohibited lane, lane reserved for priority vehicles, unmarked lanes);

– the regulation, vital component of coordination, that chooses the mode of lane management (static allocation in the event of heavy traffic or dynamic allocation in the event of infrequent priority seeking). It does not systematically intervene in management (automatic functioning is preferred), but only to change the management mode;

– the lanes receiving information regarding the propagation of both vertical (variable message signs) and horizontal (on the road) signaling;

– the system of dynamic management of so-called priority roads management includes the following main components: collection of information, management of priorities, management of lanes, and diffusion of information;

– the information transmission system (the information network).

---

3 PC Criter: traffic info of Greater Lyon. Coraly: coordination and regulation of traffic on the fast lanes of the Lyon region. Bison futé: forecasts regarding road traffic in France, information regarding road circulation: traffic jams, holiday departures/returns, services.

6.10.2. *HMI perspective*

In relation to the users identified in the system perspective, it is important to deal with the user aspect as soon as possible, by designing and implementating appropriate human-machine interfaces: as observed, the active users (requestors – beneficiaries of the system), passive users (subjected to the system), the deciders (regulation command center) and all the users via vertical and horizontal signaling must receive useful information to act appropriately. It is essential that this information and these actions occur in accordance with the work context and the corresponding requirements:

– in the vehicle compatibility with the double task – driving and managing, in a regulation work station for example, it is efficiency which dominates;

– when information is displayed outside, it has to be compatible with meteorological constraints of visibility – legibility.

The design of these HMI therefore also constitutes an important part of the system and conditions its acceptability. The approaches described in Chapter 11 dealing with the adaptation of HMI (plasticity approach), or again in Chapter 3 with the personalization of information are to be taken into account.

6.11. Examples of initiatives and projects in direct or indirect link with the e-Truck and e-Bus concepts

In order to show that the work described previously corresponds to more general concerns, which are considered worldwide to be very important, we relate a number of these projects, in particular those in which Renault Trucks is involved.

6.11.1. *LUTB and i-Trans competitiveness clusters*

The competitiveness cluster LUTB [LUT] was created in 2006. It aims to meet the challenges raised by the increase in the needs of mobility, people and goods in an urban environment. Its objective is to associate the world of research with that of business in line with this aim. The structure is based on five research and development programs, as follows:

– motorization and driveline: consists of developing a high performance, silent, reliable propulsion engine respectful of the environment, for different urban applications and hybrid motorizations;

– integrated safety and security: improve the safety of users and increase the security of people and goods transport;

– vehicle architecture and comfort: design urban vehicles of the future to meet the challenges of sustainable development and urban mobility;

– transport system: come up with global solutions, including the interaction between vehicles, infrastructure and urban systems, in a context of sustainable development;

– modeling and management of mobility: understand the dynamic of the mobility of people and goods, in urban zones and outlying suburbs.

The e-Truck and e-Bus studies previously described were carried out as follows: the first before the integration of the LIESP into the LUTB and the two others, the subjects of which come from *Think Tanks* of the programme 4 "Transport system", served as studies prior to the projects started by several partners and since approved by LUTB and submitted to national calls for tender.

The i-Trans is another competitiveness cluster [I-T] which brings together the main participantss of industry, of research, and training in the field of the rail industry and innovative ground transport present in the Nord-Pas de Calais and Picardie regions. It has the aim of meeting the challenges of international competition in the context of the intensification of freight and traveler exchanges. Its goal is to deal with problems of design, construction, competitive operation and the maintenance of innovative transport systems in terms of market share, innovation, growth and attractivity.

It covers four fields of action:

– interoperability for the rail sector;

– inter-modality for freight or traveler transport;

– intelligence of transportation systems (ITS);

– innovation for economic development.

Several industrial branches are involved: rail, automobile, ports, rivers and logistics.

6.11.2. *Examples of European projects linked to the e-Bus and e-Truck issues*

The subject of public transport is too important for constructors to be able to ignore the progress which needs to be made. As the cost of research and the need for coordination, in particular in terms of legislation on all levels, is considerable, the European Commission is not able not to support research and development in this subject. Nonetheless in a competitive context the research financed by the European community concerns pre-studies, *proofs of concepts*, that are then picked up by each industrialist to make them into products, naturally protected by confidentiality. We give hereafter a few significant projects directly linked to the issue studied before showing what a large manufacturer is doing internally (still within the limits and in respect of imposed confidentiality).

6.11.2.1. *CVIS project*

The objective of the CVIS (*Cooperative Vehicle-Infrastructure System*) project [CVI] (2006-2010) was to create a unified technical solution enabling all vehicles and elements of infrastructure to communicate with each other in a continuous and transparent manner, using a series of media and with the augmented environment. It is a question of enabling a range of potential cooperative services to work on an open application system in the vehicle and roadside equipment. To do this, it is necessary to define and validate an open architecture and a system concept for a certain number of cooperative applications, and to develop components which are common to the cooperation of supporting real requests and services for the drivers, operators, the industry and other major participants. It is necessary to deal with aspects such as acceptance by users, the privacy and security of data as well as the interoperability of the system, but also the induced risks, in particular for driving and the responsibilities involved. The needs for public order, the costs, the advantages and disadvantages and economic models are also on the agenda, as well as the deployment strategies.

In the main aspects respectively linked to the basic technology, to the cooperative applications involved and to the choice of test and deployment sites, the CVIS subprojects have the objective of generating the main following results:

– a multi-channel terminal able to maintain a continuous internet connection with all the users, including mobile telephone, the Wi-Fi network channels, infrared over short distance, ensuring full operability in communication between different components of the vehicle and systems of traffic management;

– an open architecture linking the system on board the vehicle and the system of telematic services management situated at the side of the road, which must easily be able to be updated and adjusted to enable the consideration of varied client-server technologies. It prefigures a response to our project of dynamic roads;

– techniques for the sophisticated positioning of vehicles and the creation of local dynamic maps, based on satellite positioning, radio triangulation and the latest methods of referencing and localization;

– extended protocols for vehicle, road and environment monitoring enabling the vehicles to share and verify their data with other vehicles or infrastructures which are close by, and with a service located at the side of the road;

– the design of basic applications and software tools for the cooperative management of the urban network, the cooperative management of itineraries and the dynamic management of lane allocation for buses, to facilitate the work of drivers and provide a cooperative aid to travelers on the interurban routes, for the reservation and management of parking zones and loading of utility vehicles, the monitoring and guiding of dangerous goods and controlling the access of vehicles to sensitive zones.

Presentation of CVIS principles http://www.cvisproject.org/

Figure 6.15. *Schematization of the CVIS project*

The deployment of a range of tools in the form of models, directives and recommendations in the sectors of franchise and interoperability are also targeted, as well as: the safe, secure design, which can tolerate faults; the validation of usefulness, profitability and acceptance by users; the elaboration of cost models, profits, economic models, risk and responsibility models; cooperative systems as tools for town policy and deployment road maps.

The CVIS project has broken down the complex aspects which must be dealt with in order to fulfill its objectives by structuring its activities into three sub-projects: basic technology, reference applications, on site tests. The first two blocks can occur in parallel, by developing basic characteristics for software and hardware, then the integration can lead to the deployment of more and more integrated test benches, in order to be able to carry out practical tests in the CVIS test sites.

6.11.2.2. *BESTUFS I and II, CityLog Projects*

The BESTUFS I project (*BEST Urban Freight Solutions*) [BES] (2000-2004) first of all targeted the deployment of a collaboration network in the context of a concerted action aiming to share and exchange experiences and knowledge with colleagues who are in similar positions in other towns as a prerequisite for starting common projects. This project facilitated the establishment of personal relations and the broadening of contact networks in the field of urban freight transport for all the interested parties, with no commitment or formal structures.

The next project, entitled BESTUFS II [BES] (2005-2008) was based on the observation that the most innovative urban areas, which apply the city logistical solutions (CLS), tend to be in large towns or capital cities. These larger urban communities have the resources to access the support of innovative transport solutions, participate in city networks and exchange knowledge and experience. The small and medium sized urban areas are, in this regard, at a disadvantage and often act in a limited range, as they are comparatively isolated, seen from a European perspective. It is also common that their local representatives encounter language problems which limit them in the study of the experiences of other European cities.

The partners of BESTUFS II identify such difficulties and aim to broaden the existing BESTUFS network to include medium sized zones in Europe. If diffusion of information to all is a priority objective, particular attention is given to transmission to small urban areas and its use within them. It was the intention of BESTUFS II to establish a series of practical CLS guides and to translate into national languages to be able to be used as raw material by the BESTUFS II representatives in the field. It is a matter of establishing a bridge of knowledge and exchange of experience between the local and European communities.

This need for testing and dissemination of good practices is the subject of several European projects, such as CityLog (7th PCRD project, notified in 2008 and which began in September 2009 for a three year period) [CIT]. The main partners of the project are Fiat, Iveco, TNT, Volvo, Piemont, Berlin Europlateform. The city of Lyon is participating in the experiment with Berlin and Turin, for the question of deliveries in city, with the objective of testing three innovative solutions:

– evolutive vehicle (logistics and routing/dynamicity/interoperability of vehicles);

– loadable modules;

– delivery and collection (recovery).

Among the solutions experimented with, the use of the tricycle for the "last kilometer" is part of the project. We see that the project attempts to cover the whole life of a parcel: long distance routing by large truck, then decanting and delivery in town either by trucks or vans, even motorbikes or tricycles. All of these aspects correspond to specific instances of the generic vision expressed by e-Truck and the different avenues of which must be explored and appreciated from the point of view of utility, usability and technical, political and in particular social acceptability. The role of mobile computing is vital.

6.11.2.3. *FREILOT project*

The European FREILOT project (*Urban Freight Energy Efficiency Pilot*) [FRE] was launched in April 2009 for a duration of two and a half years, with the objective of improving the energy efficiency of goods transport in an urban environment. The fuel consumption of delivery vehicles indeed depends on a number of factors among which is the performance of the vehicle, the driving style, the load being transported. It is a pilot project, not a research project, aiming to carry out tests of integration and use in the field, of solutions from the CVIS research project described above. The FREILOT project has an integration approach with four stakes:

– energy efficiency at crossroads, giving priority to heavy vehicles (reduction of the very polluting *stop-and-go*s);

– the regulation of the acceleration and speed levels thanks to embedded speed restriction systems;

– assistance to eco-driving, thanks to advanced navigation systems, reducing the risk of accidents;

– the temporal and spatial management of goods delivery areas.

The project is based on the experimentation in four European towns (Bilbao, Helmond, Lyon, Krakow), of fixing priorities for heavy vehicles at certain crossroads – at certain defined times – in addition to the equipment of vehicles with acceleration and speed limiters. Furthermore, the four metropolises will put a service for the dynamic reservation of delivery areas at the disposal of the deliverers, enabling the reduction of time searching for a parking area, and consequently the risk of congestion. This experimental project therefore corresponds to a particular instantiation of the generic vision expressed by e-Truck.

ERTICO ITS Europe, which is managing the project, gave itself the objective of reducing fuel consumption by 25%, and therefore also CO_2 emissions, thus contributing to the improvement of the quality of the air. If the results of this pilot-project match expectations, the FREILOT project and the intelligent transport systems that it deploys, should eventually be extended to other European metropolises.

6.11.2.4. *FIDEUS project*

The European project FIDEUS (*Freight Intelligent Delivery of Goods in European Urban Spaces*) [FID 05], [FID 08] of the 6th PCRD, has provided a framework for the study of new urban distribution modes implying a permanent dialog between on the one hand a logistical base and the truck driver and on the other hand the driver and city traffic management system.

Launched in 2005 for three years, this research program had the ambition of developing a new design for the organization of urban transport of goods, which, while improving their efficiency, preserves the quality of life in cities. FIDEUS has associated numerous partners including vehicle and equipment manufacturers (Renault Trucks, IVECO, ECA), transporters (DHL and TNT), cities (Lyon, Hannover, Barcelona) and university laboratories (University of Westminster, Fraunhofer Institute).

In this context, in January 2008, Renault Trucks tested a vehicle carrying advanced technical solutions for urban delivery in the Lyon area. This vehicle was premiered next to Hybrys, an innovative concept-vehicle using hybrid technology. Renault Trucks developed a delivery vehicle with increased performance in terms of environment conservation, safety, security and driver comfort.

Designed from a medium duty 190 hp Midlum (12T of GW) with a Euro 4 engine (compatible with the Euro 5 levels applicable in 2009), the vehicle is characterized by a very low noise level, 3 dB (A) below the regulatory requirements and a reduced level of polluting emissions, with an added -3 dB(A) when a so-called "low noise mode" is activated.

In addition, a complete telemetric system (navigation, positioning, identification of goods by RFID, communication with the base, etc.) informs the driver and the vehicle when the truck enters an environmental urban zone, the objective for this prototype vehicle being to demonstrate that it is possible to activate in an active manner (and passively in the future) functionalities enabling low sound and gaseous emissions (CO_2 and conventional pollutants).

Finally, the driver's task is facilitated by the ergonomics of on-board commands, by a system of automatic unlocking of all openings (including those which give access to loading), of the tailgate, and "no hands" starting by the vehicle's pushbutton. It also benefits from an electronically controlled parking brake which enables new functionalities such as an automatic parking mode and an aid for hill starts to be associated.

The bodywork and its equipment have been specially developed to carry out loading and unloading operations with ease and with reduced noise levels. The signaling of the vehicle and the lighting of the work zones have been reinforced; a camera placed behind linked with backup radars ensures safety during maneuvers.

Renault Truck's Midlum was driven in the Lyon agglomeration, used in real life conditions by the transporter DHL (Figure 6.16). After Greater Lyon, the vehicle was also successfully tested in Barcelona in March 2008, for night-time delivery experiments.

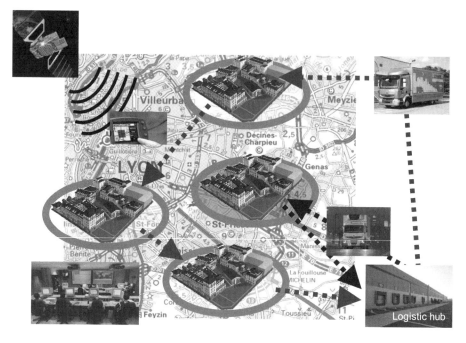

Figure 6.16. *Monitoring and management of delivery truck movements in the context of experiments in the FIDEUS project*

6.11.3. *Examples of projects specific to Renault Trucks*

The last project described above shows where the limit is between a European *proof of concept* and its adaptation by each manufacturer. Renault Trucks thus went ahead with the integration of the FIDEUS designs and with their embodiment in one of its vehicles. This transformation from a cooperative project financed by the European community to the specific and marketable materialization is a logical progression. Nonetheless this transformation is naturally protected by legitimate confidentiality.

We describe, mostly in the form of visual presentations, a few specific points of this approach, points for which Renault Trucks has lifted confidentiality. The first example deals with the layout of the truck interior (Figure 6.17).

Control lever for the clutch and the volume behind the steering wheel

A truck control panel, showing different error messages:
open door, low battery, low fuel level …

Control panel of a truck with the speedometer in the center.
Driving Controllers are on the steering wheel

Figure 6.17. *Example of the layout of the inside of a truck*

The second example deals with the different ways of laying out the driver's seating area and more generally the cab, taking into account the size of the truck and its activities (Figure 6.18).

View of the inside of a distribution truck with curved control panel for a better access to controls	Insight into storage possibilities in a control panel. A remote control enables access to information and entertainment functions

View of the inside of a long distance transport truck	Storage possibilities in the centre of the Renault Kerax truck

View inside a small distribution truck	Control panel in a small distribution truck with the navigation screen

Driver in a long distance cab with a rest area behind the seat	

Figure 6.18. *Layout of the driver's seating area and more generally of the cab*

The third example deals with the use of ICT for the remote diagnosis of engines for purposes of tuning and maintenance (Figure 6.19).

Figure 6.19. *ICTs in tuning and maintenance of trucks*

There follows a few more global projects being conducted by Renault Trucks.

6.11.3.1. *VIF project (interactive vehicle of the future)*

The VIF project enabled the development of an interactive demonstrator driver – vehicle – infrastructure – control center to optimize the safety and security of transport, the energy efficiency and the environmental footprint, the management of the connected "players" (vehicles and infrastructures) (Figure 6.20).

Figure 6.20. *HMI of the interactive vehicle of the future*

In this context, telematics, as seen by the transport operator, leads to a solution which enables the optimization of the productivity of operations through access to information relating to the vehicle, the driver and loading in real time and remotely, (Figure 6.21).

Figure 6.21. *Telematics as seen by the transport operator*

The integration of new possibilities offered by telematics must be tested before being implemented. The stage of studying driver and operators acceptability is based on the use of driving simulators (Figure 6.22).

Scoop Project: driving simulator allowing the driver to be placed in virtual "real" conditions to study the ergonomics of new systems of driving and operating aid	View of the driving simulator of the Volvo group located in Lyon: the image is projected on a big screen; the simulator enables tests of human-machine interactions in safe conditions

Figure 6.22. *Examples of driving simulators*

6.11.3.2. *CHAUFFEUR2 Project*

The CHAUFFEUR2 project [CHA] had the objective of studying how to connect two vehicles together and ensure the safety of the trip. This project enabled interactive demonstrators to be developed (Figure 6.23) relative to the concepts of "autonomous" vehicles, without the driver intervening. Firstly, each vehicle is maintained on a trajectory (*lane keeping*) and at a distance from the upstream vehicle (*safe distance keeping*); secondly, each vehicle is interacting in relation with other equipped vehicles, the first vehicle being the leader and the others being followers that are connected by virtual bars.

Safe distance keeping	Lane keeping

Figure 6.23. *Two autonomous vehicle functions allowing connected vehicle "trains"*

Major aspects relative to HMI have been studied, as well as *X-by-Wire* technology [DEL], which replaces the traditional mechanical or hydraulic links between the driver's controls and the steering and breaking mechanisms by various electromechanical actuators, emulators for activating the pedals and steering wheel, and a distributed network of electronic command modules. The components of the traditional steering and breaking systems (steering column, pump, flexible pipes, fluids, belts and servo brake/master cylinder) entirely disappear from the environment sensors, the processors of vehicle electronic systems and drive train. The electronically controlled steering and braking systems enable greater fuel savings. The elimination of hydraulic fluids benefits the environment. The use of only a few components simplifies the assembly and enables a greater flexibility in terms of the design of the cab.

In the absence of the constraints of mechanical assemblies, it becomes possible to still improve the driver's controls. In addition, their adapted design enables the controls to be easily transformed from left handed steering to right handed steering.

6.11.3.3. *SAFE TUNNEL project*

The SAFE TUNNEL project had the aim of making the vehicle, the infrastructure and tunnel management interact by connecting them together to aid operating tunnel safety. This project enabled interactive demonstrators to be developed in particular allowing the study of access to the tunnel in the approach zone, the remote control of the vehicle or also the control of speed and distance between two vehicles in the tunnel (Figure 6.24).

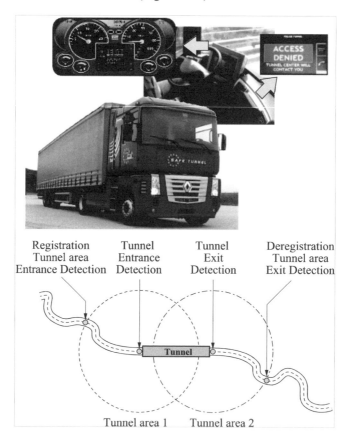

Figure 6.24. *Connection between the vehicle, the infrastructure and the tunnel operation*

6.12. Conclusion

In this chapter we have attempted to give a progress report on the place of ICT in mass transport of the future, both for people (buses) and goods (trucks). We addressed both the issue of single vehicles, or vehicle fleet, in view of increasing their efficiency in use. Without wishing to be exhaustive, but rather representative, we first of all analyzed the situation, then gave a description of the different possible contributions. Then we restricted ourselves to the study of the embedded computer, both fixed and mobile, and to the corresponding HMI. We were also able to review the different activities occurring in the truck and the bus and in their surroundings, and we have suggested supporting them, either by a fixed computer, used in priority as a driving aid, or by a wearable computer supporting activities which occur in mobility by necessity or convenience. Among these, maintenance & diagnosis to prevent or repair breakdown is of particular importance. Its contextualization need is undeniable, as well as the need to learn the steps to carry out at the right moment (just in time). *M-Learning* (mobility learning) therefore also has a central role. This work of analysis and proposition, carried out with the students of the Ecole Centrale of Lyon, led to us conducting three studies in collaboration with Renault Trucks and in the context of the LUTB competitiveness cluster, the latter two being pre-studies for collaborative projects between several partners within the LUTB. To finish, we gave a report of several European projects directly linked to the issue presented, as well as of (non confidential) work carried out in Renault Trucks. We hope that we have given the reader a fairly complete vision of the current situation concerning this issue.

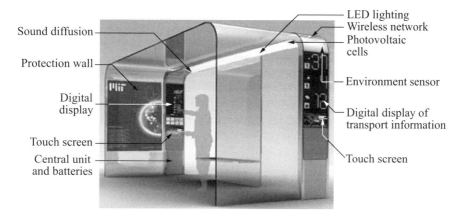

Figure 6.25. *Communicating urban bus shelter according to [MIT]*

Of course there are numerous other possible approaches, projects, or avenues worth exploring. We can very briefly give three:

– the role of the urban bus shelter in the vision of a global ICT system, has not yet been completely explored; it is true that it was attempted at MIT [MIT] (Figure 6.25), but there is no doubt a lot to be done to give it an appropriate role;

– the problem of splitting between long distance routing and local distribution, including "the last kilometer", is a logistical problem, but the role of ICT (contextualized and wearable) is vital in this. Numerous studies and experiments are progressing but also still need to be conducted;

– more globally the identification and the structuring of services largely still remains to be done, to lead to an open system with easily cofigurable services. An initial modeling is put forward in Figure 6.26. Here also, there is still a long way to go.

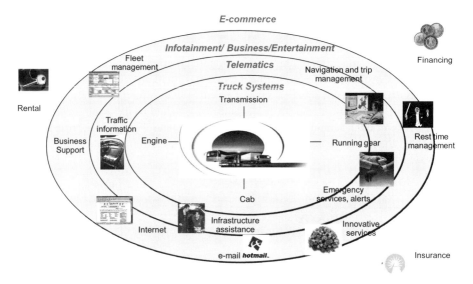

Figure 6.26. *The crown structure of new services*

6.13. Bibliography

[BES] BESTUFS, www.bestufs.net/index.html.

[BOR 01] BORCHERS J., *A Pattern Approach to Interaction Design*, John Wiley & Sons, New York, USA, 2001.

[CAL 03] CALVARY G., COUTAZ J., THEVENIN D., LIMBOURG Q., BOUILLON L., VANDERDONCKT J., "Unifying Reference Framework for Multi-Target User Interfaces", *Interacting with Computers*, 15(3), pp. 289-308, 2003.

[CHA] CHAUFFEUR 2: Automated road transport and vehicles under electronic control, www.lynuxworks.com/solutions/industrial/in-action/chauffeur2.php.

[CHA 07] CHAMPALLE O., DAVID B., MASSEREY G., CHALON R., "Du modèle de tâches à la configuration de l'ordinateur porté", *Revue d'Interaction Homme-Machine*, vol. 8, no. 1, pp. 149-181, 2007.

[CIT] CityLog, www.city-log.eu/home.

[CVI] CVIS, www.cvisproject.org/.

[DAV 91] DAVID B.T., LABIALE G., OUADOU K., "Integrated Environment for Ergonomic Studies of on-board display, International Symposium on Automotive Technology & Automation", *24th ISATA, Road Transport Informatic/Intelligent Vehicle Highway*, Florence, Italy, 20-24 May 1991.

[DAV 06] DAVID B., MASSEREY G., CHAMPALLE O., CHALON R., DELOTTE O., "A wearable computer based maintenance, diagnosis and repairing activities in Computer Augmented Environment", *Proceedings of EAM06: European Annual Conference on Human Decision-Making and Manual Control*, Valenciennes, France, 27-29 September, 2006.

[DAV 07a] DAVID B., MASSEREY G., CHAMPALLE O., YIN C., GAGNE O., CHALON R., "L'ordinateur porté et la réalité augmentée dans les activités de diagnostic – maintenance – réparation", *7e Congrès international de génie industriel*, Trois-Rivières, Quebec, Canada, 5-8 June 2007.

[DAV 07b] DAVID B., CHALON R., "IMERA: Experimentation Platform for Computer Augmented Environment for Mobile Actors", *Proceedings of WiMob*, New York, USA, 2007.

[DAV 07c] DAVID B., CHALON R., Yin C., "e-Truck : les TIC au service du camion", *Proceedings of International Workshop LT2007: Logistique & Transport*, Sousse, Tunisia, 2007.

[DEL 04] DELOTTE O., DAVID B., CHALON R., "Task Modeling for Capillary Collaborative Systems", *ACM SIGCHI Workshop TAMODIA*, pp. 15-22, Prague, Czech Republic, 2004.

[DEL] Delphi, une technologie X-by-Wire pour l'Europe, www.prnewswire.co.uk/cgi/news/release?id=73324.

[DEY 00] DEY A.K., Providing Architectural Support for Building Context-Aware Applications, PhD thesis, Georgia Institute of Technology, December 2000.

[ECL 06] ECL, Compte-rendu des travaux des élèves sur la problématique e-Truck du cours UML et le Développement Logiciel, Ecole centrale de Lyon, France, May 2006.

[FID 05] FIDEUS, www.urba2000.com/urba2000/URBA2000_FIDEUS_general.htm.

[FID 08] Infos-Industrielles, www.infos-industrielles.com/dossiers/1465.asp.

[FIN 03] FINKENZELLER K., *RFID Handbook: Fundamentals and applications in contactless smart cards and identification*, John Wiley & Sons, New York, USA, 2003.

[FOR] FORUM Systèmes & Logiciels pour les NTIC dans le transport, www.inrets.fr/services/manif/ForumNTIC/.

[FRE]   FREILOT,   www.fr.transport-expertise.org/index.php/2009/05/10/lyon-comme-ville-dexperimentation-pour-le-projet-europeen-freilot/.

[I-T] I-Trans, Pôle de compétitivité, www.i-trans.org/

[LAB 92] LABIALE G., DAVID B.T., OUADOU K., "L'interface "intelligente" d'informations et de communications dans le poste de conduite automobile", in: BRISSAUD M., GRANGE M., NICOLOYANNIS N. (eds), *Intelligence artificielle et sciences humaines*, Hermès, Paris, France, 1992.

[LAB 93] LABIALE G., OUADOU K., DAVID B.T, "A software system for designing and evaluating in-car information system interfaces" in: STASSEN H.G. (ed.), *Analysis, Design and Evaluation of Man-machine Systems*, Pergamon Press, Oxford, 1993.

[LAB 94] LABIALE G., OUADOU K., DAVID B.T., "Ergonomic requirements of an in-car adaptable interface", *Proceedings of 12th Congress of the International Ergonomics Association*, Toronto, Canada, 15-19 August 1994.

[LUT] LUTB Pôle de compétitivité, www.lutb.fr/Presentation.410.0.html.

[MAS 06] MASSEREY G., CHAMPALLE O., DAVID B., CHALON R., "Démarche d'aide au choix de dispositifs pour l'ordinateur porté", *Actes du colloque ERGO'IA 2006, L'humain comme facteur de performance des systèmes complexes*, Biarritz, France, 11-13 October 2006.

[MIT] MIT's futuristic, networked bus stop design, http://boingboing.net/2009/05/21/mits-futuristic-netw.html.

[MEY 06] MEYER C., CHALON R., DAVID B., "Caractérisation de situations de M-Learning", *Actes TICE 2006*, Toulouse, France, 23-25 October 2006.

[MOU 06] MOUSSA F., KOLSKI C., RIAHI M., "Analyse des dysfonctionnements des systèmes complexes en amont de la conception des IHM : apports, difficultés, et étude de cas", *Revue d'Interaction Homme-Machine (RIHM)*, vol. 7, no. 2, pp. 79-111, 2006.

[NOD] NODENOT T., Etude du potentiel du langage IMS-LD pour scénariser des situations d'apprentissage : résultats et propositions, www.inrp.fr/archives/colloques/scenario2006/actes/nodenot.pdf.

[NOU 07] NOUVIER J., Entrez dans le monde des ITS = Enter the world of ITS, Lyon: CERTU, cédérom TU CE12 10450 disponible auprès du département SYStèmes du CERTU, 2007.

[OMA 03] O'MALLEY C., *Mobile Learning Guidelines for Learning in a Mobile Environment*, UoN, www.mobilearn.org, 2003.

[PAT 00] PATERNO F., *Model-Based Design and Evaluation of Interactive Applications*, Applied Computing Series, Springer, London, 2000.

[PLO 04] PLOUZNIKOFF N., ROBERT J.-M., "Caractéristiques, enjeux et défis de l'informatique portée", *IHM'04, International Conference Proceedings Series*, pp. 125-132, ACM Press, Namur, Belgium, 2004.

[SRI 05] Srivasta L., "Ubiquitous Network Societies: The Case of Radio Frequency Identification", Background paper, *ITU Workshop on Ubiquitous Network Societies*, Geneva, Switzerland, 2005, www.itu.int/ubiquitous/.

[TAP 09] Tapscott D., *Grown up Digital: How the Net Generation is Changing Your World*, McGraw Hill, Maidenhead, United Kingdom, 2009.

[WEI 91] Weiser M., "The Computer for the Twenty-First Century", *Scientific American*, 265(3), pp. 94-104, September 1991.

[WEL 93] Wellner P., Mackay W., Gold R., "Computer Augmented Environments: Back to the Real World", *Special Issue of Communications of the ACM*, vol. 36, no. 7, 1993.

Chapter 7

User-centered Approach to Design an Adaptive Truck Driving Assistance: Detection of Vulnerable Users in Urban Areas

7.1. Introduction

The safety of vulnerable road users is an important issue in terms of public health. Indeed, statistical studies on road safety show that more pedestrians and cyclists are killed than motor vehicle users in an urban environment in France (66.9% of those killed [CHA 08]). More globally, statistics show that in numerous countries pedestrians, cyclists and bus passengers are the user groups which are at the greatest risk of being involved in a serious accident [TRA 04]. Finally, the majority of accidents involving a vulnerable user and a heavy vehicle have fatal consequences for the vulnerable user.

With a poor awareness of the requirements and constraints linked to driving heavy vehicles, vulnerable users frequently adopt unsafe attitudes and behaviors when in proximity to such vehicles, particularly in an urban environment (see Figure 7.1). Furthermore, the presence of trucks often causes negative, even aggressive, reactions from the others in the town. Thus, proximity to the population and the struggle for occupation of public space have a direct impact on road safety, linked to the circulation of trucks in town, as well as to the idea the public has of

Chapter written by Annick MAINCENT, Hélène TATTEGRAIN, Marie-Pierre BRUYAS and Arnaud BONNARD.

these vehicles and their drivers. Key elements of the system, the drivers who make deliveries are faced with various tasks under constant time pressure and in an extremely complex and hostile environment. Confronted with these multiple constraints, the driver-deliverers are subjected to heavy mental burdens that reinforce the benefit of developing driving aid systems to prevent accidents to vulnerable users.

Figure 7.1. *Industrial vehicles and vulnerable road users in an urban environment: a difficult cohabitation*

In light of these observations, the VIVRE2 project (Industrial Vehicles and Vulnerable Road Users), subsidized in 2005 by the National Research Agency in the context of the PREDIT[1] and approved by the competitiveness cluster LUTB2015[2], aimed to design and evaluate technological solutions for implementation in industrial vehicles. Such devices should significantly reduce the number of accidents involving people and industrial vehicles in an urban environment.

In an unfavorable economic context, the choice of low-cost solutions is an absolute necessity for the distribution of innovative solutions in trucks (see also Chapter 6). Moreover, before developing and installing the innovative driving aid systems in industrial vehicles, it is essential to adopt a research approach based on the real needs and activity of the drivers. This type of approach enables the feasibility of such systems to be specified and the relevance and efficiency to be tested on a driving simulator.

This chapter presents the approach adopted in the VIVRE2 project for the design of driving aid systems: from the specification of assistance strategies and the

---

1 National Research and Innovation Program in Ground Transport.
2 Lyon Urban Truck and Bus 2015.

human–machine interfaces (HMIs), based on contextual analyses; to the implementation of technical solutions and their evaluation on a dynamic truck simulator.

7.2. Methodological principles for an anthropocentric design

The principle retained during the design of the VIVRE2 system was an anthropocentric approach. This approach favors the identification, description and explanation of various components of human functioning in interaction with technical systems, such as assistance systems, for driving a vehicle. It is on this level that the pluridisciplinary approaches make sense, by associating the benefit of human sciences to that of engineering sciences.

7.2.1. *New assistance technologies and the driving of an industrial vehicle*

In the field of road safety, the driver has always been considered the component of the system that is at the origin of the majority of malfunctions. This is why making road transport safer, the driving of industrial vehicles less strenuous and aiding their insertion into road traffic requires us to have tools to aid decisions that, in an environment is likely to be complex, can diffuse information adapted to the context (for example, signal the presence of a pedestrian in a blind spot). It also requires us to automate an increasing number of tasks that make up the driving activity, even automatically activate decisive functions (for example, having emergency breaking or immobilizer). For a more general approach to the current concerns in terms of human–machine interactions in trucks and buses of the future, we refer the reader to Chapter 6.

The design approach of the VIVRE2 system is based on the idea that the actions of the driver must, in some cases, be able to be relayed by automatic devices capable of re-establishing driving conditions that conform to criteria required by security. It is not a matter of substituting the human with a machine, but rather defining a sphere of protection that allows technological systems to intervene each time they are more sufficient than the human decision [HAN 99].

Nonetheless, the rapid expansion of new technologies brings new problems, particularly cognitive in nature, which it is advisable to take into consideration from the design stage. Paradoxically, the addition of "intelligent" systems in vehicles often increases the workload of drivers [MA 05] and the multiplication of informative feedback can have a dispersive impact on attention and, consequently, safety [PAR 97].

Generally, the main objective of driving aids is to improve security, all the while favoring driving comfort (*safety enhancing technologies*). They are developed to facilitate the driving activity and to use the performances of the vehicle as best as possible [LEE 97], all the while maintaining an optimal level of security for the driver and road environment [MIC 93]. However, the past few years have seen the appearance of numerous embedded systems, which are more or less dependent on the vehicle but do not have a safety objective (*safety impacting technologies*); this is the case with the cell phone or fleet management tools. These different tools, regularly used by drivers in the context of work activity, have the effect of multiplying sources of distraction [LAN 04], [STR 04] and consequently increasing the risks of accidents [MCE 07]. A recent American study carried out with bus and heavy goods vehicle drivers also put forward the dangerous nature of certain subtasks associated with the use of the cell phone, such as texting [HIC 10].

Thus, the driver must not only steer his vehicle while ensuring the responsibility of the goods transported and the safety of other road users, but also manage a multitude of systems, provide instructions, monitor the environment, communicate with the outside, etc. It is therefore necessary to pay particular attention to the functioning strategies of assistance systems as well as to the interfaces that will enable interactions between the human and machine, while taking into account the real activity of the driver and the behaviors of people traveling around the vehicle. This human-centered approach, must be applied from the design of systems, at the risk of developing systems that are poorly adapted to users and therefore underused, even rejected or avoided [MAL 07].

From this perspective, the VIVRE2 project consortium adopted a pluridisciplinary systemic approach to user-centered design (UCD), which takes into account the issue of the security of vulnerable people by integrating the contextual, human and technological factors.

7.2.2. *The user-centered design approach*

Classic in ergonomics, the UCD approach is based on the notion of *acceptability,* which corresponds to the "degree" of integration and appropriation of an object in a context of use [BAR 09]. Acceptability is conditioned by the *usability* characteristics of the object [NIE 93]. Fisher [FIS 01] broadened this notion of usability to the field of adaptive systems: "to make systems more usable, more useful, and to provide users with experiences fitting their specific background knowledge and objectives".

Traditionally, design models are based on the development model in V³, which was enhanced by Kolski [KOL 98] by including two stages of ergonomic evaluation for the specification and design phases. The iterative approach, such as has been recommended by Gould and Lewis [GOU 85] and Popovic [POP 99], included the evolutive specifications enabling us to integrate the results that come from analyses of the activity over the course of development. A certain consensus concerning the UCD approach was reached with the creation of the ISO 13407 standard ([MAG 01], Figure 7.2). Nonetheless, even if this iterative design approach is essential, it is not always possible to implement several iterations due to a lack of time or funds.

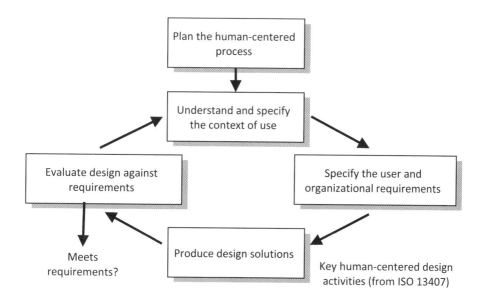

Figure 7.2. *Human-centered design process [MAG 01]*

The preliminary work of the VIVRE2 project consisted of implementing the UCD approach in the design of the assistance system (see Figure 7.3) by integrating the constraints of a pluridisciplinary development and the time necessary to carry out the ergonomic and behavioral analyses essential to definition of the real needs of users and the situations to assist. To this end, a first planning stage enabled all the analyses to be defined that need to integrate the driver and the contexts of use. This stage ensured the choice of necessary tools to guarantee the efficiency of the

---

3 V Cycle: software design method comparing the development phases and associated test phases.

approach, by minimizing the occupation of the driving simulator. These tools enabled the application of several iterative cycles in development of the system by integrating the results of the analyses progressively, according to their availability.

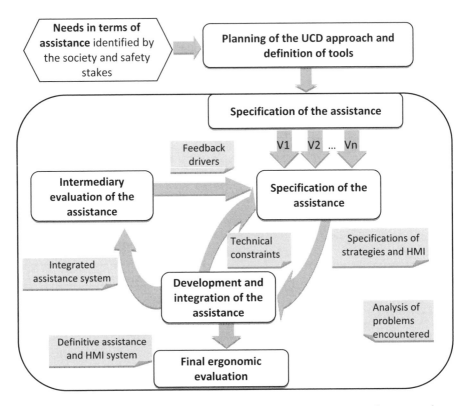

Figure 7.3. *UCD approach used for the design of the VIVRE2 system on a driving simulator*

Traditionally, the UCD approach anticipates the iterative realization of contexts of use at each new evolution of the system. In the case of the VIVRE2 project, apart from the first series of analysis of driver-deliverer activities in a natural situation with no assistance system, the intermediary evaluations of the system being developed were carried out in a table and on a driving simulator (the realization of a demonstrator did not enter into the scope of this project). Moreover, given the time constraints, it was impossible to wait for the termination of contextual analyses to initiate the first development cycle. The results were therefore integrated progressively according to their availability, to define increasingly precise functional specifications of the assistance. At the beginning of the project, these were basic (types of user to be detected, type of information and control delivered by the assistance). They became clearer and, in the end, became scenarios of use of the system, including the sequential description of system/driver interactions.

The key stage of the approach was specification of the assistance, with the involvement of all partners. It enabled the specifications to evolve according to results of the analysis of the contexts of use and intermediary evaluations, as well as the technical constraints encountered during the development and integration of the assistance. During this stage, included in the "development-evaluation-specification" cycles of a classic text, the engineers adjusted the specifications according to preliminary texts on the simulator carried out by the ergonomists (which enabled the evaluation of system modifications in terms of efficiency and usability in the context of the driving task). Shorter cycles between development and specification were added to meet needs according to the technical possibilities.

7.3. Contextual analyses in natural situations

The first stage of the UCD approach previously shown consisted of an analysis of the contexts of application of the VIVRE2 system.

The issue of the design of driving assistance is within the context of a "multi-composite" dynamic road system. The "components" of this system are not only technological objects (vehicles, infrastructures), but also and especially humans, whether they are truck drivers or vulnerable road users. Thus, the difficulty of the realization is intimately linked to the knowledge and consideration of these different users, each traveling according to their own agenda and goals. (For example, the pedestrian who is shopping and crosses the road to take advantage of an offer on the other side of the road who is unaware of the vehicle, whereas the driver, preoccupied with his itinerary search, is not expecting this risky behavior. Another notable example is that of the cyclist, who tries to overtake the truck on the pavement side, taking advantage of space the driver has made to make his turn.)

Thus, developing a driving aid system, making it possible to avoid accidents between an industrial vehicle and vulnerable users implies not only knowledge of the activity of the drivers, but also knowledge of their interactions with vulnerable users and that of the attitudes and behaviors of the latter who are potentially the cause of accidents. This is why this stage consists of a series of analyses of driver-deliverers activities in a natural situation, completed by a study of the behaviors and attitudes of vulnerable users during their journeys in an urban environment.

7.3.1. *Analysis of the activity of driver-deliverers*

A specific knowledge of the activity of driver-deliverers carrying out daily deliveries in town should enable us to specify the characteristics of the assistance system in terms of strategies (passive, informative and/or active) and restitution modes (HMIs) as well as the different situations potentially requiring assistance. In view of this, activity analyses were carried out according to the rounds of 15 driver-deliverers on board their usual vehicle (average age: 40 years old).

The methodological approach adopted was based on gathering the verbalizations of drivers *in situ* and on recording events in the environment and driver behaviors that can be observed during their rounds in the centre of the town of Lyon (see Figure 7.4). Individual interviews with the drivers made it possible to specify the idea that they have of vulnerable users in an urban environment and to define their needs and expectations in terms of driving assistance [MAI 11].

Figure 7.4. *Images taken during analyses of the activity of driver-deliverers*

The drivers expressed having been under permanent stress due to the high time pressure that is inherent to delivery requirements, but also due to the constant risk of accidents with vulnerable users. According to drivers, the latter are rarely aware of the inherent difficulties of driving a heavy vehicle, particularly of the blind spots around the truck that make their detection difficult if not impossible (behind, lateral blind spot). They are generally unaware of the difficulty of maneuvers due to the length (turn right, parallel parking) and weight of the vehicle (breaking). Furthermore, the observations recorded *in situ* showed that vulnerable users too often adopt behaviors that contravene their safety. For example, impromptu crossing in front of the moving truck, when the priority is to the vehicle or outside a pedestrian crossing; cyclists and motorcyclists who edge alongside the vehicle; pedestrians not taking into account the warning sound signaling that the truck is reversing, etc.

The day we followed the drivers begins at 5 o'clock in the morning. After having collected the list of clients they will have to deliver to, they verify the loading of the truck and check the order according to which the round is organized, taking into account time requirements set by the client or various constraints that they know of from their experience of the round (access times in pedestrian sectors, market days, proximity to a school, etc.). Once these verifications and preparations have been made, they can begin. The activity of driver-deliverers includes two different periods, for an average round of 20 deliveries over around 10 hours in an urban environment: the driving phases represent around 31% of the work time and the stationary and delivery phases represent the remaining 69%. The driving periods are themselves distributed in two phases:

– travel to and from the depot to the delivery site, in peri-urban zones, for which the average recorded speed is 60 km/h; and

– travel in urban delivery zones, for which the average recorded speed is 14km/h.

The latter comprises a large number of low-speed maneuvers. For each driver we have recorded around seven to 10 reverse maneuvers, two to six turn-around maneuvers, nine double parking maneuvers, two parking-in-a-pedestrian-zone maneuvers) and numerous interactions with vulnerable users, essentially pedestrians and cyclists.

Three actions concerning problems of multi-activity at the wheel that regularly recur throughout the round were identified:

– the *itinerary search,* often without the help of a navigation system;

– *use of the cell phone*: the drivers use their telephone to ask a colleague something about a client or a delivery place or to help a colleague in the same way;

– *consulting the delivery slips*.

These actions can be carried out during a delivery stop, during a stop at a red light or while driving. These multiple constraints led to drivers having a heavy physical and cognitive workload, to which a high level of stress was added. The association of these conditions can have negative repercussions individually in terms of attention, driving behaviors and health, as well as collectively in terms of impact on road safety. The system developed will naturally need to take into account these observations, insisting in particular on the ergonomics of HMIs that must not increase the driver's workload.

Finally, the spontaneous reports gathered during the analyses highlighted a real need in terms of *assistance with vision at the rear of the vehicle*. A large majority of drivers (13 out of 15) spontaneously suggested the installation of a camera at the rear of the truck with feedback to a screen installed on the dashboard to the left in the field of vision of the driver. The central position was rejected as the driver never looks at the centre of the dashboard when he is reversing. More globally, they were not opposed to the installation of assistance systems for the detection and prevention of accidents with vulnerable users, but they insisted on the need to have a reliable system that is not "constantly beeping". Moreover, in so far as their activity often includes the itinerary search, most of them deem that the installation of a navigation system coupled with rear vision would enable them to use the same screen for both systems and limit the use of cell phones while driving.

Let us specify that the trucks used for the delivery activities generally did not have an assistance system to facilitate maneuvers in town. For the detection of vulnerable users, they only had lateral wing mirrors (two per side) and did not have a rear vision or front view mirror.

Given these observations, it seems that an assistance system destined for the detection and prevention of accidents with vulnerable road users, in addition to the benefit in terms of road safety, should significantly improve the work conditions of industrial vehicle drivers in towns.

7.3.2. Behaviors and risk taking of vulnerable users that cause critical situations

In order to specify the nature of the interactions between vulnerable users (essentially pedestrians and cyclists) and trucks, which are at the origin of potentially critical situations, the analyses of the activity of drivers were completed by studying the risky behaviors of vulnerable users [MAI 08]. The objective of this study was the evaluation of the danger associated with around 15 road situations in an urban environment and the risk-taking of users when set in these situations. Evaluation was carried out by a panel of 142 subjects (from 12 to 77 years of age, male and female).

An original projective tool, based on video sequences filmed in an urban environment (town centre of Lyon), was built to enable the subjects to contextualize dynamic situations as well as possible. Scenes were selected based on accident research data from various regional and national databases[4], specific studies [BRE 03] and results of analysis of driver activities. They are particularly focused on situations of crossing straight areas, pedestrians walking on the road and low-speed truck maneuvers in a pedestrian area. The scenes were presented on a DVD that could be played on a computer (PC or Mac) or a living room DVD player. The

---

4 BAAC (Report of the Analysis of Corporal Accidents) and the ARVAC (Association for the Register of Traffic accident victims in the Rhone region of France).

subjects had 30 to 45 minutes to watch the DVD and complete the paper-pen questionnaire[5] that accompanied it (Figure 7.5).

Figure 7.5. *Study of travel in town, experimental condition*

The results have shown that the main aspects that come into play in the representation of a dangerous situation are mainly linked to the infrastructure in which it unfolds (area open to traffic versus pedestrian area). On one hand, transgression of the Highway Code linked to the infrastructure, and, in particular, crossing outside pedestrian crossings, which are the major cause of accidents involving pedestrians in towns, is recognized as being a real danger, and due to risk taken by the user. (This does not stop the pedestrians questioned from frequently adopting these risky behaviors.) On the other hand, and rightly so, the pedestrian area is a protected environment for pedestrians who consider that they have priority at all times and seem to be unaware of the existence of a potential risk (it is not rare to observe pedestrians passing and even stopping behind a truck without considering the warning signal to say that it is reversing). However, though in principle reserved to pedestrians and by extension to vulnerable users (except motorcyclists), at certain times these areas must be shared with trucks that are making deliveries. It therefore seems that the safety of vulnerable users in a pedestrian area rests mainly on the behavior of drivers, who will need to intensify their attention *vis-à-vis* users moving around their vehicle.

Finally, the fact that more than half of subjects admit to adopting potentially risky behavior in certain situations shows that the behaviors of vulnerable users cannot, in many cases, be anticipated by truck drivers. (Examples of these behaviors

---

5 The DVD and questionnaire that accompanies it are protected by article L. 122-4 of the intellectual property code (legal deposit: January 2007).

include, walking in front of a moving truck, thinking that it has unlimited breaking abilities; overtaking a truck on the inside thinking there is enough time to pass before it turns; not taking into account the backup signal, etc.)

7.4. Specification of the assistance

All the results previously obtained enabled us to initiate the key stage of the approach, i.e. develop the specifications of the assistance.

The VIVRE2 system was designed to assist drivers in many critical situations involving vulnerable users, pedestrians and cyclists, and industrial vehicles in an urban environment at a low speed. From a functional point of view, a critical situation is a situation requiring information feedback from the systems (informative system) associated with an adjustment of the driving action from the driver and/or system (active assistance). Thus, before more specifically defining the assistance strategies of systems and human–machine systems by enabling the application, it was essential to identify these situations.

7.4.1. *Identification of cases of use*

The study was based on the results of analyses carried out at the previous stage completed by accident research reports. The situations retained are representative of accidents that are statistically the most frequent and situations to which drivers are confronted daily and that they describe as being particularly stressful. This is the case, in particular, when reversing industrial vehicles, for which the drivers observed the need for assistance during the analysis of activities clearly expressed (vision and detection of users). It is the same for situations of sudden crossing by a pedestrian during a distribution round. Finally, the turning right with a cyclist in the right blind spot was highlighted by the services in charge road safety in Paris, who have been confronted with a renewed upsurge of this type of accident since the implementation of the VéLib service (free service bicycles) and the services operating urban buses (KEOLIS in Lyon).

In total, three classes of situation (C1 to C3) and six critical situations were retained (S1 to S6, see Table 7.1): the situations of reversing and at the start, going forward and at the start, turning right after a traffic light and overtaking a user on the road (pedestrian or cyclist) going the same way (Figure 7.6).

SITUATION	TRUCK MANEUVER	POSITION OF THE USER
C1 – REVERSE		
	S1: Start 0-5 km/h	Stationary pedestrian 0 km/h
	S2: Reversing maneuver 0-10 km/h	Pedestrian in movement 2-3 km/h
C2 – FORWARD		
	S3: Start 0-5 km/h	Stationary pedestrian 0 km/h
	S4: Exit double parking 5-15 km/h	Pedestrian in movement 2-3 km/h
	S5: Overtaking a user on the road 20/40 km/h	Cyclist in movement 5-10 km/h
C3 – TURN RIGHT going FORWARD		
	S6: Turn right slowly 0-20 km/h	Cyclist in movement 5-10 km/h

Table 7.1. *Description of critical situations retained for evaluation of the system*

Figure 7.6. *Examples of critical situations recorded in an urban environment*

All these situations were tested in three scenarios that supported an experiment on the ergonomic and functional evaluation of the system on the driving simulator of Renault Trucks.

7.4.2. *Specifications of assistance strategies*

The objectives of this stage were to determine the principles and functioning strategies of the system and the warnings as well as their output modes.

The system developed comprises two modes of assistance, defined according to the interaction level of the system with the driver:

– a mode that we can qualify as "passive" or "informative": the system delivers information or warnings, without acting on the piloting;

– a so-called "active" or "automated" mode that takes into account the behaviors and intentions of the driver: the system temporarily takes charge of piloting the vehicle.

From a functional point of view, the "informative" mode is based on the detection of vulnerable users by different sensors, according to situations encountered. Devices of direct or indirect vision and light and sound warnings enable the driver to be warned of a potential risk, all the while letting him take the initiative of action.

The "active" mode, associated with the informative mode, includes three levels of action (speed regulator, emergency breaking and immobilizer), the setting off of which differs according to the criticality levels of the situation:

– The situation is critical when the trajectory of the vulnerable user is heading towards and is close to the truck: only the speed is limited by the system.

– The situation is very critical when the trajectory of the vulnerable user crosses that of the truck. In this case, the system takes control of the vehicle (emergency breaking or immobilizer).

The two functioning modes of the system have limitations that are inherent to their specificity. The informative mode only works between 0 and 60 km/h; and the active mode between 0 and 30 km/h. The immobilizer does not stop the engine working, but the movement of the vehicle, engineer working and speed engaged.

7.4.3. Specifications of the human-machine interface (HMI)

This third phase, in dissociable from and complementary to the previous one, aimed to specify physical and functional characteristics of the HMI enabling the transmission of information and warnings from the different detection systems. The HMI of the VIVRE2 system is a multimodal interface that includes visual and sound components. All these components are piloted by the VIVRE2 system and organized according to the assistance strategies determined.

Given the specificities of the expected assistance, i.e. covering three zones around the vehicle, the HMI of VIVRE2 is in fact made up of three distinct devices (see Figure 7.7, top section) each comprising visual feedback on a screen (rear and lateral) or by mirror (front view mirror), a directional luminous alarm and a sound alarm. The luminous diodes (Figure 7.7, top half) are intuitive interfaces only used to attract attention and direct the gaze of the driver in a given direction. The driver must not try to understand the significance of the signal, but should look in the direction of the light to check and confirm the presence of an obstacle via the means of the available HMIs.

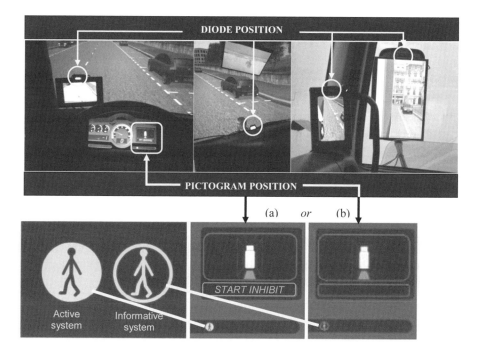

Figure 7.7. *Visual interfaces for the rear, front and lateral zones*

These interfaces are completed by a common visual interface. Composed of several information pictograms (Figure 7.7, bottom half), this interface is integrated to the display cluster of the dashboard. The display is a function of the activated assistance mode (Figure 7.7): (a) active mode; and (b) informative mode.

The pictograms enable the zone in which a user is detected to be signaled, the activated assistance mode (immobilizer, emergency breaking, regulator) to be specified and the system that is functioning (active/informative) to be indicated. These displays are meant to alert the driver and provide him with an explanation, as the need may be, when a system is set off.

7.5. Development and integration of assistance solutions on a driving simulator

From a functional point of view, the system integrated in the simulator must:

– recuperate data on the simulation environment (position of mobile objects around the vehicle, actions of the driver, dynamics of the vehicle);

– simulate the outputs of the perception sensors regarding these data (estimation of the position of vulnerable users detected in the frame of reference of each sensor);

– generate a map of the environment based on different simulated sensors (representation of the position of all vulnerable users in the frame of reference of the truck);

– define the warnings and/or active controls necessary for the assistance system (selection of information to give to the driver and of the adapted warning level according to the behavior of the driver);

– generate warnings or controls in the simulation environment (piloting of physical interfaces, such as screens, diodes and loud speakers).

7.5.1. *Implementation of the user-centered design approach*

To implement the UCD approach, the development process (Figure 7.6) was broken down into three stages in the laboratory (development, integration and tests) and two on the simulator (intermediary and final evaluations):

– The "development of the assistance" stage enables us to create the module of the assistance system that defines the active warnings or controls with the help of models of the environment and the driver. This stage enables the development of all the algorithms of the decision module that, based on a map of the environment containing all the objects around a vehicle, defines the type of assistance required (warning, taking control of the vehicle) and its level of intrusion.

– The "testing of the assistance" stage is done on two levels. Either the whole assistance system is validated on pre-recorded data, or the decision module of the assistance alone is validated thanks to a tool that "generates a dynamic scenario" by use case taking place temporally with the help of a dynamic scenario. Each case being a fragmented and static part of the solution, this tool enables us to take into account the temporal evolution of the situation and to integrate all the needs of the cases into a single, homogenous and coherent system. The example below presents the interfaces of the dynamic scenario generator for a situation that required emergency breaking:

- the left part of Figure 7.8 is a view from above the positions of the vehicle and the vulnerable user as well as the open spaces covered by detection zones;

- the right part of Figure 7.8 shows that the temporal speed and acceleration curves as well as the activation levels of the active assistances (level 0: no active assistance, level 1: regulator, level 2: emergency breaking) and informative (level 0: no assistance, level 1: visual, level 2: visual and sound).

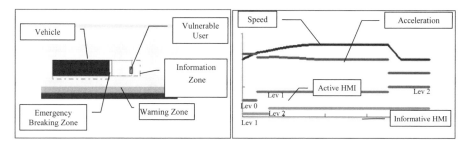

Figure 7.8. *Interfaces of the dynamic scenario generator for emergency breaking*

Finally the "integration of the assistance" stage enables the model to function on real data coming from the driving simulator. The outputs of perception sensors are simulated from this data to generate a map of the environment and they translate the type of assistance required as well as its level in terms of activation orders in the HMI (lighting of visual interfaces, triggering of sound interfaces, activation of active controls). All the functionalities have been integrated in an integration platform used either in "online" mode (connected to the driving simulator), or in "offline" mode (enabling it to replay previously recorded data).

The necessary iterative cycles (Figure 7.9) have finally been defined. The definition cycles (D cycles) enable us to take into account the evolving specifications that come from the refinement of the analysis of contexts and integrate the technical constraints encountered in the development stages. The validation cycles (V cycles) enable the developments to be validated. Three in total, the V cycles become increasingly long as the development progresses:

– The short V1 cycle enables the coherence of the functioning of the assistance to be identified over all use cases by using the scenario simulation tool, which includes all the models that implement the assistance strategies. This tool therefore enables implementation of the strategy of a given scenario after each evolution of the module for selection of the adapted aid and testing of the repercussion on others.

– The V2 cycle, which lasts a long time, allows validation of the functioning of assistance with the integration platform on real pre-recorded data ("offline" mode). Initially, the integration of modules for the simulation of sensors and the module implementing assistance strategies as well as communication between modules are validated. Then, assistance is tested on pre-recorded data.

– The V3 cycle, which is longer still as it requires the use of the simulator. It enables the integration of the assistance to be validated, in particular for communication with the driving simulator, thanks to the integration platform which functions in "online" mode (that is to say on the data transmitted in real time) and intermediary evaluations of different versions of the assistance in critical scenarios to be carried out.

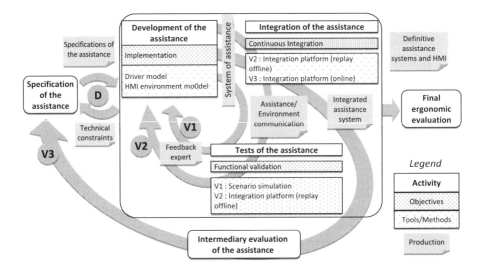

Figure 7.9. *Development process of the VIVRE2 system according to a UCD approach*

7.5.2. *Description of an adaptive solution*

The architecture of the system was developed by using an "adaptive technological" type approach, i.e. that adapts the functioning of the system to take into account the behavior of the driver in a given situation [BEL 05]. For this, a model of the intention of the driver was implemented. This model is used by the assistance like any input on a par with the data of the perception of the external environment.

7.5.2.1. *Vulnerable user detection zones*

The system selects the type of assistance with the help of two available information sources: information on the possible position of vulnerable users (in front, behind, or on the right-hand side of the vehicle) and information regarding the actions of the driver (Figure 7.10). This information is then compared to the intentions of the driver, which are inferred from a "driver intention model", in order to determine the adapted assistance strategy, and then to run the HMI.

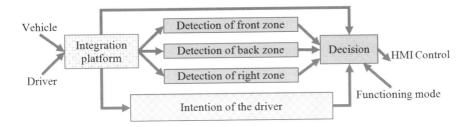

Figure 7.10. *Architecture of the assistance*

The functioning principle of the VIVRE2 system is based on an assistance strategy that varies according to the proximity of vulnerable users. For this, the space around the vehicle has been segmented into three decision zone families (Figure 7.11):

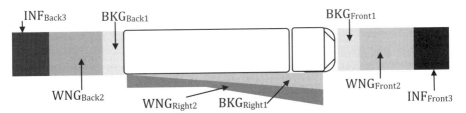

Figure 7.11. *Decision zones of the functioning of the assistance*

– The "emergency braking, braking" (BKG) zone corresponds to situations in which a user is in immediate danger. It is applicable to the front, back, and right spaces of the vehicle.

– The "warning" (WNG) zone corresponds to situations in which a user is in danger if the driver does not react quickly enough. It is applicable to the front, back, and right spaces of the vehicle.

– The "information" (INF) zone, corresponds to situations in which a user is in deferred danger: he could be in danger in the next few seconds if the driver has not detected him. It is applicable to the front and back spaces of the vehicle.

7.5.2.2. *Driver intention model*

In addition to the consideration of the presence and proximity of vulnerable users around the vehicle, the VIVRE2 systems function differently depending on the behavior of the driver, by estimating whether or not he has taken the danger into account [TAT 10]. The behaviors of the driver were categorized according to several intention levels by breaking down the starting of the vehicle into four phases for which the information given to the driver can be different (Figure 7.12):

– stop: the driver is not doing anything to indicate a maneuver;

– selection of the direction of the maneuver: the driver shows his intention to initiate a maneuver;

– starting: the driver initiates a maneuver; and

– moving forward: the driver carried out a maneuver.

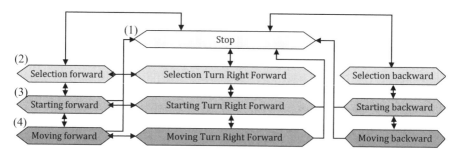

Figure 7.12. *Driver intention model for the activation of the system*

The model retained comprises three intention levels that are involved during the realization of three maneuvers identified in the scenarios described in Table 7.1 ("moving forward", "reversing" and "turn right while moving forward"). Nine states therefore combine these two criteria (situation to be covered and activity phases of the driver) and the tenth corresponds to "stop" (see Figure 7.12).

As the assistance strategies during the forward maneuvers are different depending on whether the driver turns right (consideration of the vulnerable users coming along the right-hand side of the vehicle) or not (consideration of the vulnerable user in front of the vehicle only), the states are duplicated. Moreover, these states are connected as the evolution of "moving forward" to "turn right" can occur without going via the "stop" stage, which is not the case for the change between "going forward" and "reversing".

The advantage of this type of model is twofold. First, it takes into account the intentions of the driver that are inferred based on his behavior in real time, for example, when the driver shifts into reverse, the speed is lower than a given threshold and the accelerator is greater than a given threshold, the intention is "back selection". This requires the different states of the driver to be defined and then the objective measures which could differentiate them to be searched for. Second, this model provides a semantic of the activity that can be understood whatever the discipline: the ergonomics will be able to validate the functioning of the HMI according to the states of the driver and the technologists can work on the algorithms allowing their identification. Any change in technology on the vehicle (for example a change of the gearbox type) will only affect this second aspect.

7.5.2.3. *Decision tables*

The spatial partition defined around the vehicle in terms of detection zones and the characterization of the activity of the driver defined in 10 states enables a finite number of possible input states to be obtained. Two decision tables (one for informative functioning and the other for active functioning) with two dimensions (activity and decision zone) show the level of assistance provided for each combination: no assistance (NoAss), non intrusive information (INF), a warning (WNG) or active assistance (emergency braking–BKG-start inhibit-SIN-).

These tables also enable the evolution of situations to be apprehended by taking into account the evolution of the maneuver resulting from the behavior of the driver (decision to start, starting, move forward) and the evolution of the movement of a vulnerable user.

Decision		Driver's Intention				
Vuln. User front area	Vuln. User right area	Selection Fwd	Starting Fwd	Moving Fwd	Selection RightFwd	Starting RightFwd
		Progress of manoeuvre →				
Near		No Ass	INFfront	WNGright	No Ass	INFfront
Near	Near	No Ass	INFfront	WNGright	INFright	WNG front right
Near	Very Near	No Ass	INFfront	WNGright	INFright	SINright

Table 7.2. *Extract from a decision table*

For example, in the presence of a vulnerable user in the near front zone (Table 7.2, line 1), the information delivered evolves from an absence of assistance if the intention model is in the "selection" state, to an unobtrusive informative assistance (solely visual if the intention model is in the "Starting" state), then to a stronger informative assistance (visual and sound) if the intention model is in the "moving forward" state. The intensity of alarms therefore intensifies as the maneuver progresses. However, if the intention model remains in the same state, for example the "Starting turn right going forward" (Table 7.2, column 7), and a vulnerable user appears in the near right zone (Table 7.2, line 2, column 2), the visual information as well as the sound alarm is set off (WNG). If this user is moving towards the very near right zone (Table 7.2, line 3, column 2), the system will activate the immobilizer (SINright). This double reading enables us to gain an overview of the progress of situations in time and thus to ensure coherence of the functioning of the assistance according to the evolution of the situation.

7.6. Evaluation of solutions on a driving simulator

Once the iterative validation cycles V1 and V2 are finished (see Figure 7.3), the next stage, dedicated to the validation of the system developed, was carried out on the dynamic truck simulator of Renault Trucks (SCOOP[6]). It occurred in two steps (V3 cycle, Figure 7.3). An initial intermediary phase enabled the modifications and/or adjustments that need to be carried out to be identified, as much for the assistance strategies and HMIs as for the progress of virtual situations. The second phase constituted the experimental part dedicated to the final ergonomic evaluation of the HMIs and assistance strategies. Each phase progressed according to a distinct experimental procedure.

For these tests, the simulator was equipped with a "Renault Midlum" type cab, mounted on a dynamic platform at an optional possible six degrees (Figure 7.13, left-hand side). The interactive vehicle (simulated vehicle) was a "carrier" type truck (Figure 7.13, right-hand side), representative of a large number of town distribution vehicles.

Figure 7.13. *FIDEUS demonstration truck (with a Midlum cab) and platform of the driving simulator equipped with a Midlum cab*

---

6 Driving simulator for the optimization and objectification of performances.

The virtual urban environment (City NG) used for the tests was defined and designed, especially for the VIVRE2 project and the experimentation scenarios required the adjustment and mastering of complex interactions, in real time, between mobile simulation elements (pedestrians and cyclists) and the interactive vehicle.

7.6.1. *Intermediary evaluation by experts*

The intermediary evaluation was carried out with four drivers that had experience of driving a truck (1,000 to 3,000 km/per year), three test technicians, experts in system tests, and an ergonomist from Renault Trucks. Its objectives were: first the development of simulation scenarios requiring the activation of the assistance; second the functional evaluation and the adjustment of VIVRE2 system in situation; and finally the realization of an initial ergonomic evaluation of the assistance strategies and the HMIs.

The test protocol consisted of two parts. The first part enabled drivers to test the behavior of the system for around 30 minutes on the simulator. The different HMIs were evaluated both when stationary and in movement (reversing or going forward). In the second part of the protocol, the drivers completed different questionnaires dedicated to the ergonomic evaluation and more specifically, see Table 7.3, to:

– the positioning and legibility of visual feedback, screens and diodes;

– the understanding of visual and sound information;

– the utility, understanding, relevance and efficiency of information;

– the utility and relevance of emergency braking;

– the potential hindrance provoked by the functioning of the system.

An interview complemented these questionnaires, recording the comments and suggestions of drivers regarding the improvement of the system and its components.

In addition to the essential developments for carrying out the final evaluation, this phase enabled us to solve problems linked to interactive situations on the simulator and to improve the first version of the HMI (adjustment of the view of the rear camera, positioning of the screen, adjustment of the luminosity of diodes and the volume of sound warnings, modifications of the characters of the visual interfaces of the display cluster for better legibility, etc.).

7.6.2. *Final evaluation by professional drivers*

The intermediate evaluation was immediately followed by a new phase of specification and development in order to update the HMIs and the assistance strategies for the final evaluation stage.

This final stage of the VIVRE2 project aimed to evaluate the relevance, functioning principles and strategies of the system as well as that of their restitution mode (visual interfaces and alarms). From an ergonomic point of view, the VIVRE2 system was evaluated by drivers in terms of usability and acceptability, perceived utility and efficiency as well as understanding of assistance strategies. The mental work-load caused by use of the system in the active and informative mode was measured for each subject, and compared to a driving situation with no system.

Fifteen male professional drivers (average age: 45) participated in the trials. For each of them, the experimental procedure consisted of four sessions lasting one hour each and spread over four non-consecutive days. These four sessions were carried out on a complex and dense urban circuit and enabled three conditions to be tested: a "familiarization" condition, a condition with "informative system only" and a condition with "informative and active system". Each condition consisted of a different itinerary, simulating a delivery round in a town with different maneuvers to carry out in order to be able to park. Six test situations were reproduced in each condition to enable the subjects to evaluate the system in different cases of use and to test its efficiency by counting the number of accidents that are "potentially" avoided. In order to control the impact of learning, the itineraries and test situations were presented to subjects randomly. Moreover, the situations were positioned in different places on the circuit for each experimental condition. Finally, each situation was replicated at least twice per condition with and without criticality and presented in a random way. For example, reversing to park in a pedestrian zone or a cul-de-sac, condition 1 was carried out without a vulnerable user behind the truck and condition 2 had one or two pedestrians having a discussion behind the truck. Each session was made up of a "moving forward" part on the simulator followed by an "ergonomic evaluation" part. The mental work-load of drivers was evaluated with the help of a modified version of the NASA TLX[7] [HAR 88]. This method was adapted for the situations of evaluation of assistance systems for driving a truck on a simulator [MAI 11]. The dimensions taken into account in this version are attention, visual requirements, auditory requirements, disturbance (here caused by the

---

7 The NASA Task Load index is a multidimensional method destined for subjective evaluation of the workload felt by an operator. The first three dimensions represent the damage imposed on the subject by the task (mental, physical and time requirements) and the three others account for the interactions of the subject with the task (performance, effort and frustration). The test provides a global weighted score of the workload and enables identification of the specific task for a given task or system.

VIVRE2 system), stress and performance. The tools destined for the evaluation of systems were made up of observation grids completed in real time by the researcher (number of users detected, knocked over, avoided, times when the system was set off) and questionnaires in the form of Likert[8] scales (see Table 7.3). A final questionnaire at the end of the experiment asked the drivers to choose which system they would advise installing on future trucks regularly circulating in an urban environment. These questionnaires were completed by feedback in the form of an individual psychological interview with each driver. The objective of this interview was to check that situations during which the drivers had potentially knocked over a vulnerable user had not caused a psychological shock.

PROPOSALS	DESCRIBERS	
What do you think of active braking?		
Active braking is	*from* Awkward	*to* Not awkward
In terms of security active braking is	*from* Inefficient	*to* Efficient
The use of active braking in driving is	*from* Unpleasant	*to* Pleasant
With active braking driving it is	*from* Disrupted	*to* Facilitated
Globally active braking is	*from* Useless	*to* Essential
What do you think of the pictograms on the display?		
For safety, pictograms are	*from* Inefficient	*to* Efficient
During driving, display of pictograms is	*from* Awkward	*to* Not awkward
With pictograms, driving is	*from* Disrupted	*to* Facilitated
Globally pictograms are	*from* Useless	*to* Essential
The information given by pictograms is	*From* Incomprehensible	*to* Comprehensible
Globally what do you think of the rear detection system?		
The use of the system seemed	*from* Difficult	*to* Simple
For maneuvers the system is	*from* Unpleasant	*to* Pleasant
Globally the system is	*from* Useless	*to* Essential
With the system, the maneuvers in town are	*from* Disrupted	*to* Facilitated
In terms of safety, the system is	*from* Inefficient	*to* Efficient

Table 7.3. *Examples of questions comprising the Likert scales*

The results of this evaluation on a simulator were very conclusive regarding all the dimensions that were chosen. The auto-evaluation of the mental work-load of

---

8 Our Likert scales were presented in the form of a continuous line 10 cm in length, without graduation and with a description at each extremity. The descriptions are antonyms and the drivers had to position themselves by drawing a mark with a pencil on the line that they felt best reflected their evaluation.

drivers did not show a significant increase during driving with the system, particularly with the dimensions of visual and auditory loads, of stress and disturbance. The results obtained on a driving simulator will need to be checked in real situations during the development of the system on the vehicle.

The assistance and information strategies of the VIVRE2 system were perfectly understood and globally accepted by all the drivers. As for the choice of system that the drivers would advise installing on trucks of the future, all the subjects chose visual feedback on a screen for the rear zones and the right side blind spot as a minimum and more than two-thirds chose the complete informative system (visual feedback plus light and sound warning). Opinions diverge more regarding the front view mirror: some drivers use it without reserve, whereas others deem that the size of the truck tested enables them to see directly in front of the bonnet. For drivers who did not select the complete system, the choice of luminous and/or sound warnings seems to be according to the preferential processing channel. Around a third of subjects preferred only visual warnings and a quarter preferred only sound warnings.

Results were more mixed regarding the choice of the complete and "ideal" VIVRE2 system. These results reflect an important individual variability that cannot be smoothed out due to the small size of the cross section. This variability is particularly noticeable when taking account of the covering zone considered. Globally, a significant result emerges for the *front and back zones* of the vehicle: All the drivers chose the start inhibit and 75 to 85% completed it with the emergency braking. Whatever their choices, all the drivers associated the active system with visual information feedback. However, the *rejection of the regulator* is significant for a large part of drivers (90 to 100% rejected the regulator, depending on the zone covered).

Finally, in terms of objective efficiency, for all the simulation protocols for all subjects, the VIVRE2 system enabled 89% of potentially critical situations to be avoided.

These results, for the most part positive from an ergonomical (acceptability and usability), cognitive (comprehension and mental load) and functional point of view, enabled us to conclude that the system could be developed in its current form on demonstration vehicles, subject to a few modifications (regulator to be revised, for example).

In conclusion, the VIVRE2 system, as it was designed and tested, has a certain advantage in reducing the number of accidents involving vulnerable road users and industrial vehicles in an urban environment. Nonetheless the development of such a system requires even more iterative evaluation phases of functional and ergonomic evaluations, in real conditions of delivery activity and in real driving situations, which does not enter into the scope of this project.

7.7. Conclusions and viewpoints

From the point of view of design, the approach implemented was UCD. Its focal development point was the needs of users and this enabled the design of a system that was well accepted by the latter. The iterative UCD cycle meets the needs of regularly re-examining the specifications. However, though the traditional approach involved sometimes very costly developments, it turned out to be necessary to find solutions enabling developments carried out in parallel by different teams working on the project. We therefore proposed a methodology integrating the new validation cycles to reduce the costs of tests. These cycles allowed the results of the analysis of driver activities carried out in parallel, and the different stages of the process such as they are described by [MAG 01] to be taken into account.

The phases of specification of the user needs led to the definition of typical situations that required specific assistance: two reversing situations (in movement and when starting to move), two situations of moving forward (in movement and when starting to move), a situation of turning right after starting at a light, and an situation of overtaking a vulnerable user on the road going in the same direction. The assistance system retained consisted of an immobilizer, emergency brake and a speed regulator, completed by visual informative feedback by rear and side cameras and by flashing lights and sound warnings in the cab. The ergonomic evaluation phase on a simulator was necessary to lead to the proposal of this adaptive system. Designed to diminish the number of accidents between vulnerable users and industrial vehicles in an urban environment, it is based on dynamic assistance strategies according to driver behaviors and the behaviors of vulnerable user(s) in a given situation. Evaluated in a virtual world by a panel of truck drivers, the VIVRE2 system has proven its efficiency on a driving simulator: thanks to the system, 89% of accidents were avoided over the course of the experiments. Moreover, the results of the ergonomic evaluation attest that the system should be well accepted by drivers and that its use should not lead to a cognitive and informational overload.

In conclusion, the generic methodological framework presented in this chapter proved its efficiency and met both objectives of the project and will be used in future projects to design an aid system on a simulator that based on the needs of the driver that uses perception technology.

This type of approach can be extended to the design of demonstrators in real driving situations. Thus, a follow up of this work proposes deploying the results broadening the field of application to urban buses and to all the users involved (pedestrians, cyclists, following vehicles). It can also be used to demonstrate the technical feasibility of the VIVRE2 system on two demonstrators: one truck demonstrator and one bus demonstrator. Assistance solutions will also be put forward for other users (vulnerable users and vehicles in proximity).

7.8. Bibliography

[BAR 09] BARCENILLA J., BASTIEN J.M.C., "L'acceptabilité des nouvelles technologies: quelle relation avec l'ergonomie, l'utilisabilité et l'expérience utilisateur?", *Le Travail Humain*, vol. 72, no. 4, pp. 305-310, 2009.

[BEL 05] BELLET T., TATTEGRAIN-VESTE H., BONNARD A., "Risk of collision and nehavior adequacy assessment for managing human-machine interaction", *Human-Computer Interaction International Congress*, Las Vegas, Nevada, USA, July 22-27 2005.

[BRE 03] BRENAC T., NACHTERGAËLE C., REIGNER H., Scénarios types d'accidents impliquant des piétons et éléments pour leur prévention, Study Report INRETS n° 256, Collections of l'INRETS, Arcueil, France, 2003.

[CHA 08] CHAPELON J., LAGACHE M., *Grands Thèmes de la Sécurité Routière en France: Édition 2008*, la Documentation Française, Paris, France, 2008.

[FIS 01] FISHER G., "User modeling in human computer interaction", *Journal of User Modeling and User-Adapted Interaction*, vol. 11, no. 1-2, pp. 65-86, 2001.

[GOU 85] GOULD D.J., LEWIS C., "Designing for usability: key principles and what designers think", *Communications of the ACM*, vol. 28, no. 3, pp. 300-311, 1985.

[HAN 99] HANCOCK P.A., PARASURAMAN R., "Driver centered issues in advanced automation for motor vehicles", in: R. PARASURAMAN and M. MOULOUA (eds), *Automation and Human Performance*, Lawrence Erlbaum Associates, Mahwah, USA, 1999.

[HAR 03] HART S.G., STAVELAND L.E., "Development of a multi-dimensional workload rating scale: Results of empirical and theoretical research", in: HANCOCK P.A., MESHKATI N. (eds), *Human mental workload*, pp. 139-183, Elsevier, Amsterdam, The Netherlands, 2003.

[HIC 10] HICKMAN J.S., HANOWSKI R.J., BOCANEGRA J., Distraction in Commercial Trucks and Buses: Assessing Prevalence and Risk in Conjunction with Crashes and Near-crashes, Report FMCSA-RRR-10-049, 2010.

[KOL 98] KOLSKI C., "A call for tender around the proposal of an HCI-enriched model", *ACM SIGSOFT Software Engineering Notes*, vol. 23, no. 3, pp. 93-96, 1998.

[LAN 04] LANSDOWN T.C., BROOK-CARTER N., KERSLOOT T., "Distraction from multiple in-vehicle secondary tasks: vehicle performance and mental workload implications", *Ergonomics*, vol. 47, no. 1, pp. 91-104, 2004.

[LEE 97] LEE J.D., "A functional description of ATIS/CVO systems to accommodate driver needs and limits", in: Y. IAN NOY (ed.), *Ergonomics and Safety of Intelligent Driver Interfaces*, pp. 63-84, Lawrence Erlbaum Associates, Mahwah, USA, 1997.

[MA 05] MA R., KABER D.B., "Situation awareness and workload in driving while using adaptive cruise control and a cell phone", *International Journal of Industrial Ergonomics*, vol. 35, no. 10, pp. 939-953, 2005.

[MCE 07] MCEVOY S.P., STEVENSON M.R., WOODWARD M., "The prevalence of, and factors associated with, serious crashes involving a distracting activity", *Accident Analysis & Prevention*, vol. 39, no. 3, pp. 475-482, 2007.

[MAG 01] MAGUIRE M., "Methods to support human-centred design", *Int. J. Human-Computer Studies*, vol. 55, no. 4, pp. 587-634, 2001.

[MAI 11] MAINCENT A., *Des Sciences Humaines aux Sciences de l'Ingénieur: Comportements Humains, Activités Finalisées et Conception de Systèmes d'Assistance à la Conduite d'un Véhicule Industriel*, Editions Universitaires Européennes, Sarrebruck, Germany, 2011.

[MAI 08] MAINCENT A., BRUN L., MARTIN R., "Pedestrians' representations about risky behaviours in urban areas", *Proceedings of International Conference on Traffic and Transport Psychology*, Washington, USA, September 1-4, 2008.

[MAL 07] MALTZ M., SHINAR D., "Imperfect in-vehicle collision avoidance warning systems can aid distracted drivers", *Transportation Research Part F*, no. 10, pp. 345-357, 2007.

[MIC 93] MICHON J.A., *Generic Intelligent Driver Support. A Comprehensive Report on GIDS*, Taylor & Francis, London, 1993.

[NIE 93] NIELSEN J., *Usability Engineering*, Academic Press, San Diego, CA, USA, 1993.

[PAR 97] PARASURAMAN R., RILEY V., "Humans and automation: use, misuse, disuse, abuse", *Human Factors*, vol. 39, no. 2, pp. 230-253, 1997.

[POP 99] POPOVIC V., "Product evaluation methods and their importance in designing interactive artefacts", in: W.S. GREEN and P.W. JORDAN (eds), *Human Factors in Product Design: Current Practice and Future Trends*, Taylor and Francis, London, 1999.

[STR 04] STRAYER D.L., DREWS F.A., "Profiles in driver distraction: effects of cell phone conversations on younger and older drivers", *Human Factors*, vol. 46, no. 4, pp. 640-649, 2004.

[TAT 10] TATTEGRAIN H., BONNARD A., "Advantages of a driver model use in the design of a driving assistance system to prevent collisions between deliver trucks and vulnerable road users", Paper presented at *Human Centred Design for Intelligent Transport Systems Berlin*, April 2010.

[TRA 04] TRANSPORT CANADA, "La sécurité des usagers de la route vulnérables: un enjeu mondial", paper presented at: *Sécurité Routière et Réglementation Automobile*, World Health Day, Paris, France, 2004.

Chapter 8

Menu Sonification in an Automotive Media Center: Design and Evaluation

8.1. General context

The automobile needs to transmit to its driver, and its occupants, a certain amount of information relative to driving and the use of life systems on board (aid with navigation via GPS or radio, for example). The passenger compartment of the car thus becomes an increasingly demanding environment in terms of sensory attention; as Ho and Spence write in the introduction of [HO 08]: "*the act of driving represents a highly complex skill requiring the sustained monitoring of integrated perceptual and cognitive inputs*".

Information is most often presented in a visual form, with the help of signals and display boards on which texts and graphics appear. The auditory modality is also mobilized when it is advantageous compared to the visual mode. This is particularly the case when the driver gets out of the vehicle and has therefore little chance to look at the instrument panel (the sound warning "forgotten light" is part of this category). Another example is when an important message – which will require a rapid reaction from the driver – appears on a display: the sound then attracts the gaze towards the visual (the sound alarm "door open while moving" corresponds to this scenario). On this subject, it is interesting to note that the reaction to a visual prompt (reaction time of around a second) is globally greater than that caused by an auditory prompt. The automobile constructor nonetheless tries not to overload the passenger compartment with sound alarms, as sound in contrast to sight, is harder to

Chapter written by Nicolas Misdariis, Julien Tardieu, Sabine Langlois and Séverine Loiseau.

ignore and can therefore very quickly become cumbersome: it is therefore advisable to use it wisely.

That being said, driving – the main task to carry out when on board the vehicle – requires very sustained visual attention. The tasks on board, secondary to driving, must therefore be able to be carried out without impairing visual concentration to the detriment of driving. This is why the auditory modality is, *in theory*, beneficial in assisting the driver in the use of multimedia systems, particularly when they offer increasingly varied functions. The benefit of these is also in the fact that they can be transposed to other domains where the notions of control and shared attention are also strategic, for example a plane cockpit or a control (or supervision) room.

Resorting to the auditory modality to help navigation in these systems therefore meets a first priority challenge on board the vehicle: to ensure driving safety. The second challenge, of an ergonomic nature, is to create a sound human-machine interface that is easy to learn and use: it will need to be intuitive so that the driver can appropriate it quickly, without the risk of his driving being affected when he is using the multimedia system. Finally, a well designed sound interface, based on quality sounds, will have the effect of contributing to the global perception of the quality of the vehicle.

In view of this, we are interested in the audification of an embedded system like an on-board computer (here called a *multimedia center*), allowing navigation in an information structure that is a part of the vehicle (functioning, navigation, etc.), includes personal data (music, photos, etc.) and mainly uses the auditory modality to leave the driver with all the concentration required by the driving situation. Integrated in a scientific approach, this study will focus on three main phases:

– analysis: includes a phase involving a state of the art from the field leading to the definition of functional specifications and the choice of design method;

– creation: this phase is associated with a composer / sound designer, the realization of sounds being carried out by implementation of the selected method;

– validation: this is a phase of evaluation of the result on the basis of *ad-hoc* methodology and in relation to the initial specifications.

This chapter presents this approach by giving details of the different stages of the process. After a presentation of the general context and the issue specific to the targeted application, the bibliographical study provides elements of state of the art that have enabled us to define an original design model. Then, after a summary of the approaches and methodological constraints relating to the experimentation in the domain of sound perception, the evaluation results of the model are discussed. In the conclusion, a discussion is opened regarding the general form of the results obtained, as well as the different possible axes to extend this work.

8.2. Specifications of the problem: identification of functions

8.2.1. *Hierarchical menu*

The frame of the study in which we place ourselves is the standard structure of the hierarchical menu mentioned in section 8.3 (particularly in [BRE 98a]). Its tree-like architecture consists of nodes and branches that establish parental relations between the different nodes.

From a general point of view, the first node of the structure (generally represented at the top) is called the "root" and is the starting point for the tree. Each node inherits properties from the node placed directly above it ("parent" node) and gives its properties to all the nodes that are placed directly below it in the hierarchy ("child" nodes); furthermore, nodes that come from the same parent are called "brothers" (or "sisters") and an "ancestral" node is a node which is linked to all the nodes situated on a lower level. In addition, a child only has a single direct parent, which implies that there is a unique path from one point of the tree to another. Figure 8.1 represents this hierarchical structure symbolically where: A is the root of the tree; B is the parent of D and E; B and C are the children of A; F, G and H are brothers (or sisters); and A is the ancestor of all the nodes of the tree, from B to L (see [SHA 01], for more details on the formalisms of trees).

In the case that concerns us, the architecture and taxonomy of the tree are slightly adapted and modified according to the application targeted. The nodes represent families of content (called "menus") and possess lower hierarchical levels ("sub-menus") the specific content of which therefore naturally inherits the content of their ancestors. Similar to a classic library process that progress, for example, in the following manner: Geography > World > Africa > Western Africa > Mali. Moreover, the structure used for the application does not really have a root, since the highest level already contains several menus. Finally, each level can be considered as a list in its own right, therefore regrouping all the brother elements, in which it is possible to move horizontally without having to go via the shared higher level: to go back to the analogy of a library, it is thus possible to reach the different continents without having to systematically go via the parent menu (World). However, the structure respects one of the fundamental properties of the tree: the unique nature of the path between two points of the tree. Indeed, each list is ordered and its progress systematically begins from the first element; thus, still using the library analogy, going to Oceania boils down to using the following path: Geography > World > Africa / America / Asia / Europe / Oceania. Figure 8.2 specifies the hierarchical structure adapted to the application targeted in the study.

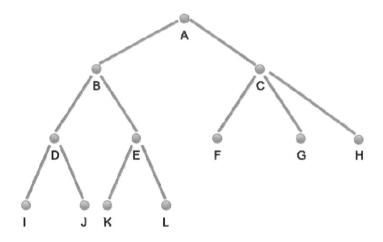

Figure 8.1. *Symbolic representation of a tree structure*

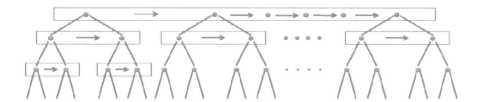

Figure 8.2. *Details of the tree structure adapted to the targeted application*

In practice, the targeted application is an automobile multimedia center that can resemble a cell phone or *smart phone* type environment and that therefore groups together the everyday personal data of a standard situation of this type of system (schedule, contacts, music, etc.) to which data specific to the application environment are added: the automobile. Furthermore, given the application context this time – while driving – nodes of the tree are made inaccessible by taking into account the incompatibility of certain menus with the attention required for automobile driving (for example, looking at a series of photos or watching a video is not permitted). In the end, the structure has three levels of hierarchy starting from six main menus: *Communication, Navigation, Vehicle, Music, Images*, and *Videos*. Figure 8.3 presents the taxonomy and organization of the system used in the study as well as the different constraints that are imposed.

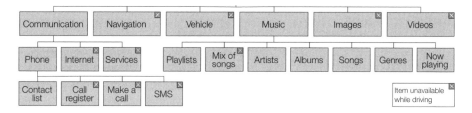

Figure 8.3. *Presentation of the structure used in the rest of the study*

8.2.2. *Sonification*

Introduced in the 1990s, in particular by Kramer [KRA 94], sonification is a process of information transmission and representation of data via the auditory modality; it can be seen as the equivalent of visualization for the visual modality (we indeed sometimes speak of audification to define the most basic approach of sonification). According to [VIA 07], "sonification […] aims to exploit the auditory modality by translating visual information in a sound form in order to limit the overload of information provided by the graphic interfaces. In the case of abstract data flows, observation by audition is better than vision for locating temporal structures". This technique, which enables the reading of data, is therefore particularly well adapted to contexts where visual attention is solicited as a priority.

Sonification techniques are based, first of all, on three fundamental concepts (more details being given in section 8.3):

– The notion of "*earcon*", synthetic sound for which the sound/meaning relationship is arbitrary – or symbolic – and must therefore be learned by the user. This idea was initially introduced by Blattner [BLA 89]. The benefit of earcons is that it can easily represent a hierarchical structure by playing on the modulation of sound and musical characteristics: pitch, tone, rhythm, duration, etc.

– The notion of "*auditory icon*" introduced by Gaver [GAV 86], which establishes a direct – or metaphorical – link with the object or concept that it represents, by referring to a sound from our daily environment (for example, the sound of crumpled paper when the desktop recycle bin is emptied). The auditory icon is therefore almost directly comprehensible to the user. An implementation of this approach can be found in particular in the works of Barrass [BAR 97] or Conversy [CON 98], [CON 00].

– The notion of "*spearcon*" – contraction of "speech" and "earcon" – is based on a vocal synthesis compressed in time, but at a constant pitch; as if a person was speaking faster – therefore compressing, even deleting, certain syllables – but keeping the same tone. The recognition of the word or group of words is not necessarily ensured, but the spearcon plays the role of an unequivocal footprint. This notion was initially introduced by Walker [WAL 06] in order to compensate for the limitations of a sonification based on earcons or auditory icons (difficulty in creation and learning, in particular for earcons). Regarding this, the works of Walker, particularly those carried out with Palladino [PAL 07] on a cell phone menu, put forward the learning capabilities of spearcons.

Other than these three basic approaches – and by moving further away from the case where the sound has only a warning role only, informing in a binary manner as to the activation state of a system (for example, the ringtone of the cell phone that is the same whoever is calling) – sonification can also take into account the interactivity aspects inherent to communication between the human and the machine. In this case it is based on more complex techniques, the detail of which is given in [HER 04], [HER 08], such as:

– The so-called "parameter mapping" approach that consists of linking the value or nature of data to acoustic characteristics of the signal (intensity, pitch, duration, rhythm, tone attributes, etc.). The typical implementations of this approach are, for example, the Geiger counter or sound devices to aid parking, where information regarding distance between the car and the obstacle is converted on a rhythmical scale.

– The so-called "model-based" approach that does not directly consider the conversion of data into sound, but, initially, the conversion of data into a device (or instrument capable of producing a sound); the exploration of data being achieved through the interaction between this device and the user-explorer. This is, for example, the case of a device such as *Shoogle* (quoted in [HER 08]), which converts messages received on a cell phone into as many elements (grains or balls) of a maracas-type instrument that the user activates by shaking the device, thus linking the tone of the phone – which has become an instrument – to the number of waiting messages. This approach, which is relatively new, is based on computing abilities to model physical objects (virtual reality) or on technological abilities to instrument tangible objects (augmented reality). In the end, it is therefore not a matter of the manner in which the data manage the sound but rather the manner in which these same data are instrumentalized.

It is important to note that the issue of sonification is largely addressed internationally within the ICAD (International Community on Auditory Display)[1] community and more recently in the context of the European COST-Action SID (Sonic Interaction Design)[2], which deals more specifically with the emerging aspects of interactive sonification.

---

1 www.icad.org.
2 www.cost-sid.org.

8.2.3. *The wider issues of the problem*

On the basis of previous definitions, sonification of the hierarchical menu used for targeted application (multimedia automobile center) therefore has several design issues. Indeed, the information transmitted by the auditory modality must consider both the semantic content of menus as well as the navigation position within the structure. It is therefore possible to specify in this case the main functions the sonification approach must satisfy:

– The clarification and the differentiation of the *meaning of menus*: each menu is associated with a family of sounds that must ensure a good coherence within the same menu, but also enable a good distinction between the different menus (for example, *Communication* relates to several modes of communication and is different to *Navigation,* which deals with data relative to various orientation and geo-localization tools).

– Information of *vertical position*: the sound associated with a menu must be able to show the level of depth in the structure (for example, *Directory* is the son of *Telephone* and has *Communication* as an ancestor).

– Information of *horizontal scrolling*: for a given hierarchical level, the sound associated with each brother node must be able to show the level of progress in the corresponding list (for example, *Albums* is situated before *Tracks* and after *Artists* in the list that comes from *Music*).

8.3. State of the art

This state of the art puts forward a summary of the main work dealing with the sonification of hierarchical menus, mainly carried out by researchers who come from the previously mentioned ICAD community (see section 8.2.3) and the ACM/CHI[3] (Association for Computing Machinery/Computer–Human Interaction) community. The first part addresses the question of sound representation of the hierarchical relationships within a menu, i.e. the representation of an item within a menu by a horizontal and vertical positioned sound. The second part presents work on the sound representation of the semantic content of items, i.e. the representation of the object or concept that the item is referring to by a sound. The third part presents work that tries to reconcile these two types of representation, which will enable the introduction of the original mixed model, which is the object of this chapter.

---

3 www.sigchi.org.

8.3.1. *Sound representation of the hierarchical level*

8.3.1.1. *Earcons*

The notion of earcon was introduced by the works of Blattner *et al.* [BLA 89] and corresponds to a sound used to carry an information in a non verbal way. The relationship between the earcon and the meaning is posed arbitrarily and must therefore be learned by listeners. The authors thus propose the construction of earcons based on musical motifs of which five parameters enable the signification of the motif to be varied: the dynamic (i.e. the range of the variation of intensity); the rhythm (i.e. the temporal organization of sounds); the pitch (fundamental frequency); the tone (i.e. the type of instrument used), and the register (i.e. the range of variation in pitch).

Brewster [BRE 95a] then proposed a series of specifications for the creation of earcons on the basis of these five parameters to which spatialization and sound effects are added. For a given level of hierarchical depth, these different musical parameters enable the elements that make up this level to be differentiated:

– level 1: the use of different tones of instruments, the register and spatialization (e.g.: stereo position);

– level 2: use of different rhythms, tempos and durations;

– level 3 and lower: use of the pitch, intensity, different chords and sound effects (e.g. reverberation) to differentiate items.

8.3.1.2. *Hierarchical earcons according to Brewster*

On the basis of the parameters described above, Brewster [BRE 98a] tested different methods to represent the hierarchical structure of a menu comprising several levels of depth.

An initial level of earcons for a small hierarchy of files is presented in Figure 8.4. The files that come from the same family share the same tone, and the files of the same type share the same rhythm.

Brewster then proposes a method to represent a hierarchy of files this time comprising four levels of 27 nodes. The hierarchy and associated sounds are represented in Figure 8.5. This figure shows that level 2 is represented through three parameters: the tone, the stereo position and the register. For levels 1 and 2, the sound associated with each item is continuous. Then, level 3 uses rhythm to differentiate each sub-menu, which inherits the properties of the item above. Three different rhythms are used, as presented in Figure 8.5. Level 4 is a replica of level 3 with a more rapid repetition of motifs.

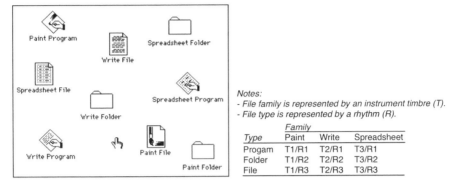

Figure 8.4. *Example of a small hierarchy of files, adapted from [BRE 98a]*

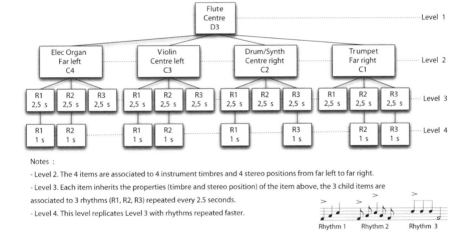

Figure 8.5. *Sonification principles of a hierarchy on four levels, adapted from [BRE 98a]*

A variation of the method of hierarchical earcons is also put forward by Brewster: *compound earcons* (see also [BRE 98b]). The hierarchy is numbered similarly to chapters: 1, 1.1, 1.2, 2, 2.1, 2.2, etc. Then, to each number, and the dot "." corresponds a tone of instrument (see Figure 8.6). Each item is then represented by the concatenation of tones that thus form a sequence. The mixed earcons therefore function a bit like Morse code, i.e. by a construction of complex messages based on a finite number of items that make up an alphabet.

The advantage of this method is that it allows any hierarchy. However, the major inconvenience is that compound earcons become increasingly longer as we descend in the hierarchy; the user must then listen to the earcon until the end. During the use of long sequences, recent effects can also appear, i.e. the memorization of the last elements of the sequence to the detriment of the first elements.

A possible solution to decrease the length of sequences is to simultaneously play the different parts of the mixed earcon (i.e. by mixing). This is the work of *parallel earcons* presented by Brewster in [BRE 95b], and the results of which show recognition levels identical to those obtained with mixed earcons presented in succession.

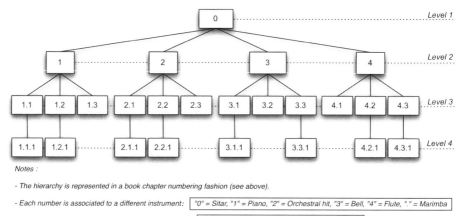

Notes :

- The hierarchy is represented in a book chapter numbering fashion (see above).
- Each number is associated to a different instrument: "0" = Sitar, "1" = Piano, "2" = Orchestral hit, "3" = Bell, "4" = Flute, "." = Marimba
- Each item is represented by a sequence of sounds, e.g.: 3.1.1 = Bell - Marimba - Piano - Marimba - Piano
- The note used is a C3, 0.3 seconds long.

Figure 8.6. *Representation of the hierarchy by mixed earcons, adapted from [BRE 98a]*

8.3.1.3. *Hierarchical earcons according to Leplâtre*

In [LEP 00], [LEP 02], Leplâtre proposes an adaptation of Brewster's method for the sonification of hierarchical menus in a cell phone. The author develops four main principles for the sonification of menus on the basis of these musical parameters.

Principle 1 – differentiation of families of items grouped together in semantic families. To carry out this differentiation, the author uses four parameters:

– Tone: sounds from a "synthesizer" type are used.

– Envelope, i.e. the temporal evolution of the amplitude of the sound: the envelope here is divided into three parts, the duration of which can be modified: the time the sound increases (*attack*); the duration during which the sound is maintained (*sustain*); and the duration for the sound to die (*release*).

– Register: the author uses three different registers: low, medium or high.

– Type of musical motif: chord, arpeggio (notes of a chord play sequentially), or both superimposed.

For example, the *Call register* menu consists of six sub menus that it is possible to group together in two semantic categories: history of calls (*Missed calls*, *Received calls*, *Dialed calls*) and actions on the messages (*Erase lists*, *Call duration*, *Costs*). For the first category, the three associated earcons are three arpeggios on a high register. The three earcons listened to one after the other form a descending progression, i.e. from the highest to the lowest. For the second category, the three associated earcons are also arpeggios, but this time on a low register and the progression of the three earcons is ascending.

Principle 2 – the earcons inform us as to the level of hierarchical depth of items, in the following manner:

– The duration of an earcon associated with an item depends on the depth of this item in the hierarchy: the lower an item in the hierarchy, the shorter the duration of the earcon.

– Similarly, the number of notes used in an earcon diminishes the lower an item is at in the hierarchy.

– A brief percussive sound, different for each level of hierarchical depth, is played at the same time as the earcon. This sound enables an immediate indication of the level of an item.

For example, the earcon associated with the *Call Divert* menu is a chord that consists of three notes; the earcons associated with the items of the level below are two-note chords; and then one note for the items that are below them.

Principle 3 – the relative position of an item in a list is represented by the position of the earcon within a melodic or harmonic progression associated with the list. For example, when a list of items is represented by earcons, the succession of which forms an ascending melodic progression, the position of an item in the list will be directly represented by the position of the earcon in the melodic progression.

Principle 4 – the number of notes used for the earcon represent the number of sub menus contained in this menu. Example: the five sub-menus of the *Settings* menu respectively consist of 2, 0, 5, 4 and 6 sub menus (see Figure 8.8). The number of notes in the five associated earcons then directly reflects these different components.

These four principles are interesting as they enable the creation of earcons whose structure is more closely linked to the level of depth of an item as well as its position within a list. Indeed, the two types of scrolling (vertical and horizontal) are directly represented by sound parameters (duration and melodic progression). We can, however, criticize the absence of a real perceptive evaluation of the function fulfilled by earcons, as well as a semantic representation of items that nonetheless still remain very arbitrary (i.e. associate an item with a tone of one instrument rather than another).

8.3.1.4. *Auditory scrollbars: sonification of the scrolling*

The scrollbar is the element of the interface that enables us to scroll down a long list of items or a document consisting of several pages. Several works have put forward sonification of the scrollbar in order to represent the (relative or absolute) position in a list and/or the scroll direction.

Brewster [BRE 94] thus proposes two principles for the sonification of scrolling in a long document:

– for scrolling down or up, the use of a brief "beep" at a frequency of 130 Hz $(C3)^4$ or 2093 Hz $(C7)^5$ respectively;

– to show the position in the document, the use of a continuous organ sound as a background, the volume of which increases during 150 milliseconds when a new page is passed. From the top to the bottom of the document, the pitch varies from 1975 Hz $(B6)^6$ to 130 Hz (C3).

The results of tests show a decrease in the mental work load (mental requirement, physical requirement, temporal requirements, effort, performance and frustration) and an improvement in terms of rapidity of navigation in the document.

More recently, Yalla and Walker [YAL 08] tested four different designs for the sonification of scrolling in a long list of items (list of the names of an address book). The earcons are followed by item announced by vocal synthesis.

Design 1 = *single tone*:

– each element in the list is accompanied by a beep;

– the progression of the pitch depends on the polarity of the pitch, i.e. ascending or descending (both possibilities are tested separately);

---

4 C3 represents the 3rd note of C on a standard piano keyboard (88 keys).
5 C7 represents the 7th note of C on a standard piano keyboard.
6 B6 represents the 7th note of B on a standard piano keyboard.

– the pitch slot is constant (two octaves); the pitch gap between two consecutive items therefore depends on a number of items.

Design 2 = double tone:

– same beep as for a *single tone* followed by a beep corresponding to the first item on the list (if scrolling up) or last item on the list (if scrolling down).

Design 3 = proportional regrouping:

– a single beep before the vocal synthesis (same as design 1);

– only eight notes used (C, D, E, F, G, A, B, C – starting from C4[7]);

– if there are only eight items, there is one note per item;

– if there are more than eight items, there is a grouping together, one note for each group of N/8 items. If N is not a multiple of eight, the last group takes the rest.

This design makes it possible to have an idea of the size of the menu after scrolling the first items.

Design 4 = alphabetical regrouping:

– only for the lists classed alphabetically;

– maximum of 26 notes, one note for each letter of the alphabet. For example: all the items beginning with A are indicated by the same note.

A comparison of these four different designs is carried out thanks to preference tests and the results are presented in section 8.5.4.4.

8.3.2. *Sound representation of the semantic content*

8.3.2.1. *Vocal synthesis*

An initial approach to representing the semantic content of an item in a menu thanks to a sound consists of saying the word, whether by vocal synthesis (*Text To Speech* or *TTS*) or by a recording from a speaker. This approach is largely used in the case of systems destined for people who are blind or who have impaired vision.

This principle is also used in a project called *earPod* [ZHA 07], targeting a system to aid scrolling for a portable music player (like an iPod): the user scrolls

---

7 C4 represents the 4th note of C on a standard piano keyboard.

down items in the menu by sliding his finger on a circular *trackpad*[8], and each element is announced by vocal synthesis.

This approach has the advantage of not requiring any learning, but it does have one limitation: the listener must know the language used for the enunciation of the word.

8.3.2.2. *"Spearcons" (speech earcons)*

This notion was introduced by Walker [WAL 06] in order to compensate for the limitations of a sonification based on earcons or auditory icons (see section 8.3.3). Among these limitations, the author mentions for example the arbitrary side of the earcon/item relationship, which requires an explicit learning, and the rigidity of this system as it is difficult to carry out changes in the hierarchy once it has been sonified.

The *spearcon* associated with a menu item is then obtained in the following manner. The item is first of all announced by vocal synthesis; then it is modified by *time stretch*, with conservation of the pitch of the original word. The rate of time stretch is not fixed *a priori*; it is chosen according to the length of the original word and the level of intelligibility that we wish to keep. Indeed, the spearcon is not necessarily recognizable as a word.

A spearcon thus represents an item in a unique manner as it is made from the word of the item, and the similarities between the items are translated by similarities between spearcons. For example, the three items "save", "save as", "save as web page" will be associated with similar spearcons as they all start with the same word. The results of the evaluation are satisfactory (see section 8.5.4.3), as a spearcon only needs to be listened to once on average in order to be learned.

8.3.2.3. *Auditory icons*

The notion of auditory icons was introduced by Gaver [GAV 86] to describe a sound that represents an object (or an action) by referring to a sound in our environment. In some cases, the sound can be directly linked to the object or the action (e.g. the *Camera* item is represented by the sound of a clicking shutter). But in most cases a metaphorical link is established between the sound and the object that it represents: for example, a sound of paper being thrown into the bin means the deletion of a file on a computer. In contrast to earcons, auditory icons require very little learning as they refer to sounds known to all.

---

8 http://www.dgp.toronto.edu/~sszhao/earPod.html.

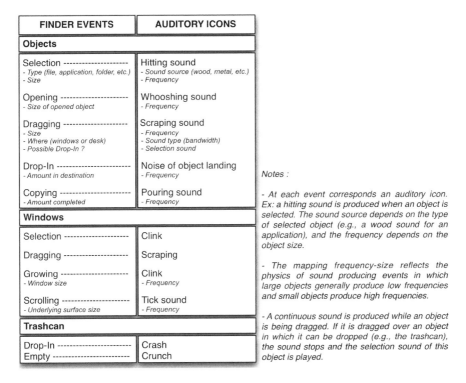

FINDER EVENTS	AUDITORY ICONS
Objects	
Selection ------------------- - Type (file, application, folder, etc.) - Size	Hitting sound - Sound source (wood, metal, etc.) - Frequency
Opening --------------------- - Size of opened object	Whooshing sound - Frequency
Dragging -------------------- - Size - Where (windows or desk) - Possible Drop-In ?	Scraping sound - Frequency - Sound type (bandwidth) - Selection sound
Drop-In --------------------- - Amount in destination	Noise of object landing - Frequency
Copying --------------------- - Amount completed	Pouring sound - Frequency
Windows	
Selection --------------------	Clink
Dragging ---------------------	Scraping
Growing ---------------------- - Window size	Clink - Frequency
Scrolling --------------------- - Underlying surface size	Tick sound - Frequency
Trashcan	
Drop-In ---------------------- Empty -------------------------	Crash Crunch

Notes :

- At each event corresponds an auditory icon.
Ex: a hitting sound is produced when an object is
selected. The sound source depends on the type
of selected object (e.g., a wood sound for an
application), and the frequency depends on the
object size.

- The mapping frequency-size reflects the
physics of sound producing events in which
large objects generally produce low frequencies
and small objects produce high frequencies.

- A continuous sound is produced while an object
is being dragged. If it is dragged over an object
in which it can be dropped (e.g., the trashcan),
the sound stops and the selection sound of this
object is played.

Figure 8.7. *Sound icons used in Gaver's SonicFinder, adapted from [GAV 89]*

Gaver thus proposed a sound interface for a computer based on the use of sound icons: the SonicFinder [GAV 89]. Sounds accompany each action of the user, for example the selection of a file is accompanied by the sound of an object being hit. The properties of sounds are then associated with certain properties of the interface (for example, the type of file selected is represented by a type of material for the object that is hit). Figure 8.7 represents auditory icons and the associated actions in the SonicFinder. In contrast to Brewster's example (see section 8.3.1), the SonicFinder also informs us as to the size of the file by associating the sound to the size of the object being hit (and therefore the frequency of the produced sound). However, the SonicFinder does not give information regarding the hierarchical relationships between files.

Works by Barrass [BAR 97] resulted in a spin-off of the original method to define the parameters of an icon that was to be used to carry a given piece of information. His method is based on large-scale surveys (via the Internet, for example) where people are questioned regarding their experiences with the sounds of every day life. By analyzing the results, the author proposes to define the sound icons that group together the traits that were the most common to the experiences of the people questioned.

More recently, Conversy [CON 00] introduced the notion of premastered sound icons. These consist of sound icons with certain acoustic properties that can vary according to the information that is to be conveyed. The author proposes, for example, the sonification of computing processes that occur as background tasks [CON 98]. For this he uses a simulation of sounds emitted by the wind: white noise filtered by a narrow-band noise[9], whose central frequency varies according to the state of the process.

8.3.3. *Mixed approaches*

8.3.3.1. *Earcons and vocal synthesis*

Vargas and Anderson [VAR 03] propose combining earcons and vocal synthesis in order to sonify a user interface in an automobile. The interface enables control of the different accessories of the car (e.g. radio, lights, etc.). The authors chose to use earcons to represent the hierarchy of the menu and vocal synthesis to represent the semantic content of items. The main menu includes four main menus (lights, windscreen wiper, ventilation and radio), the name of the item is announced each time it is visited, and the earcon is diffused before the vocal synthesis.

The description of the associated earcons is as follows:

– each family of the basic level is accompanied by the tone of an instrument: lights = piano, windscreen wiper = singing, ventilation = bells, radio = brass. Alternate use of arpeggios and chords;

– each sub level inherits from the instrument and notes of the level above. The differentiation of each item is carried out according to the rhythm and melody;

– the hierarchical level is given by a brief percussive sound diffused before the earcon.

Compared to the use of simple vocal synthesis (without earcons), the evaluation of this system shows that even if the navigation is slower, users have a more efficient navigation in terms of the number of times they press on the keys.

8.3.3.2. *Manipulation of vocal synthesis parameters*

Shajahan and Irani [SHA 07] propose an original method of navigation aid in a hierarchical menu, thanks to vocal synthesis including the parameter synthesis (e.g.

---

9 White noise processed through a band-pass filter.

the pitch or the speech rate) are manipulated to indicate the hierarchical position of items in the menu.

In an initial experiment, a small hierarchy is studied, and three parameters of vocal synthesis are manipulated: the average pitch of the voice (*Average pitch*, AP); the pitch range of the voice (*Pitch range*, PR); and the rate of speech (*Speech rate*, SR). On the basis of these parameters, two sets of sounds were tested:

– set 1: depth is given by the average pitch (AP) and the pitch range (PR); horizontal scrolling is given by the pitch rate (SR);

– set 2: depth is shown by the speech rate (SR), and horizontal scrolling by the average pitch (AP).

Results show a marked decrease in the number of navigation errors when this type of sound is used, compared to simple vocal synthesis without a parameter variation. This example thus shows that we can efficiently combine a representation of semantic content of menu items (here by vocal synthesis) with a representation of hierarchical relationships within that menu.

8.3.4. *Discussion*

A bibliographical review of the methods employed for the sonification of hierarchical menus has been presented. The challenge consisted of associating a sound with each item in order to represent both the position of the item in the hierarchical structure of the menu; and the semantic content of this item or the family of items to which it belongs.

The presented works propose the representation of the hierarchical level using earcons, i.e. abstract sound signals constructed so as to conduct the desired information. These earcons are built on the basis of sound parameters (e.g. tone, pitch, rhythm or duration), which enables the hierarchical relationships that exist between the menu items to be represented. These prove to be very efficient in representing the position of the item in the hierarchy as it enables us to map hierarchical relationships on the different sound parameters [BRE 98a], [LEP 00], [LEP 02]. Earcons prove to be inefficient, however, when it is a matter of representing the semantic content of an item or family of items. Two other methods are then presented to compensate for this limitation: *spearcons* [WAL 06] and *auditory icons* [GAV 86]. In this case, the sound signals are more efficient and intuitive as they represent the semantic content either directly in the case of spearcons or metaphorically for auditory icons. A "mixed" approach that combines earcons with the hierarchical representation and vocal synthesis or sound icons for the semantic representation should enable us to obtain the best results by benefiting from both types of approaches. This nonetheless raises new problems, particularly in the way in which both types of information can be superimposed. Little work is going in this direction and it is this type of approach that we have chosen to implement and that we describe hereafter.

8.4. Method of sound design: hybrid model for the sonification of a hierarchical menu

This section presents the model developed for sonification of the hierarchical menu that mixes two basic approaches, which are metaphorical and symbolical, to result in an original hybrid approach that could meet the functionalities of the targeted application. Both instances of the model, which will serve for the rest of the study, are presented and clarified.

8.4.1. *Proposition of a hybrid model: original mixed approach*

The generic model chosen for the application is a mixed model that links the ability of auditory icons to directly suggest a meaning and the ability of earcons to codify more abstract data, such as the position in space of the tree. Both of these notions are thus dedicated to one (or several) identified functions and intervene in a preponderant way in a specific zone of the tree.

8.4.1.1. *Metaphorical approach*

The metaphorical approach (auditory icons) seems the best adapted to signify the large fundamental families of the structure. It is therefore used to sonify the six menus of the highest level. A definition of the content of each of these main menus is carried out in two steps: a semantic analysis, which reveals different notions associated with each menu; and then, where possible, a transposition in the sound domain, which attaches a sound metaphor to each of these notions. The selection of metaphors is also carried out according to their relevance *vis-à-vis* the menu considered and their degrees of legibility *vis-à-vis* a user-listener who is not *in theory* an expert. Figure 8.8 illustrates this process schematically.

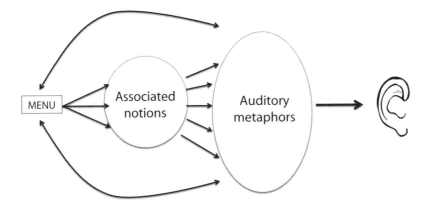

Figure 8.8. *Process of the definition of metaphors associated with the main menus*

At this stage, several obstacles can appear:

– menus that are abstract or polysemic (such as *Communication* or *Navigation*) can result in complex notions that are difficult to realize in terms of sound metaphor;

– the most common menus (such as *Music* or *Videos*) can be interpreted by pre-conceived ideas – "cliché" type notions – leading to situations that are too stereotyped and therefore less efficient in terms of interface quality ("old" or "retro" aspect not considered as being very qualitative);

– transposition in the sound domain of the idea suggested by a menu can sometimes lead to fabricated ("manufactured"), or even fictitious, images.

These problems can be partly resolved thanks to design and validation methods such as:

– initially, the production of a great many ideas, e.g. collective discussion sessions (*brainstorming*);

– the different stages of the process to test the different proposals with a panel of people enabling us to objectively select the best candidates;

– the possibility of building sound metaphors in a composite manner, i.e. by combining several basic ideas either by superposing them (mixing) or by concatenation (sequencing).

8.4.1.2. *Symbolic approach*

The symbolic approach (earcons) seems better adapted to signify the position of the hierarchical structure in space. It is produced according to the "parameter mapping" type principle, either on the basis of elements constituting the auditory icons or based on elements attached to auditory icons, designed via means of external sound synthesis motor (see the following paragraphs and section 8.4.2.1); the design parameters of earcons then being connected, in both cases, to the navigation data like spatial coordinates (x, y): vertical depth and horizontal scrolling.

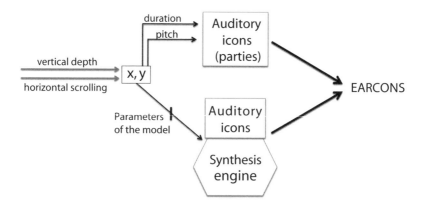

Figure 8.9. *Process of mapping data with sound control parameters*

More specifically, the parameters used in one case (case 1) are mainly the duration and pitch, and in the other case (case 2) the tone attributes directly controlled by the definition of the synthesis model (see Figure 8.9).

The second case (case 2) can thus resemble a "model-based" type approach. Indeed, the earcon is produced here thanks to a physical modeling synthesis engine that simulates a mechanical (or acoustic) system that produces a sound (e.g. a plaque hit by a mallet or a string bowed by a bow). This system is defined via parameters that directly influence the physical phenomenon which generates the sound. For example, a physical model of a plate that is hit will be defined by its dimensions (width, length and thickness) or the characteristics of the material (density, elasticity, etc.). It is to these parameters of the model that the sonification data are then linked together, thus enabling variation of the system – and therefore implicitly its associated tone – according to the navigation position.

Here, also, there are potentially several obstacles that can be removed thanks in particular to knowledge and know-how in terms of sound technologies and signal processing:

– the difficulty of extracting coherent elements from the auditory icons (segmentation) as well as the feasibility of parameters used, particularly pitch: problem – specific to sampling techniques – sound quality that comes from transposition, especially when the transposition rate becomes high;

– the complexity of the approach by physical modeling, which generally offers a greater number of physical control parameters: relevance of the choice of these parameters and, as the case may be, their rate of variation, which can initially be evaluated on a perceptive level (by asking, for example, if the variation of such a parameter is audible and enables us to efficiently discriminate one position in relation to another).

Moreover, unlike the frame of certain previous studies (see section 8.3), we have set ourselves the requirement of carrying out relatively short sounds (less than a second in total) so that the information is rapidly given and perceived to thus avoid annoying the user. This constraint first of all involves consequences for the "duration" sonification parameters but also for their choice of physical models used or certain control parameters (in particular, the physical shock damping units linked to materials and modes of the resonance of models).

8.4.2. *Two instances of the model*

The mixed model of sonification of a hierarchical menu described in section 8.4.1 was instantiated according to two distinct modalities to provide two different solutions to the application targeted by the study (automobile multimedia center), presented in detail in section 8.2.1. This stage of applied creation was also completely carried out by an "expert" in the sound domain – Andrea Cera[10], composer and sound designer.

8.4.2.1. *Hybrid solution*

The hybrid solution is based on a series of auditory icons that come from recordings of real sounds in the environment. Particular attention was given to the quality of recordings used, by carrying out selection in a professional sound bank used in audiovisual production (Sound Ideas[11]). The main associations brought to light by the six first-level main menus are following (those that were effectively retained are in bold):

– *Communication*: Morse code, telephone (dialing, ringtone), modem, computer (keyboard), etc.

---

10 brahms.ircam.fr/andrea-cera.
11 www.sound-ideas.com.

– *Navigation*: sound of water (waves, streams, torrents), sound of oars, electromagnetic waves, aquatic movement (boats, fish), etc.

– *Vehicle*: motor (starting, acceleration, stop), etc.

– *Music*: piano or guitar arpeggio, orchestral chord (percussion, strings), etc.

– *Images*: camera (clicking of the shutter, flash noise), etc.

– *Videos*: sound of the 16 mm projector (starting, scrolling, stop), etc.

The original sounds were edited and underwent processing such as segmentation, breakdown into morphologically important modules (start (*attack*), body (*sustain*), conclusion (*release*)), re-composition by eliminating the unnecessary elements, and final mixing.

The part relative to earcons in this initial (hybrid) solution was made based on two generic resonator models:

– a rectangular plate fixed to its edges (like a drum);

– a free rectangular bar (like a xylophone).

The particularity of these models – and at the same time, of this first solution – resides in the fact that the resonators thus modeled are set in motion, not by a physical exciter (such as mallet) but by a numerical exciter, in this case the signal of auditory icons. This approach operates in roughly the manner of a source/filter type process: the source, which supplies the system in energy, being the numerical excitation signal and the filter being the resonator – in this case mechanical – with all the specific modes of resonance.

Thus, the control parameters of models (linked to sonification data) depend largely on the nature of the auditory icon, which excites the resonator: dimensions, thickness of the plate (or bar), damping coefficient, density of the material, number of modes or distance between each input point (excitation) and output point (listening) are use to make, in each case, the resonator compatible with the sound file (auditory icon) used to make it vibrate.

8.4.2.2. *"Museme" solution*

The second solution implemented is directly inspired by the theories of musicologist Philip Tagg, who defines a "museme" as a minimum of musical significance composed of a simple series of pitches, rhythms, harmonies and tones [TAG 82]. On a metaphorical level (the six menus of the first level of the tree), the approach mainly tries to "mimic" the auditory icons established for the first solution. This mimicry is obtained either by directly orchestrating the initial content of icons, or by composing a musical equivalent; as follows:

– *Communication*: interval of notes played by a horn (reference to the hunting horn, used by postal couriers during the 19th Century).

– *Navigation*: imitation of the icon by means of string instruments (cello, violin) played pizzicato and flute chord which is held to make the sound of a boat's foghorn.

– *Vehicle*: imitation of the car horn by an ensemble of trombones and horns.

– *Music*: very well known musical phrase played on the flute (despite the difficulty of "representing music with music").

– *Images*: imitation of the icon by means of strings played pizzicato, of percussions and violin glissandos.

– *Videos*: musical phrase referring to an old Hollywood film (in this case, "As time goes by" taken from *Casablanca*, the 1942 American film).

The part relative to earcons in this second solution (museme) is carried out according to a standard "parameter mapping" type approach:

– the vertical depth is established both by the reduction of the duration (acceleration of the tempo) and lowering of the pitch of notes (change of the respective range of each instrument);

– horizontal scrolling is established in a more subtle way by modification of the musical content (change of the color of chords – minor/major – or simply notes).

8.5. Evaluation protocols: general evaluation methods

In the process of auditory design, the analysis of needs and evaluation of results require rigorous experimental approaches. This section initially presents the paradigms generally used in the domain of the evaluation of auditory stimuli, then the problems posed by situations of auditory interaction and finally the methods more specifically used in the context of studies on the sonification of hierarchical menus, which come from studies presented in section 8.3.

8.5.1. *Generality regarding the experimental evaluation approaches of auditory stimuli*

Just as for other sensory modalities, the experimental approaches in the auditory domain relate to different fields, such as psychophysics or cognitive psychology. On the basis of two recent and detailed reviews on the matter, ([GIO 11], [SUS 11]), this part offers a summary of the different methods made available to the experimenter to probe the phenomena linked to auditory perception.

8.5.1.1. The issue

From a general point of view, the study of auditory perception is concerned with quantities and units representative of what humans perceive when they are subjected to an auditory stimulus (percept). These units – assembled under the general term of auditory attributes – can cover simple notions that it is possible to link to physical units directly calculable on the auditory signal (intensity, duration, etc.) via the intermediary of basic metrological approaches, which globally relate to the domain of psychoacoustics. They can also cover more complex notions linked to the nature of the information contained in the sound (mentioning the source, judgment of value, etc.) that require more exploratory approaches, belonging to the field of experimental psychology.

These approaches respectively summarize the two main mechanisms of processing sensory information, which are mentioned in Chapter 29 of [SEA 07] from a general point of view and developed in [MCA 93] on issues more particularly linked to sound:

– bottom-up processing guided by attributes of the auditory stimulus;

– top-down processing guided by prior knowledge acquired about the auditory stimulus (culture, expertise, etc.).

The particularity of these approaches resides in the fact that, with a few exceptions, there is no tool for measuring – and therefore predicting – these auditory attributes, other than the human ear and the processing that is then done by the cerebral system. Their knowledge and the understanding of their links with the auditory stimuli considered therefore inescapably go via experimental procedures involving listening and judgment tasks carried out by people (called "subjects" or "participants"), whose methods are explained hereafter.

8.5.1.2. Classic methods

Classic methods involve psychophysics (and more precisely psychoacoustics) and are more generally one-dimensional, i.e. they try to establish a direct and qualitative relation between an auditory attribute (perceived unit) and a physical sound property (physical unit, also called acoustic descriptor) in order to result in a formula such as: $\Psi = f(\phi)$, where Ψ represents the perceived unit (psychological) and ϕ the acoustic unit (physical). The most common methods were ordered and categorized by Susini in [SUS 11] according to the following taxonomy:

– indirect methods:

- the **threshold method** that consists of measuring a threshold of the perception of a unit which can either be absolute or differential, leading in the second case to the notion of *just-noticeable difference* (JND), which corresponds to the smallest detectable variation in the considered unit,

– **confusion scaling method**, which consists of varying a physical unit and measuring the variation of the corresponding differential threshold;

– the direct methods:

– **ratio scaling**, which is based on the ability to carry out a numerical judgment in relation to a difference in the level of perceived sensation. This method can be implemented, either by **unit estimation** by associating a number proportional to the perceived sensation or by **unit production** by directly adjusting the perceived sensation level for a sound to a number,

– **cross modal matching**, which consists of linking a modality – e.g. auditory – via the means of another modality – e.g. haptic (for instance, evaluation of the auditory sensation of the sound level by the production of a sensation of muscular force). This method can be used in the case of situations that evolve over time.

8.5.1.3. *Exploratory methods*

When the auditory attributes are not easy to define or identify (conversely, for example, to auditory intensity or duration) or are not known before, exploratory and generally multidimensional methods are used.

In this domain, more current methods have also been listed by Susini in [SUS 11]:

– The *semantic differential method*, which consists of evaluating sounds studied on a semantic scale marked by two opposed verbal descriptions (e.g. "pleasant/unpleasant" or, in a slightly different way, "bright/non bright"). The rigorous implementation of this method requires a few pre-requisites, in particular the previous validation of the words used (also called semantic descriptors) in terms of relevance in relation to the sensation studied but also in terms of common understanding of their meaning. This method results in the description of a semantic type profile that can also be put in relation to the acoustic sound descriptors.

– The method of *dissimilarity judgment*, which consists of evaluating the similarity/dissimilarity that can be perceived between two sounds on a continuous numerical scale, by repeating the process for combinations of pairs that come from a given corpus. This method *in theory* enables us to reveal the perceptive dimensions that underlie the perception of the sounds of the corpus and is therefore based on a strong perceptive continuum hypothesis along these dimensions. Thus, this method possesses a certain number of prerequisites including, among others, certain homogeneity of stimuli that make up the corpus. Nonetheless, the associated *multi-dimensional analysis* enables us to construct the perceptive (metric) space describing the dimensions revealed by the experience and position the sounds of the corpus occupy. The process of analysis is generally completed by relating perceptive dimensions with acoustic descriptors, thus describing an acoustic space associated with the perceptive space.

– The *categorization* method, *in theory* free, is an alternative approach to the previous method and is used when the perceptive continuum hypothesis (and therefore the homogeneity of the corpus) is no longer valid. This method consists of grouping them together on the basis of similarity criteria (which can, as the case may be, be specified: in this case, the categorization is said to be "oriented"), the different sounds of a corpus, this grouping together occurring with no notion of order nor numerical value. The most current analysis associated with this method is a "cluster" type analysis that leads to a hierarchical representation in the form of a tree (*dendrogram*) describing the structural organization of elements of the corpus revealed by the experience.

8.5.2. *Specificity of the evaluation protocol of auditory HMIs*

When the use of sound and implementation of the associated investigation methods are applied to the domain of HMIs, we then talk of auditory HMIs; the objective of this application being to facilitate the use, ergonomics and relation between a user and a system ("system" is taken in the broad sense and includes both the virtual interfaces and tangible objects or physical spaces in which the user evolves). In this case, the protocols and experimental factors are influenced by two important effects that come from the limited context of psychoacoustics, such as presented in the previous section: context and interaction.

8.5.2.1. *Consideration of the context*

The degree of consideration of the experimental context defines the configuration between a so-called laboratory situation (*in vacuo*) and a real situation (*in situ*). This degree can be variable according to the type of application and experimental means that are implemented to deal with it. For example, concerning yourself with auditory HMIs in the automobile passenger compartment can lead to the deployment of a range of contextualizations ranging from a completely decontextualized situation (passive monophonic listening in a sound booth) to a realistic situation, which is therefore active (spatial listening on a 3D driving simulator playing a scenario), even real (vehicle on a track or open road). From an experimental point of view, the difficulty resides in mastering the different parameters linked to the context: the more real the test situation, the more complex it will be and therefore difficult to control. This is the case given that an ideal experimental framework is defined by mastering all the experimental parameters in order to identically reproduce it, and, as the case may be, study the possible interactions with the results obtained. To take the previous example, testing auditory HMIs in a real situation requires, among other things, the background noise inside but also outside the vehicle to be controlled.

The question of context also goes via the experimental guidelines, the role of which is to present the experiment, but also to condition the psychological and mental state of participants before the test. This instruction can be given according to different modes: verbally, by reading a text; visually via photos and/or videos, etc. On this subject, Susini *et al.* [SUS 09] showed in a general manner that the instruction format (nothing/text/text + images) influenced the perceptive judgment of an auditory sequence linked to the welcoming phase of a vehicle.

8.5.2.2. *Consideration of the interaction*

As well as their realism, the contexts of study of auditory HMIs generally have an interactive dimension. Indeed, to different degrees, in most cases a HMI resembles a perception/action retroactive cycle in which the user is inserted during the handling of the interface.

Other than the most simple cases, where sound only has an alarm role – like a simple switch with two positions (*on/off*) – this cycle can be resumed in the following manner: the use of the system produces a sound that provides auditory feedback to the user who consequently adapts his action on the system, etc. Figure 8.10 illustrates this process schematically.

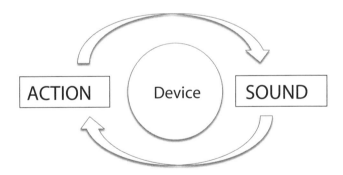

Figure 8.10. *Diagram showing the principle of the perception/action interaction cycle*

This dynamic characteristic that takes into account the temporal support of the auditory HMI, i.e. its ability to evolve over time, induces an additional complexity not only in terms of design (by analogy with the visual, it is necessary to design a series of images at a certain cadence – i.e. a film – and not a fixed and isolated image) but also in terms of experimental methodology, which upstream serves analysis of the problem and downstream the validation of ideas. As previously mentioned, see section 8.2.2, this relation between sound and interaction is an emerging issue. It is dealt with, in particular, in the context of the European COST-Action SID.

8.5.3. *Experimental approaches specific to interactivity*

From an experimental point of view, the notion of interactivity can be deployed on two different time scales:

– short term, linked the specific execution time of the task, which involves chronometric type investigation methods; and

– more long term, linked to the global time of experience, which requires alternative methods involving, in particular, some learning and even memorizing.

They are presented in succession in the rest of this section.

8.5.3.1. *"Chronometric" methods*

In the interaction process, the so-called "chronometric" methods [LEM 09] essentially measure the influence of sound in terms of reaction time (RT), movement time and more globally the time it takes to carry out the task.

The measure of the RT, for example, can be relatively complex to carry out in so far as this unit brings several aspects into play that come from theories of the signal detection and the processing of information. Thus, according to Donders' model [DON 69], the RT necessary to make a choice after an auditory stimulation successively puts in play – in a cumulative way – the simple reaction time (including the motor execution stage), discrimination time and choice time (see [SUE 07] for more details on the subject).

In this context it is important to take into account the fact that the measure of time it takes to carry out a given task must be able to be done at "iso-difficulty", i.e. by ensuring that the task of each experiment represents the same mental load for the user as closely as possible (see section 8.5.4.2 for the definition of this notion).

8.5.3.2. *Alternative methods (learning, memorization, etc.)*

When the level of human-machine interactivity is higher than for a simple reaction to an auditory stimulus, it can be relevant to concern ourselves with methods of alternative measures, taking into account more complex phenomena linked to the time of manipulation of the system. This is the case, for example, with processes for learning or memorizing a task, which requires specific experimental protocols enabling us to measure the influence of the auditory modality on these same processes.

An example illustrating this approach is the methodology developed around the device, called Ballancer, designed by Rath and Rochesso [RAT 05]. It consists of a tangible interface made up of a wooden bar on which a virtual marble rolls, the movement and position of which the user controls by tilting the bar to one side or another; the sound of the ball rolling is managed by a computer sound synthesis that enables us to modify, among other things, the size, weight and shape of the ball as well as the texture of the bar (i.e. the properties of the ball/bar contact, see [RAT 05], for more details about the device). The objective of the study is to measure the influence of auditory feedback on control of the position of the ball by the user.

The experimental method implemented to this effect is built around a scenario consisting of immobilizing the virtual ball in a given region of the bar. The experimental protocol measures improvement in the performance of the "player" over time by varying the parameters of the game (position and dimensions of the targeted zone) conjointly with the auditory parameters (properties of the ball and bar). Globally, the study shows that the auditory feedback improves the use and especially favors learning of the device (see [RAT 06], [RAT 07], [RAT 08] for more details about the methodology and results).

8.5.4. *Review of evaluation methods of the state-of-the-art studies*

This section clarifies the methods used in the works presented section 8.3 in order to measure the efficiency of the proposed sonification principles (i.e. earcons, spearcons and scrollbar). The results of the evaluation are also reported and discussed.

8.5.4.1. *Measure of the recall rate*

The recall rate here corresponds to the ability of sonified menu users to remember the item corresponding to a given earcon. Initially each item of the menu is presented with the associated earcon, then only the earcons are presented and the user must find which item on the menu they correspond to.

In an initial experiment, Brewster [BRE 98a] tests the aptitude of listeners to learn earcons associated with a hierarchy with four levels and 27 nodes (see section 8.3.1). He proposes an evaluation procedure in three phases:

– learning phase 1: the participants become aware of the hierarchy and associated sounds. Each sound is played only once;

– learning phase 2: the participants then have five minutes to learn the rules of the earcons by using the sonified menu. This stage is done without the help of the experimenter;

– test phase: 12 earcons are presented successively; the participants must associate each earcon with the node to which it corresponds in the hierarchy. Two new earcons are also presented that correspond to two missing nodes on level 4. The recall rates are thus calculated.

The results of the experiment show very high recall rates, with an average rate of 81.5%. The strongest rates are obtained for the highest hierarchy levels, and the three weakest (between 50 and 60%) are obtained for level 4 (the lowest), but no satisfactory explanation is given. Results also show a very high recognition level for the two new earcons (83% and 100%).

In a second experiment, Brewster tests the influence of the learning mode on the recall rate of earcons. Four different types of learning are then tested: individual or group, with or without sounds in the first and second learning phases. Two test sessions are put in place: the first just after the learning part and the second a week later. The result does not show an effect of time between the two sessions and the "active" learning is the most efficient, such as when subjects use the HMI themselves.

8.5.4.2. *Measure of the number of times keys are pressed*

The number of times keys are pressed here corresponds to the number of times the user presses on a key of the keyboard (e.g. the keyboard of a cell phone) to reach the item of the menu that he is looking for. This allows us to know whether the user is carrying out an optimal path between the starting and the arrival points in the menu.

Leplâtre [LEP 02] proposes a method for evaluating the efficiency of the sonification of a cell phone menu based on this type of measure. Two participant groups are compared: Group 1 with sonification and Group 2 without sonification (i.e. only the key-press beep are present).

The evaluation method is divided into two phases:

– for both groups, the subjects must carry out 56 tasks: actions to carry out in menus, or elements of the menu to be found. In Group 1 only, the participants carry out two additional "blind" tests, i.e. the cell phone screen is off and the participants can only see the keys of the telephone.

– A NASA-TLX (Task Load Index[12]) questionnaire is given to the participants to fill in at the end of the experiment. This subjective questionnaire enables participants to estimate the task according to six areas: mental requirement, physical requirement, temporal requirement, effort, performance and frustration. A global mental task score is calculated based on these responses.

The data gathered are the number of times the keys are pressed, the average time between two keys being pressed and the number of errors. The results are as follows:

– the keys are pressed fewer times and there are fewer errors for Group 1;

– there is no difference between the two groups regarding the time between two keys being pressed;

– performances become better as the experiment progresses, and in a more significant manner for Group 1;

– globally the participants appreciated the sounds.

Helle and Leplâtre [HEL 01] then propose an evaluation of a sonified cell phone. The participants use the phone for three weeks and then fill in a questionnaire about the emotional and hedonic aspects of their experience with the phone and associated sounds.

8.5.4.3. *Efficiency of spearcons*

Paladino and Walker [PAL 07] evaluated the efficiency of spearcons (see section 8.3.2.2) in the rapidity of navigation thanks to a measure of the time taken to find an element of the menu as well as the number of errors. The results show that spearcons enable a quicker navigation than earcons or auditory icons. Dingler *et al.* [DIN 08] then evaluated the efficiency of learning spearcons associated with a list of common things (e.g. bird, wind, flute, etc.) or a list of functions of a cell phone (New message, Add recipient, Open, etc.). Two experiments were put in place, described below.

Experiment 1:

– Training phase: the participant listens to 30 items from a list, in both possible conditions: vocal synthesis followed by the earcon or followed by the spearcon.

– Test phase: a sound is presented (earcon or spearcon); the participant must find which item it corresponds to in the list. If the participant makes a mistake, the correct answer is played (i.e. the vocal synthesis followed by the auditory clue).

---

12 http://humansystems.arc.nasa.gov/groups/TLX/.

– These two phases are repeated until the participant no longer makes any mistakes.

– This same procedure is carried out with the second list of items.

Experiment 2:

– After having done experiment 1, the same participants listen to the 60 spearcons alone (without the vocal synthesis) and are asked to write the corresponding word.

– Six new participants who did not do experiment 1 are asked to do the same.

The results of experiment 1 show that the average number of tries necessary to obtain a perfect score is much lower for spearcons than for earcons. Indeed, a single try on average is enough to obtain a perfect score with spearcons, versus 4.5 (list of things) and 6.5 (cell phone list) tries on average with earcons.

Experiment 2 shows that for the 60 spearcons, 59 are recognized by the participants of experiment 1 and 38 by new participants.

These works therefore show that spearcons are much more efficient in terms of learning as it is in fact relatively easy to recognize the corresponding word. In other words, the transformation of a word into a spearcon still makes it fairly intelligible.

8.5.4.4. *Other types of tests*

In order to test the different sonification modes of scrollbar (see section 8.3.1.4), Yala and Walker [YAL 08] use subjective preference tests. They ask participants to choose the sonification method that they prefer from four different design modes. The tests are carried out both with blind people and people who are able to see.

The results of the preference tests are as follows:

– the *single tone* design has a better score than the *double tone*;

– the proportional design obtains a better score than the alphabetical design;

– there is no difference in preference between the two types of polarity (i.e. ascending or descending pitch);

– generally, blind and non-blind participants find sounds useful. People who are blind from birth are less enthusiastic, whereas others are very keen on having this kind of solution.

8.6. Methodology adopted for evaluation of the system and initial results

In light of the different standard experimental approaches presented in section 8.5, a methodology was developed to evaluate the sonification model of the system that is targeted for application to the multimedia center of an automobile passenger compartment. This evaluation was done thanks to verbalized subjective appreciations and by means of objective measures that led to initial results concerning the performances of use of the system.

8.6.1. *Recall of the experimental frame*

As mentioned in section 8.2.1, the targeted application is the multimedia center of an automobile passenger compartment presenting a hierarchical structure with six main basic menus and three depth levels (see Figure 8.3 for the schematic representation of the system):

1. Communication

→ Telephone → Directory / Call History / Dial a N° / SMS;

→ Internet;

→ Telematic services.

2. Navigation

3. Vehicle

4. Music

→ Playlists / Track mix / Artists / Albums / Tracks / Genres / Now playing.

5. Images

6. Videos

Thus, the navigation in this structure is augmented by auditory information on the basis of fundamental sonification approaches as well as instances of the mixed original model as it is presented and clarified in section 8.4.2; three different sound collections (called "libraries" (LIBs)) are hereby developed:

– LIB1: so-called "hierarchical" library corresponding to the "hybrid" instance of the mixed model; it assigns a combination of auditory icon and earcon to each menu, weighted according to the type of menu and its place in the structure (see section 8.4.2.1 for more details on the construction of this instance of the model).

– LIB2: so-called "hierarchical" library corresponding to the "museme" instance of the mixed model. It assigns an orchestrated auditory icon (museme) to each of the six main menus and assigned the variations of these musemes following certain design principles of an earcon type to sub-menus such as, for instance, the variation of duration, pitch or rhythm (see section 8.4.2.2 for more details on the construction of this instance of the model).

– LIB 3: so-called "vocal" library using the traditional principle of voice synthesis implemented according to a TTS type approach. This library constitutes a sort of reference in so far as on one hand it corresponds to a limited case of sonification. (It is generally agreed that sonification only deals with the non verbal but TTS can be seen as degenerative case of the spearcon approach, i.e. with a compression rate of zero.) On the other hand, it represents a method currently used in a standard way in this type of situation. Vocal synthesis is carried out here using the voice of Alice from the TTS Acapela[13] synthesis (see [LAN 10] for more details on this implementation).

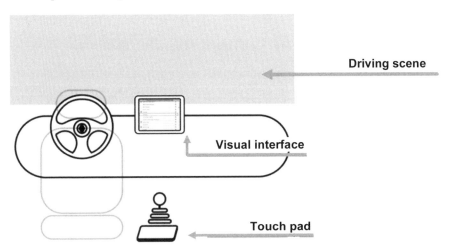

Figure 8.11. *Diagram of the driving simulator*

Finally, in practice, navigation occurs on a prototype model by means of a touch trackpad that acts as a surface interface connected to a visual interface and, as the case may be, in the context of a driving simulator (made up of: automobile seat, steering wheel, gearbox, pedals, frontal screen for visual simulation and stereophonic system for restitution of the auditory atmosphere) offering a situation of moving a winding road where the optimum speed is approximately 90 km/h. The

13 http://www.acapela-group.com/.

touch pad is positioned to the right of the driver (in front of the gearbox) and the visualization screen of the model is positioned at the top in the centre of the dashboard – the usual position for a navigation screen (see Figure 8.11).

8.6.2. *Goals and hypotheses of the experiment*

From a general point of view, the stakes of the first phase of model validation are as follows:

– verify, out of context, the comprehension and quality of sounds of hierarchical libraries (LIB1 and LIB2);

– verify, in context (simulated driving), the acceptability and efficiency of sounds;

– gather the opinions of users regarding the different approaches of auditory guiding.

On this basis, the hypotheses formulated prior to the experiment can be resumed by the following statements:

– sonification enables navigation tasks to be carried out more rapidly (**H1**);

– sonification limits gaze diversion and enables a better focus on driving (**H2**);

– hierarchical sounds can support better long-term use, from the point of view of lassitude, than vocal synthesis (**H3**);

– the "museme" withstands better long-term use, from the point of view of lassitude, than the "hybrid" instance (**H4**).

8.6.3. *Description of the protocol*

The experimental evaluation protocol involved the participation of 24 people ("participants") equally distributed in gender (11 women, 13 men), aged from 21 to 48 according to a quasi uniform distribution (21-28 years old: 5; 29-34 years old: 8; 35-40 years old: 6; 41-48 years old: 5). All were employees in the field of automobile industry and have had their driving licence for at least two years. The test progresses in seven stages (average total length of around 90 minutes):

1. General presentation of the system, progress and evaluation instructions.

2. Free evocation phase on two hierarchical libraries (LIB1 and LIB2). The experimenter plays the sounds of each library, one after the other; at the end of each listening phase, the participant voices what the sound means to him and the function that it could represent.

3. The experimenter presents the model (auditory and visual), asks the participant to evaluate the coherence felt in the sound/function relation, then to evaluate the continuity of the auditory item in each functional universe (i.e. the coherence felt between a main menu and its different sub menus), on the two hierarchical libraries (LIB1 and LIB2).

4. Individual choice of the preferred hierarchical library (LIB1 or LIB2).

5. Familiarization with the touch pad and model associated with the hierarchical library chosen in the previous phase.

6. Realization of the six ongoing tasks on the model in a situation of simulated driving:

- T1: select the phone number (pre-recorded) of a shopkeeper [hairdresser],

- T2: select the phone number (pre-recorded) of a home delivery service [Pizza Rapido],

- T3: launch a first track in the player ["Divine idylle" by Vanessa Paradis],

- T4: launch the second track in the player ["Superstition" by Stevie Wonder],

- T5: play a first artist [Gare du Nord],

- T6: play a second artist [Ray Charles].

These tasks were repeated in the three following conditions:

– C1: the use of the hierarchical library LIB1 or LIB2 chosen at stage 4;

– C2: the use of the vocal library LIB3;

– C3: no auditory guiding with a minimal library (LIBm) comprising only structure sounds (error, empty list or scroll sounds).

Furthermore, counterbalancing of conditions and tasks is carried out in order to control the order effect. For each task, the experimenter notes:

– the time to complete the task: each task is timed;

– the driving comfort level felt on a scale of 6 points (4 = very uncomfortable, 5 = uncomfortable, 6 = quite uncomfortable, 7 = quite comfortable, 8 = comfortable, 9 = very comfortable) – corresponding to the standard 1 to 10 scale of comfort; here reduced to the more common points (i.e. from 4 to 9);

– the perceived frequency of gaze diversion from the road: after each task, the participant evaluates the frequency that his gaze is diverted from the road during the realization of the task, on a scale on 4 points (1 = rarely, 2 = a little, 3 = often, 4 = very often);

7. Response to a questionnaire enabling the participants to verbally explain their preferences and judgment strategies.

8.6.4. *First results obtained*

Two main categories of results were obtained at the end of this test compiling both subjective data (for example, evocation, preference or level of sensation felt) and objective data (for example, duration of the realization of tasks). One is relative to the perceived quality of sonification and the other measures the efficiency of the proposed auditory guidance.

From the point of view of subjective judgment:

– The free verbalization phase (stage 2) enables us to have an idea about the evocative power of sounds. Thus, in the hybrid library (LIB1), only the *Telephone* sound is correctly associated with the function by the majority of participants (74%). The *Images* sound is understood by 43% of participants, whilst the *Communication* sound suggests functions such as *Telephone* and *Internet* linked to the same functional universe as *Communication*. The other sounds are rarely associated with the right function, and the *Navigation* sound is recognized by none of the participants. The majority of sounds suggest diverse functions. However, nearly half of the participants associate the *Music* sound to an error sound (like those found in computing environments).

In the museme library (LIB2), no sound is correctly associated with the function that it represents. The *Music* sound, which is the most recognized, is recognized by 30% of participants. Most sounds are spontaneously associated with warning or error sounds.

In summary, we observe that globally, few sounds are freely associated with their function.

– The sound/function association phase (stage 3) corresponds more than the previous phase to the manner in which users would discover the system in a real situation (i.e. by reading items on the screen at the same time as listening). In this case, the observation made is that after discovery of the model, sounds are judged to be globally coherent with the function that they represent; in particular hybrid sounds (LIB1) *Communication*, *Vehicle* and *Images* and the museme sounds (LIB2) *Music* and *Videos*. However, in the hybrid library, half of the participants consider that the *Music* sound is not all adapted to the function; and in the museme library, it is the *Images* and *Communication* sounds that are not considered adapted to the function by half of the participants. Table 8.1 summarizes the general results of this stage.

Hybrid library (LIB1)	Museme library (LIB2)
☺ **Communication (63%)** ☺ **Vehicle (42%)** ☺ **Images (38%)**	☺ Music (54%) ☺ Videos (54%)
☺ Navigation (☺ 25% / ☹ 33%) ☺ Videos (☺ 21% / ☹ 21%)	☺ Navigation (☺ 21% / ☹ 33%) ☺ Vehicle (☺ 25% / ☹ 33%)
☹ Music (63%)	☹ Images (63%) ☹ Communication (50%)

Table 8.1. *Evaluation of the sound/function coherence*
for the hybrid and museme libraries

– In addition, stage 3 can also enable us to judge the continuity of the auditory item during in-depth navigation in the *Communication* or *Music* menus. Regarding this, for the museme library (LIB2), continuity is judged satisfactory by most of the participants in the *Music* (83%) and *Communication* menus (96% in the sub-menus of *Communication* and 92% in the *Telephone* sub-menus). For the hybrid library (LIB1), this continuity of auditory theme is only judged satisfactory in the *Music* menu (96%) and the *Communication* sub menus (96% each); however, 42% of participants find that the *Telephone* sub-menu is not homogeneous.

That being said, in the general comments formulated during this stage, it is interesting to highlight that some lament the lack of the evocative nature of sounds in the last level of the menu, involving difficult memorization. Nonetheless, 29% of participants highlight and appreciate that the depth of the menu is given by the simplification of sounds when we go deeper into the structure.

– Finally, concerning the preference among the two hierarchical libraries, the majority of participants (79%) orientated their choice towards the hybrid library (LIB1) versus a distinct minority (13%) for the museme library (LIB2). More specifically, the hybrid library is preferred as it is judged to be more explicit, suggestive, intuitive and therefore capable of facilitating memorization, learning and familiarization with the system. Let us nonetheless note that 8% of participants would like a mix of both libraries keeping the musemes sounds *Music* and *Videos* and completing with the remaining sounds from the hybrid library.

From the point of view of guiding efficiency, the context of the study is as follows:

– two independent variables (categorized):

- the sonification condition: three conditions (C1 to C3, specified previously),

- the experimental task: six tasks (T1 to T6, specified previously);

– three dependent variables (measured):

- the duration of the realization of tasks,

- the perceived driving comfort,

- the perceived frequency of the gaze diversion.

Variance analyses (95% confidence interval) on independent variables allowed us to define which have a significant influence on data gathered. These analyses correspond to an experimental plan with repeated measures, of which the inter-subject variables identified are the gender and age class. Moreover, Fisher tests enabled us to compare different variable modalities (e.g. hierarchical library versus vocal library versus minimal library for the variable sonification condition). Furthermore, it is worth noting that the analysis of data concerns the latest of the three conditions tested by participants (the order of conditions being evenly distributed to all subjects) in order to overcome a presentation order effect and concentrate on the situation where the subject is familiarized with the system as well as is possible.

The observations thus made for the three types of measures, enable us to respectively come to the following conclusions:

– An almost significant effect of sonification on the time to complete tasks is observed [$p=0.047$]. The Fisher test shows that the only difference is in the vocal library (LIB3), which has a longer execution time than the minimal library (LIBm) [$p=0.02$]. However, the hierarchical library (LIB1/LIB2) has similar times to vocal and minimal libraries [$p=0.9$ and $p=0.08$, respectively] (see Figure 8.12, for the graphic representation of data).

– A significant influence of the sonification condition on the perceived level of comfort [$p<0.0001$]. Participants judge their driving to be more comfortable with the vocal library (LIB3) than when auditory guiding is deactivated (LIBm) [$p<0.0001$].

Time to complete a task

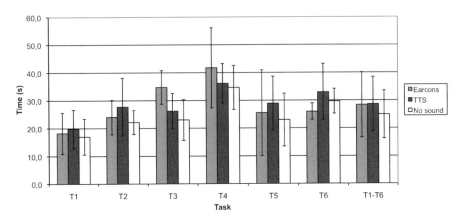

Figure 8.12. *Completion time (average, standard deviation) per task (T1 to T6), on average (T1-T6), for the conditions C1 ("Earcons") C2 ("TTS") and C3 ("No sound")*

However, no significant effect of the hierarchical library (LIB1/LIB2) was observed on the perception of driving comfort: this was felt to be similar between hierarchical library versus minimal library [p=0.2], and hierarchical library is perceived as less comfortable than vocal library [p=0.002] conditions (see Figure 8.13, for the graphic representation of data).

Driving comfort while performing the task

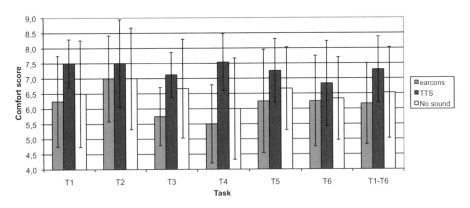

Figure 8.13. *Perceived comfort (average, standard deviation) per task (T1 to T6), on average (T1-T6), for conditions C1 ("Earcons"), C2 ("TTS") and C3 ("No sound")*

– A globally significant effect of the sonification condition occurred with the perception of gaze diversion [p<0.0001]. Participants had the impression of diverting their gaze more often from the driving scene when auditory guiding was stopped (LIBm) than when the vocal library was activated (LIB3) [p<0.0001]. However, no significant difference was observed between the minimal library and the hierarchical library [p=0.2] but the hierarchical library induces more perceived diversion than the vocal library [p=0.006] (see Figure 8.14 for the graphic representation of data).

Perception of gaze diversion

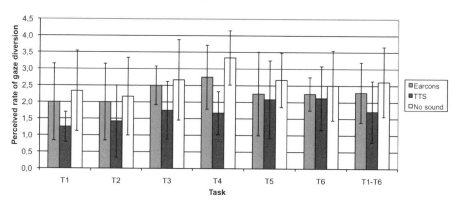

Figure 8.14. *Perceived gaze diversion (average, standard deviation) per task (T1 to T6), on average (T1-T6), for conditions C1 ("Earcons"), C2 ("TTS") and C3 ("No sound")*

8.6.5. *Post-drive commentaries*

The last stage of the evaluation provided guided comments (answering a questionnaire) that enabled us to understand the judgment strategies used and the general feelings with regards to the proposed device.

First of all, vocal and hierarchical libraries were globally judged to be of good quality. The appreciation of hierarchical libraries (LIB1/LIB2) dealt essentially with sounds that were the most recognized during stage 3 (*Telephone* and *Communication* of hybrid library (LIB1); *Communication* and *Music* of the museme library (LIB2)). Conversely, the least appreciated sounds are those that suggested the least, apart from the *Vehicle* sound of the hybrid library, that was well identified but judged too tedious as it was too familiar (comparable with the noise of a motor).

Furthermore, regarding the issue of the use of long-term auditory guiding, a strong majority (92%) showed that sonification made driving safer, but that it did not enable the visual interface to be removed (83%). Thus, 71% of participants thought they would continue to use auditory guidance in the vehicle for the long-term. In addition, an identical proportion (71%) prefered to continue to use the same auditory library rather than changing it in order to conserve the benefit of learning ("to benefit from the automatic mechanism", or "to change would be a handicap"). In terms of use strategy, a few participants would use the vocal library (LIB3) during the discovery phase of the system – a more explicit library, requiring no learning – and would then use one of the hierarchical libraries for the long term (LIB1/LIB2) that are less tedious, shorter, more pleasant and personalized. After appropriation of the system, hierarchical libraries would thus be used by 35% of participants, the vocal library by 30% of participants and another 30% would opt for a mixed library (hierarchical plus vocal), vocal being used to replace the non-explicit sounds of the last menu level. Only one person (5%) preferred the non-sonified condition.

8.6.6. *Conclusions*

In summary, with regards to the starting hypotheses (H1 to H4) and in the current state of the evaluation process of the approach, the partial conclusions that can be drawn are as follows:

– the idea that sonification enables us to carry out navigation tasks more rapidly is not yet validated; indeed, the duration of tasks is identical with or without one of the hierarchical libraries (LIB1/LIB2) and longer with the vocal library (LIB3);

– the idea that sonification enables better attention to driving is partially validated but could be consolidated with more objective measures (like eye tracking, for example);

– the idea that hierarchical libraries support long-term use better than vocal libraries is *in theory* validated only for the first levels of the hierarchical structure; the idea the museme library (LIB2) supports long-term use better than the hybrid library (LIB1) is *in theory* not validated, even if the museme library globally has a better continuity for the auditory theme; the evocative aspect of sonification used in the hybrid library seems to be preferred by users.

8.7. Discussion and perspectives

8.7.1. *Discussion*

The domain of auditory HMIs is meeting increasingly common auditory contexts: we have gone from a visual "civilization" to an audio-visual one. This transition can be explained by an accumulation of visual information in HMIs, thus causing a kind of saturation of the visual channel. It is therefore necessary to use other modalities (auditory, haptic, etc.) to convey information to the user. It is not only a question of unloading the visual modality by replacing visual information by transposition to the auditory domain. It is also a matter of understanding and using the specificities of the auditory modality in order to create complementarities with the visual modality. Among the specificities of our auditory system there is, for example, a weaker reaction and integration time than for the visual channel, a panoramic perception at 360°, the impossibility of "closing ones ears", etc. It is thus necessary to take the specificities in the sonification of HMIs into account.

This approach is all the more relevant in the context of automobile driving, which requires visual attention to be focused on the road scene. As numerous studies show, one of the main causes of road accidents is linked to a lapse in the attention of the driver, which can be caused by a distraction, inattention or interference due to a secondary task (for a detailed review of the literature, please refer to [LEM 08]). The rapid expansion of new technologies means that we are finding ourselves increasingly involved in actions exterior to driving: making phone calls, listening to music or navigating menus on the onboard computer. It is this last point that we have addressed in this chapter. Indeed navigation in the onboard computer requires us to look at the control screen in the dashboard, which carries an obvious risk since when the driver is looking at the screen he is no longer looking at the road.

Our objective was therefore to develop a navigation principle involving search "by ear", by proposing a sonification of actions and items of the onboard computer menu of an automobile. State of the art enabled us to highlight the main principles of auditory creation for the sonification of hierarchical menus. The works presented can be grouped according to three approaches:

– The auditory representation of the position of an item within the hierarchy of the menu thanks to earcons, i.e. abstract auditory signals synthesized by auditory parameters defined previously. This method is very efficient as it is based on direct mapping of the hierarchical relations on the different auditory parameters, but does not enable us to represent the semantic content of the item.

– The semantic representation of the item or family of items thanks to vocal synthesis or auditory icons, i.e. sounds that come from our daily environment and represent the item directly or metaphorically. These sounds are, in principle, very intuitive and require very little learning.

– A mixed approach that combines the advantages of the first two approaches. Few works deal with this, but it is this approach that we have chosen to develop our sonification model.

We have thus developed a new mixed approach for the sonification of a hierarchical menu. This model links the ability of auditory icons to transmit meaning directly with the efficiency of earcons for the representation of hierarchical relations between items. Each of the six main level menus is therefore represented by an auditory icon, the choice of which is based on different criteria: quality of sound, relevance of the icon in relation to the represented notion and homogeneity of auditory icons. The construction of earcons is then based on auditory synthesis by a physical model, the parameters of which map the hierarchical position of each item. Thus, each item in the menu is associated with a sound that comprises two types of information: semantic (metaphorically with the auditory icon) and hierarchical (symbolically with the earcon). Two instances of this new model were put forward by the sound designer integrated in the project: a "hybrid" solution, the originality of which resides in the manner in which the auditory icon and the earcon are *fused*; and a "museme" solution for which the semantic information of the item is ensured by an orchestrated version of the auditory icon.

A model of the auditory HMI was then created to evaluate the ergonomics of this new model and compare it with sonification based only on vocal synthesis. The results of the test enable the following conclusions to be drawn:

– The model does not enable us to carry out navigation tasks more rapidly. This result is in line with the results of Leplâtre and Brewster [LEP 00] regarding the menu of a cell phone. However, it seems to us that in the case of automobile driving the main stake consists of navigating menus without looking at the screen, even if that means a slower navigation.

– A large majority of users deem that the model enables safer driving and better visual attention to the driving scene. This result is obtained subjectively, and it will now be relevant to implement objective methods in order to quantitatively evaluate the efficiency of the model. Among the methods generally used to evaluate attention in automobile driving, we can quote eye tracking, for example [SOD 02] or measuring on a driving simulator (e.g. measure of the reaction time to braking [SUM 00]).

– In the long term, users prefer the hybrid to the museme instance, as the proposed sounds are judged to be more evocative.

– The model obtains better results than vocal synthesis for the acceptance of sounds in the long term.

8.7.2. *Viewpoints*

The results obtained during the study presented in this chapter confirm the benefit of auditory guidance in an automobile multimedia system. Though sonification of the system does not enable us to navigate and access data more quickly, participants prefer to keep it, as in the end, their driving appears to be safer. The proposed sounds must be evocative, and for all levels of the hierarchical menu. The auditory vocal guidance gives the impression of more comfortable driving and less frequently diverting the gaze from the road.

Furthermore, the majority of participants (71%) disclosed their intention to keep auditory guidance in the long term. This result, obtained after a short use of sounds (around 30 minutes of driving) is to be moderated by the result gathered by Helle and Leplâtre [HEL 01] on a cell phone on which well-designed earcons were installed: at the end of three weeks, half of the participants had taken the sounds off, judging them to be too awkward in public spaces, too long and too high pitched. It is true that the context here is different: the automobile environment is less open to the outside, and the auditory technology available on an embedded multimedia system is much greater than that of the cell phone used by these authors. A longitudinal evaluation (lending of an equipped vehicle during a defined period) would enable us to observe the effect of auditory guidance on the appropriation of the system and to study the evolution of its use in the long term.

In view of this, it therefore seems that the study of the benefit of auditory guidance deserves to be pursued. To this end, we will base our work on the results obtained during the study presented in this chapter: we will use hybrid sounds evocative of the content for the first levels of the interface, then vocal synthesis for the lower levels. The evaluation of the sonification thus created will ideally be done with the help of eye tracking measures of the time the gaze is diverted, and will involve long observations in order to harness the quality of the appropriation of sounds and the possible tediousness that could lead drivers to switch off sounds after a certain period of use.

Finally, it turns out at the end of this first study that the intervention of an composer/sound designer is and remains essential for the creation of hierarchical sounds associated with the items in menus. Indeed, even if the design of sounds is controlled by technical and functional constraints, the creativity and artistic singularity of an sound "expert" seems necessary, specifically to get the best out of these constraints and achieve satisfactory solutions, both on an ergonomic and qualitative level. For this, the sonification approach – or more generally that of sound design – can begin to generalize a design approach based on models such as the one developed in this chapter, by progressively moving away from doing things case-by-case.

8.8. Bibliography

[BAR 97] BARRASS S., Auditory information design, PhD thesis, The Australian National University, 1997.

[BLA 89] BLATTNER M.M., SUMIKAWA D., GREENBERG R.M., "Earcons and icons: their structure and common design principles", *Human-Computer Interaction*, vol. 4, no. 1, pp. 11-44, 1989.

[BRE 94] BREWSTER S.A., WRIGHT P.C., EDWARDS A.D.N., "The design and evaluation of an auditory-enhanced scrollbar", in: B. ADELSON, S. DUMAIS, and J. OLSON (eds.), *Proceedings of CHI'94*, ACM Press, Addison-Wesley, Boston, Massachusetts, USA, pp. 173-179, 1994.

[BRE 95a] BREWSTER S.A., WRIGHT P.C., EDWARDS A.D.N., "Experimentally derived guidelines for the creation of earcons", in: *Adjunct Proceedings of HCI'95*, Huddersfield, UK, 1995.

[BRE 95b] BREWSTER S.A., WRIGHT P.C., EDWARDS A.D.N., "Parallel earcons: Reducing the length of audio messages", *International Journal of Human-Computer Studies*, vol. 43, no. 2, pp. 153-175, 1995.

[BRE 98a] BREWSTER S.A., "Using non-speech sounds to provide navigation cues", *ACM Transactions on Computer-Human Interaction*, vol. 5, no. 2, pp 224-259, 1998.

[BRE 98b] BREWSTER S.A., CAPRIOTTI A., HALL C.V., "Using compound earcons to represent hierarchies", *HCI Letters*, vol. 1, no. 1, pp. 6-8, 1998.

[CON 98] CONVERSY S., "Wind and wave auditory icons for monitoring continuous processes", in: *Summary Proceedings of ACM CHI 98 Conference on Human Factors in Computing Systems*, pp. 351-352, Los Angeles, USA, 1998.

[CON 00] CONVERSY S., Conception d'icones auditives paramétrées pour les interfaces homme-machine, PhD thesis, University of Paris-Sud XI, France, 2000.

[DIN 08] DINGLER T., LINDSAY J., WALKER B.N., "Learnabiltiy of sound cues for environmental features: auditory icons, earcons, spearcons, and speech", in: *Proceedings of the International Conference on Auditory Display (ICAD)*, Paris, France, 2008.

[DON 69] DONDERS F.C., "On the speed of mental processes", *Acta Psychologica*, no. 30, pp. 412-431, 1969 (translation of: *Die Schnelligkeit psychischer Processe*, first published in 1868).

[GAV 86] GAVER W., "Auditory icons: using sound in computer interfaces", *Human-Computer Interaction*, vol. 2, no. 2, pp. 167-177, 1986.

[GAV 89] GAVER W., "The SonicFinder: an interface that uses auditory icons", *Human-Computer Interaction*, no. 4, pp. 67-94, 1989.

[GIO 11] GIORDANO B., SUSINI P., BRESIN R., "Experimental methods for the perceptual evaluation of sound-producing objects and interfaces", in *Sonic Interaction Design Book*, MIT Press, 2011.

[HEL 01] HELLE S., LEPLÂTRE G., MARILA J., LAINE P., "Menu sonification in a mobile phone - a prototype study", in: *Proceedings of the International Conference on Auditory Display (ICAD)*, Espoo, Finland, 2001.

[HER 04] HERMANN T., HUNT A., "The discipline of interactive sonification", in: *Proceedings of International Workhop on Interactive Sonification (iSon)*, Bielefeld University, Bielefeld, Germany, 2004.

[HER 08] HERMANN T., VISELL Y., WILLIAMSON J., MURRAY-SMITH R., BRAZIL E., "Sonification for sonic interaction design", *ACM Conference on Human Factors in Computing Systems (CHI'08) Workshop on Sonic Interaction Design*, Florence, Italy, 2008.

[HO 08] HO C., SPENCE C., *The Multisensory Driver: Implications for Ergonomic Car Interface Design*, Ashgate Publishing, Farnham, UK, 2008.

[KRA 94] KRAMER G., "Some organizing principles for representing data with sound. Dans Auditory display", in: *Sonification, Audification, and Auditory Interfaces*, pp. 185-221, Addison-Wesley, Upper Saddle River, NJ, USA, 1994.

[LAN 10] LANGLOIS S., LOISEAU S., TARDIEU J., CERA A., MISDARIIS N., "Evaluation de la sonification d'un système multimédia automobile", *Actes de 22ème Conférence internationale francophone sur l'Interaction Homme-Machine (IHM)*, Luxemburg, pp. 173-180, ACM New-York, 2010.

[LEM 09] LEMAITRE G., HOUIX O., VISELL Y., FRANINOVIC K., MISDARIIS N., SUSINI P., "Toward the design and evaluation of continuous sound in tangible interfaces: The Spinotron", *International Journal of Human-Computer Studies*, vol. 67, pp. 976-993, 2009.

[LEM 08] LEMERCIER C., CELLIER J.M., "Les défauts de l'attention en conduite automobile: inattention, distraction et interférence", *Le travail Humain*, vol. 71, no. 3, pp. 271-296, 2008.

[LEP 00] LEPLÂTRE G., BREWSTER S.A., "Designing non-speech sounds to support navigation in mobile phone menus", *Proceedings of International Conference on Auditory Display (ICAD)*, pp. 190-199, Atlanta, USA, 2000.

[LEP 02] LEPLÂTRE G., The design and evaluation of non-speech sounds to support navigation in restricted display devices, PhD thesis, University of Glasgow, Scotland, 2002.

[MCA 93] MCADAMS S., BIGAND E., *Thinking in Sound: The Cognitive Psychology of Human Audition*, Oxford University Press, Oxford, 1993.

[PAL 07] PALLADINO D.K., WALKER B.N., "Learning rates for auditory menus enhanced with spearcons versus earcons", *Proceedings of International Conference on Auditory Display (ICAD)*, Montreal, Canada, 2007.

[RAT 05] RATH M., ROCCHESSO D., "Continuous sonic feedback from a rolling ball", *IEEE MultiMedia*, vol. 12, no. 2, pp. 60-69, 2005.

[RAT 06] RATH M., "On the relevance of auditory feedback for subjective and objective quality of control in a balancing task", *Proceedings of the 2nd ISCA/DEGA Tutorial and Research Workshop on Perceptual Quality of Systems (PQS)*, pp. 85-88, Berlin, Germany, 2006.

[RAT 07] RATH M., "Auditory velocity information in a balancing task", *Proceedings of the International Conference on Auditory Displays (ICAD'07)*, pp. 372-379, Montreal, Canada, 2007.

[RAT 08] RATH M., SCHLEICHER D.R., "On the relevance of auditory feedback for quality of control in a balancing task", *Acta Acustica United with Acustica*, vol. 94, pp. 12-20, 2008.

[SEA 07] SEARS A., JACKO J.A., *The Human-Computer Interaction Handbook: Fundamentals, Evolving Technologies and Emerging Applications* (2nd Edition), 2007.

[SHA 01] SHAFFER C.A., *A Practical Introduction to Data Structures and Algorithm Analysis: Second Edition*, Prentice Hall, Upper Saddle River, NJ, USA, 2001.

[SHA 07] SHAJAHAN P., IRANI P., "One family, many voices: Can multiple synthetic voices be used as navigational cues in hierarchical interfaces?", *International Journal of Speech Technology*, vol. 9, no. 1-2, pp. 1-15, 2007.

[SOD 02] SODHI M., REIMER B., LLAMAZARES I., "Glance analysis of driver eye movements to evaluate distraction", *Behavior Research Methods, Instruments, & Computers 2002*, vol. 34, no. 4, pp. 529-538, 2002.

[SUE 07] SUEID C., De l'urgence perçue au temps de réaction: application aux alarmes sonores, PhD Thesis, University of Paris VI, France, 2007.

[SUM 00] SUMMALA H., "Brake reaction times and driver behavior analysis", *Transportation Human Factors*, vol. 2, no. 3, pp. 217-226, 2000.

[SUS 09] SUSINI P., HOUIX O., MISDARIIS N., SMITH B.K., LANGLOIS S., "Instruction's effect on semantic scale ratings of interior car sounds", *Applied Acoustics*, vol. 70, no. 3, 2009.

[SUS 11] SUSINI P., LEMAITRE G., MCADAMS S., "Psychological measurement for sound description and evaluation", in: *Measuring the Impossible – Theory and Methods of Measurements with Persons*, Taylor and Francis, London, 2011.

[TAG 82] TAGG P., "Teoria degli affetti", *Analyzing Popular Music: Theory, Method and Practice, Popular Music*, no. 2, pp 37-67, 1982.

[VAR 03] VARGAS M.L.M., ANDERSON S., "Combining speech and earcons to assist menu navigation", *Proceedings of International Conference on Auditory Display (ICAD)*, Boston, USA, pp. 38-41, 2003.

[VIA 07] VIAUD-DELMON I., BRESSON J., PACHET F., BEVILACQUA F., ROY P., WARUSFEL O., "EarToy: Interactions ludiques par l'audition", *Actes des Journées d'Informatique Musicale (JIM)*, Lumière University Lyon II, Lyon, France, 2007.

[WAL 06] WALKER B.N., NANCE A., LINDSAY J., "Spearcons: speech-based earcons improve navigation performance in auditory menus", *Proceedings of International Conference on Auditory Display (ICAD)*, Queen Mary University of London, London, UK, 2006.

[YAL 08] YALLA P., WALKER B.N., "Advanced auditory menus: design and evaluation of auditory scroll bars", *Proceedings of ASSETS'08*, Halifax, Nova Scotia, Canada, October 13-15 2008.

[ZHA 07] ZHAO S., DRAGICEVIC P., CHIGNELL M., BALAKRISHNAN R., BAUDISCH P., "earPod: Eyes-free menu selection with touch input and reactive audio feedback", *Proceedings of the ACM Conference on Human Factors in Computing Systems (CHI)*, pp. 1395-1404, 2007.

Chapter 9

Consideration of the Travel Time Experience in the Conceptual Models of Personalized Interactive Applications

9.1. Transport: a field with particular needs in terms of personalization of information

With the multiplication of information sources on numerous fixed or mobile technical platforms (computer, PDA, smart phone, terminal, etc.), the user can access information at any time wherever he is. Nonetheless, faced with a multitude of accessible information, the user needs tools enabling him to access the right information at the right time. This is all the more true in the field of transport, where the user needs to access mobility information for the duration of his trips [VIA] (see Chapter 1). It is also essential to allow the interactive applications to adapt to users and become as individualized as possible based on a complete knowledge of each user. This happens via a personalization of information and services [VES 05] but also by taking into account specificities of the environment in which the application is used; this must enable analyses of needs to center on the user and not the system [COO 07]. In the field of transport, it is only recently that researchers have examined the issue of the time it takes users for a trip and more specifically their often diverse expectations, which are in constant evolution [FLA 05]. As far as we know, this point has never been taken into account in the context of a method or tool in the creation of applications specific to the field of transport, but is essential if we want to be able to meet the needs and expectations of users.

Chapter written by Arnaud BROSSARD, Mourad ABED, Christophe KOLSKI and Guillaume USTER.

However, finding a solution to this issue is not enough. Indeed, with increasingly complex applications, it is also necessary to be able to create reusable application models enabling new applications to be generated based on proven models; this will enable us to accelerate developments and increase their reliability. This is what is proposed by the model-driven approach, which is currently associated with a huge research movement. In our works, we have attempted to summarize these needs and constraints, in order to put forward a method and tools enabling to us take into account the use of travel time in public transport by the user, in the context of a model-driven approach, to develop personalized interactive applications.

9.2. The modeling of applications and consideration of the needs of users in the context of personalizing interactive applications

9.2.1. *Modeling of applications and the MDE approach*

Model-driven engineering (MDE) is becoming the new paradigm in terms of the development of ICT applications [FAV 06], [HAI 06], [SCH 06]. Its objective is to enable the creation of ICT applications based on conceptual models, particularly those based on an assembly of conceptual models; each model dealing with a well-defined business issue. From a systemic approach by ICT applications, each model represents a different point of view of a same business process, such as access safety, the distribution of tasks between stakeholders, etc. Also, a business process is seen as an ensemble of tasks enabling a user to reach a specific goal (visualize the next departure, renew a transport subscription, etc.).

An important notion of MDE is that of the conceptual model. As far as we are concerned, we have retained the definition given by the *Object Management Group* (OMG) for the *computation independent model* level of the *model-driven architecture* (MDA) approach [OMG 03] that corresponds to a level of conceptual models: "*the CIM [computational independent model] model is a view of the system from the sole point of view of the IT elements which enable it to be realized. The CIM model does not show the details of the structure of systems. A CIM model is sometimes called a domain model and a vocabulary which is familiar to experts in this domain is used to specify it*".

The objective of conceptual methods is to enable experts in the field, who are not ICT specialists but business specialists, to themselves define the models of the business processes that they use and want to see used again in an ICT application. In the rest of the chapter, for greater clarity we will use the term business expert instead of field expert.

The passage of conceptual models to practical applications occurs via a succession of model transformations based on an MDA type approach; see Figure 9.1. In fact, the model transformations represent the main asset of the MDA methodology as they are the ones that are a reflection of the know-how and the methodologies used within a development structure. This is why the OMG recommends modeling model transformations themselves in order to ensure quality and to ensure the durability of agreed investments in the implementation of an MDA approach. This requirement is very well explained in [CLA 04]. As far as we are concerned, we are interested from the point of view of the human-machine interactions (HMI).

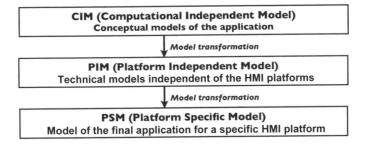

Figure 9.1. *Global representation of the MDA approach from the point of view of the HMI*

Through the use of three abstraction levels, the MDA approach aims to separate the functional logic associated with application of the technology used in order to carry a task out. The objective is to delete the link between the functional aspects of applications and the associated coding, thus facilitating their interoperability, all the while making them less sensitive to technological evolutions. The passage from one level to another is done with the help of model transformations, enabling each stage to enrich the models of the previous level with the necessary and sufficient technical information. This transformation is today carried out automatically or semi-automatically with the help of tools such as VIATRA (*VIsual Automated model TRAnsformations*) or ATL (*Atlas Transformation Language*)[1]. As there are many tools enabling us to carry out model transformations, we can refer to [CZA 06] for a presentation and a classification of them.

In the context of the modeling of interactive applications, few works have initially put forward a true MDA-type approach, even though the benefit of using this type of approach has been demonstrated [PER 07], [SOT 05], [SOT 06],

---

1 Both accessible on the website, http://www.eclipse.org/projects/project_summary.php? projectid=modeling.gmt.umlx).

[STA 06], [VAN 05]; numerous research projects are currently ongoing. In the rest of this chapter, we will not present a new modeling method but focus on our method for modeling interactive applications based on business processes [BRO 07] to show how it is possible to integrate the notion of the travel time experience of travelers during their journeys in the context of the conceptual modeling of an interactive application [BRO 09], [UST 09].

9.2.2. *Modeling of the user in interactive applications*

To provide information and services that are relevant to the user, it is necessary to be able to identify and characterize him. This knowledge of the user implies resolving two issues [ANL 06], [RAZ 03]:

– That of the storing of information gathered for each user. This is generally done via user profiles that contain, for each user, all the information which is specific to him [AMA 99].

– That of tools and methods to be implemented in order to gather this information. This gathering can be done explicitly via the use of questions the user is asked [SHA 95]. It can also be done implicitly (automatically) by the system, i.e. with no intervention from the user [GOE 00] via an analysis of the user's behavior and the history of interactions with the user. Finally, it can be done in a mixed manner, the user confirming the information suggested by the system.

However, if we want to be capable of adapting applications to the user, the storing of information about the user and its direct use in applications is not enough. It is in fact necessary to change the way in which applications are designed by adopting an approach to interactions centered on the user and first of all on the goals that he has when using each application [COO 07]. It is also necessary to find other ways of interacting with him in order to enable a more rapid adaptation of applications. In order to do this, one of the possible solutions is to recognize the emotions of the user [COW 01], i.e. to recognize the emotional context when the application is used.

9.2.3. *Definition and limitations of the consideration of context*

Before defining the notion of context in the field of transport, it is essential to start by specifying the notion of context in a global manner. In order to do this, we will use the definition in [DEY 00], [DEY 01]: *"Context represents all the information which can be used to characterize a situation or an entity. An entity is a person, a place or an object that is considered as significant in the interaction between the user and the application, including the user and the application itself. A system is sensitive to the context if it uses the context to provide information or services that are relevant to the user; the relevance being evaluated according to the user's ongoing task".*

In the frame of an interactive application, consideration of the context can occur on two levels:

– At the human-machine interface. In this case, we will speak of plasticity. Thus, for [THE 99] plasticity is: "the ability of interfaces to adapt to their context of use with respect to their usability. The context of use is defined as the triplet user, platform and environment" (see also Chapter 11).

– In the content where we will talk about context awareness, defined as [ABO 99]: "the use of context to provide appropriate information and/or services to the user; the context being any information which can be used to characterize the situation of an entity which can be a user, an environment, a physical or IT object".

In the frame of an MDE-type approach, the question that arises is how to take into account the context on a conceptual level, i.e. how to make the context sufficiently abstract for it to be independent of the technology and sufficiently practical for it to be used with conceptual models. Starting from existing works on the subject, we were able to determine several different ways to deal with the characterization of contexts:

– The first, used by [TAD 06], consists in only defining a limited and specified number of contexts. By being based on an ensemble of rules, it then becomes possible, all the time, to associate one and only one specified context to the application.

– The second, used by [CHE 04], based on the previous solution, suggests introducing the notion of context ontology. Each element of context (place, time, technical ability, etc.) has its own ontology. It is the inference engine for all these ontologies that enables the active context to be determined.

– The third consists in linking the notion of context to the user's ongoing activities. Thus, certain works [BAR 04] propose basing the adaptation to context according to the user's ongoing business processes. Other works propose integrating the notion of intention at the user level in the adaptation to context [PAS 99]. It is, according to these works, the only way of having a contextual adaptation that really takes into account the needs and expectations of users.

If these solutions put forward different visions for the consideration of context, they nonetheless have a certain number of similarities:

– they all possess a rules engine, or "intelligent" components enabling the actions that are to be carried out to be defined according to changes occurring in the context;

– they are all based on a conceptual definition of the context enabling the technical elements to be separated, which takes into account the context of applicative elements that are sensitive to context. For the majority of solutions used today, this abstraction is done with the help of an ontology of context;

– the consideration of the context can only be done via the definition and use of predefined specific rules. An application can only react to the context, if it is anticipated from the design stage that it will react, and it has been specified during the creation of the application how to react.

These different constraints regarding the use of the notion of context in a conceptual model being established, we will now present a type of context specific to the field of transport, which is the consideration of the travel time experience of users.

9.2.4. *User model and transport: consideration of users' travel time experience*

In the field of transport, travel times have long been considered a waste of time [FIC 70] during which the activities carried out, such as reading or talking to a neighbor, are only done by the traveler to pass the time [ORA 97]. However, one study [MAR 99] showed that the transport time was only perceived as wasted time by 40% of users. From this observation, research sought to differentiate the act of travel from the activities carried out during the trips [JEN 08], [LYO 05], [MOK 01] and then to characterize the activities carried out during the travel times by grouping them together in categories, in a heuristic vision of the issue.

Thus, an initial categorization [FLA 05] proposes distributing the activities according to three groups:

– productive activities, such as reading, writing, etc.;

– relaxing and transition activities, such as listening to music, observing the landscape, etc.;

– sociable activities, which enable travelers to start a communication with one or more individuals.

Another possible categorization is that based on a sociological and anthropological study carried out in the context of the Viatic.Mobilité project [VIA], [UST 09]. The conclusions of this study, partly presented in Chapter 1, propose distribution of travelers into four distinct groups divided into two axes according to their use of travel time; see Figure 9.2.

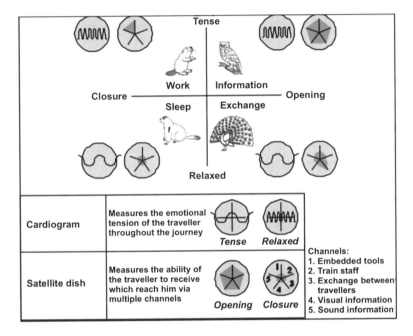

Figure 9.2. *The categories of travel time experience by travelers identified in the context of the Viatic.Mobilité project (see Chapter 1)*

In this categorization represented by a bestiary:

– the *beaver* represents the person that has a productive activity (reading or writing a report, reading over a lesson, learning a language, etc.);

– the *owl* represents the person who is lost or is searching for information (consulting line maps, searching for the next connection, etc.);

– the *peacock* represents the person who communicates with others (talking with his neighbor, sending SMS, etc.);

– the *marmot* represents the person who is sleeping, relaxing, snoozing, watching the landscape go by, etc.).

In the context of our works, we have used the categorization put forward in the context of the Viatic.Mobilité project for consideration of the use of travel time by users in application models.

It is important to note here that this categorization, which is based on a field study, is only a heuristic vision of the issue. Thus, the choice of the number of categories, as well as the definition of each category, was done in order to be able to identify as many common behaviors as possible. The use of such an approach, if it enables the issue to be simplified, also implies the existence of a grey area at the boundaries between the different categories.

It does not enable us, *in theory*, to be able to ensure a certain and unambiguous identification of which category the user belongs to. That being said, it represents an initial approach to the issue of considering the notion of time use during travel by users of public transport.

9.3. Specificities in the field of transport in the framework of a method of modeling personalized interactive applications

9.3.1. *Introduction*

To take into account the travel time experience of the user in application models, it is first essential to be able to correctly identify the activities associated with each category. Then, it is necessary to define how we can know, at any time, in which category the user is. Finally, it is necessary to be able to take into account this notion of category of travel time experience by the traveler in the application models, particularly the conceptual models.

9.3.2. *A different approach to the analysis of needs*

In the classical methods of analysis proposed in the context of systemic-type approaches, such as Merise [NAN 01], Cartesian, such as SADT (Structured Analysis and Design Technique) or IDEF0 (Integration Definition for Function Modeling) [ANG 99], object-oriented, such as UP (Unified Process) [JAC 99], RUP (Rational Unified Process) [KRU 00] or 2TUP (Two Track Unified Process) [ROQ 07], the organization of tasks only considers a functional logic centered around a goal to be reached and only marginally takes into account the user. We propose adding a new stage to the different analysis stages of these methods; see Figure 9.3. Initially, once all the tasks have been identified, it will consist of grouping them together into business processes; i.e. an ensemble of tasks enabling us to determine a business goal from the point of view of the user and/or the point field of business in which the application is used (a business process can call on several users).

Once the processes have been identified, it is necessary to distribute them into the different categories of users' travel time experience; each process can be part of one or several different categories. Then, it is necessary to adapt each process to the different categories of travel time use; i.e. to possibly redefine the content of each task according to the different categories of travel time experiences associated with the business process.

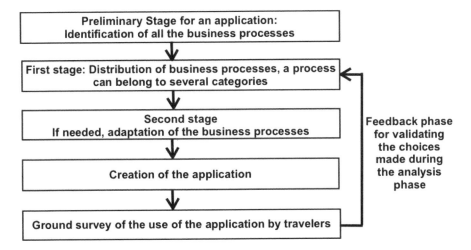

Figure 9.3. *The specific part of analysis associated with the consideration of categories of travel time use*

At this level, we are not creating new business processes, but, as we will show further on the chapter, we are using information regarding the category to which a user belongs (*Peacock, Beaver, Marmot* or *Owl*) to adapt certain tasks or enable the execution of certain tasks only associated with a category in particular. Thus, if we take a business process associated with the creation of a new trip, for example, it will automatically be able to be linked to the work schedule of the user if he is a *beaver* type whereas this link will be optional if he is a *peacock*-type user. Each adaptation needing to correspond to a real user need, it will not be carried out systematically; certain business processes will be able to be given for all users, such as for example the printing of a metro line map.

If the distribution of categories and their adaptation is done at the analysis phase, it is important to anticipate a feedback phase enabling the choices that were made to be validated. In order to do this, once the application has been deployed, it is necessary to carry out surveys in the field to analyze the real uses of each business process. If there is a difference, it will be necessary to return to the analysis phase and, if necessary, adapt the distribution of business processes in the different categories and/or modify the adaptation to categories made in each business process.

As a result, the distribution of business processes in each category and their adaptation must be a pluridisciplinary work in which different disciplines are involved, as much in the field of ICT as in that of social sciences. At this level we must therefore have a decompartmentalization of disciplines, and this is probably one of the major challenges for the integration of the notion of travel time experience in interactive applications in the field of transport.

9.3.3. *Categories of the travel time experience of users*

Dealing with the categories of travel time experience in conceptual models can be done on several levels in the context of our model-driven modeling approach [BRO 08]:

– in the business rules, like all criteria of the user profile;

– in the business process models;

– in the static interaction models.

The business rules [OMG 05] enable part of the business logic of business processes to be extracted, making them easier to modify. A definition of the business rules is given by [BRG 00]: "*A business rule is a declaration which can be evaluated and that defines or restricts certain aspects of the business. It has the aim of affirming the business structure or to control or influence the behavior of the business. For a given project, the business rules are atomic, that is to say that they cannot be redefined into smaller elements*".

In the context of our approach, we have defined three types of business rules:

– so-called validation rules, the evaluation of which returns a Boolean-type value (true or false);

– selection rules, the evaluation of which returns a value that can be a chain of characters, a date or a number;

– action rules, the evaluation of which will set off a particular action.

With business rules, the use of information regarding the category of travel time experience of the user is incorporated as with any other information in the profile. To give an example, we can see a validation-type business rule "*IsABeaver*" below that enables us to determine whether the user is part of the *beaver* category.

For reasons of legibility, the formalism of the definition of rules has been simplified:

```
<rule name="IsABeaver" type="Validation">
    <condition>
            <clause>
            <element type="Profile" value="UserCategory"/>
            <comparator type="equal"/>
            <rightmember type="FixedValue" value="Beaver"/>
            </clause>
    </condition>
</rule>
```

With business process models, the use of information regarding the category of travel time experience of a user is determined relative to the selection elements of the tasks to be carried out in the business process. If the selection criterion has little chance of evolving over time, it can be used directly in the business process.

In the opposite case, it will be necessary to use a business rule. Figure 9.4 presents, in a simplified business process, an element of selection that as a selection criterion, uses the value of the element of the user's profile containing his current category of travel time experience to trigger a specific task for each category.

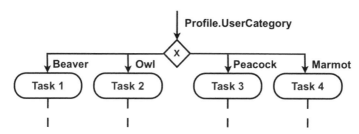

Figure 9.4. *Example of travel time use categories in a business process (based on a BPMN-type formalism [BPM 04])*

For static interaction models, the information contained in the profile of the user is only used via business rules at the level of the properties of display of interaction elements, such as:

– the *IsVisibleRule* property that is used to determine whether the interaction element is visible to the user;

– the *ISUsableRule* property, which is used to determine whether or not the interaction element can be handled by the user.

Figure 9.5 gives an example of a text-type input field (*UserName*), the content of which will not be able to be modified if the evaluation of the *IsABeaver* business rule, which enables determination of whether or not the user is in the *Beaver* category, comes back false.

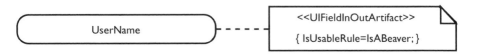

Figure 9.5. *Example of use of a category of travel tine in a static interaction model (based on a BPMN-type formalism)*

9.3.4. *The issue of identification of category changes*

Now that we have shown how, at a conceptual level, it is possible to take into account the category of travel time experiences of users, one question remains to be dealt with: how to take the changes of categories into consideration in real time, or more exactly as quickly as possible, in the applications?

In the context of our approach, each user must belong to one and only one category at all times. This implies that at the start of the application, we automatically allocate the user to a category; which is specific to each application. This enables us to allocate a default behavior to each application.

Based on the moment the user handles the application, the category change can occur:

– *explicitly*: the user choosing the category to which he belongs. This is an option that can be useful at the time of starting the application, if the category is automatically chosen by default. It is not a good solution if the user must himself define his category changes before being able to access certain parts of the application;

– *implicitly*: the application itself choosing when to make the change according to predetermined criteria.

In the event where the change is carried out implicitly, it can be done according to several elements:

– The change happens automatically in a certain manner, following the use of a well determined functionality in the application. For example, if the user consults a map, we can presume that he is lost and that he is therefore in the *Owl* category. Similarly, if he accesses his work schedule, we can presume that he is working and is therefore in the *Beaver* category. Practically, this type of change is managed at the level of the modeling and more specifically at the level of the business processes in which it is possible to carry out a category change following a user action.

– The change can also occur in an uncertain manner, based on contextual information that the application and the platform are able to recuperate and manage. Thus, if the user is no longer using the application and if a sensor means that we know he is talking, we can presume that he is in the *Peacock* category. Similarly, if the user is no longer using the application and a sensor determines he has not spoken nor moved for more than five minutes, we can presume that he is in the *Marmot* category. This type of adaptation is close to the works of [SIE 03] that, basing themselves on information obtained from sensors, propose carrying out a dynamic contextual adaptation according to the modifications of the exterior environment and the physiological states of the user.

If the change according to the actions of the user is done systematically in a sure way, the change in the function of contextual information occurs following an uncertain methodology based a certain number of heuristics. In any case, the automatic change of category is done according to probabilistic methods that are based on a certain number of criteria that enable us to define, for sure, whether or not they belong to a specific category. For this to happen, the criteria must be measurable and quantifiable and in particular must be fixed in the context of the execution of each application. Thus, if we take our example of the duration of non-use of the application as a criterion for category change, we have:

– duration of non-use >2 min = possibility of changing category to *Peacock*;

– duration of non-use >5 min = possibility of changing category to *Marmot*.

This simple example shows a limitation of the approach in the sense that, if we only use these criteria, when the duration of non-use is greater than 5 min it is impossible to define which category the user is in (*Peacock* or *Marmot*?).

To limit error risks during category changes, for each business process we propose to associate a confidence level with regards to the different categories. This confidence level can take on a value between 0 (the user is definitely not in this category) and 1 (the user is definitely in this category). For example, when the user consults the list of the latest films that have just come out at the cinema, we can in principle define with certainty that he is not in the *Beaver* category (confidence level fixed at 0.0) but more probably in the *Peacock* category (confidence level fixed at least at 0.5). In the event where a degree of confidence is not explicitly associated with a category, it is considered as being equal to 0.0.

In order to determine the different levels of confidence for a specific business process, during the phase of needs analysis presented in Figure 9.3 we propose to use a three-step approach:

– determination of the confidence levels during the initial phase of user needs definition;

– analysis of results of the field studies regarding the real use of applications;

– adaptation of the confidence levels, if necessary, and a return to the first stage.

The use of confidence level with the business processes used is not enough to determine for sure whether a change in category needs to be carried out or not. In fact it is also necessary to know the previous category of the user as well as the activities that he was doing before using the new business process. This is carried out via the use of a history of category changes for each user. In this history, each process change is saved with the time of the change as well as the confidence level associated with this change; and this for all four categories. For each category, it is then possible to determine a global confidence level with the help of the following formula:

$$\sum (\text{confidence level}) \times (\text{time in minutes in the history of category changes})$$
for each business process in the history of category changes

By using this formula, the current category of the user is defined as being the category that has the highest global confidence level.

COMMENT 9.1:– if the user selects a business process with a confidence level equal to 1 for one of the categories, the category of the user is immediately changed and the history of the category changes is reset.

One of the main problems that can occur with the use of this formula for the determination of the global level of confidence resides in the fact that if we do not fix a time limit on the level of information contained in the history, the system will become decreasingly relevant to the level of detection of category changes. Thus, if a user remains in the *Beaver* category for an hour and he launches a new business process linked with the *Peacock* category, the change in category can only occur a certain time after this new process has been used, which can be quite long. This is why we have fixed a limited lifespan for each piece of information stored in the history of category changes. As determined by the sociological and anthropological study conducted during the Viatic.Mobilité project [UST 09], a category change can be considered as being almost sure after a maximum estimated length of around 7 minutes. This is this delay that we have taken as the maximum length of information storage in the history of category changes. Beyond this, only information concerning the confidence levels regarding the last process used are conserved in the history.

In order to avoid a continuous evaluation of the global confidence level for each category, the calculation is only carried out every 20 seconds and when a business process changes. This delay, which was determined by sociologists and anthropologists based on field studies, enables us to ensure a good balance between the need to limit the calculation burden on information systems and the need to regularly determine the category changes.

In the context of our approach, it is possible to only use sure methods of category change for certain applications and for other applications only uncertain methods. Similarly, it is possible to use both or none if the application is not sensitive to the category of travel time use by the user.

9.3.5. *Summary and discussion*

Today, with the multiplication of nomad ICT systems and available information, the automatic adaptation of applications to their context of use is a requirement [WAG 02]. In the context of a user-based approach, part of the notion of context is based on the needs and expectations of users in relation to their ICT systems. As such, in the field of transport, an element of context that the applications must be able to take into account is the notion of travel time experience of users.

In this chapter, based on the categorization suggested in Figure 9.3, we have put forward a global method for taking this element of context into account via:

– a new approach to the analysis of needs;

– an integration of the adaptation to this element of context in the conceptual models in the context of an IDM-type approach;

– methods for the consideration of category changes, whether these changes occur explicitly or implicitly.

Although this enables this type of adaptation to be dealt with, a question still remains unanswered: how relevant is the consideration of this contextual element and, more specifically, how relevant are the adaptations to be carried out?

By analyzing the relevance of the use of different menu typologies within an application (static menus, adaptable menus, adaptive menus), works have shown that the automatic adaptations were not always the ideal solution when making menus more relevant and easier to use [FIN 04]. In the context of the consideration of the travel time experience of users in applications, we can ask whether it is relevant to automatically make adaptations or whether it is necessary to let the user make his adaptations himself. Similarly, we can ask ourselves, in the context of an automatic adaptation, about the relevance of changing categories several times in a single trip.

In the context of our study we do not yet have answers to these issues as they can only be found via studies carried out in the field in real conditions of use. Also, consideration of the use of travel time by the user in applications is within a continuous cycle made up of four phases (see Figure 9.6) that are fairly similar to that put forward in the Deming wheel or PDCA cycle (Plan, Do, Check, Act) [DEM 86]:

– phase 1: planning of adaptations;

– phase 2: integration of adaptations in the applications;

– phase 3: observation in the field of the relevance of adaptations;

– phase 4: analysis of observations. We keep what is working well, which we will not modify and we isolate what is not working well, that we will therefore modify, before returning to phase 1.

The foundations of our approach being laid, we now present a few examples of its use in order to illustrate its different principles.

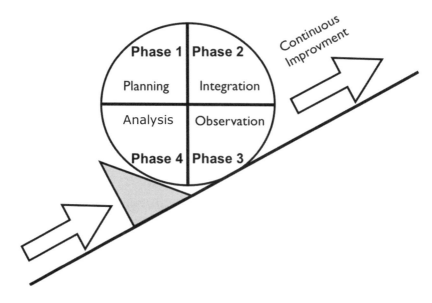

Figure 9.6. *The principle of continuous improvement of the relevance of adaptations with consideration of the use of travel time by users in applications*

9.4. Application of the method

9.4.1. *Presentation of the Viatic.Mobilité project*

Our research works are within the context of the ANR Viatic.Mobilité project [VIA] (see Chapter 1).

This project aims to implement a service of mobility help for public transport users.

This service has the objective of proposing mobility information, but also of agreement by expressing the informational needs of a person who is on a trip in a logical manner.

It will also present the particularity of being accessible throughout the user's journey: at his home, in the multimodal exchange clusters (place of passage from one mode of transport to another) and on board a transport vehicle (Figure 9.7).

In the rest of this chapter, we will present a few examples developed in the context of the project.

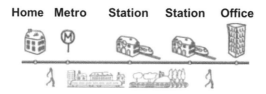

Home   Metro   Station   Station   Office

Figure 9.7. *The continuity of the journey in the Viatic.Mobilité project*

9.4.2. *An example of HCI personalization*

In the context of the Viatic.Mobilité project, the user accesses information via a portal from which he can choose the activity he wishes to carry out. In this portal, he can carry out a certain number of operations that are common to all users such as, for example, to connect himself, modify his profile or send a message to the application support service. He can also access of services grouped together according to the different categories of the travel time experience.

Thus, in an initial, simplified portal (Figure 9.8) he can access the following groups of services:

   – communication (associated with the *Peacock* category);

   – transport information (common to all categories);

– general information (associated with the *Owl* category);

– leisure (associated with the *Marmot* category);

– work (associated with the *Beaver* category).

In this example, the distribution of services in the different categories is the result of the analysis phase specific to the use of travel time by users. This enabled us to determine the confidence levels for each category and for each group of services; see Table 9.1.

Figure 9.8. *Example of an access portal simplified to the Viatic.Mobilité application*

Group of services	Beaver	Owl	Peacock	Marmot
Communication	0.4	0.3	0.8	0.1
Transport information	0.5	0.7	0.2	0.3
General information	0.5	0.4	0.2	0.3
Leisure	0.1	0.2	0.4	0.8
Work	0.9	0.1	0.1	0.1

Table 9.1. *Definition of the confidence levels for each group of services in the simplified Viatic.Mobilité portal*

In this example, access to a service group is considered as being a change in the active business process and will be identified as such in the history of category changes. Given the distribution of confidence levels, the category change could require a certain amount of time to really be taken into account.

During the Viatic.Mobilité project, due to a lack of time it was only possible to conduct a limited number of experiments with test users. This did not enable us to provide a definitive conclusion regarding our global approach, but we did identify three initial avenues for improvement:

– the semantic characterization of the category of travel time experience of users is not easy to define for sure, as each participant within the work groups can make his own interpretation of the needs analysis results;

– the definition of the confidence levels for each category is currently more experimental than scientific, and it has not yet been possible for us to define a collection of rules to determine them in a confident manner;

– the validation of the approach by carrying out surveys in the field is not easy as each surveyor may have his own perception of different categories; certain situations perhaps leading to different conclusions depending on the surveyors.

That being said, a certain number of results have been able to be determined:

– the use of confidence levels enables us to have results for the applications that are closer to the real behaviors and needs observed by the surveyors in the field;

– the number of incorrect changes in categories of travel time experience within an application is limited.

In fact, the main problem identified during the field surveys was the difficulty in having reliable information about the category of the user when he is not using the application. This can lead to poor category choices and/or a certain adaptation time to determine the real category of the user.

9.4.3. *An example of business process personalization: the organization of a trip*

To illustrate the case of the adaptation of a business process to the category of travel time experience, we will present the example of a business process, the aim of which is to enable the display of information associated with the next departure of the user. The analysis of needs has given rise to the identification of two different adaptations of the business process. The first, linked to the *Beaver* category, enables the display of information concerning the trip to be linked with the information contained in the work schedule of the user in order to give him information regarding the reason for the trip and about the next rendezvous. The second, common to all other categories, only displays information associated with the trip itself. In the application, access to this process could be possible, in a *Windows*, *Icons*, *Menus*, *Pointing Device-* or WIMP-type interface, with the help of a menu option or a button. Based on this, an action could be set off that would use a selection criteria based on the category of the user (key-word *Profile.UserCategory*) to display either a group of interaction elements called *UIGroupNextDepartPro* if it is of the *Beaver* category (see Figure 9.10) or a group of interaction elements called *UIGroupNextDepartGen* for the other categories.

Figure 9.9 shows an extract from the associated business process model centered on the selection of a group of interaction elements to be displayed according to the category of the user.

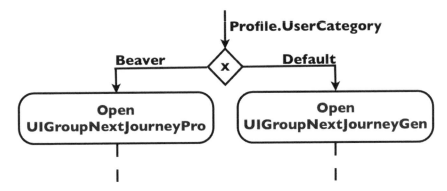

Figure 9.9. *Extract from the business process associated with the display of information regarding the user's next trip*

In the two example screens in Figures 9.10 and 9.11, in order to take into account the fact that it is impossible to be sure of the category of the user, we have added the possibility of enlisting an action via the use of the *Modify display* button. This enables us to change the display content from one type to another.

Thus, a user will be able to explicitly ask to have a screen output that is normally associated with the *Beaver* category although he is in another category and a user of the *Beaver* category will be able to ask to have the output screen associated with other categories.

This manner of proceeding enables us to consider possible category changes that could not otherwise be detected during the execution of a business process and via an explicit choice of the user.

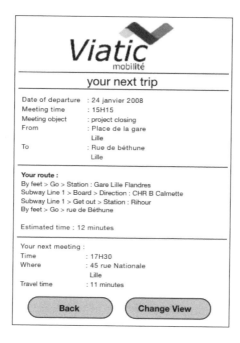

Figure 9.10. *Screen associated with the display of the next trip for a user of the Beaver category (addition of information regarding the next trip at the bottom of the screen)*

Figure 9.11. *Screen linked to the display of the next trip for a user who is not of the Beaver category*

9.4.4. *Extension of the approach to other business domains*

Having seen this first example, it is important to know whether our approach can be extended to business domains other than public transport. In theory the answer is yes, as from a sociological and anthropological point of view [UST 09] it always seems possible, whatever the business domain concerned, to determine an attitude in relation to the experience *vis-à-vis* time. For example, time can be used to acquire new skills, collect information, create new documents or for personal needs. In fact, the real problem resides in the determination of categories that can be associated with the time experience of the user in the business domain concerned. Regarding the Viatic.Mobilité project, this can be carried out via sociological or anthropological studies in the field. As the categories defined in each business domain have a certain probability of being different, the question that arises is how to link them together? This is a question that is all the more critical as a user can use applications belonging to various different business domains at the same time.

To answer this question, we propose using semantic links between the categories of the different business domains considered. As it is not always possible to envisage direct links between two categories of two different business domains, we propose using weightings between 0 and 1 for each link. This enables semantic distances between the categories of the two business domains considered to be defined. Table 9.2 gives an example of a definition of this type of relationship between two different business domains.

		Category of travel time use			
		Beaver	**Owl**	**Peacock**	**Marmot**
Categories of the user's experience in relation to time in the field of journeys for pleasure (non professional journeys according to [ARS 09])	Relax	0.0	0.1	0.3	0.8
	Meet people/visit friends or family	0.1	0.3	0.8	0.1
	Discover new things	0.1	0.5	0.4	0.1
	Do stress relieving activities	0.0	0.2	0.6	0.0
	Shopping	0.2	0.3	0.4	0.0

Table 9.2. *Definition of semantic links on the categories of user experience in relation to time for two different business domains (coefficients not validated experimentally in the current state of our works)*

Due to a shortage of time, we have not yet had the time to implement this type of semantic approach between two business domains via experiments. That being said, this semantic approach was validated, from the point of view of its global principle, within the Viatic.Mobilité project by sociologists and anthropologists who considered it to be relatively simple to understand and handle, all the while being relevant to the fact that, in principle, the user only rarely goes from one state to a completely different one.

9.4.5. *Summary and discussion*

Via these examples, we have shown that our approach could potentially enable us to take into account the travel time experience of the user on several levels in applications:

– as an element enabling the content of all the business processes associated with the application to be distributed and defined;

– as a selection criterion, directly or via a business rule, enabling choices within a business process to be defined and therefore within the conceptual models of the application.

These examples also enable the current limitations of the approach to be identified:

– The importance of the preliminary analysis phase, to distribute and adapt the different business processes, which is based on a pluridisciplinary approach that is often difficult to set up.

– The difficulty of exactly knowing the real category of the travel time experience of the user; the category changes only being made via interactions carried out by users, the other elements being ignored. Thus, talking to a neighbor after having worked on a dossier is a typical example of a category change that is ignored by the application as it is impossible to identify in the current state of our works. Nonetheless, we have a certain number of preliminary ideas for the use of existing sensors to take into account category changes, such as the use of sound sensors to identify passage to the *Peacock* category. All of these avenues still need to be validated, however, as the choice of relevant sensors and the definition of ensembles of associated values for each category represent an important focus of research that we have only just started to address.

– Finally, there is a real issue with the characterization of categories and the number of them. In the context of our works, we have used four categories of user classification, but other works have put forward three [FIC 70] and nothing says that there should not be more than four categories. With the characterization of categories, the aim of which is to specifically define the criteria enabling a user to be identified as being part such-and-such a category, the difficulty resides in the definition of criteria that are discriminatory enough to avoid all ambiguity when a category is associated with a user. The characterization and definition of the number of categories, which can only happen based on sociological, psychological and anthropological studies carried out in the field, are also dependent on lifestyles and cultures and can therefore evolve in time and space; the issue is knowing how to take these evolutions into account.

All these limitations and constraints represent avenues of research that specifically require a multidisciplinary approach.

9.5. Conclusion

The consideration of the user in applications becomes an increasingly important criterion in the context of the development of new ICT applications. Numerous works have studied various issues, such as the notion of user profile, information personalization and elements that are attached to it or the mood of the user. To our knowledge, however, there are no works that have attempted to provide an answer to the consideration of the attitude of the traveler during his trips on public transport or, more specifically, the consideration of travel time experience (time used for working, communicating or resting).

In the context of our works, via the use of different sociological and anthropological studies, we provide a first approach to the consideration of the travel time experience within applications. Thus, we propose to add new stages to the phase of needs' analysis, which is a prerequisite for all ICT development, for it to take into account the notion of travel time experience during the creation of different business processes associated with the application. Then, in the context of an MDA approach, we propose solutions to take into account the travel time experience within conceptual models of the application. Finally, we propose a solution to take into account the category changes, either in an explicit or implicit manner, when the user is using the application. If our works still leave a lot of questions unanswered, they represent, in our opinion, interesting progress in the field of interactive personalized applications in public transport in so far as developments are based on the users and their needs in terms of mobility and not on systems, whether these are embedded or not.

9.6. Bibliography

[ABO 97] ABOWD G., ATKESON C., HONG J., LONG S., KOOPER R., PINKERTON M., "Cyberguide: a mobile context-aware tour guide", *ACM Wireless Network*, vol. 3, pp. 421-433, 1997.

[AMA 99] AMATO G., STRACCIA U., "User profile modeling and applications to digital libraries", *Proceeds of Third International Conference on Research and Advanced Technology for Digital Libraries*, pp. 184-197, Paris, France, 1999.

[ANG 99] ANG C.L., "Enactment of IDEF0 Modes", *International Journal of Production Research*, vol. 37, no. 15, pp. 3383-3397, 1999.

[ANL 06] ANLI A., Méthodologie de développement des systèmes d'information personnalisés : Application à un système d'information au service des usagers des transports terrestres de personnes, PhD thesis, University of Valenciennes and Hainaut-Cambrésis, France, 2006.

[ARS 09] ARSENEAULT P., Portrait Sociodémographique et Comportement de Voyage des Québécois par Segment Démographique, Rapport final, Chaire de Tourisme Transat, Ministère du Tourisme, Montreal, Quebec, 2008.

[BAR 04] BARDRAM J.E., "Activity-based support for mobility and collaboration in ubiquitous computing", *Proceeds of the Second International Conference on Ubiquitous Mobile Information and Collaboration Systems*, Riga, Lithuania, pp. 101-115, 2004.

[BPM 04] BPMI, *Business Process Modeling Notation version 1.0*, 2004, Available at http://www.bpmn.org, accessed 5.5.11.

[BRG 00] THE BUSINESS RULES GROUP, *Defining Business Rules: What Are They Really?* (4th edition), 2000, Available at: http://www.BusinessRulesGroup.org, accessed 5.5.11.

[BRO 07] BROSSARD A., ABED M., KOLSKI C., "Modélisation conceptuelle des IHM: Une approche globale s'appuyant sur les processus métier", *Ingénierie des Systèmes d'Information - Revue des Sciences et Technologies de l'Information*, vol. 5, pp. 69-108, 2007.

[BRO 08] BROSSARD A., *PERCOMOM:* Une méthode de modélisation des applications interactives personnalisées appliquée à l'information voyageur dans le domaine des transports, PhD thesis, University of Valenciennes and Hainaut-Cambrésis, France, 2008.

[BRO 09] BROSSARD A., ABED M., KOLSKI C., USTER G., "User modeling: the consideration of the experience of time during journeys in public transportation", *ACM Mobility Conference, 6th International Conference on Mobility Technology, Applications and Systems*, ACM Press, Nice, France, September 2-4, 2009.

[CHE 04] CHEN H., FININ T., JOSHI A., "Semantic web in the context broker architecture", *Proc. Second IEEE International Conference on Pervasive Computing and Communication, PerCOM'04*, pp. 277-286, Orlando, USA, 2004.

[CLA 04] CLARK T., EVANS A., SAMMUT P., WILLANS J., *Applied Metamodelling: A Foundation for Language Driven Development Version 0.1*, Société Xactium, 2004.

[CZA 06] CZARMESKI K., HELSEN S., "Feature-based survey of model transformation approaches", *IBM System Journal*, vol. 45, no. 3, pp. 621-645, 2006.

[COO 07] COOPER A. REIMANN R., CRONIN D., *About Face 3: The Essentials of Interaction Design*, Wiley Publishing, Indianapolis, USA, 2007.

[COW 01] COWIE R., DOUGLAS-COWIE E., TSAPATSOULIS N., VOTSIS G., KOLLIAS S., FELLENZ W., TAYLOR J.G., "Emotion recognition in human-computer interaction", *IEEE Signal Processing Magazine*, vol. 18, no. 1, pp. 32-80, 2001.

[DEY 01] DEY A, "Understanding and using context", *Personal and Ubiquitous Computing*, vol. 5, pp. 4-7, 2001.

[DEM 86] DEMING W.E., *Out of the Crisis*, MIT Center for Advanced Engineering Study, Cambridge, USA, 1986.

[DEY 00] DEY A., ABOWD G., "Towards a Better Understanding of Context and Context-Awareness", *Proc. CHIA'00 workshop on Context-Awareness*, 2000.

[FAV 06] FAVRE J.-M., ESTUBLIER J., BLAY-FORNARINO M., *L'Ingénierie Dirigée par les Modèles*, Hermès, Paris, France, 2006.

[FIC 70] FICHELET M., FICHELET R., MAY N., *Contribution à une Psychosociologie des Comportements Urbains*, Ministère de l'Equipement et du Logement, Paris, France, 1970.

[FIN 04] FINDLATER L., MCGRENERE J., "A comparison of static, adaptive, and adaptable menus", *Proc. Conference on Human Factors in Computing Systems*, pp. 89-96, ACM Press, CHI, Vienna, Austria, 2004.

[FLA 05] FLAM M., "A qualitative perspective on travel time experience", *5th Swiss Transport Research Conference, STRC-2005*, Switzerland, 2005.

[GOE 00] GOECKS J., SHAVLIK J., "Learning users' interests by unobtrusively observing their normal behavior", *Proc. International Conference on Intelligent User Interfaces*, pp. 129-132, 2000.

[HAI 06] HAILPERN B., TARR P., "Model-driven development: The good, the bad and the ugly", *IBM System Journal*, vol. 45, no. 3, pp. 451-461, 2006.

[JAC 99] JACOBSON I., BOOCH G., RUMBAUGH J., *The Unified Software Development Process*, Addison-Wesley Longman, Boston, USA, 1999.

[JEN 08] JENN J., LYONS G., "The gift of travel time", *Journal of Transport Geography*, vol. 16, no. 2, pp. 81-89, 2008.

[KRU 00] KRUCHTEN P., *The Rational Unified Process: an Introduction* (2nd Edition), Addison-Wesley Professional, Boston, USA, 2000.

[LYO 05] LYONS G., URRY J., "Travel time use in the information age", *Transportation Research Part A: Policy and Practice*, vol. 39, no. 2-3, pp. 257-276, 2005.

[MAR 99] MARZLOFF B., GLAZIOU S., *Le Temps des Puces*, Editions Carnot, Bourges, France, 1999.

[MOK 01] MOKHTARIAN P.L., SALOMON I., "How derived is the demand for travel? Some conceptual and measurement considerations", *Transportation Research Part A*, vol. 35, pp. 695-719, 2001.

[NAN 01] NANCI D., ESPINASSE B., *Ingénierie des Systèmes d'Information: MERISE, 2ème Génération*, Vuibert, Paris, France, 2001.

[OMG 03] OMG, *MDA Guide v1.0.1*, OMG, 2003. Available at: http://www.omg.org/cgi-bin/doc?omg/03-06-01, accessed 5.5.11.

[OMG 05] OMG, *Semantics of Business Vocabulary and Business Rules (SBVR)*, 2005, available at: http://www.omg.org/technology/documents/bms_spec_catalog.htm, accessed 19.6.11.

[ORA 97] ORAIN H., "Du côté des trajets", in: JUAN S., LARGO-POIRIER A., ORAIN H., POLTORAK J.-F. (eds), *Les Sentiers du Quotidien – Rigidité, Fluidité des Espaces Sociaux et Trajets Routiniers en Ville*, pp. 97-119, L'Harmattan, Paris, France, 1997.

[PAS 99] PASCOE J., RYAN N., MORSE D., "Issues in developing context-aware computing", *Proc. International Symposium on Handled and Ubiquitous Computing, HUC'99*, pp. 208-221, Karlsruhe, Germany, 1999.

[PER 07] PÉREZ-MEDINA J.L., DUPUY-CHESSA S., FRONT A., "A survey of model engineering tools for user interface design", *Proc. 6th International Workshop on TAsk Models and DIAgrams TAMODIA'2007*, pp. 84- 97, Toulouse, France, 2007.

[RAZ 03] RAZMERITA L., User Model and User Modeling in Knowledge Management Systems: An Ontology-based Approach, PhD thesis, University of Toulouse, France, 2003.

[ROQ 07] ROQUES P., VALLEE F., *UML2 en Action* (4th edition), Eyrolles, Paris, France, 2007.

[SCH 06] SCHMIDT D.C., "Model-driven engineering", *Computer*, vol. 39, no. 2, pp. 25-31, 2006.

[SHA 95] SHARDANAND U., MAES P., "Social information filtering: algorithms for automating "word of mouth"", *Proc. CHI'95 Conference*, pp. 210-217, ACM Press, Denver, USA, 1995.

[SIE 03] SIEWIOREK D., SMAILAGIC A., FURUKAWA J., MORAJEVI N., REIGER K., SHAFFER J., "Sensay: A context-aware mobile phone", *Proceedings of the Seventh IEEE International Symposium on Wearable Computer*, ISWC'03, pp. 248-249, New York, USA, 2003.

[SOT 05] SOTTET J.-S., CALVARY G., FAVRE J.-M., "Ingénierie de l'interaction homme-machine dirigée par les modèles", *Actes IDM'05, Premières Journées sur l'Ingénierie Dirigée par les Modèles*, Paris, France, June 30-July 1 2005.

[SOT 06] SOTTET J.-S., CALVARY G., FAVRE J.-M., COUTAZ J., "IHM & IDM: Un tandem prometteur", *Poster, Ergo'IA 2006*, Biarritz, France, 2006.

[STA 06] STAHL T., VÖLTER M., BETTIN J., HAASE A., HELSEN S., *Model-Driven Software Development*, John Wiley & Sons, Chichester, UK, 2006.

[TAD 06] TADJ C., NGANTCHAHA G., "Context handling in a pervasive computing system framework", *Mobility '06, Proc. 3rd International Conference on Mobile Technology Application & Systems*, Bangkok, Thailand, ACM, 2006.

[THE 99] THÉVENIN D., COUTAZ J., "Plasticity of user interfaces: frameworks and research agenda", *Proc. IFIP 13th International Conference on Human-Computer Interaction, Interact'99*, pp. 110-117, Edinburgh, UK, 1999.

[UST 09] USTER G., JUGUET S., TALON G., "The Viatic concept: information technology for intelligent travelers", *ITS-T Conference 2009*, Lille, France, October 20-22 2009.

[VAN 05] VANDERDONCKT J., "A MDA-compliant environment for developing user interfaces of information systems", *Proc. 17th Conference on Advanced Information Systems Engineering, CAiSE 2005*, pp. 16-31, Porto, Portugal, 2005.

[VES 05] VESANEN J., What is Personalization: A Literature Review and Framework, Working Paper W-391, Helsinki School of Economics, Finland, 2005.

[WAG 02] WAGNER M., BALKE W., HIRSCHFELD R., KELLERER W., "A roadmap to advance personalization of mobile services", *Proc. 10th International Conference on Cooperative Information Systems, CoopIS 2002*, Irvine, USA, 2002.

[VIA] VIATIC.MOBILITÉ project website. Available at: http://viatic.inrets.fr, accessed 5.5.11.

Chapter 10

Towards New Interactive Displays in Stations and Airports

10.1. Introduction

In train, tram, bus stations and airports, the supply of information to passengers is an essential task for the smooth running of their journey. However, the multitude of information present in these places often leads to a multiplication of display devices and overloads passengers with information that does not necessarily concern them. This can only lead to the confusion of users and a lot of time spent searching before finding the desired information. This is particularly true in the case of public display devices, such as the display screens that can be found in airports; see Figure 10.1. This type of screen displays information concerning all available flights, whereas a passenger considered individually will only be interested in one flight. This therefore leads the user to carry out an information search that can be all the more tedious when there is a great deal of information present.

Based on the principle that there is no point in presenting a person with information that does not concern him, our objective is to make sure that the presentation of information is targeted at the users who receive it. We therefore suggest designing an *opportunistic* system for presenting information, which only provides information to the users situated in its proximity.

Chapter written by Christophe JACQUET, Yacine BELLIK and Yolaine BOURDA.

Figure 10.1. *At Paris-Charles de Gaulle airport, this wall of information
displays information about more than 150 flights*

The objective is to provide information to these mobile users either by using
private devices that they can carry with them (PDA, cell phone, portable multimedia
player, etc.), or if they do not have one, using public devices that they might
encounter during their journey (pubic information screens, loudspeakers). Let us
remark that it is not a matter of presenting personal information on public devices
but rather carrying filtering public information so as to present only that which
could be of interest to users in close proximity[1].

All users, whoever they may be, are confronted with difficulties when they need
to obtain information and direct themselves in an unknown environment.
Nonetheless, there is a category of people for whom these tasks are particularly
delicate: those with sensory handicaps. Indeed, the information devices are not
necessarily adapted to them. Therefore, an information screen will be of no use to a
blind person; similarly, a deaf person will not perceive information broadcast by
loudspeaker.

---

1 If a single user is present in front of a screen, information that was initially of a public
nature can take on a private nature and therefore pose confidentiality problems. In this case,
one possible solution consists of displaying a few information items so as to preserve the
individuals' privacy. This point will be discussed in the conclusion.

We therefore suggest placing *multimodality* at the center of our system: the devices will be able to use different output modalities. Furthermore, a given device will provide information to a user only if the output modalities of the first are compatible with the input modalities of the second. This way we will, for example, avoid information destined to a blind person being transmitted by a video monitor. Let us note that we are only concerned with *output* interaction, and not with input: for us it is solely a matter of *providing* information to users.

10.2. Related work

Several systems have already been put forward to provide contextual information to mobile users during their journeys. For example, CoolTown [KIN 01] shows web pages to users depending on their location. The main application of this type of system consists of providing information to users regarding their environment, for example, "where is the closest pizzeria?" [HUL 97]. Generally, information is broadcast by small portable devices: for example the Cyberguide [LON 96], a tourist guide for museums, uses the Newton PDA from Apple.

We therefore join the vision of ubiquitous computing [WEI 93], in which computerized devices are capable of talking to each other without technological constraint. However, transporting and handling a portable device is always a constraint. The concept of *ambient intelligence* [DUC 01], [RAM 07] picks up on ubiquitous computing, and adds to it a desire to interact in a *natural, calm* and *intelligent* way with the user.

This idea is well adapted to the world of transport, as a passenger is often preoccupied by his journey and hampered by luggage, which makes the use of a handheld device difficult and unpleasant. An interaction that is as *natural* as possible with the environment would therefore be preferable. In view of this, we can decide to use devices *present in the places visited*.

This choice was in made in the Hello.Wall [STR 05] system, which consists of a wall capable of displaying information that is of general interest when no one is in proximity, and to provide more personal information when a user makes an explicit interaction. A *public* device is therefore used to transmit *personal* information, which can raise issues regarding privacy [VOG 04]. Hello.Wall resolved this problem by not displaying *clear* information, but abstract motifs made up of around 100 cells that were either lit up or turned off. There are public motifs, which are meant to be known to everyone, and private motifs, the significance of which is known only to the recipient.

In the context of a traveler information system, we cannot only rely on abstract motifs: it is necessary to present information that is clear and comprehensible to all. Therefore, if we retain the concept of interaction that involves the device only when the user approaches it, we need to imagine new solutions for the issue of respecting privacy. An assessment of this point will be given in the conclusion of this chapter.

10.3. Targeted characteristics of the system

10.3.1. *Opportunism*

From the point of view of the user, our system will need to be capable of providing him with relevant information during his journeys. The fact that this presentation of information is done in a *fortuitous* manner, over the course of the movements of the user is called *opportunism*. The information will be provided via appliances that we call *presentation devices*, which are already available in public spaces: video screens, loudspeakers, lit signs, etc. Nonetheless, we could also imagine private presentation devices, such as for example an earpiece.

This opportunism involves the availability of means to detect users: the system must, for example, be able to determine who is in front of a screen. Various technologies can be used: detection of Bluetooth appliances [EAG 05], cell phones, specialized localization systems such as Ubisense [STE 05], or radiofrequency identification (RFID) sticker reader situated in the tickets themselves. Without making a technological choice, we simply presume in what follows that the notion of proximity between two objects is known to the system in a reliable manner.

10.3.2. *Multimodality*

People who have a sensory handicap, especially visual, are often treated separately in order to offer them solutions that are adapted to their sensory abilities [JAC 04]. In contrast, an ambient environment aims to interact with its users in a natural manner, so most often uses multimodal interfaces. Under these conditions, a handicapped person, for example, no longer constitutes a separate case, but simply one user profile *among others* [EMI 05]. Our system will therefore be multimodal, so as to treat all users on an equal footing.

In the domain of multimodality, we use Bellik's vocabulary [BEL 95]: a *mode* corresponds to the nature of a means of communication, therefore to one of the human senses – visual, auditory, tactile, etc. A modality is a practical form of a mode. For example, using the auditory mode, we can give the following modalities: speech, sound, song, etc.

10.3.3. *Adaptation*

The diversity of interactions that multimodal interfaces offer, their flexibility as well as their intuitive and natural nature, make them apt to target different user categories. These properties also give them important abilities enabling them to accommodate frequent modifications that the physical environment can undergo and optimally exploit the physical resources of the systems that it hosts. Consequently, they become particularly interesting to use in the context of an ambient environment that is subject to frequent evolutions. This is why we envisage adaptation from the point of view of multimodality. Our system will need to "intelligently" exploit all the modalities that it could have at its disposal, to communicate a piece of information to a user [RIS 05], [ROU 06].

10.4. The KUP model

Over 30 years, several models of software architecture have been suggested. Among those, we can cite model-view-controller (MVC [KRA 88]), presentation-abstraction-control (PAC [COU 87]) or Arch [BAS 92]. These architectures emphasize two components:

– The *model* of information to be presented. It represents the abstraction of the problem to be dealt with, in the form of business data and logic. It is directly linked to the *functional core* of a given application (name given by ARCH; PAC calls it *abstraction*). In our model, we will denote this component K, as it provides knowledge.

– A practical, even physical, implementation of the *interface* with the user as well as the associated interactions (*view-controller* for MVC; *presentation* for PAC). In our model, we will denote this component P, as we are concerned with output only – the *presentation* of information.

10.4.1. *Source of knowledge, users and presentation mechanisms*

In order to design a system corresponding to the description that was given in section 10.3, we introduce a new architecture model for our system. As well as the two aforementioned entities K and P, this model includes a third entity entitled U, corresponding to the logical representation of the user. Indeed, in the context of the design of our mobile and opportunistic system, it seems advisable to separate two kinds of actions:

– the *supply* of a piece of information by the functional core to the user;

– the *presentation* of this information destined for the user.

This way, the system can *gather* information opportunistically as and when it is discovered, and memorize it, *even if at that time there is no available presentation device*. The presentation occurs later on, also opportunistically, when the user is in proximity of a presentation device. The decorrelation between the two phases is the condition required for the doubly opportunistic behavior of the system.

To obtain this decorrelation, the functional core must not be directly linked to the presentation device: there must be an intermediary between them. Otherwise, the supply and presentation of information would necessarily be linked. U, corresponding to the user, will be situated at the center of the model in order to allow decoupling between the supply of information by the K entities (knowledge sources) and their presentation by P entities (presentation devices), hence the name KUP.

10.4.2. *Comparison with the existing models*

The KUP model is doubly original compared to the existing models as:

– it includes an active software representation of the user (U), whereas this is absent or reduced in classic models. This software representation goes far beyond the simple characterization of users by a profile or preferences;

– this software entity representing the user is at the center of the model and thus gives the user a dominant position: all communication within the model will henceforth transit via this *user* software entity.

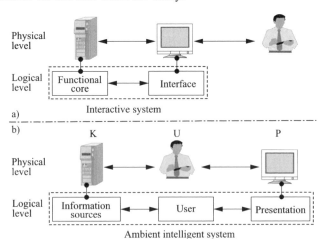

Figure 10.2. *Architecture models used in Human-Computer Interaction: a) classical model in which the user is not explicitly represented; and b) KUP model in which the user is placed at the center of the ambient intelligence system*

Thus, the KUP model is different from classical models (ARCH, Seeheim, PAC, MVC, etc.) due to the fact that in the latter the user is always outside the system; he is never explicitly represented as an active entity. In the KUP model the user entity U is the central entity; see Figure 10.2.

10.4.3. *Notion of proximity*

In order to construct an opportunistic system based on meetings between entities, we need to formally define the corresponding notions of *proximity*.

10.4.3.1. *Perceptual space*

Informally, we wish to define the *perceptual space* of a physical entity *e* as being the collection of points in space where *e* can perceive another entity that is present. For example, for a user entity the perceptual space could correspond to its visual field. However, this definition is too restrictive because:

– The different senses of a user have different characteristics. For example, the field of vision of a human being does not correspond to their zone of auditory perception. Thus, a screen situated 2 m behind will not be perceived by a given user, whereas a speaker device will be.

– Perception depends on the *attributes of modalities*. For example, a cell phone ring tone emitted at 50 m will not be perceived by a human being, whereas the sound of a siren will easily be.

Consequently, the informal definition of the notion of perceptual space given beforehand is too limited. It must be completed to take into account modalities and instantiations of the latter. To do this, we introduce an additional notion: *multimodal space*, or m-space for short. An m-space is the Cartesian multiplication of the physical space *E* by all the instantiations of usable modalities. For example, let us assume that the usable modalities for an entity are:

– *ringtone*, with a *volume* attribute continuously varying between 0 and 100;

– *text*, with a *size* attribute continuously varying between 10 and 60 points and a *color* attribute that can take the three discrete values of *red*, *green* and *blue*.

In this case, an element of the m-space could be the point that has coordinates of 46°23''32' N, 1°02''56' E, with a point size of 23 for text and the color green.

It is now possible to formally define the *perceptual space* of a physical entity. It consists of a subset of an m-space M, which corresponds to the *points* perceivable to the entity. If the entity moves, its perceptual space will be modified: in most cases, it will naturally *follow* its entity.

For example, if we carry out a projection of the perceptual space of a user, *u*, according to the visual modality and with constant attributes (e.g. with a given character size), we obtain a *visual field*. A visual field is represented in Figure 10.3: information displayed on screens A and B are perceived by user *u*, but not those displayed by C.

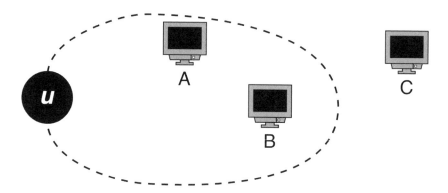

Figure 10.3. *Special case of perceptual space: visual field of a user, u*

10.4.3.2. *Space of influence*

We now have all the necessary notions for the definition of *reciprocal* notion of perceptual space. Perceptual space characterizes the perceptions of an entity, in other words its *inputs,* i.e. its behavior as a *multimodal receiver*. However, an entity can also be a *multimodal emitter*, i.e. present output multimodal characteristics. Just as input characteristics are portrayed by perceptual space, output characteristics are portrayed by what we call the *space of influence*.

Formally, we define the *space of influence* of an entity *e vis-a-vis* an entity *d* as being all the points *x* of the physical space *E* from which *d* can perceive *e*, i.e. for which *e* belongs to the perceptual space of *d* when *d* is situated in *x*.

The space of influence is defined *in relation to a receptive entity*: as the perceptual spaces are different for each entity, the perception of an *emitter* in a given point in space will or will not be possible depending on the entity considered. It is therefore impossible to define a space of influence in absolute terms. Figure 10.4 deals with the simple case where the only modality considered is visual text.

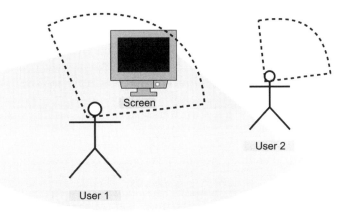

Figure 10.4. *User 1 can perceive the screen (as it is in his visual field, in dots), but this is not the case for user 2. Thus, only the former is in the space of influence of the screen (gray zone)*

10.4.3.3. *Sensory proximity: the generative element*

In the KUP model, all interactions between entities appear following a particular event: that is called *sensory proximity*. This event occurs when an entity e_1 enters into or leaves the perceptual space of another entity e_2[2]. Given the previous definitions of perceptual space and space of influence, it is important to note that this sensory proximity covers two aspects. First, it refers to spatial proximity referring to the distance that separates the two entities as well as their respective orientations. Second, it refers to the capacities in terms of the input/output modalities of the two entities considered. Thus, a blind user approaching within 50 cm of a screen will not set off a sensory proximity event. It will be the same for a user situated at the same distance who can see, but who has his back to the screen.

10.4.3.4. *An opportunistic model for the presentation of information*

The KUP model enables the information supply phase to be separate from its presentation phase. When a user (U) penetrates the space of influence of an information source (K), this source provides one or several relevant pieces of information. It is possible that at the moment when the user receives the information, no presentation device (P) is in proximity (as in sensory proximity). However, as the user is mobile, it is possible that a presentation device penetrates his perceptual space later on. This will then cause a sensory proximity event that will have the effect of setting off the process of information presentation on the device in question.

---

2 This is equivalent to saying that entity e_2 enters into the space of influence of e_1.

10.4.4. *Semantic units*

The information emitted by information sources is said to be composed of *semantic units* (abbreviated as s.u.). A semantic unit corresponds to elementary information that can be transmitted over a network and can be expressed in at least one modality. For example, a semantic unit can carry information corresponding to the boarding gate of a passenger in an airport or to the time of the next train going in the desired direction.

Semantic units are meant to be expressed on a presentation device and according to a given modality. It is therefore necessary to associate practical content in the modality in question. However, the *automatic* generation of content is a research project in its own right [ZOC 02]: we will not explain these processes in detail. For us, the generation of practical content is seen as a *black box*, the input of which is specified (practical modality), and of which we use the output (practical content). Figure 10.5 summarizes the process of practical content generation for a given semantic unit, according to different modalities.

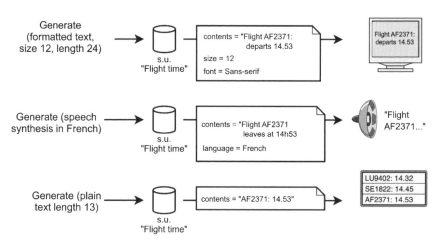

Figure 10.5. *Generation of practical content: the same semantic unit (s.u.) generates different practical content for each instantiated modality*

10.5. Agent architecture

In our view of ambient intelligence, we have three types of entities (K, U and P) but there can be many instances of them. Furthermore, we do not set any mobility constraint. We presume that the three types of entities can be mobile. We wish to give the personnel in the places where the system is deployed the possibility of reorganizing the layout of the information sources, to move presentation devices, to bring in new ones if a particular event occurs, etc., without having to configure anything. The presentation devices must be capable of adapting themselves to change without a human intervention being necessary. This is why decentralized software architecture based on the notion of an agent is required in this instance. Each of the three types of entities mentioned previously corresponds to a type of agent:

– user agent (U): acts as active software representation of human users;

– information agent (K): corresponds to the software declination of information sources – it provides information to the user agent;

– presenter agent (P): constitutes a software interface with the physical presentation devices.

Thus, the world of agents constitutes a "mirror" of the real world regarding our three entities of interest. We presume that all agents can communicate with each other. Communication can be via wireless networks such as Wi-Fi. The relationships of sensory proximity in the physical world are mirrored in the world of agents. For example, if user a perceives a presentation device b, then the same relationship will exist between the associated agents. Agents are reactive: they are dormant most of the time and react when particular events occur. In practice, a given agent a can react to three kinds of events:

– another agent b comes towards a[3];

– agent b, who was close to a, has just moved away from it;

– a has just received a message via the network, coming from a random agent c, which is not necessarily close to a.

Thus, if the agents were to find themselves on their own in the system, nothing would ever happen. Agents have reactive behaviors when the physical entities that embody them move. This means that the proactivity of the system is ensured by physical entities, in particular human entities: it is the latter that will generally move around, and from there set off a cascade of reactions in the system.

10.6. Allocation and instantiation in KUP

Allocation consists of selecting the most adequate presentation modality for a given semantic unit (depending on the user, the device and the information to be presented). As for instantiation, it concerns the definition of the most adequate values for the attributes of the selected modality [ROU 06]. In KUP, the allocation

---

3 In the sense of sensory proximity.

and instantiation of modalities is done in a decentralized manner. Given the disseminated nature of entities involved in an ambient intelligence system, it is advisable to adopt a decentralized approach, in line with the architecture induced by the previously described agents. Thus, when an entity U penetrates the space of influence of an entity P, the two agents associated with these entities will negotiate to determine the most adequate modality (and its instantiation) to use in order to present information to U. This negotiation process is based on the notion of *profiles*. A profile is a set of weights assigned to modalities and their instances. Profiles are defined in relation to an arborescent taxonomy of modalities, common to the three types of entities. Figure 10.6 gives an example of a partial taxonomic tree of output modalities.

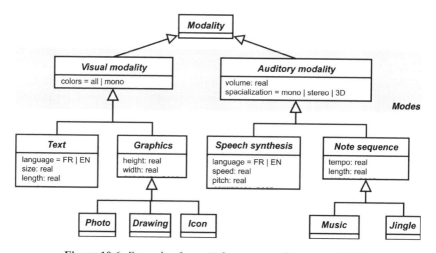

Figure 10.6. *Example of a partial taxonomy of output modalities*

Each entity defines a weighting tree that it will superimpose over the taxonomic tree of modalities[4]. The principle of a weighting tree is simple: it consists of adding weights to a taxonomic tree in order to express the abilities, preferences and constraints of users, devices and semantic units. A weight is a real number between 0 (included) and 1 (also included). It can be situated in two different places:

– *At a node*: the weight then applies to the sub-tree that has this node as its root. A weight of 1 means that the modalities of sub-trees are accepted, or even desired; whereas a weight of 0 means that the corresponding modalities are refused or not

---

4 Except for K entities, which define a weighting tree for each semantic unit that they produce. Indeed, each semantic unit is likely to be able to express itself according to its own modalities. Consequently, in the case of K entities, the weighting trees are attached to semantic units produced and not to the entity that generates them.

desired. The intermediary values enable the expression of intermediary levels between these two extremes, so as to express levels of preference.

– At an attribute: we then specify a function defined over all the possible values of this attribute and with values in the real interval [0, 1]. This function indicates the weight given to each possible value of the attribute. The meaning of these weights is the same as before. Thus, the values of attributes close to 1 are desired; whereas values close to 0 are not, and a weight of 0 might even be refused.

A profile (such as previously mentioned) is defined as being a weighting tree, the root of which corresponds to the root of the taxonomy of modalities. Figure 10.7 gives an example of a partial profile. It could correspond to a blind English-speaking user, who would much rather have auditory modalities to visual ones: the corresponding weights are shown in white on a black background, next to the nodes. Weighting functions are shown for a few attributes: depending on whether attributes are with continuous variations or with discrete values, the weighting functions are themselves continuous or discrete.

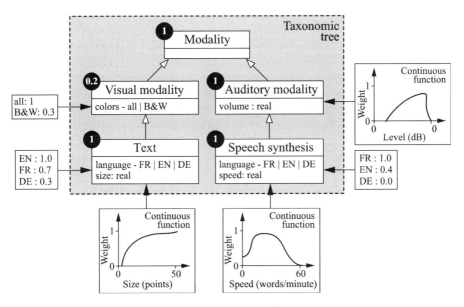

Figure 10.7. *Example of partial profile (weighting tree)*

Given a user *u*, a presentation device *d* and a semantic unit *s,* the definition of the most adequate modality (and its instantiation) to present *s* to *d* over *u,* is realized by carrying out the intersection of the three respective weighting trees. This intersection mechanism [JAC 06b] ultimately produces a new weighting tree, the leaves of which indicate the candidate modalities. All that needs to be done then is to choose the modality that has the greatest weight and to instantiate it by using the values of attributes having obtained the strongest ratings. However this situation corresponds, in reality, to the simplest case: that of a unique semantic unit, a unique user and a unique presentation device. In the more general case, where several users are in proximity to the device or, conversely, several devices are in proximity to the user (or even in the case where several users are in the proximity of the same devices), more complex algorithms have been implemented so as to have several devices collaborate with one another [JAC 06a]. This aims to ensure a global coherence of the distribution of presentations while guaranteeing a minimum level of satisfaction to any of the users.

10.7. Implementation

We have implemented these models and algorithms in the form of a platform called PRIAM (*PResentation of Information in AMbient intelligence*). As mentioned above, this platform is built according to agent architecture. The agents are implemented in Java, which enables them to run in various hardware and software environments. Furthermore, they can easily exchange messages through the network via the *remote method invocation* (RMI) mechanism, which is integrated in Java.

As the implementation of full-scale experimentations is relatively hard and takes a lot of time, we started by making a simulator that allows the final components of an application to be tested, without having to deploy them in real conditions as early as the first trials (see Figure 10.8). This simulator enabled us to verify the correct behavior of the algorithms. For example, Figures 10.8b and 10.8c put two users in play (someone who is blind and someone who is not), as well as a screen and a sound device. When the user who can see presents himself, the screen and the sound system can give him information (b). However, when the blind person comes close, the screen does not display anything as its output modality is not compatible with the profile of the blind person (c).

In this example, we note that the multimodal behavior of the PRIAM platform conforms to what we have specified before. Indeed, when choosing the presentation method of a semantic unit, the system chooses a modality adapted to the user, depending on the presentation devices present in proximity.

All the aspects of the algorithms can be tested in this manner, with the necessary number of presentation devices, users and information sources. For example, Figure 10.9 presents an example of a simulation of the instantiation process of modalities. Depending on the distance between a given user and the screen, the attributes of instantiation are different. Thus, the text is displayed in larger characters when the user is further away from the screen.

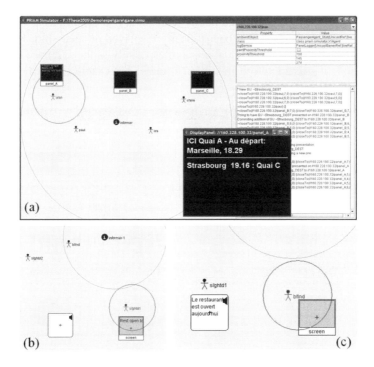

Figure 10.8. *The simulator of the PRIAM platform*

10.8. Experiments

Initially, the simulator enabled us to verify the correct working of our algorithms. However, we then chose to evaluate the real benefit of our system: we therefore carried out two laboratory experiments with human subjects; these are described in [JAC 09].

The first concerns the display of a list of flights in an airport. In this case, several users are meant to be in the proximity of a single presentation device. The second reproduces a train station environment, in which each subject must go to the platform where his train is about to depart. In this case, a single user successively interacts with several physical presentation devices.

In these experiments, we have not sought to evaluate the multimodal character of our platform: these aspects were able to be tested thanks to the simulator described above. The two experiments described below had the objective of evaluating the real benefit of our system in terms of time necessary for a given task to be accomplished. In total around 20 subjects participated in these experiments. The detection of users was carried out with the help of a system of infrared badges

[JAC 07]. The use of badges would not be realistic in real conditions as users would be obliged to carry an electronic badge clearly displayed on their shirt. However, it was well adapted to an experimental context, especially as the system was sensitive to orientation: it was therefore possible to know, for example, whether or not a person was watching a screen.

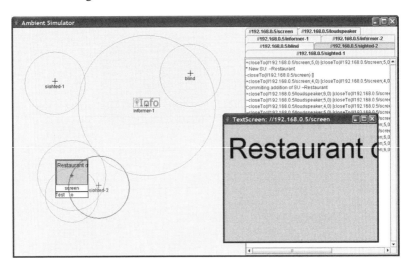

Figure 10.9. *When the distance increases, the instantiation process chooses different values for the attributes: the size of the text increases*

10.8.1. *The "departing flights" experiment*

In this experiment, we displayed a list of information items among which each of the subjects must look for a precise item that concerns him. Our idea was to compare the time taken by a user to find the information, depending on whether the list was static (a paper list or static screen), or personalized and dynamic, i.e. managed by the PRIAM platform. We also wished to measure the influence of the number of people found around the display zone on research time. Indeed, we predicted that the more people there are in front of the screen, the harder the information search will be for each of them.

The information displayed concerns flights in an airport terminal. It is made up of triplets (flight, time, boarding gate). A screen displays this information. Initially, it is static (control experiment), then it becomes dynamic (version using PRIAM). During each exercise, we provide the user with a flight number as well as a departure time. The user then has to find the letter of the corresponding boarding gate on the screen and make a written note of it. On the screen, the flights are classified in chronological order; see Figure 10.11.

10.8.1.1. *General description*

At a given signal, one to eight subjects approach a screen and try and find a particular piece of information. When one of them has identified their piece of information, they memorize it, raise their hand and immediately move away from the board. They then write this information on a paper form that was given to them at the beginning of the experiment. This way, by filming the progress of the experiment, see Figure 10.10, we were easily able to measure the search time of each user. This quantity is defined as being the time that separates the user entering the "scene" of the experiment (i.e. the zone situated in proximity to the display device) and the moment when they raise their hand.

Figure 10.10. *The subjects come close to the screen and then raise their hand once they have found the information*

The forms completed by the users enabled us to verify the exactitude of the information we found. Cases of errors were very rare and did not enable us to establish useful statistics regarding the conditions in which they arose. In fact, the majority of errors were from a single user, who we will qualify as "distracted".

We first of all carried out a "control" experiment in which the list of information was static. Then, we introduced dynamic lists: in this case, the information displayed by screens only concerns users situated before it. The detection of users by the system was carried out with the help of the infrared badge system.

10.8.1.2. *Control experiment*

First of all, users looked for information concerning their flight among a fixed number of pieces of information. We carried out two experiments.

10.8.1.2.1. Search for one piece of information among 12

The results of this experiment are presented in Table 10.1.

Number of people	Average time (s)	Standard deviation	Minimum time	Maximum time
1	3.00	0.00	3.00	3.00
2	4.00	2.00	2.00	6.00
3	4.00	1.41	3.00	6.00
4	4.63	1.22	2.00	6.00
5	5.80	0.98	4.00	7.00
6	8.67	4.38	4.00	17.00
7	7.67	2.56	5.00	13.00
8	6.88	4.28	4.00	18.00

Table 10.1. *Search time for a boarding gate on a static screen, series 1*

10.8.1.2.2. Search for one piece of information among 20 (Figure 10.11)

The results of this experiment are presented in Table 10.2.

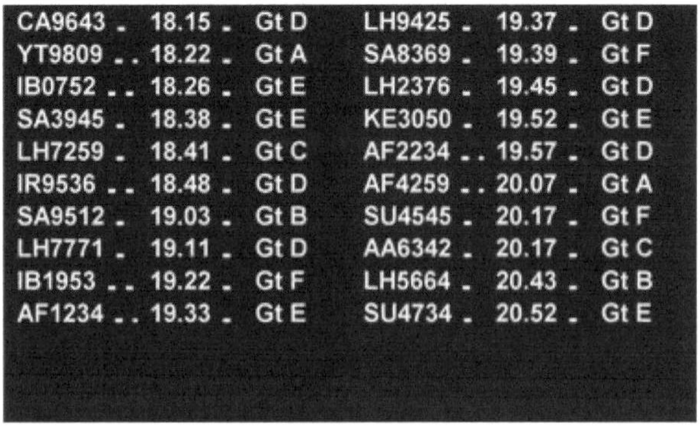

CA9643 . 18.15 . Gt D	LH9425 . 19.37 . Gt D
YT9809 .. 18.22 . Gt A	SA8369 . 19.39 . Gt F
IB0752 .. 18.26 . Gt E	LH2376 . 19.45 . Gt D
SA3945 . 18.38 . Gt E	KE3050 . 19.52 . Gt E
LH7259 . 18.41 . Gt C	AF2234 .. 19.57 . Gt D
IR9536 .. 18.48 . Gt D	AF4259 .. 20.07 . Gt A
SA9512 . 19.03 . Gt B	SU4545 . 20.17 . Gt F
LH7771 . 19.11 . Gt D	AA6342 . 20.17 . Gt C
IB1953 .. 19.22 . Gt F	LH5664 . 20.43 . Gt B
AF1234 .. 19.33 . Gt E	SU4734 . 20.52 . Gt E

Figure 10.11. *Static display of a series of flights*

Number of people	Average time (s)	Standard deviation	Minimum time	Maximum time
1	6.00	0.00	6.00	6.00
2	5.00	1.00	4.00	6.00
3	4.67	0.47	4.00	5.00
4	8.00	2.65	5.00	14.00
5	7.40	3.26	3.00	11.00
6	8.00	4,52	5.00	17.00
7	8.43	2.92	5.00	13.00
8	6.00	2.20	3.00	10.00

Table 10.2. *Search for a boarding gate on a static screen, series 2*

We remark that the times have a tendency to be longer when the number of people simultaneously present increases, without this tendency being very clear cut. We also note that the search times among 20 pieces of information are a lot longer than searches among 12 pieces of information.

10.8.1.3. *Dynamic version*

Here we only display information relative to the users situated in proximity to the screen, see Figure 10.12. Let us note that it could happen that two users are searching for the same information (they are meant to take the same flight). In this case, in dynamic mode, the screen was even less loaded than in the previous experiment. The results are given by Table 10.3.

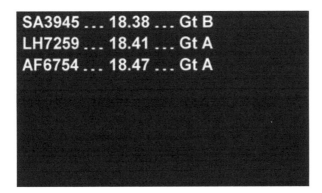

Figure 10.12. *Dynamic display of flights relative to users in proximity*

Number of people	Average time (s)	Standard deviation	Minimum time	Maximum time
1	1.50	0.50	1.00	2.00
2	2.75	1.92	1.00	6.00
3	2.83	0.69	2.00	4.00
4	3.31	1.49	0.00	6.00
5	3.00	1.73	0.00	6.00
6	2.82	1.85	1.00	7.00
7	3.29	1.94	0.00	7.00
8	4.06	2.34	1.00	10.00

Table 10.3. *Search time for a boarding gate on a dynamic screen*

These results led to the following conclusion: the search for a piece of information is much quicker when only information relative to users in the immediate proximity is presented; see Figure 10.13.

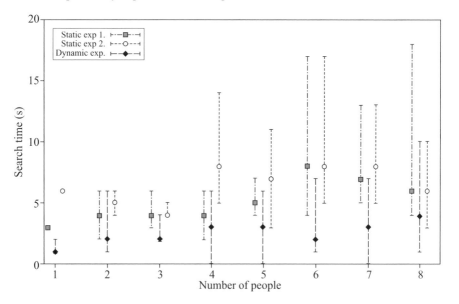

Figure 10.13. *Comparison of the search times for a flight in terms of the number of people simultaneously present. For each case studied, a segment figures on the graph: it indicates the minimum and maximum times. The point situated in the segment represents the average time. For legibility reasons, results of static experiment No. 1 are slightly staggered to the left, whereas those of static experiment No. 2 are slightly staggered to the right. The results of the dynamic experiment are therefore between the results of these two static experiments*

10.8.1.4. *Subjective perception of the experiment*

We handed our subjects a questionnaire in order to analyze their perception of this experiment. First of all, most of the users preferred the dynamic versions of these exercises: in general, they found it "practical", "easy", and even "amusing". The search for information generally seems easier to them, as there are fewer items to scan over, and so therefore less *noise* to drown out the information of interest. Let us note nonetheless that most of our subjects were in their 20s, and so were definitely more receptive to dynamic behaviors than the population on average. Thus, a somewhat older person definitely preferred static displays, all the while defining herself as having a "linear"[5] behavior.

However, some people were troubled by an aspect of the dynamic display: the fact that the list was periodically reorganized (at each arrival or departure of a user in proximity to the display device). Indeed, a given row would sometimes move suddenly on the screen (due to the arrival of a new user and the permanent maintenance of the classification of rows), as the user was reading it. These fluctuations gave a *flashing* effect that was quite disruptive for users. In section 10.9, we introduce the outlines of the solution to solve this problem.

The methods used for information search were very typical. Most of the subjects started by looking for the time of departure, then checked it with the help of the flight number (or singled out the flights leaving at the same time).

Most users think that this system can be useful in practice. However, they highlight the fact that its advantages are visible only when a small number of users are found in proximity to the screen. Indeed, if a large number of users are grouped together, the screens will generally display a great deal of information, and therefore the gain will be nil compared to a static system. In this vein, one of the subjects made us realize that it would be necessary to avoid passers-by, who are not interested in the information, from disrupting the display of the screens.

10.8.1.5. *Implementation notes*

Up until now, we have seen the way the information search experiment was carried out with the help of the PRIAM platform. In this section, we look more in detail at how this experiment was implemented in our platform, in particular in terms of agents. The presentation mechanism consisted of a simple computer with a large screen (17 inches). For reasons of simplicity, and in order not to depend on a network connection for carrying out the experiment, all agents ran on this laptop. The following agents were implemented:

---

5 This person appreciates one-dimensional searches and narrations. For example, this person does not like cartoons due to their lack of linearity, which they find disturbing.

– An information agent tasked with providing information to different users. Like all other PRIAM agents, this agent had a constructor capable of creating an instance based on a series of attribute-value pairs. In the experiment, this agent read an XML file describing the informational content to be used. This information agent provided its semantic units to all known user agents: its space of influence was therefore equal to the usage space of the system.

– The potential users were simply represented each by one of PRIAM's standard user agents. Eight of these agents were therefore instantiated.

– A presenter agent capable of displaying information. We used a presentation device adapted to the presentation of tabbed data, called *DisplayPanel*.

We also defined a class of semantic units meant to represent flight information. These semantic units were capable of generating a practical content intended for a textual presentation device, for example the *DisplayPanel*. In order for the user agents to detect the proximity of the screen, we created a localization service adapted to our badge system. As soon as the infrared receiver detected a badge in proximity, the agents corresponding the screen and to the user in question received a proximity notification.

10.8.2. *Experiment: "finding one's way in a station"*

The previous experiment demonstrated the benefit of our system in the search for an information item in a list, including several users simultaneously. We are now looking to evaluate how it can constitute an aid during the search for a direction. As an example, we use the typical configuration of a train station; see Figure 10.14. A reception hall enables access to an underground pass (or a footbridge), which in turn gives access to different platforms via the intermediary of stairs. In the reception hall, a general display panel indicates the departure times and platforms of all trains. Moreover, at each staircase, a monitor is situated in the underground passage: it recalls the list of departing trains on the corresponding platform.

This organization can seem fairly complete, and perfectly able to guide the traveler. For example, when a user arrives in a train station, he starts by consulting the general display panel, which gives him his platform number. He can then use the underground passage. At the staircase that leads to its platform, a monitor confirms his destination. However, this schema does not take into account travelers in transit. Indeed the latter get off the train on one of the many platforms and must head for another platform. Without additional information, they must therefore either:

– go to the hall, consult the general display panel, and then once again take the underground passage to go to their platform of destination;

– head to a random destination in the underground passage, at the risk of turning back to go and explore the other direction if they were not going the right way. Indeed in this case they have on average one chance in two of getting it wrong.

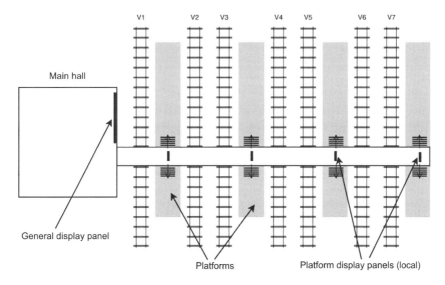

Figure 10.14. *Typical layout of a train station*

These strategies are not optimal in either case as travelers have to carry out unnecessary movements. Not only are these movements tiring, especially when carrying luggage, but they are also *stressful* if the connection time is short. It would therefore be useful to have an information system that indicates their destination platform from the start, without them having to carry out unnecessary trips. Admittedly, vocal messages about connections, broadcast on arrival of trains in the station, are meant to accomplish this, but they are often not understood or even heard by the travelers. On the screens of the underground passage, *in addition to the usual information* (departing trains on the corresponding platform), we therefore propose to display information relating to the trains of users who approach these screens.

10.8.2.1. *General description*

We have installed five screens (in reality laptops) in a corridor of our laboratory, according to the configuration given in Figure 10.15. Each of these screens corresponds to a platform, numbered from A to E. Users can go from one of the extremities of the corridor (landmark 0 and 2), or a "median" position (landmark 1). This median starting position is not found precisely in the middle of the corridor, but it is justified by the configuration of the place.

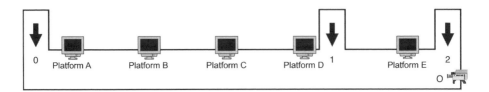

Figure 10.15. *Installation carried out for the direction search experiment: the underground passage of train station was figured in the corridor of our laboratory*

In two cases (static screens that only display the departing train on their platform, or dynamic screens that display personalized information), we wish to study the movement made by users to find their platform, according to the different possible starting points. As in the previous experiments, we filmed[6] the experimentations so as to later "segment" the movements of users; see Figure 10.16. During this segmentation, we identified two kinds of elementary movements:

– advance from platform Q1 to platform Q_2. We denote this movement $Q_1 \rightarrow Q_2$. Example: $A \rightarrow B$; and

– turn around at platform A. We denote this movement Q ↺. Example: C ↺.

These two types of elementary movements enable the trajectory of users to be described completely. It seems much more relevant to us to carry out such a segmentation than to measure the time taken by users to reach their destination platform, as this time can depend on how fast the user moves, which is not a relevant parameter for our study. Indeed, we do not want the measurements to be distorted by the subjects walking relatively quickly. In each experiment, the users had to search for the platform for the train to Lyon, starting from one of the three landmarks 0, 1 and 2. Once they had found it, they needed to stop in front of the corresponding screen and raise their hand. For the utilization of results, we first of all introduce the notion of the *length* of a path. The length of a path is equal to the number of elementary movements on this path. We can then define the *relative length* of the path traveled by a user as being equal to the ratio of the length L_U of the path actually traveled by the user by the length L_O of the optimal path[7]. For example, let us assume that the user goes from landmark 1 to platform B. The optimal path is:

$$1 \rightarrow C, C \rightarrow B$$

---

6 The camera was situated at the observation position marked O in Figure 10.15.
7 The *optimal path* is that which has the fewest elementary movements.

Figure 10.16. *Extract from the film of the direction search experiment*

We therefore have $L_O = 2$. Let us now assume that the user travels the following path:

$$1 \rightarrow C, C \rightarrow D, D \rightarrow E, D \circlearrowleft, E \rightarrow D, D \rightarrow C, C \rightarrow B$$

In this case, $L_U = 7$. The relative length L_R of this path is therefore $L_U/L_O = 7/2 = 3.5$. This relative length enables any path traveled to be compared with the optimum, without the distance between the start and end points coming into play. We therefore judge that it is a good metric for comparison between different experiments.

10.8.2.2. *Experiments with a user*

In these experiments, a single user at a single point in time was looking to find his way.

Control experiment. In this experiment, the screens only displayed information concerning the platform that corresponded to them (Figure 10.17). The results are given in Table 10.4. We can observe a great disparity in results:

– When the user goes from one of the extremities of the corridor (landmarks 0 or 2) the average relative length is 1, which shows that in this case the journeys are optimal. Indeed, all that is necessary in this case is to go down the corridor in the only possible direction, and the user will inevitably end up at his platform of destination, without the risk of making a mistake.

– When the user starts from the middle of the corridor (landmark 1), the average length in our experiments was 2.75: the journeys are far from being optimal, as the user can choose either direction, and therefore has a one in two chance of making a mistake.

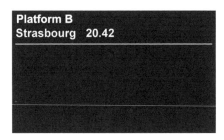

Figure 10.17. *Static display of a departing train on a given platform*

Subject	Start	Dst	Movement	L_U	L_O	L_R
a	2	E	2 → E	1	1	1.0
b	1	E	1 → D, D → C, C → B, B → A, A ↺, A → B, B → C, C → D, D → E	9	2	3.5
c	0	E	0 → A, A → B, B → C, C → D, D → E	5	5	1.0
d	1	E	A → D, D → C, C → B, B → A, A ↺, A → B, B → C, C → D, D → E	9	2	3.5
a	1	B	1 → D, D → E, E ↺, E → D, D → C, C → B	6	3	2.0
b	2	B	2 → E, E → D, D → C, C → B	4	4	1.0
c	1	B	1 → D, D → E, E ↺, E → D, D → C, C → B	6	3	2.0
d	0	B	0 → A, A → B	2	2	1.0
a	0	C	0 → A, A → B, B → C	3	3	1.0
b	0	C	0 → A, A → B, B → C	3	3	1.0
c	2	C	2 → E, E → D, D → C	3	3	1.0
d	2	C	2 → E, E → D, D → C	3	3	1.0

Table 10.4. *Results of the experiment searching for directions with the help of static screens. The double horizontal lines are used to separate the different series of experiments*

Dynamic version. In this version, the screens display in addition information that concerns users situated in proximity (see Figure 10.18). The departure times of the trains of the latter, as well as their platform numbers and arrows that indicate the directions to follow, complete the basic static display.

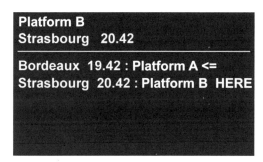

Figure 10.18. *Display of a train departing from a given platform, completed by dynamic information relative to users situated in proximity. This display is to be compared with that of Figure 10.17*

Subject	Start	Dst	Movements	L_U	L_O	L_R
a	1	B	$1 \rightarrow D, D \rightarrow C, C \rightarrow B$	3	3	1.0
b	1	B	$1 \rightarrow D, D \rightarrow C, C \rightarrow B$	3	3	1.0
c	1	B	$1 \rightarrow D, D \rightarrow C, C \rightarrow B$	3	3	1.0
d	1	B	$1 \rightarrow D, D \rightarrow C, C \rightarrow B$	3	3	1.0
e	1	B	$1 \rightarrow D, D \rightarrow C, C \rightarrow B$	3	3	1.0
a	1	E	$1 \rightarrow D, D \rightarrow E$	2	2	1.0
b	1	E	$1 \rightarrow D, D \rightarrow E$	2	2	1.0
c	1	E	$1 \rightarrow D, D \rightarrow E$	2	2	1.0
f	1	E	$1 \rightarrow D, D \rightarrow E$	2	2	1.0

Table 10.5. *Results of the direction search experiment with the help of dynamic screens*

As in the previous experiment, users starting from the corridor extremities (landmarks 0 and 2) were already following optimal trajectories. We did not reiterate these experiments and we concentrated on the experiments in which subjects started from the middle of the corridor (landmark 1). The corresponding results are given in Table 10.5. We can note that in all cases the movements are optimal. On average, the use of a dynamic system brought the relative length of the journeys departing from landmark 1 from 2.75 to 1.00.

10.8.2.3 *Experiments with several users*

We have also studied the behavior of this installation when several users simultaneously searched for their respective platforms. Three users each had to search for a different direction, corresponding to a departing train on one of five platforms. We started by carrying out a control experiment in which the screens were static, and only displayed the destination of the next train to arrive at their platform. The results are given in Table 10.6.

Subject	Start	Dst	Movements	L_U	L_O	L_R
a	1	A	1 → D, D → E, E ↻, E → D, D → C, C → B, B → A	7	4	1.75
b	1	B	1 → D, D → C, C → B	3	3	1.00
c	1	E	A → D, D → C, C → B, B → A, A ↻, A → B, B → C, C → D, D → E	9	2	4.50

Table 10.6. *Results of the direction search experiment including several users with the help of static screens*

The average relative length for this experiment was 2.42, which once again shows that the journeys taken were less than optimal. Thus, subjects b and c went in the wrong direction from the offset. We then began the experiment again in dynamic mode. The results are given in Table 10.7.

Subject	Start	Dst	Movements	L_U	L_O	L_R
a	1	A	1 → D, D → C, C → B, B → A	4	4	1.0
b	1	E	1 → D, D → E	2	2	1.0
c	1	B	1 → D, D → C, C → B	3	3	1.0

Table 10.7. *Results of the direction search experiment by several users with the help of dynamic screens*

In this case, all the journeys are optimal. Thus, even when several users are present, the use of PRIAM to provide users with dynamic and personalized information enables them to save precious time when they are on the move.

10.8.2.4. *Implementation notes*

The implementation followed the same principles as the flight search experiment. We have used the following agents:

– an informative agent tasked with providing each user with the semantic unit corresponding to their destination;

– a few standard user agents: one is enough in the event where a single user travels the length of the underground passage; for the experiment with three users, we have implemented three of these agents;

– five presenter agents, each responsible for one of the screens.

During the practical realization of the experiment, we used five notebook computers to represent the five screens, all the while keeping the same architecture. However, in order to avoid problems related to network connections between computers[8], we preferred to duplicate the informative agent and the user agents *on each of the five notebook computers*.

In summary, each computer therefore contained:

– a copy of the informative agent;

– a copy of all the user agents linked to the infrared localization system;

– the corresponding presenter agent.

As a general rule, such a duplication of agents could pose a problem, as different *instances* of the same agent could be found in different states, which would be incoherent.

However, in the very restricted framework of our experimentation, this did not disrupt the global functioning of the system, as the user agents implemented did not have any particular *states*.

10.9. Conclusions and perspectives

We have introduced a conceptual model for the presentation of multimodal information to mobile users, the natural application of which is in train stations and airports. This model is accompanied by algorithms for the choice of modalities according to the abilities of the interactive devices and the users. This model and its algorithms were implemented in the PRIAM platform, which enabled us to conduct experiments in pseudo-real conditions. These experiments have shown the benefit of carrying out a selection as to what information is presented in public places, depending on the people situated in front of the presentation devices.

The people who participated in our experiments often told us that they had been unsettled by modifications in the content of the screen, which were too frequent.

---

8 Even though at the beginning of this chapter we formulated a hypothesis stating that all the entities would be realized by a wireless network, we preferred not to make our experiments dependent on possible problems linked to the network.

When it is necessary to reorganize the display of a screen, it will in consequence be necessary to anticipate transitions between the old organization and the new one. For example, if it is necessary to add a new line between two previously displayed lines, it is possible to very slowly move the lower part of the screen so as to carefully make room for the necessary space, rather than bluntly switch from one display to the next. If it is necessary to delete a line it is possible to progressively reduce its size. Here we will be able to reuse animation techniques validated in the field of Human-Computer Interaction. It would also be interesting to introduce priorities between the information presented. Thus, the information relative to the immediate departures or to the disappearance of people could appear first. Similarly, priority could be given to users depending on what their subscription or their handicap is.

The display of selected information according to the people present can raise issues of respecting privacy. We have seen that our system aims to make a selection from among many pieces of information. Consequently, if a single user is present in a given place, an individual hidden in proximity can infer private information based on a system's presentation, as he knows that it will only concern the user in question. Let us remark that this problem disappears when two or three users are present, if different information concerns them: it is then no longer possible to attribute the presented information to such and such a person.

For example, let us presume that a monitor displays the destinations of the travelers situated in proximity. If several people are present, the monitor will display a few destinations, and it is not possible to infer anything about anybody. If a single person is present, then only their destination will be displayed, which could be a problem. To remedy this inconvenience, it is possible to introduce a "scrambling" of information. In the aforementioned case, we can for instance decide that when fewer than two or three relevant pieces of information are to be presented, one or two additional pieces of information, which are random and non relevant, will also be presented. This way, revealing information relative to a passenger who presents himself alone in front of a screen is avoided.

10.10. Bibliography

[BAS 92] BASS L., FANEUF R., LITTLE R., MAYER N., PELLEGRINO B., REED S., SEACORD R., SHEPPARD S., SZCZUR M., "A metamodel for the runtime architecture of an interactive system", *SIGCHI Bulletin*, vol. 24, no. 1, pp. 32-37, 1992.

[BEL 95] BELLIK Y., Interfaces Multimodales: Concepts, Modèles et Architectures, PhD thesis, University of Paris-Sud 11, Orsay, France, 1995.

[COU 87] COUTAZ J., "PAC, an object-oriented model for dialog design", *Proceedings INTERACT 87 - 2nd IFIP International Conference on Human-Computer Interaction*, North-Holland, pp. 431-436, 1987.

[DUC 01] DUCATEL K., BOGDANOWICZ M., SCAPOLO F., LEIJTEN J., BURGELMAN J-C., Scenarios for Ambient Intelligence in 2010. Final Report, Information Society Technologies Advisory Group (ISTAG), European Commission, 2001.

[EAG 05] EAGLE N., PENTLAND A., "Social serendipity: mobilizing social software", *IEEE Pervasive Computing*, vol. 4, no. 2, pp. 28-34, 2005.

[EMI 05] EMILIANI P.-L., STEPHANIDIS C., "Universal access to ambient intelligence environments: Opportunities and challenges for people with disabilities", *IBM Systems Journal*, vol. 44, no. 3, pp. 605-619, 2005.

[HUL 97] HULL R., NEAVES P., BEDFORD-ROBERTS J., "Towards situated computing", *Proceedings of ISWC '97*, IEEE Comp. Soc., pp. 146, Washington, DC, US, 1997.

[JAC 04] JACQUET C., BELLIK Y., BOURDA Y., "A context-aware locomotion assistance device for the blind", *People and Computers XVIII – Design for Life*, Springer-Verlag, London, UK, pp. 315-328, 2004.

[JAC 06a] JACQUET C., BELLIK Y., BOURDA Y., "Dynamic cooperative information display in mobile environments", *Proceedings of the 10th International Conference on Knowledge-Based & Intelligent Information & Engineering Systems, KES 2006*, pp. 154-161, Bournemouth, UK, 2006,

[JAC 06b] JACQUET C., BELLIK Y., BOURDA Y., "KUP, un modèle pour la présentation multimodale et opportuniste d'informations en situation de mobilité", *Ingénierie des Systèmes d'Information (ISI), special edition, Adaptation et Gestion de contexte*, vol. 11, no. 5, pp. 115-139, 2006.

[JAC 07] JACQUET C., "IRIS: identification d'utilisateurs par badges infrarouges", in: *Actes d'IHM*, ACM Press, pp. 287-290, 2007.

[JAC 09] JACQUET C., BELLIK Y., "Présentation ciblée d'informations dans les moyens de transport", *Génie Logiciel*, no. 91, pp. 27-34, 2009.

[KIN 01] KINDBERG T., BARTON J., "A web-based nomadic computing system", *Computer Networks*, vol. 35, no. 4, pp. 443-456, 2001.

[KRA 88] KRASNER G., POPE S., "A cookbook for using the model-view controller user interface paradigm in Smalltalk-80", *Journal of Object Oriented Programming*, vol. 1, no. 3, pp. 26-49, 1988.

[LON 96] LONG S., KOOPER R., ABOWD G., ATKESON C., "Rapid prototyping of mobile context-aware applications: The cyberguide case study", *Proceedings of the 2nd Annual International Conference on Mobile Computing and Networking*, ACM Press, pp. 97-107, 1996.

[RAM 07] RAMOS C., "Ambient intelligence – A state of the art from an artificial intelligence perspective", *Progress in Artificial Intelligence*, Lecture Notes in Computer Science, no. 4874, pp. 285-295, 2007.

[RIS 05] Rist T., "Supporting mobile users through adaptive information presentation", *Multimodal Intelligent Information Presentation*, Springer, London, pp. 113-141, 2005.

[ROU 06] Rousseau C., Bellik Y., Vernier F., Bazalgette D., "A framework for the Intelligent Multimodal Presentation of Information", *Signal Processing*, vol. 86, no. 12, pp. 3696-3713, 2006.

[STE 05] Steggles P., Gschwind S., "Ubisense – a smart space platform", *Adjunct Proceedings of the Third International Conference on Pervasive Computing*, vol. 191, pp. 73-76, Munich, Germany, 2005.

[STR 05] Streitz N.A., Röcker C., Prante T., Van Alphen D., Stenzel R., Magerkurth C., "Designing smart artifacts for smart environments", *IEEE Computer*, vol. 38, no. 3, pp. 41-49, 2005.

[VOG 04] Vogel D., Balakrishnan R., "Interactive public ambient displays: transitioning from implicit to explicit, public to personal, interaction with multiple users", *UIST '04*, Santa Fe, NM, USA, ACM Press, pp. 137-146, 2004.

[WEI 93] Weiser M., "Some computer science issues in ubiquitous computing", *Communications of the ACM*, vol. 36, no. 7, pp. 75-84, 1993.

[ZOC 02] Zock M., Sabah G., "La génération automatique de textes", in: M. Fayol (ed.), *Production du Langage*, Hermès, Paris, France, pp. 263-285, 2002.

Chapter 11

Transport: a Fertile Ground
for the Plasticity of User Interfaces

11.1. Introduction

Until the first decade of the 21st Century, User Interfaces (UIs) were designed for a predetermined context of use, i.e. for a specific class of users, using a given platform (generally a workstation), in a fixed physical and social environment (e.g. at a desk). The UI was rigid, created for this specific context of use (<user, platform, environment>). This context was presumed to be fixed, known from the design stage, and intervened at the entry point of design methods [ISO 99]; see Figure 11.1. Ambient intelligence creates a new paradigm: henceforth, the user is thought of as mobile, evolving in a dynamic environment consisting of heterogeneous interaction resources and being able to opportunistically target new goals. From this point on, the hypothesis of fixed context of use is no longer valid and the rigidity of the UI is no longer acceptable.

This chapter deals with the plasticity of UIs in ambient intelligence. Plasticity denotes the ability of UIs to adapt to the context of use while respecting the user-centered properties. Two viewpoints are developed: on the one hand, the point of the end-user; on the other hand, the point of view of the system for the engineering of plastic UIs. Both viewpoints are illustrated in the field of transport.

Chapter written by Gaëlle CALVARY, Audrey SERNA, Christophe KOLSKI and Joëlle COUTAZ.

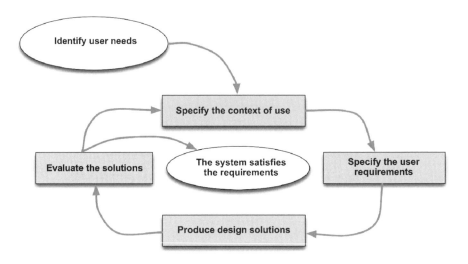

Figure 11.1. *User-centered design for a context of use specified before the design process takes place: ISO norm 13407 (figure translated from [ISO 99])*

The following section structures the key elements of UI evolution in ambient intelligence [CAL 06], [CAL 07a], [CAL 07b]. Section 11.3 shows how UI plasticity acts as an integrator for these evolutions from a user's perspective. Plasticity is then illustrated in the field of transport, which proves to be an extremely fertile application framework. Section 11.4 adopts the system viewpoint. Section 11.5 presents a problem space that covers both the user's and the system's viewpoints. A number of questions remain open, giving rise to numerous issues for further research.

11.2. Evolution of human-computer interaction

Calvary *et al.* [CAL 06] identified the key elements for the metamorphosis of human-machine interaction in ambient intelligence. This section proposes a review of this and organizes its dimensions according to three factors: the diversity of interaction resources, their dynamicity and human control.

11.2.1. *Diversity of interaction resources*

Lyytinen and Yoo [LYY 02] structure the evolution of information technology (ICT) according to two axes (see Figure 11.2a): *mobility* and *integration* into the physical world. *Mobility* refers to the success of pocket computers (personal assistants, smart phones, games consoles, etc.). *Integration* into the environment designates the progressive evanescence of the computer in the physical world: our everyday objects are augmented with digital properties, and take part in the interaction [THE 07]. For example, the vehicle, depending on the situation, is informed of or signals an accident (see Figure 11.2b), and then sends this information to other vehicles [DEL 09], [DEL 10]; or newspapers (see Figure 11.2c) complement textual information with video on demand [MAE 09].

Mobility and integration into the environment can be combined. Thus, the European GLOSS (*GLObal Smart Spaces*, 2001-2004) project imagined the coupling of a personal digital assistant (PDA) with an augmented wall to display information to the individual relating to his journey (see Figure 11.3b): the PDA contained road information; the public wall, connected to the PDA, displayed additional information about the weather forecast and the transport strike at the destination. More recently, Maes and Mistry [MAE 09] envisioned the possibility for the traveler who is late, going to the airport by taxi, to project information in real time relating to his flight onto his boarding pass (see Figure 11.3a)[1].

Such prototypes hypothesize a software and material infrastructure for perception, information and/or action. This information can be public and/or personal, offered by the current location and/or carried by the user. Borkowski [BOR 04] uses the control between a video projector, on one hand, and a camera fixed to the ceiling, on the other, to make every piece of paper an interactive display surface. Conversely, the SixthSense wearable motion interface [MAE 09] is based on a pico-video projector and a camera worn as a necklace. This principle of wearable ICT was conceived by [ANT 02], who proposed the display of tabular information on the fingers of a hand, in this case information relating to hotels (see Figure 11.3c). Today, this idea is implemented in the Skinput system [HAR 10].

The variety of display surfaces (in size, width, transparency, etc.), the existence of other output modalities (audio, for example) and at the same time the diversity of input modalities make the *morphology of the interaction* a subject of utmost importance. UIs are no longer reduced to classical intermediate players and are no longer necessarily centralized in a single PC. They go:

– *from graphics to multimodal* form, involving other human senses than sight and touch, for example;

– *from WIMP (Windows, Icons, Menus, Pointing devices) to post-WIMP*, going beyond the WIMP: windows can be round, directly handled by a finger;

---

1 See also [SIX].

– from centralized to distributed, where components of the UI are spread over several surfaces: for example, a remote control on a PDA and content displayed on a wall [MYE 01].

The combination of this diversity with temporal relationships gives the study an additional complexity: that of the variability of interaction resources.

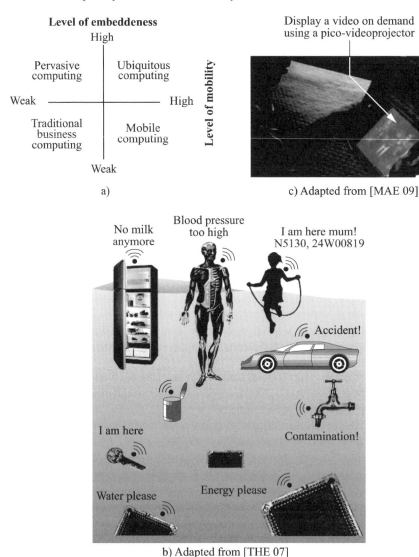

Figure 11.2. *From the evolution of ICT to that of the interaction media*

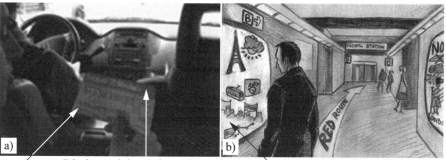

| Transport ticket | Display real time information on objects using a pico-video projector (here flight delayed by 20 minutes) | Augmented wall enabling the display of useful information for a traveler equipped with a PDA |

Figure 11.3. *Evolution of ICT: combination of the mobility and integration axes: a) taken from [MAE 09] and adapted; b) project GLOSS; and c) according to [ANT 02]*

11.2.2. *Dynamicity of interaction resources*

In conventional ICT, turning a computer on or off results in starting or stopping applications. In ambient ICT, processing is more subtle: the interactive space of the user changes as soon as a computation, interaction or communication resource appears or disappears. Such a change can be an opportunity to redistribute applications across the available resources. UIs thus go from *sedentary to nomadic* [CAL 06]; the migration of applications, whether it be partial or total, being placed under the *explicit* or *implicit* user control, and this at various levels of granularity.

For example, Ubiloop [SER 09], see Figure 11.4, enables a person to report incidents (a broken bus shelter, a damaged self-service bicycle, etc.), and enables the communities to deal with them. Depending on the interaction device used by the person, a photo of the damage can be taken and attached to the notification of the incident. The local administration receives the notifications. For easier public decision making, the photos can be moved to an interactive table that will facilitate the grouping of incidents according to their level of priority; see Figure 11.4a. Moving the PC towards the table is explicitly asked for by the user (administrative member of staff), consequently leading to *redistribution* of the UI.

a) Migration of incidents pictures   b) Picture taking
onto an interactive tabletop   service availability

c) GPS localization   d) Localization on a map   e) Manual localization

Figure 11.4. *Ubiloop, an example of UI redistribution and remodeling*

(a) Sedan-Bouillon as a centralized version on PC: the UI is comprised of a title, a navigation bar and content

(b) Meta-UI that proposes redistribution of the UI between the PC and PDA (identifiers: log_Lionel_0 or log_Lionel_1)

(c) After redistribution, the navigation bar has disappeared from the PC. It appears remodeled on the PDA and it is displayed horizontally (instead of vertically) below the title

Figure 11.5. *Sedan-Bouillon, a plastic Website [BAL 04]*

For the individual, UI adaptation to the interaction device is performed automatically: photo taking is only proposed to the person if his cell phone is equipped with a camera, see Figure 11.4b. The localization of the incident is automatic when the cell phone has a GPS, see Figure 11.4c. Otherwise it is manually done by checking on a map whether the cell phone has a map of the place, see Figure 11.4d or, if not, by specifying the address of the place, see Figure 11.4e.

If after connecting his PC to Sedan-Bouillon, Lionel connects to this same site from a PDA, then this double connection is detected and a redistribution proposal is made to him: a *negotiation* UI pops up that explains to Lionel that he can distribute the site, as he sees fit, between the PC and the PDA, see Figure 11.5b. The redistribution is done according to workspaces (the zones). By ticking the appropriate check boxes, Lionel specifies the allocation of the various workspaces to the different platforms. This additional UI enables the dynamicity to be placed under human control. These supervision UIs, which enable users to program their ambient spaces, are called "meta-UIs" by [COU 06]. The redistribution then proceeds, recomposing the UI under the control of the user, see Figure 11.5c.

In addition to dynamic adaptation triggered by the dynamic discovery of interaction resources, two other variables need to be considered:

– the variability of *information* provided by services that appear and disappear opportunistically; and

– the variability of the user's *intention* as the result of a change of place or the arrival of a particular information.

11.2.3. *User control*

It can be important for the user to have control of the UI adaptation process. One possible approach is so-called end-user programming, which makes it possible for "non-ICT specialists" to develop their own services and systems. Although end-user programming was initiated 30 years ago [SMI 77], this area of research is being rediscovered in the context of ambient intelligence.

Research in end-user programming first sought to define simplified notations: scripting textual (*HyperTalk*) or graphical languages (*Visual AgenTalk*) [REP 04], programming by demonstration and by example [CYP 93], as well as the construction of macros (similar to emacs). These techniques were essentially applied to targeted areas such as Computer-Aided Design [GIR 92], spreadsheets [BUR 03], bio-informatics [LET 05] or, like Alice [CON 97] and HANDS [PAN 02], to the learning of programming. Recently, research has opened up to the Web, with the possibility for users to build macros: with Koala, a user saves his actions on a

Webpage (for example, the input for the field of a form). He can replay these actions and publish them on a wiki to share them with members of his community (who can then reuse the pre-filled in forms) [LIT 07].

Works on the programming of ambient spaces by the final user are still in the early stages. In Speakeasy, the user can build queries for searching interaction resources (devices, services, etc.), filtering them based on the specification of the type of information they provide, with the objective of combining these resources in ways that had not been anticipated by the developers of the system [NEW 02]. With Jigsaw, users build simple programs by assembling pieces of a puzzle, such as "if someone rings the doorbell, take a photo and transfer it to the PDA" [ROD 04]; see Figure 11.6a. It seems to be possible to extrapolate this principle to the world of transport or mobility, with assemblies such as: "provide a warning when passing an interesting site; take photos and send them to grandpa and grandma so that they can follow the journeys of their grandchild(ren) almost in real time". This extrapolation is broader than the adaptation to interaction resources: it also adapts to informational content.

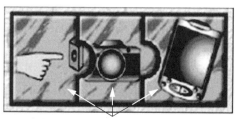

a) Construction of interactive programs
by assembly of three digital components or services

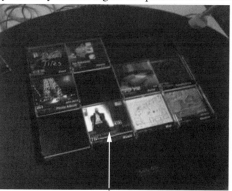

b) Construction of interactive programs by
assembly of physical tablets indentifiable by RFID

Figure 11.6. *Two examples of programming by the end-user:*
a) Jigsaw [ROD 04]; and b) DataTiles [REK 01]

The media-cubes [BLA 01], ICAP [SOH 06] and CAPella [DEY 04] tackle similar problems regarding combining interaction resources, with the difficulty of creating a productive alliance between the physical and digital worlds. Whereas in Jigsaw the user manipulates the digital world, in other approaches, such as [HIN 00] and DataTiles [REK 01] (see Figure 11.6b), the physical world comes first: for example, in DataTiles, the composition of physical tiles enables the user to express complex commands. The tiles are equipped with a radiofrequency identification (RFID) sensor that enables them to be identified in a unique way, as in [KUB 09]. They are augmented with the display of numerical data. In [TAY 09], motion defines the function of the object: the bar of soap becomes a telephone or a screen depending on how it is held. However none of them includes a Whyline-like development tool to support debugging [MYE 06].

UI adaptation to variability for the good of the human while supporting human control is a challenging issue for UI plasticity.

11.3. User interface plasticity: user viewpoint

This section adopts the viewpoint of the user. It defines the property of plasticity from the point of view of use and illustrates it in the field of transport.

11.3.1. *Definition*

Generally speaking, the property of plasticity refers to the ability of an entity for adaptation as the result of a change that has occurred in this entity or its environment. In human-computer interaction (HCI), plasticity is defined as the ability for *adaptation* of a UI to *a change in context of use* while respecting the *value* expected by the user [DÂA 07]. Three keywords structure this definition: the notions of adaptation, context of use and value.

Context is a set of information. This set is structured. It is shared, evolves, and serves interpretation [WIN 01]. The nature of the information, and how it is interpreted, depend on the finality. For UI plasticity, the finality is UI adaptation. As a result, the *context of use* is defined as the <user, platform, environment > triplet where:

– the user denotes the user of the interactive system. He can be described by his skills in the application domain, ICT, etc., as well as by general data (age, size, etc.);

– the platform captures the hardware and software necessary for the interaction. Typically, the input and output devices are to be considered;

– the environment refers to the physical space where the interaction takes place. It can be described by light, sound, social, etc. conditions.

The *value* refers to a set of user-centered properties. In HCI, this notion of value is put forward by Cockton [COC 04], [COC 05]. He believes that usability is not sufficient: it must be confronted with the true expectations of the user. The example that he gives is that of heating management [COC 04]. The systems are possibly usable in the sense that they are easy to use and learn but none really meets the true desire of the user, which is to make a saving. The user does not program his heating system for fun. It is to reduce his bill. A good system should therefore show him how much he has saved. By extrapolation to the domain of transport, the incentive to use a mode of public transport or a combination of several personal and/or public modes (for example, take ones car to go to the station, then the train, then the tram, then walk) to go from point A to point B (refer on this subject to Chapter 1) can rest on a number of value criteria. These criteria can be those related to savings, time gained, or the possibility of traveling, or not, in connected mode during the trip. All of this must take into account the possible handicaps of the user, with the desire to be informed of the possible delays in the network, of the weather forecast (if it is raining, I'm not going to take my bicycle), etc. in real time.

In economy, value is defined as a unit that increases when the user's satisfaction increases or total spending decreases. Here, no judgment of value is established, consequently leaving the possibility of:

– whether or not to integrate the notion of cost;

– whether or not to support it with existing reference sources in the field of HCI, or in that of software ergonomics, whether normalized or not (for example ISO/IEC 9126), general references, attributing special attention to acceptability, utility and usability (e.g. typical reference sources such as [ABO 92], [BAS 93], [BRA 03], [CON 99], [DIX 93], [GRA 96], [NIE 94], [PRE 94], [SCH 97], [SHA 91], [STE 09], [VAN 99] or specific references (such as [MON 05], [NOG 08] for the web or [LOP 04] for adaptation).

For choosing the appropriate properties, the domain-dependent functions as well as the adaptation process need to be considered. For example, observability [GRA 06] is a criterion of general value. It applies to both the application domain and the adaptation process (and therefore successively to the UI and possibly to its meta-UI). In contrast, interaction continuity [TRE 03] measured, for example, by the number of physical actions the user has to repeat after UI adaptation, or inter-usability (i.e. "the facility with which users can transfer and adapt what they have learnt from their previous uses of a service when they access it with a new medium") [KAR 05] – also called horizontal usability [SEF 04] – are value criteria specific to the adaptation process.

As illustrated in Ubiloop (section 11.2.2), adaptation can consist of a remodeling and/or a redistribution of the UI. The remodeling can be more or less deep, affecting the task of the user (his objective or the procedure) or be limited to surface modifications (restructuring or restyling). The redistribution can be total or partial, leading to a centralized or distributed UI.

The following section illustrates the plasticity in the domain of transport in a scenario that suggests an ensemble of research perspectives in this field.

11.3.2. *Illustration in transport*

Prelude: Pierre, who lives and works in Grenoble, France, must go on a business trip in the countryside near Toulouse for a company seminar. He must travel with Christine, a work colleague. They must take a train and then a bus to reach the location of the seminar. On his smart phone, Pierre has a very complete personal space, particularly for his trips: he stores all the information necessary for his journey (electronic train ticket, electronic bus ticket, hotel reservation, address of the seminar, etc.).

Moment No. 1: Pierre and Christine are in the augmented compartment of the train. Whereas some people are playing chess on the interactive table placed in front of their seats, Christine prefers to work on a project she is writing. She has already started filling in the description form: title, summary, number of hours, project manager, etc. She gets out her laptop computer. She begins by rereading the text and decides to show it to Pierre to get his opinion. As they are working, the battery of Christine's PC runs low. The form is then switched to the interactive table located in front of them. They can thus continue to work.

Analysis: a change occurred in the user platform (its battery was running out). This change caused a redistribution of the UI to enable the user to continue her task (expected value).

Moment No. 2: Pierre and Christine arrive in Valence, where they have to change trains. When they arrive on the platform, they learn that their connecting train will be late. Using his smart phone, Pierre consults the times of the next trains. There is a long wait so they will not arrive in time to take their bus to Toulouse. They must find an alternative solution. They head towards the Wi-Fi-enabled business lounge and sit down at an interactive table. The system suggests keeping the actions linked to personal data on the smart phone and to carry out actions concerning the journey on the table. Pierre accepts. Information regarding the different stages of their journey is displayed on the table. By pressing on "Toulouse", they can consult the solutions available to get to the seminar. The system suggests renting a car rather than taking the bus. Using his smart phone, Pierre drags and deposits personal information to fill in the car hire form. The presentation adapts itself to the platform.

Analysis: as the display surfaces of the platforms are heterogeneous, moving data requires a remodeling of the UI.

Moment No. 3: Pierre and Christine finally get onto their connecting train. Pierre consults his smart phone to see their seat numbers. They are in the augmented compartment; an interactive table is available to users. Pierre goes towards it. The system suggests moving information to the table. Virtual scissors then appear on Pierre's smart phone that enable him to cut out the information he wishes to move to the interactive table. He chooses to display information relating to their journey on the table. A 3D view of the compartment of the train is displayed. Pierre can navigate through the compartment by tilting and turning his smart phone. He locates the seat numbers. Pierre takes advantage of this to visualize a map of the route. Christine and Pierre can interact at the same time: Pierre consults information regarding Toulouse station whereas Christine looks at where the seminar is and locates the hotel they have reserved.

Analysis: it is the proximity of the user to the table that triggers the adaptation.

Moment No. 4: Once in Toulouse, Pierre and Christine collect the hire car. Pierre connects his smart phone to the vehicle system. The vehicle system asks him if he wants his "car preferences" to be transmitted to the hire car. Pierre chooses two options when he is driving: on the one hand, the display of text messages on the dashboard and on the other hand, the vocal transmission of road information. Pierre and Christine take the fast lane. The car system orally transmits the authorized speed to them. They have been going for about half an hour when Pierre receives a text message. The message is displayed on the dashboard: it is their colleagues from Grenoble telling them that they have stopped a bit further on to visit a farm with local products. Pierre and Christine decide to join them.

Analysis: the display of text messages adapts itself to the available platforms.

11.4. User interface plasticity: system viewpoint

This section is concerned with engineering UI plasticity. It recalls the key periods illustrated in the field of transport.

11.4.1. *Retrospective*

Since its definition in 1999 [THE 99], plasticity is explored incrementally, in three phases.

First stage: in the first decade of the 21st Century, adaptation was studied in terms of multi-targeting: it consisted, at the design stage, of generating different versions of the UI for the different targeted contexts of use (typically, large screens versus small screens). This work was stimulated by:

– development and maintenance costs induced by the production of as many UI versions as contexts of use anticipated before the design stage; and

– the difficulty in ensuring ergonomic consistency between versions when developments are carried out in a partitioned manner.

This sales pitch was in answer to the *varied* nature of the context of use according to a system viewpoint: that of the designer confronted with multi-target UI engineering [THE 01]. We label these works as the passage from *mono-targeting* to *multi-targeting*.

Second, the *variable* nature of the context of use is integrated into the research agenda, thus making the leap from *multi-targeting* to *plasticity:* designing for several key contexts of use identified in the phase before the design stage is not enough. Changes in context of use must be addressed. The European CAMELEON project (2001–2004)[2] covers these two increments (from mono-targeting to plasticity) with a bary centre nonetheless on multi-targeting. In particular, user-centered properties are not considered. The contexts of use and the changes in contexts of use are identified at the early phases. As a result, UIs are prefabricated, as for the Sedan-Bouillon demonstrator (section 11.2.2).

Third, the *unpredictable* nature of the context of use is integrated into the research agenda. From then on, it is no longer just a matter of perceiving the context of use and switching to the most appropriate prefabricated UI but generating, if necessary, an appropriate UI. The adaptation process then becomes more prominent. It can be based on approaches from artificial intelligence, including automatic symbolic learning techniques for decision modeling as in [HAR 08], [HAR 09]. The following section illustrates this viewpoint in a scenario linked to the field of transport[3].

---

2 http://giove.isti.cnr.it/cameleon.html.
3 This scenario could be extended to be linked with elements of personalization, as described in Chapter 3.

11.4.2. *Illustration in transport*

Prelude: Nathan, living in Grenoble, is on a business trip to Montpellier. Despite his tiredness, he decides to take his car rather than public transport. On his smart phone, Nathan has a very complete personal space, particularly for his trips (according to the same principle as Pierre in the illustration in section 11.3.2).

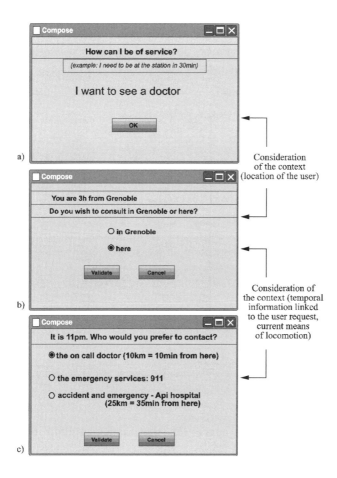

Figure 11.7. *Dynamic generation of UIs by taking into account information linked to the context of use (adapted from [GAB 09])*

Moment No. 1: Nathan is not very far from Montpellier. He is at the steering wheel and feels faint. He must see a doctor. He uses his smart phone (see Figure 11.7a) to express his needs.

Analysis: the plastic system takes into account contextual information to progressively provide Nathan with a reasonable solution (see Figures 11.7b and 11.7c).

Moment No. 2: Nathan has arrived in Montpellier. His feeling of illness is now more intense. He prefers to park and go by foot or by any other means available (bus, tram, etc., depending on the possibilities due to the late hour) to get to the on-call doctor. Once again, he uses his smart phone to express his query.

Analysis: the plastic system takes contextual information into account in order to suggest the most appropriate route to Nathan (see Figure 11.8).

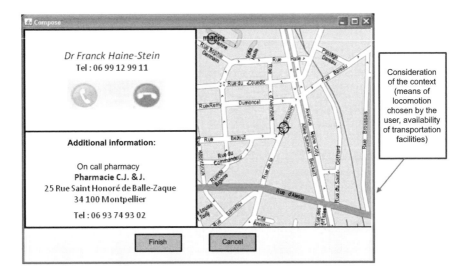

Figure 11.8. *Another example of dynamic generation of UIs by taking into account information linked to the context of use (adapted from [GAB 09])*

11.5. Towards a problem space for the implementation of plastic user interfaces

Several problem spaces have been proposed for UI plasticity [CAL 07a]. These spaces identify the key dimensions for supporting the analysis, design, implementation and/or evaluation of plastic UIs. Figure 11.9 proposes a simplified version of [CAL 07a]. This version is intended for UI designers. The objective is two-fold: to help them to imagine innovative solutions; and to think about the engineering. If this space does not claim to be exhaustive, it nonetheless compiles a number of questions that have been explored in the literature or that are to be investigated. Its originality is to attribute a semantic to point 0 and to the form of the diagram obtained by the characterization of a plastic UI in this space: the greater the distance to the centre, the more subtle the plasticity, making it potentially complex to implement. Our problem space is organized into sectors according to the external or internal properties under consideration.

11.5.1. *User viewpoint: external properties*

External properties are organized into four sectors according to: the nature of the domain-dependent UI with which the user interacts; the change of context at the origin of the adaptation; the changes instigated in the UI; and the control given to the user regarding to the adaptation process (see Figure 11.9).

Domain-dependent UI: in general, the UIs that are considered for plasticity are simple, such as forms. The problem space makes a clear distinction, in terms of complexity, between the adaptation of form-based and command lines UIs and the adaptation of direct manipulation and post-WIMP UIs. This axis is concerned with UI remodeling. The second axis refers to UI distribution. It distinguishes the adaptation of centralized versus distributed UIs, the distribution being coarse grained (inter-task) versus fine grained (intra-task). Coarse grain means that a task is entirely carried out on a given platform. Conversely, fine grain implies that a same task requires the use of several interaction devices (for example in Ubiloop where part of the UI is on the PC and the other part is on an interactive table).

Context: in line with the definition of context of use, three axes make up this sector. The user dimension specifies whether the adaptation is done in relation to an archetypal model of the targeted user versus the effective interaction the user or, even more generally, his activity. The platform distinguishes simple configurations composed of a single entity (e.g. a PC) versus homogeneous (e.g. two PCs) or heterogeneous platform assemblies (e.g. a PC and an interactive table, as in Ubiloop). The environment, which goes beyond open environments (e.g. a street), and closed spaces (e.g. an office), covers some potential complexity related to users' mobility.

Effects of the adaptation: the occurrence analyses the moment when the adaptation happens. With coarse grain, it can intervene between two sessions. It can also occur between two user tasks or even, with smaller grain, between two physical actions on interaction devices. The task dimension defines the range of the adaptation in terms of the user's task: is it limited to the user's task?

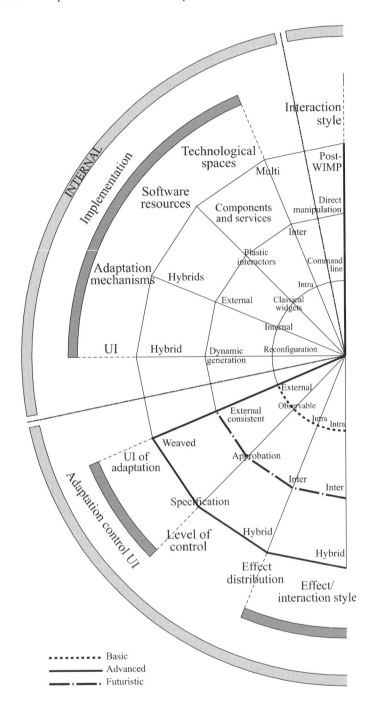

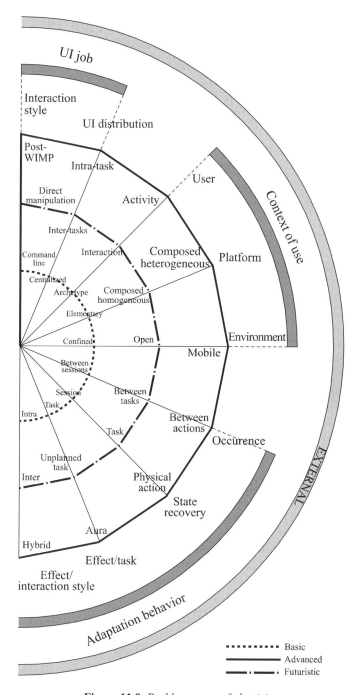

Figure 11.9. *Problem space of plasticity*

Does it consist of enabling an unplanned task as in section 11.4.2 or does it extend to the full personal information space? In terms of remodeling, does adaptation preserve the UI interaction style (command lines, direct manipulation versus post-WIMP)? If so, the adaptation is said to be intra-style. Inter-style refers to a change in style (e.g. from post-WIMP to direct manipulation). More complexly, styles can be combined (one post-WIMP part on the table; one command line part on the PC). In terms of distribution, the state of the UI (centralized, distributed inter-task versus intra-task) can be maintained (intra) or modified. The modification can be the passage from one state to another (inter) or to the combination of states (mixed). The state recovery refers to the eventual loss of physical actions during the adaptation process. At the session grain, the user must repeat all of his past actions. The action grain saves and restores any physical action whether the task is achieved or not.

Control of the adaptation: as a minimum, according to software ergonomic rules the user must be able to observe the adaptation process. For example, in Ubiloop the council staff member sees the photos move progressively from the PC to the interactive table. A more subtle degree of control anticipates that the system will propose adaptation (here, the moving of photos) to the user. The latter approves the proposition or not. In a more controlled manner, as in Sedan-Bouillon, the user can specify the adaptation and control the UI that is consequently fabricated or reused. Whatever the degree of control, a UI (and a meta-UI if it exists) therefore makes the adaptation process observable and possibly controllable by the user. The meta-UI, which makes the domain-dependent UI observable and controllable, may be external to this domain-dependent UI, with no interaction style constraint, as is the case in Sedan-Bouillon: it is a window in its own right, heterogeneous in style. Alternatively, the meta-UI may be external and consistent in interaction style with the domain-dependent UI, or it can be woven into the domain-dependent UI, e.g. integrated into the window (in the case of graphical UI) of the domain-dependent UI, possibly requiring the plasticity of the domain-dependent UI!

If the dimensions described in this section are perceivable to the user, they all translate into software requirements. These requirements are not necessarily perceived by the user. These internal properties are discussed next.

11.5.2. *System viewpoint: internal properties*

Internal properties are organized along four dimensions; see Figure 11.9. First is the UI: is this subject to adaptation, reconfigured or is another UI generated or even a hybrid configuration produced? In the latter case, the UI is the assembly of components from the original UI and of generated parts. Second, are the adaptation mechanisms embedded in the source code of the UI? If not, are they external to the

UI and taken care of by a middleware? Or is it a hybrid configuration that inter-operates internal and external parts?

Third, does the generated UI instantiate classical *widgets* provided by the usual toolboxes (e.g. Swing) or does it resort to specialized *widgets* for plasticity (e.g. COMET [DEM 07])? It is worth noting that the software components of larger grain size can also be dynamically recruited to serve as a basis for the composition of UIs [BAL 08].

Finally, from a technological point of view, are the technological spaces conserved? Intra means that the pre- and post-adaptation UIs are implemented within the same technological spaces (e.g. HTML). Inter refers to a change in technological spaces (e.g. from HTML to OpenGL). Mixed would denote a combination of technological spaces.

11.6. Conclusion and perspectives

In the rich, complex domain of interactive systems, UI plasticity is a particularly promising and challenging research area. This chapter has given a representative overview of UI plasticity while showing that transport is a fertile ground for its application. The chapter opened with the evolution of HCI in relation to the diversity and dynamicity of interaction resources, including their control by humans. Where possible, these different aspects have been illustrated with transport applications, and more generally with users' mobility.

The concept of UI plasticity was defined from the perspectives of the user and the system. Two voluntarily restricted, but representative, scenarios related to transport have been explored to illustrate the potentials of UI plasticity. Both show the central role of context.

A problem space was outlined to provide designers, developers and evaluators with an overview of aspects of UI plasticity that should be considered and combined for the development of future interactive systems.

Numerous research issues have been identified. UI composition by end-users is one of the foremost challenges. If keeping the user in the loop seems reasonable from the point of view of human factors, the approach seems equally reasonable from the point of view of engineering. The automation of evaluation of the quality of a UI requires the formalization of ergonomic criteria, the definition of metrics and the implementation of evaluation functions. These challenges are at the foreground of plasticity, but more generally are also at the cutting edge of academic teachings as well as industrial practice in HCI. Indeed, [SER 10] shows that thinking plasticity can improve the quality of even rigid UIs. Plasticity is clearly a challenge of growing impact that has yet to reveal its full importance.

11.7. Acknowledgements

This work was carried out in the context of the ANR MyCitizSpace project (2007–2010). We would in particular like to thank Olivier Nicolas (the coordinator at Génigraph) and Florence Pontico (Midi-Pyrénées Region) for their valuable help.

11.8. Bibliography

[ABO 92] ABOWD G.D., COUTAZ J., NIGAY L., "Structuring the space of interactive system properties", in: LARSON J., UNGER C. (eds), *Engineering for Human-Computer Interaction*, Elsevier Science Publishers, Amsterdam, The Netherlands, pp. 113-126, 1992.

[ANT 02] ANTONIAC P., PULLI P., KURODA T., BENDAS D., HICKEY S., SASAKI H., "Wireless user perspectives in Europe: Handsmart mediaphone interface", *Wireless Personal Communications*, vol. 22, pp. 161-174, 2002.

[BAL 04] BALME L., DEMEURE A., BARRALON N., COUTAZ J., CALVARY G., "CAMELEON-RT: A software architecture reference model for distributed, migratable, and plastic user interfaces", in: MARKOPOULOS P., EGGEN B., AARTS E. *et al.* (eds), *Computer Science, vol. 3295, Ambient Intelligence: Second European Symposium, EUSAI 2004*, pp. 291-302, Springer-Verlag Heidelberg, Eindhoven, The Netherlands, November 8-11 2004.

[BAL 08] BALME L. Interfaces homme-machine plastiques: Une approche par composants dynamiques, Thesis, Joseph Fourier University, Grenoble I, France, 2008.

[BAS 93] BASTIEN J.M.C., SCAPIN D., Ergonomic Criteria for the Evaluation of Human-computer Interfaces, INRIA technical report, no. 156, INRIA, June 1993.

[BLA 01] BLACKWELL A.F., HAGUE R., "AutoHAN: An architecture for programming the home", *Proc. Of the IEEE Symposium on Human-Centric Computing Languages and Environments*, Stresa, Italy, pp. 150-157, 2001.

[BOR 04] BORKOWSKI S., LETESSIER J., CROWLEY J., "Spatial control of interactive surfaces in an augmented environment", *European Conference on Human Computer Interaction, EHCI 04*, Hamburg, Germany, July 2004.

[BRA 03] BRANGIER E., BARCENILLA J., *Concevoir un Produit Facile à Utiliser*, Éditions d'Organisation, Paris, France, 2003.

[BUR 03] BURNETT M., COOK C., PENDSE O., ROTHERMEL G., SUMMET J., WALLACE C., "End-user software engineering with assertions in the spreadsheet paradigm", *Proc. ICSE 2003*, pp. 93-103, Portland, USA, 2003.

[CAL 06] CALVARY G., COUTAZ J., DAASSI O., GANNEAU V., BALME L., DEMEURE A., SOTTET, J.-S., "Métamorphose des HCI et plasticité: Article de synthèse", in: E. BRANGIER, C. KOLSKI, J.R. RUAULT (eds), *10e Conférence ERGO-IA, L'Humain comme Facteur de Performance des Systèmes Complexes*, ESTIA & ESTIA.INNOVATION, pp. 79-86, Biarritz, France, October 11-13, 2006.

[CAL 07a] CALVARY G., Plasticité des Interfaces Homme-Machine, Habilitation à Diriger des Recherches, Joseph Fourier University, Grenoble 1, France, November 2007.

[CAL 07b] CALVARY G., COUTAZ J., "Métamorphose des HCI et plasticité", *Revue d'Interaction Homme-Machine (RHCI)*, vol. 8, no. 1, pp. 35-59, 2007.

[COC 04] COCKTON G., "From quality in use to value in the world", *IACM Proc. CHI 2004, Late Breaking Results*, pp. 1287-1290, 2004.

[COC 05] COCKTON G., "A development framework for value-centered design", *ACM Proc. CHI 2005, Late Breaking Results*, pp 1292-1295, 2005.

[CON 97] CONWAY M., PAUSCH R., "Alice: easy to learn interactive 3D graphics", *ACM SIGGRAPH Computer Graphics*, vol. 31, no. 3, pp. 58-59, 1997.

[CON 99] CONSTANTINE L.L., LOCKWOOD L.A.D., *Software for Use: A Practical Guide to the Models and Methods of Usage-Centered Design*, Addison-Wesley, New York, USA, 1999.

[COU 06] COUTAZ J., "Meta-user interfaces for ambient spaces", Invited speaker. *Proc. of TAMODIA 2006*, Springer, pp. 1-15, Hasselt, Belgium, October 2006.

[CYP 93] CYPHER A., *Watch What I Do*, MIT Press, Cambridge, USA, 1993.

[DÂA 07] DAASSI O., Les Comets: une Nouvelle Génération d'Interacteurs pour la Plasticité des Interfaces Homme-Machine, Thesis, Joseph Fourier University, Grenoble I, France, January 2007.

[DEL 09] DELOT T., CENERARIO N., ILARRI S., LECOMTE S., "A cooperative reservation protocol for parking spaces in vehicular ad hoc networks", *6th International Conference on Mobile Technology, Applications and Systems (Mobility Conference 2009)*, ACM Digital Library, Best Paper Award, Nice, France, September 2009.

[DEL 10] DELOT T., CENERARIO N., ILARRI S., "Vehicular event sharing with a mobile peer-to-peer architecture", *Transportation Research Part-C*, vol. 18, no. 4, pp. 584-598, 2010.

[DEM 07] DEMEURE A. Modèles et Outils pour la Conception et l'Exécution d'Interfaces Homme-Machine Plastiques, Thesis, Joseph Fourier University, Grenoble I, France, October 2007.

[DEY 04] DEY A., HAMID R., BECKMANN C., LI I., HSU D., CAPPELLA A., "Programming by demonstration of context-aware applications", *Proc. ACM Conference on Human Factors in Computing Systems (CHI)*, pp. 33-40, ACM Press, 2004.

[DIX 93] DIX A., FINLAY J., ABOWD G., BEALE R., *Human-Computer Interaction*, Prentice-Hall, Upper Saddle River, New Jersey, USA, 1993.

[GAB 09] GABILLON Y., CALVARY G., MANDRAN N., FIORINO H., "Composition dynamique d'Interfaces Homme-Machine : Besoin utilisateur ou Défi de chercheur?", *Proc. HCI 2009, 21ème Conférence de l'Association Francophone sur l'Interaction Homme-Machine*, International Conference Proceedings Series, ACM Press, pp. 61-64, Grenoble, France, October 13-16 2009.

[GIR 92] GIRARD P., Environnement de Programmation pour non Programmeurs et Paramétrage en Conception Assistée par Ordinateur: Le Système Like, Mémoire d'HDR, University of Poitiers, France, November 1992.

[COC 96] GRAM C., COCKTON G., *Design Principles for Interactive Software*, Chapman & Hall, London, 1996.

[HAR 08] HARIRI M.-A., Contribution à une méthode de Conception et Génération d'Interface Homme-machine Plastique, PhD thesis, University of Valenciennes and Hainaut-Cambrésis, Valenciennes, France, June 2008.

[HAR 09] HARIRI M.-A., LEPREUX S., TABARY., KOLSKI C., "Principes et étude de cas d'adaptation d'HCI dans les SI en fonction du contexte d'interaction de l'utilisateur", *Ingénierie des Systèmes d'Information (ISI), Networking and Information Systems*, vol. 14, pp. 141-162, 2009.

[HAR 10] HARRISON C., TAN, D. MORRIS, SKINPUT D., "Appropriating the body as an input surface", *Proceedings of the 28th Annual SIGCHI Conference on Human Factors in Computing Systems, CHI '10*, pp 453-462, ACM, Georgia, Atlanta, USA, April 10-15, 2010 .

[HIN 00] HINCKLEY K., RAMOS G., GUIMBRETIERE F., BAUDISH P., SMITH M., "Stitching: Pen gesture that span multiple displays", *Proc. UIST 2000*, ACM Press, pp. 91-100, 2000.

[ISO 99] ISO, Human Centered Design Processes for Interactive Systems, ISO 13407, 1999.

[KAR 05] KARSENTY L., BOTHEREL V., "Analyse empirique de l'inter-utilisabilité d'un service multisupport Web et téléphone", *Actes des Deuxièmes Journées Francophones sur l'Ubiquité et la Mobilité (UbiMob'05)*, ACM Press, Grenoble, France, 31 May-3 June 2005.

[KUB 09] KUBICKI S., LEBRUN Y., LEPREUX S., DOS SANTOS P., KOLSKI C., CAELEN J., "New human-computer interactions using tangible objects: application on a digital tabletop with RFID technology", in JACKO J.A., *Proceedings of the Human-Computer Interaction, 13th International Conference, HCI International 2009, San Diego USA, July 19-24*, LNCS 5612, pp. 446-455, Springer-Verlag, 2009.

[LET 05] LETONDAL C., "Participatory programming: Developing programmable bioinformatics tools for end-users", in: H. LIEBERMAN, F. PATERNO, V. WULF (eds), *End-User Development*, Springer/Kluwer Academic Publishers, 2005.

[LIT 07] LITTLE G., LAU T., LIN J., KANDOGAN E., HABER E., CYPHER A., "Capture, share, automate, personalize business processes the web", *Proc. CHI 2007*, ACM Press, pp. 943-946, 2007.

[LOP 04] LOPEZ-JAQUERO V., MONTERO F., MOLINA J.P., GONZALEZ P., "A seamless development process of adaptive user interfaces explicitly based on usability properties", *Proc. EHCI04*, pp. 289-291, Hamburg, Germany, July 2004.

[LYY 02] LYYTINEN K., YOO Y., "Issues and challenges in ubiquitous computing". *Communications of the ACM*, vol. 45, no. 12, pp. 62-65, 2002.

[MAE 09] MAES P., MISTRY P., "Unveiling the "Sixth Sense", game-changing wearable tech", *TED 2009*, Long Beach, California, USA, 2009.

[MON 05] MONTERO F., GONZALEZ P., LOZANO M., VANDERDONCKT J., "Quality models for automated evaluation of web sites usability and accessibility", *Proc. International Hyperlink COST 294, Workshop on User Interface Quality Models UIQM '2005, Interact workshop*, pp. 37-43, Rome, 2005.

[MYE 01] MYERS B., "Using hand-held devices and PCs together", *Communications of the ACM*, vol. 44, no. 11, pp. 34-41, November 2001.

[MYE 06] MYERS B., WEITZMAN D.A., KO A.J., CHAU D.H., "Answering why and why not questions in user interfaces", *Proc. SIGCHI Conf. Human Factors in Computing Systems CHI'06*, ACM Press, pp. 397-406, Montreal, Quebec, Canada, 2005.

[NEW 02] NEWMAN M.W., SEDIVY J.Z., NEUWIRTH C.M., EDWARDS W.K., HONG J.I., IZADI S., MARCELO K., SMITH T.F., "Designing for serendipity: supporting end-user configuration of ubiquitous computing environments", *Proc. Designing Interactive Systems (DIS)*, London, pp. 147-156, 2002.

[NIE 94] NIELSEN J., "Heuristic evaluation", in: NIELSEN J., MACK R.L. (eds), *Usability Inspection Methods*, John Wiley & Sons, New York, USA, 1994.

[NOG 08] NOGIER J.F., *Ergonomie du Logiciel et Design Web – Le Manuel des Interfaces Utilisateur* (4th edition), Dunod, Paris, France, 2008.

[PAN 02] PANE J.F., A programming system for children that is designed for usability, PhD Thesis, Carnegie Mellon University, 2002.

[PRE 94] PREECE J., ROGERS Y., SHARP H., BENYON D., HOLLAND S., CAREY T., *Human-Computer Interaction*, Addison Wesley Publication, Wokingham, 1994.

[REK 01] REKIMOTO J., ULLMER B., OBA H., "DataTiles: A modular platform for mixed physical and graphical interactions", *Proceedings of CHI'01*, pp. 269-276, ACM Press, Seattle, USA, 2001.

[REP 04] REPENNING A., IOANNIDOU A., "Agent-based end-user development", *Communications of the ACM*, vol. 47, no. 9, pp. 43-46, September 2004.

[ROD 04] RODDEN T., CRABTREE A., HEMMINGS T., KOLEVA B., HUMBLE J., AKESSON K.P., HANSSON P., "Configuring the ubiquitous home", *Proc. ACM Symposium on Designing Interactive Systems*, ACM Press, Cambridge, USA, August 1-4, 2004.

[SCH 97] SCHNEIDERMAN B., *Designing User Interface Strategies for Effective Human-Computer Interaction* (3rd edition), Addison-Wesley, Reading, USA, 1997.

[SEF 04] SEFFAH A., JAVAHERY H., *Multiple User Interfaces, Cross-platform Applications and Context-aware Interfaces*, Wiley & Sons, New York, USA, 2004.

[SER 09] SERNA A., PINEL S., CALVARY G., "La plasticité des HCI en action : un exemple de téléprocédure plastique", *Conférence HCI'2009*, pp. 359-362.

[SER 10] SERNA A., CALVARY G., SCAPIN D., "How assessing plasticity design choices can improve UI quality: a case study", *Proc. EICS'10*, pp. 29-34, Berlin, Germany, 2010.

[SHA 91] SHACKEL B., "Usability-context, framework, design and evaluation", in: *Human Factors for Informatics Usability*, pp. 21-38, Cambridge University Press, Cambridge, 1991.

[SIX] SIXTHSENSE, Pranav Mistry, Media Lab, MIT, http://www.pranavmistry.com /projects/sixthsense.

[SMI 77] SMITH D.C., *Pygmalion: A Computer Program to Model and Stimulate Creative Thought*, Basel, Birkhauser Verlag, Stuttgart, Germany, 1977.

[SOH 06] SOHN T.Y., DEY A.K., "iCAP: An informal tool for interactive prototyping of context-aware applications", *Proc. Int Conf Pervasive Computing 2006*, pp. 974-975, Dublin, Ireland, May 2006.

[STE 09] STEPHANIDIS C., *The Universal Access Handbook*, CRC Press, 2009.

[TAY 09] TAYLOR B.T., BOVE V.M., "Graspables: grasp-recognition as a user interface", *Proc. 27th Int Conf Human Factors in Computing Systems (CHI'09)*, ACM Press, pp. 917-926, 2009.

[THE 99] THEVENIN D., COUTAZ J., "Plasticity of user interfaces: framework and research agenda", in: A. SASSE and C. JOHNSON (eds), *Proc. Interact99*, pp. 110-117, IFIP IOS Press Publication, Edinburgh, Scotland, 1999.

[THE 01] THEVENIN D., Adaptation en Interaction Homme-Machine: le cas de la Plasticité, Thesis, Joseph Fourier University, Grenoble I, France, 2001.

[THE 07] THE ECONOMIST, "When everything connects: the coming wireless revolution", *The Economist*, April 2007.

[TRE 03] TREVISAN D., VANDERDONCKT J., MACQ B., "Continuity as a usability property", *HCI 2003 – 10th Int. Conf. Human-Computer Interaction*, vol. I, pp. 1268-1272, Heraklion, Greece, June 22-27 2003.

[VAN 99] VAN WELIE M., VAN DER VEER G.C., ELIËNS A., "Usability properties in dialog models", *6th International Eurographics Workshop on Design Specification and Verification of Interactive Systems DSV-IS99*, pp. 238-253, Braga, Portugal, June 2-4, 1999.

[WIN 01] WINOGRAD T., "Architecture for context", *Human Computer Interaction*, vol. 16, pp. 401-419, 2001.

List of Authors

Mourad ABED
LAMIH
University of Lille-Nord de France
University of Valenciennes and
Hainaut-Cambrésis
France

Mohamed AHMED NACER
LSI
USTHB
Algiers
Algeria

Yamine AÏT AMEUR
LISI, ENSMA
Poitiers
France

Idir AÏT SADOUNE
LISI, ENSMA
Poitiers
France

Abdouroihamane ANLI
DSI
University of Paris 1
Panthéon-Sorbonne
France

Thierry BELLET
IFSTTAR-LESCOT
Bron
France

Yacine BELLIK
LIMSI-CNRS
Paris-Sud 11 University
Orsay
France

Arnaud BONNARD
IFSTTAR-LESCOT
Bron
France

Yolaine BOURDA
SUPELEC Systems Sciences (E3S)
Department of Computer Science
Gif-sur-Yvette
France

Serge BOVERIE
Continental Automotive France
Toulouse
France

Guy BOY
Human-Centered Design Institute
Florida Institute of Technology and
NASA Kennedy Space Center
USA

Arnaud BROSSARD
Aplon France
Anzin Saint Aubin
France

Marie-Pierre BRUYAS
IFSTTAR-LESCOT
Bron
France

Gaëlle CALVARY
Grenoble INP
Laboratoire d'Informatique de
Grenoble (LIG)
France

René CHALON
LIESP
Ecole Centrale de Lyon
France

Joelle COUTAZ
Grenoble INP
Laboratoire d'Informatique de
Grenoble (LIG)
France

Bertrand DAVID
LIESP
Ecole Centrale de Lyon
France

Bernard FAVRE
Volvo Technology, Renault Trucks
Lyon
France

Emmanuelle GRISLIN
LAMIH
University of Lille-Nord de France
and University of Valenciennes and
Hainaut-Cambrésis
France

Jean-Michel HOC
IRCCyN, CNRS
Nantes
France

Christophe JACQUET
SUPELEC Systems Sciences (E3S)
Department of Computer Science
Gif-sur-Yvette
France

Nadjet KAMEL
LRIA
USTHB
Algiers
Algeria

Christophe KOLSKI
LAMIH
University of Lille-Nord de France
and University of Valenciennes and
Hainaut-Cambrésis
France

Sabine LANGLOIS
Renault
Guyancourt
France

Séverine LOISEAU
Renault
Guyancourt
France

Annick MAINCENT
SONOVISION, LIGERON division
Lyon
France

Nicolas MISDARIIS
STMS Ircam-CNRS-UPMC
Paris
France

Linda MOHAND OUSSAÏD
LISI/ENSMA
Poitiers
France
and
Centre de Recherche sur
l'Information Scientifique et
Technique
Algiers
Algeria

Pierre MORIZET-MAHOUDEAUX
CNRS Heudiasyc
Compiègne University of Technology
France

Assia MOULOUDI
Capgemini Finance & Services
Paris-La Défense
France

Audrey SERNA
INSA de Lyon
and
UJF-Grenoble 1
Laboratoire d'Informatique de
Grenoble (LIG)
France

Julien TARDIEU
URI Octogone
University of Toulouse II Le Mirail
France

Hélène TATTEGRAIN
IFSTTAR-LESCOT
Bron
France

Guillaume USTER
IFSTTAR -ESTAS
University of Lille-Nord de France
France

Annette VALENTIN
Consultant
Paris
France

Index